Security Technologies and Social Implications

Security Technologies and Social Implications

Edited by

Garik Markarian

Emeritius Professor, School of Computing and Communications
University of Lancaster
Lancaster, UK

Ruža Karlović

Police College
Police Academy, Ministry of Interior
Zagreb, Croatia

Holger Nitsch

Department of Policing of Bavarian Police
Fürstenfeldbruck, Germany

Krishna Chandramouli

Venaka Media Limited
London, UK

IEEE PRESS

WILEY

Published by John Wiley & Sons, Inc., Hoboken, New Jersey.
Published simultaneously in Canada.

For general information on our other products and services or for technical support, please contact our Customer Care Department within the United States at (800) 762-2974, outside the United States at (317) 572-3993 or fax (317) 572-4002.

Wiley also publishes its books in a variety of electronic formats. Some content that appears in print may not be available in electronic formats. For more information about Wiley products, visit our web site at www.wiley.com.

Library of Congress Cataloging-in-Publication Data
Names: Markarian, Garik, editor. | Karlović, Ruža, editor. | Nitsch,
   Holger, editor. | Chandramouli, Krishna, editor.
Title: Security technologies and social implications / edited by Garik
   Markarian, Ruža Karlović, Holger Nitsch, Krishna Chandramouli.
Description: Hoboken, New Jersey : Wiley, [2022] | Includes bibliographical
   references and index.
Identifiers: LCCN 2022029632 (print) | LCCN 2022029633 (ebook) | ISBN
   9781119834144 (hardback) | ISBN 9781119834151 (adobe pdf) | ISBN
   9781119834168 (epub)
Subjects: LCSH: Law enforcement–Technological innovations.
Classification: LCC HV7936.A8 S39 2022 (print) | LCC HV7936.A8 (ebook) |
   DDC 363.2/3–dc23/eng/20220805
LC record available at https://lccn.loc.gov/2022029632
LC ebook record available at https://lccn.loc.gov/2022029633

Cover Design: Wiley
Cover Image: © Light/Getty Images

Set in 9.5/12.5pt STIXTwoText by Straive, Pondicherry, India

Contents

List of Contributors

Evgenia Adamopoulou
Institute of Communication and
Computer Systems, National
Technical University of Athens,
Athens, Greece

Theodoros Alexakis
Institute of Communication and
Computer Systems, National
Technical University of Athens,
Athens, Greece

Sebastian Allertseder
Department Police, University
of Applied Sciences for
Public Services in Bavaria,
Fuerstenfeldbruck, Germany

Luigi Briguglio
R&D Department, CyberEthics Lab.,
Rome, Italy

Valeria Cesaroni
R&D Department, CyberEthics Lab.,
Rome, Italy

Krishna Chandramouli
Multimedia and Vision Research
Group, School of Electronic
Engineering and Computer Science,
Queen Mary University of London,
London, UK

and

Venaka Media Limited,
London, UK

Konstantinos Demestichas
Institute of Communication and
Computer Systems, National
Technical University of Athens,
Athens, Greece

Katja Eman
Faculty of Criminal Justice and
Security, University of Maribor,
Maribor, Slovenia

David Faure
Thales, Courbevoie, France

Sven-Eric Fikenscher
Department of Policing
(CEPOLIS), University of
Applied Sciences for Public Service
in Bavaria,
Fürstenfeldbruck, Germany

David Fortune
SAHER (Europe),
Harju maakond, Estonia

Rok Hacin
Faculty of Criminal Justice and
Security, University of Maribor,
Maribor, Slovenia

Bilal Hassan
Multimedia and Vision Research
Group, School of Electronic
Engineering and Computer Science,
Queen Mary University of London,
London, UK

and

Faculty of Engineering &
Environment, Northumbria
University London Campus,
London, UK

Grigore M. Havârneanu
Security Division, International
Union of Railways (UIC),
Paris, France

Roxana Horincar
Thales, Courbevoie, France

Andrea Iannone
R&D Department, CyberEthics Lab.,
Rome, Italy

Ebroul Izquierdo
Multimedia and Vision Research
Group, School of Electronic
Engineering and Computer Science,
Queen Mary University of London,
London, UK

Ruža Karlović
Police Academy, Police University
College, Zagreb, Croatia

Ioannis Kompatsiaris
Information Technologies Institute,
Centre for Research and Technology
Hellas, Thessaloniki, Greece

Garik Markarian
Emeritus Professor University of
Lancaster and CEO of Rinicom
Intelligent Solutions Riverway
House, Morecambe Road Lancaster
LA1 2RX, UK

Thomas Marquenie
KU Leuven Centre for IT & IP Law,
Leuven, Belgium

Natasha McCrone
RiniSoft Ltd, Sliven, Bulgaria

Sotirios Menexis
Information Technologies
Institute, Centre for Research
and Technology Hellas,
Thessaloniki, Greece

Gorazd Meško
Faculty of Criminal Justice and
Security, University of Maribor,
Maribor, Slovenia

Wilmuth Müller
Fraunhofer IOSB,
Karlsruhe, Germany

Charlotte Jacobe de Naurois
Thales, Courbevoie, France

Holger Nitsch
Department of Policing (CEPOLIS),
University of Applied Sciences
for Public Service in Bavaria,
Fürstenfeldbruck, Germany

Carmela Occhipinti
R&D Department, CyberEthics Lab.,
Rome, Italy

Guenter Okon
Institut für musterbasierte
Prognosetechnik, ImfPt.,
Oberhausen, Germany

Damir Osterman
Ministry of Interior Research and
Innovation, Zagreb, Croatia

Dirk Pallmer
Fraunhofer IOSB,
Karlsruhe, Germany

Nikolaos Peppes
Institute of Communication and
Computer Systems, National
Technical University of Athens,
Athens, Greece

Laura Petersen
Security Division, International
Union of Railways (UIC),
Paris, France

Katherine Quezada-Tavárez
KU Leuven Centre for IT & IP Law,
Leuven, Belgium

Konstantina Remoundou
Institute of Communication and
Computer Systems, National
Technical University of Athens,
Athens, Greece

Arif Sahar
CENTRIC, Sheffield Hallam
University, Sheffield, UK

Thomas Schweer
Institut für musterbasierte
Prognosetechnik, ImfPt.,
Oberhausen, Germany

Andrew Staniforth
SAHER (Europe), Harju
maakond, Estonia

Ines Sučić
Institute of Social Sciences Ivo Pilar,
Zagreb, Croatia

Theodora Tsikrika
Information Technologies Institute,
Centre for Research and Technology
Hellas, Thessaloniki, Greece

Stefanos Vrochidis
Information Technologies Institute,
Centre for Research and Technology
Hellas, Thessaloniki, Greece

Xindi Zhang
Multimedia and Vision Research
Group, School of Electronic
Engineering and Computer Science,
Queen Mary University of London,
London, UK

Preface

While working in a law enforcement environment, I realized that societies are changing very quickly. To protect citizens is the main objective for law enforcement, and it is important to take all changes and developments in the society and also of deviant behavior into consideration. For police education, that means a constant observation of the developments concerning societal, technological, tactical, economical, and legal changes. Technological innovation advanced rapidly within the last few decades and also changed all the other aspects mentioned earlier. In particular, the dark web, deep web, Web 2.0, and drones pose threats that have not been known before.

Policing has to keep up with the challenges of new threats by the use of new technologies, but societal implications have also to be taken into account. Every innovation brings not only positive aspects but also possible new threats to the security of the society. Therefore, it is of utmost importance that the education of law enforcement keeps pace with the newest developments of crime in all aspects.

Current threats to the safety and security of citizens of free and democratic societies come from radicalization, terrorism, cybercrime, drone threats, threats to the misuse of personal data, digital identity theft, disinformation, fake news, and many more. Law enforcement has the duty and obligation to counter these threats, to imagine possible future threats and by doing so, to protect the democratic and civil society from these threats by countering them with appropriate measures. The education sector plays a major role in this. As my long experience with policing showed, there is always a connection to the social sciences in deviant behavior, also within the use of new technologies. I see it as important to connect these two major sciences to effectively fight threats to the civil society. Furthermore, to be up to date, it is important to take current research on technological and societal developments into account.

I am glad to see that in this book, the nexus of social science and technology for law enforcement agencies is perfectly represented. As an experienced lecturer and head of a policing education organization, I emphasize the combination of different disciplines in the way it is presented here. The given range is very broad and it is an eye-opener for law enforcement to see all the innovations done by research. Technological and social science research do not exclude themselves. The combination of both provides a solution for the education of law enforcement and successful future policing to ensure the safety and security of citizens in a democratic and open society.

Ingbert Hoffmann
Head of the University of the Bavarian Police

Introduction

Scientific innovation in the area of security solutions for citizen safety has leapt ahead following the exponential increase in the capability to collect, store, and process information from various sources. The enhancements in the field of device connectivity through networking and their onboard computational power have enabled algorithmic intelligence to be deployed both at the cloud and also at edge devices. Such computing systems have also extended beyond traditional modalities of data processing to include new forms of data analytics, resulting from recent innovations in artificial intelligence (AI) and machine learning (ML) solutions. The ever-increasing diverse data modalities and the ability to extract hidden patterns and relevant information through advanced data correlation have simultaneously enhanced the investigative capabilities of the law enforcement agencies (LEAs) in securing European society and citizens against foreseeable threats and terrorist attacks. The technological advancements in the field of information technology (IT) offer a sense of encouragement to equip LEAs to counter-act criminal activities carried out by perpetrators.

In contrast to the classic tools available for LEAs (such as guns, handcuffs, and other less harmful weapons), the new approach to terrorism and crime relies on the emergence of technological tools such as mobile devices, AI, social media, drones, and GIS to name a few. As crime, in general, and cybercrime, in particular, become more and more sophisticated, a combination of complex social measures are required, which include prevention, detection, investigation, and prosecution. An effective solution to this problem requires continuous synergy and innovation from interdisciplinary scientific experts and the adoption of technologies into the operational practice of LEAs. Emerging new technologies change the landscape for LEAs, providing new opportunities for improving the effectiveness of problem-solving and partnership initiatives and assisting in the implementation of organizational changes designed to institutionalize these processes. This book focuses on the development and application of new technologies that police officers could leverage as a tool for both predictive and intelligence-led investigations and recommends the best practice for incorporation of these technologies into day-to-day activities by LEAs.

The use of technologies by LEAs is mandated in two different ways: the use of legacy technologies and novel platforms specifically dedicated for LEA applications (which we will refer to as professional LEA technology platforms) and technologies introduced for other (e.g. consumer) applications but which can be utilized by LEAs enabling new activities (which we will refer to as consumer technologies). Although significant progress has been achieved in developing innovative technologies, incorporation of such technologies into decision making by LEAs is still slow due to several objective and subjective reasons. For example, the development of professional technology platforms is associated with government decisions, requires public funding, is limited to LEAs only, and is expensive and conservative (and often slow) due to its nature. On the other hand, consumer technology platforms have seen rapid development in recent years. They are driven by commercial organizations often representing the private sector and have wider acceptance by the general public who are using such solutions on a day-to-day basis. In addition, the ethical discussions on the use of pervasive technologies that are complemented with the introduction of new European regulations such as GDPR have compounded the organizational reluctance in adopting some of the scientific advancements into day-to-day operational activities of LEAs.

In this book, we discuss both professional and consumer technology platforms, which were introduced recently for LEA applications. We demonstrate the drawbacks of the existing solutions and provide a blueprint for improving the overall adaptability of innovative technologies for enhanced policing and security. We also analyze emerging consumer technology platforms and show how these could be incorporated within the existing professional technology platform and improve LEA operations.

As the breadth of research outcomes to be analyzed is too vast to be addressed in a single book, we focus on technologies developed within the HORIZON 2020 EU Security Programme, which have either recently completed or have entered the final stages of completion, in which all authors played an active role. More specifically, we describe new technologies developed by numerous HORIZON 2020 projects, such as UNITY, NEXES, PROPHETS, TENSOR, CUPS, DRONEWISE, MAGNETO, DEFENDER, and PROPHETS (just to name a few) and provide both engineering and social perspectives on these technologies.

In addition, we also analyze the speed of acceptance of these technologies considering numerous factors, such as LEA subculture, training, and recent ethical and GDPR regulations, and provide recommendations for faster convergence of technologies into the LEA decision process. In addition, as new technologies have become available to everyone, including various criminal organizations and individuals with a criminal mind, the dual role of new technologies is discussed and evaluated – on the one hand, the ability to facilitate LEAs work, and, on the other hand, providing new opportunities for criminals. This is an interesting and challenging topic, which requires a multidimensional approach, covering technological advances, legislation, regulations, and licensing, just to name a few. Typical examples include satellite navigation systems and drones, which are used by both the LEAs and criminals. However, through certain technological advances, legislation, and state control, criminals (theoretically) cannot get access to higher levels of navigation accuracy. Similarly, drones are widely used by LEAs for search and rescue operations, however, they are also used by criminals for delivering contraband to prisons. Developing complex solutions, which will allow legitimate use of drones by the general public and the LEAs while preventing criminals from using drones, is one of the open problems, which is analyzed and described in the book.

The book is organized as follows:

The aim of the first chapter is to review the current state of research on policing technology to assess the police perspective on technology role and usage. It also encountered obstacles and observed needs. The review provides an in-depth understanding of how technology is adopted in the LEAs, which factors moderate association between technology implementation and police efficiencies, and in what way integration of innovative technology in the LEAs could generate the most benefits for both police and community.

The second chapter outlines the interim legal and ethical impact assessment of the security solutions, technology, and tools by providing a preliminary evaluation of the ethical and legal concerns raised by the security practitioners in the usage of the system as well as templates and solutions to address these issues. The chapter also reviews the risks posed by the new systems, presents mitigation techniques aimed at addressing them, and provides an update on the implementation of legal and ethical safeguards in the system.

The third chapter is dedicated to improving the quality and accuracy of identity recognition and the impact of such technologies upon society. The chapter shows how research in technology can and, in some respect, must include collaboration with social sciences and social practice. More specifically, the authors of this chapter look at the challenges associated with biometrics-based solutions in no-gate border crossing point scenarios, including the procedures needed for the assessment of their social, ethical, privacy, and regulatory acceptance, particularly in view of the impact on both the passengers and border control authorities as well as the potential pitfalls of biometric technology due to fraudulent activities. In consultation with the collaborating border control authorities, the chapter reports on the formal assessment of biometric technologies for real-world acceptance to cope with the increasing demand of global travelers crossing state borders.

Chapter 4 is dedicated to soft biometrics, which is emerging as one of the promising technologies for enabling faster border crossing. It is based on the fusion of multiple modalities in a soft biometrics' framework. To showcase proof of concept, authors developed a taxonomy of soft biometrics features specific to verification at public places, including the context-aware bag of soft biometrics. More importantly, quantitative features-based verification is the main agenda along with extracting significant information from clothing and auxiliary attachments of the human body. The chapter is completed with experimental results showing a verification rate of more than 90% during multiple different experiments, confirming the great potential of soft biometrics in security research.

Chapter 5 recognizes that the illegal use of UAVs is now a serious security concern across the world as terrorists, activists, and criminals are adopting drone technology and developing new, creative, and sophisticated ways in which to commit crime, terrorism and invade the privacy of citizens. To address these current vulnerabilities, the chapter provides a detailed description of the counter-UAV systems and proposes a holistic first-responder agency command, control, and coordination strategy, underpinned by evidence-based training for the counter-terrorism protection of public spaces.

Chapter 6 is closely linked to Chapter 5 as it describes novel AI-based machine vision solutions for detection, tracking and classification of UAVs and other objects which are of interest to LEAs. More specifically, the chapter presents a framework that integrates three main computer vision technologies, namely (i) object detection; (ii) person reidentification; and (iii) face recognition to enhance the operational security of critical infrastructure perimeters. The novelty of the proposed framework relies on the integration of key technical innovations that satisfy the operational requirements of critical infrastructure in using computer vision technologies. One such requirement relates to data privacy and citizen rights, following the implementation of the General Data Protection Regulation across Europe for the successful adoption of video surveillance for infrastructure security.

Chapter 7 describes a novel tool, which aims to unify different evidence data sources, such as video, audio, text/documents, social media and Web data, telecom data, surveillance systems data, and police databases, providing a common representation model for internal data representation. Data fusion combines the collected information in order to enable actions and decisions that would be more accurate than those that were produced by a single data source.

Chapter 8 describes technical and societal issues associated with the development and implementation of communication tools and platforms which will enable secure, reliable, and ethical communication between the first responders and the general public during the CBRNE attacks or events. The chapter also describes several recommendations for next-generation Emergency Services that harmonize the use of mobile applications for purposes of emergency communications.

Chapter 9 describes the application of the geographic information system (GIS) by the LEAs in general and provides specific examples of its use by the Slovenian police. Importantly, it summarizes interviews with police chiefs on a local level describing their experiences as end users of GIS in solving antisocial problems and planning preventive activities.

Chapter 10 presents the result of a study that aims to counter the causes of online radicalization, cybercrime, and cyberterrorism. It also provides clear explanations of the definitions of four key areas: terrorism-generated content, terrorist financing, terrorist recruitment, and training and online hate speech. The results are rooted in the use of different methodologies from a variety of disciplines and the focus is on the micro, meso, and macro level. The focus of this chapter is on the vulnerability indicators on the different levels. The chapter emphasizes the importance of a multidimensional approach in the prevention of these negative security phenomena for the general public good of society.

The eleventh chapter reports on the scientific activities carried out toward the development of tools and software components that complies with the European legal and judicial regulations for authenticating and authorizing the digital evidence using advanced and complex algorithms. The chapter outlines the implementation of three technologies, namely (i) a semantic framework for tracking and recording the processing of information; (ii) the use of distributed immutable storage that protects against external malicious attacks; and (iii) the creation and storage of digital hash within a blockchain environment to enable data audit logs.

The twelfth chapter is dedicated to predictive policing, which is still a rather young but very dynamic part of criminological research and police work. In addition to the fight against ordinary crime (e.g. domestic burglary), predictive policing is becoming increasingly important in the fight against terrorism, not only in predicting terrorist attacks but also in predicting the radicalization tendencies in biographies. The chapter describes innovative instruments for analyzing the risk potential of supporters of extremist groups or individual radicalization patterns, in order to be able to forecast terrorist activities and initiate suitable operational measures in a timely manner. In addition to the undeniable advantages of such personal prognosis methods, like the increase of internal security and the prevention of politically motivated acts of violence, the chapter also considers data protection and ethical questions focusing on the opportunities and challenges of predictive policing for the LEAs of the European Union.

Finally, in the Conclusion, we summarize the findings of individual chapters, show the connection between the topics and propose some new topics for future research in the area.

1

The Circle of Change: Technology Impact on LEAs

Ines Sučić

Institute of Social Sciences Ivo Pilar, Zagreb, Croatia

1.1 Introduction

Infiltration of innovative technology into law enforcement agencies (LEAs) could be traced to the late 1990s when started the replacement process of previous forms of "intuition-led policing" by "intelligence-led policing" (Ratcliffe 2016) and then by "technologically enabled prediction-led policing" (Sandhu and Fussey 2021). These processes parallel a shift in policing priorities "from crime-fighting to public protection of ever-widening scope" and harm prevention (Heaton et al. 2019, p. 2). As policing broadens its scope, so is the concept of crime becoming more tied to different external threats under the "wider umbrella of security" (Degenhardt and Bourne 2020). As a result, LEAs are increasingly turning to new technologies to address fast-transforming settings of threats and harms more safely and efficiently, parallelly facing many transformations and challenges – from practical (Vrăbiescu 2020) over regulatory (Allen et al. 2016) to organizational (Vepřek et al. 2020).

Advances and changes in technology generated opportunities and transformations – across the criminal sphere and its impact on victims, communities, and policing. Technology provides new promising tools for LEAs in hardware – surveillance devices (e.g. CCTV, body-worn cameras, and drones); mobile devices (e.g. navigation systems and mobile phones); "Internet of Things" (e.g. wearables and smart devices), as well as in software – statistics, database coupling, data mining, and profiling (e.g. "predictive policing" and "big data" algorithms); Automatic Number Plate Recognition (ANPR); mapping (e.g. GPS and heatmaps); biometrics

Security Technologies and Social Implications, First Edition. Edited by Garik Markarian, Ruža Karlović, Holger Nitsch, and Krishna Chandramouli.

(e.g. fingerprints, DNA, and face recognition); social media and open-source intelligence (OSINT) (e.g. Ariel et al. 2018; Bradford et al. 2020; Clavell 2018; Custers and Vergouw 2015). Thus, LEAs, for some time now, are functioning in an intense information environment (Lorenz et al. 2021; Sørensen and Pica 2005). Technologies' utilization and policing routines, strategies, and decision making turned into "complex socio-technical mediations" (Fussey et al. 2021) because technologies not only alter users' behavior (e.g. Ariel et al. 2015) but users also actively identify new needs as well as problems imposed by the technology implementation (Fielding 2021; Sandhu and Fussey 2021). Thus, the impact of technology on the transformation of police practices, increase in effectiveness and efficiency seems more complex (e.g. issues of occupational tensions and trust) (Miranda 2015; Wilson-Kovacs 2021) and often not so explicit and/or not so prompt as expected (e.g. Sandhu and Fussey 2021).

One of the important reasons is also the primary purpose of a specific technology (commercial or professional), and the other is concurrent criminals' access to and usage of technology. LEAs have rationally used various commercial and private sector technological solutions, only some of which are specifically designed for them (Rajamäki et al. 2018). It is important to distinguish between technology developed for commercial purposes or/and in a commercial setting (e.g. drones, mobile phones, and cameras) and specialized technology designed exclusively for LEAs (e.g. TETRA, hot-spot maps, and databases) since each has its advantages and disadvantages. The legal and policy framework and the structural decisions made around commercial and professional technologies differ significantly, leading to many unresolved issues; for example, high costs and lengthy implementation and adoption of professionally in-house developed technology for LEAs, problems arising from private companies taking care of the data collection and analysis for LEAs, and commercial software remaining proprietary knowledge usually unavailable for external scrutiny ("black box," Sandhu and Fussey 2021).

Technology provides resourceful platforms for standard and "new" types of offenses, making crimes more sophisticated, organized, and less traceable. Digital tools now play a role in almost all crimes, and it remains debatable whether it is now beyond the capability of the current LEA to police it effectively (Horsman 2017). Since criminals usually have access to technology ahead of LEAs, they are in a constant race of trying to catch up with criminals' plans for implementing attacks against individuals and organizations, especially if the LEAs are using the same commercial technology as criminals.

Moreover, those digital tools are defined in a sociopolitical context and with certain objectives that must be acknowledged (Miró-Llinares 2020); for example, digital technologies "act as an important legal instrument and a vital part of the transnational harmonization mechanism that enhances efficiency in protecting EU external borders" (European Commission 2016; Vrăbiescu 2020, p. 11). By employing them, LEAs are balancing between obtaining international security while respecting (inter)national-(inter)state legislations on data protection, human rights, and privacy (Fielding 2021). Security concerns and predicted increase in border-crossing trends empower further border security technologization (Lehtonen and Aalto 2017) advocated by European Commission (2016). This proactive use of innovative technologies resulted in associating such technologies with securitization (in which public opinion is neglected) (Lodge 2004; Müller 2011; Skleparis 2016) and the militarization of police (technology that can have both civilian and military usage) (Martins and Ahmad 2020). Thus, besides challenges imposed on LEAs by its technical aspects, innovative technology also ruffles legal and ethical dilemmas surrounding legitimacy, accountability, and governance. Having in mind the severe and far-reaching consequences of LEAs' decisions and consequences of public mistrust and lack of confidence in police (Ariel 2016; Kounadi et al. 2015), the broader societal implications of technology implementation should be taken into consideration.

In Europe, the effects of technological developments for police organizations and citizens have not yet been comprehensively or systematically studied (see for exception: Buckingham et al. 2019; Edwards et al. 2015; Maskaly et al. 2017) and dissemination outputs resulting from Horizon 2020 projects are just emerging. Therefore, to better understand and value technology and its implications, the assessment requires a more comprehensive overview not only of empirical data on perceptions of technological solutions' endorsement by both POs and the public capturing benefits but also limitations and drawbacks, and future directions (Miró-Llinares 2020).

1.2 Study Aims and Objectives

There is a knowledge gap regarding how different police systems around Europe have adapted to digital challenges and how they cope with innovative technology demands. Thus, this chapter aims to review the results of empirical research on innovative technology adoption by different LEAs' jurisdictions in Europe in the period 2014–2021 by representing both LEAs and public perspectives on technology role and usage as well as experienced challenges and barriers.

1.3 Methodology

Studies for this rapid review were selected based on the following inclusion criteria: primary studies conducted in Europe, journal-article-type publications, written in English, and published from 2014 onward. The year 2014 was chosen as the baseline year because it is the start year of the Horizon 2020 EU Research and

Innovation program. The search was limited to peer-reviewed publications that contained empirical assessments and/or evaluations of technology implementation into LEAs, using quantitative and/or qualitative research design, conducted on humans, and presenting LEAs and/or public perspectives.

Relatively broad concepts for the research topic were chosen: "technology," "police," "LEA," "study," and "survey," and all possible combinations of these keywords were used in publication search. To narrow the search, the presence of those keywords was required in the published abstract.

Three academic databases were searched for combinations of the keywords in English-language journals: Web of Science Core Collection – excluding Chemical Indexes, Scopus, and EBSCO. The initial search process resulted in 1697 publications. Additional 32 publications were selected for inclusion based on cross-referencing, resulting in 1729 publications.

Publications revealed in the initial search were the first subject to screening for duplicates and then followed by "title and abstract" screening. Then, the full text of all potentially relevant papers was retrieved for closer examination. The inclusion criteria were applied first against the manuscripts' abstracts and then against the full-text version of the selected papers. Based on the screening and extraction process, 28 research articles were selected for analysis (Figure 1.1). Information extracted from studies included the authors' names, year of study publication, country of study, technology researched, objectives, the study design/data collection, and sample size (Table 1.A.1). Finally, findings from the included publications were synthesized using a narrative summary.

1.4 Results

1.4.1 Study Characteristics

Regarding the temporal and geographical distribution, most of the analyzed studies were published in 2020 (32%), and the majority is conducted in the United Kingdom (50%), while 20% was conducted in more than one jurisdiction. Respondents were mainly POs (75%), while public and POs were captured in two research areas. All studies were cross-sectional, and the majority of them were entirely or partially qualitative (70%). In qualitative studies, the dominant method of data collection was interviewing (70%). More than one-fifth of the research used mixed-method design (21%), and four endorsed experimental paradigms. Consequently, data were mainly collected on convenient, small samples. In two researches, data were collected from the (nationally) representative samples. In most analyzed studies, researchers were analyzing the implementation of social media (18%), smart borders (17%), diverse technologies (17%), followed by crime mapping (10%), and predictive policing (10%) (Appendix 1.A).

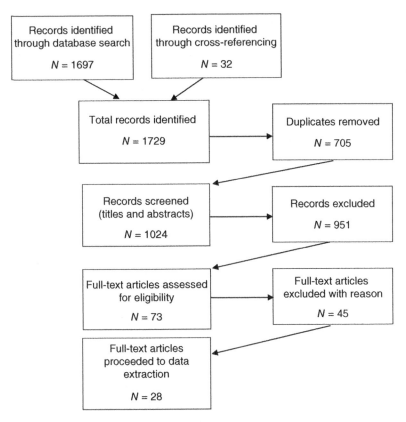

Figure 1.1 Study selection flow chart.

The following section will first summarize the results of the studies that capture technology implementation into LEAs more broadly, followed by the summary of the adoption of specific digital tools.

1.4.2 Diverse Technologies Adoption

Generally, there are optimistic views among European LEAs regarding technology implementation and adoption. However, the majority also observe obstacles in this process and would prefer to have a more comprehensive overview of the available technologies, together with more grounded information on whether and how those technologies are working before actual frontline adoption (Allen et al. 2016; Custers and Vergouw 2015; Miranda 2015).

Findings from Portugal (Miranda 2015) show that inspectors' beliefs about the positive contribution of technology to the criminal investigations' effectiveness are grounded in associating actions based on scientific evidence with objectivity, credibility, and legitimacy. Investigators expect that technology will help them resolve more sophisticated crimes, primarily those criminals commit, by using innovative techniques and strategies. The capacity of technology to (automatedly) obtain, collect, record, sort, store, analyze, and compare information through databases and online (e.g. through social networks) faster, easier, and more error-free was the most significant assistance to their work.

When it comes to technological consequences for changes in their work, some investigators predict the disappearance of traditional police work in the future and its complete replacement by innovative technological solutions (Miranda 2015). Others think that criminal investigation will not change so much and that traditional and basic police methods will remain the same. They argue that traditional detective work remains necessary even if combined with science and new technologies since there is still a need to manually ascertain the results at the end of an "automated" investigation (Miranda 2015). As one of the negativities of technology implementation, they ascertain how this trust in technology infallibility contributes to eliminating human responsibility and reducing POs' effort (Miranda 2015).

As obstacles to technology implementation in police work, inspectors mentioned: lack of technological and human resources, restrictive legislation, and the lack of collaboration in the access and sharing of information (between the scientific organization and police, and between different national police bodies, services of scientific and technical policy) due to lack of confidence from some authorities toward others, lack of knowledge about the capability of some units, the mismatch between criminal investigation and science and technology (not being aware or capable of applying some things that already exist), resistance to innovation, especially among older POs, certain conservatism and nonacceptance of new technology by legal bodies, resistance and distrust toward new (genetic) profiles (Miranda 2015).

Wilson-Kovacs' (2021) explorational study of the part-time digital media investigators' embeddedness in police investigations confirms how POs' unwillingness to use digital technologies, and for their fear of digital processes, as well as lack of seniors' support and prefer using traditional methods over innovative one, represents obstacles in technology implementation in the UK police. Custers and Vergouw (2015) internationally collected data confirmed that most respondents experienced obstacles in applying technology in policing. Especially in the domain of organization (insufficient support, guidance, and management, insight and overview, connection with international developments, financing, and technology availability), followed by legal (lack or insufficient clarity of a legal basis, especially on how to deal with personal data) and then technical obstacles (insufficient technology availability and overview of available technologies). In Wilson-Kovacs (2021) study, part-time digital media investigators also expressed their concern about the innovative technology data reliability outside a controlled (educational) environment. They complained about their workloads during specializations accompanied by big expectations, confusion about their duties, and their roles and responsibilities, as well as lack of guidance and post-training. Consequently, the support they provide to POs with technology implementation is weakened and not fully comprehended.

According to Abbas and Policek's (2021) analysis of the post-adoptive stage of mobile technology POs found several digital features (e.g. photographs, the e-signature feature, and Google Maps) as efficiency promotors, but overall do not consider that mobile devices either made their work more exciting or increase their job satisfaction. Moreover, most POs believe that organization adopts technologies that are not useful, not being convinced of the new systems' benefits. Also, especially officers of long service were dissatisfied with how new technologies are implemented (ill preparation for device usage, insufficient help, and support to officers who are experiencing problems). Additional reasons for officers' resistance and responses/adaptations during the post-adoptive stage of mobile technology were considering the devices frustrating, accessing the low quality of information, facing poor signal and connectivity, limited data storage capacity, etc. The usefulness of the device feature contributed to observed benefits. In contrast, limited IT skills, the uneasiness of getting used to new work methods, older age, inadequate reliability, and the uselessness of these features contributed to the perception of the mobile device as a threat. Generally, Abbas and Policek (2021) recommended that organizations invest in (continuous) training programs, especially for older POs, to enhance their technical skills and create a positive user experience through which the perceived usefulness of technology will be promoted.

Sumuer and Yildirim (2015) assessed factors related to acceptance of general electronic performance support systems in Turkey (EPSS – integrated into application software and provide POs with task structuring, knowledge, data, tools, and communication components to facilitate their work processes). Behavioral intentions, perception of usefulness, and positive attitudes toward using EPSS were strongly interrelated, and perceived ease of use had a significant direct influence on both perceived usefulness and attitude toward using the EPSS. Furthermore, estimation on system usefulness and easiness to use were, similarly to Abbas and Policek (2021) findings', related to (i) user personal characteristics – better computer knowledge and skills, more experience, less anxiety about using the system, enjoyment with the system, motivation to use (ii) system characteristics – simplicity and clarity of the system interface, user-friendliness, simplified data entry, performance support facilities such as access to data and information, step-by-step guidance, and automating job-related tasks; importance of relevance of the system to their job; less part of the system that produce overload; usability of the mobile personal computers – the learnability of the system, regular updates to fix problems or bugs, improve existing tools and resources, and add new functions and functionalities to the system and (iii) organizational characteristics – improvement of information technology infrastructure in terms of network and hardware in the organization – training offered for using information, for using technology infrastructure (e.g. help systems and peer and technical support), and adequate personnel management.

Custers and Vergouw (2015) international findings showed that technologies used the most by police forces are also assessed as those having the highest potential (DNA, camera surveillance/CCTV, face recognition, wiretapping, network analyses, GPS/tracking systems, biometrics, and fingerprints) and were producing the highest satisfaction and preference for its use. ANPR, virtual reality, weapon technologies, social media, and bodycams are lesser used technologies that are hardly mentioned as most satisfactory. LEAs' representatives are most interested in the future implementation of face recognition, virtual reality, drones, and GPS/tracking system, but the potential of those technologies is not estimated as high (apart from GPS/tracking systems). Allen et al. (2016) findings related to the condition of IT infrastructure in UK police forces showed that overall, most technology areas are seen as up-to-date or old-but-serviceable, in most cases, in better condition than before. As expected, the areas seen as being up to date tend to have a lower expectation of transformational change. The results highlight call handling, dispatch, custody management, crime analysis, and mapping as areas where technology was significantly described as not being up to date. As key priority areas in police forces are listed incident management, mobility/portable technologies (as opposed to fixed ones), and information governance. Reliance on collaboration in systems development with other police forces is high and assessed as a high priority, while reliance on cloud computing and outsourcing to deliver and support IT capability is low and assessed as a low priority for most police forces. These findings go against governmental efforts to strengthen collaboration between different police services and between police services and other agencies, and against considering the lack of collaboration in the access and sharing of information as an obstacle to technology implementation (Custers and Vergouw 2015; Miranda 2015). International findings (Custers and Vergouw 2015) also indicated how within and between different jurisdictions prevails an entirely different conception of what is comprised by the same type of technology (e.g. biometrics) and that there is a lack of overview of available technologies in police forces.

1.4.3 Real-Time Data Providers

It was assumed that **body-worn cameras** (BWC) facilitate new opportunities to examine (document, inform, and assess) police decisions and reduce improper decision-making enabled by subjective policing (Sandhu and Fussey 2021).

The BWC randomized-controlled trial (Henstock and Ariel 2017) showed a reduction in the prevalence and severity of police use of force used when wearing BWC but only in the cases with less aggressive force response (e.g. open-hand tactics including physical restraints and non-compliant handcuffing). The study pointed to the need to test BWC efficacy regarding the level of force response. Later, BWC study by Miranda (2021) showed that POs consistently compare the use of BWCs to other visual surveillance technologies (namely CCTV) regarding their administration and data management, showing special concern about data gathering, storing, and accessing (especially access of unauthorized third parties). POs pointed out that BWC design (e.g. bulk, dimensions, and weight), body placement (e.g. chest and head), and situational characteristics substantially impact their operations and practice and reliability in use. POs are concerned with where to place the camera, (un)intentionally moving of camera, losing it, quality of video footage (i.e. in the night economy), etc. BWC showed to be more useful in more remote (rural) areas, but these settings especially present problems of connectivity and, consequently, video-information quality. In order to ensure the suitability of BWC equipment to their operational needs, the perspectives and experience of frontline POs should be considered when designing them.

Similar to BWC, **other real-time data providers** (e.g. POI application/systems) are expected to decrease the number of situations in which POs act without information – and reduce improper decision making enabled by subjective policing.

In Lukosch et al.'s (2018) study, frontline POs assessed a "mobile location-based real-time notification system" as pragmatic and straightforward to use, valuable and usable, especially for POs new to the area. App usage also contributed to a reduction in emergency response calls. Furthermore, to keep using the application daily, POs pointed to the need for continuously updating information and the need for co-driver assistance if the application is used in the vehicle (Engelbrecht et al. 2019). However, providing POs with more information on situations through this app did not result in the expected increase in situation awareness (situation understanding) (Lukosch et al. 2018). Thus, an expected decrease in the number of situations in which POs act without information and a reduction in improper decision making enabled by subjective policing were not gained by this application.

Further testing of the location-based real-time notification system that gives POs information on the spot and lets them report incidents on location (Engelbrecht et al. 2019) revealed that system usability varies with the type of front officers' work (neighborhood patrol, surveillance, and emergency) and type of transportation (foot, car, and bicycle). The app was perceived as the most usable by neighborhood patrol agents on foot since its usage fits the most closely to their daily routine work. Again, app usage did not result in differences in situational awareness, productivity, or task load. Also, there was no difference in the app assessment due to the difference between locations in hot spot density. It was assumed that the lack of effect on situational awareness could be attributed to the higher number of notifications that raise attention demands. That lack of stress reduction could be attributed to a disruption in working roles and division of responsibilities by introducing this new system with high information density. POs liked the possibility of creating reports in their patrol area on location directly but showed concern about database fragmentation, long-term maintenance, etc. The system enabled them to visit substantially more hot spots during their shift, but some POs expressed concern over constantly tracking their location, monitoring them, and logging activity. POs preferred the mobile app over the smartwatch version. It was recommended to use additional filters to decrease the number of notifications received to lower the attention demand and that new digital tools should be implemented to improve work performance while still allowing officers to keep their preferable work routine (Engelbrecht et al. 2019).

Saunders et al. (2019), in an experimental comparison of VR training and full-live training exercise, prove that performance increased significantly within all training groups and that knowledge scores did not differ significantly across groups after the training. These results supported using VR training as a backup solution for training POs.

Bradford et al. (2020) findings from the representative sample of the London adult population indicate that the public generally approves of police use of "live face recognition" (LFR), especially when its usage is augmented by identifying potential terrorists or serious violent criminals. Citizens who worried about crime, who trusted more in police fairness and community engagement, and police legitimacy (primarily normative alignment) were more prone to accept LFR usage. The most important determinant of acceptance of police use of LFR is concern about privacy, but its effect is mediated by legitimacy (primarily normative alignment). Legitimacy also mediated all assumed associations between trust and acceptance of LFR use by police. The fact that attitudes toward police legitimacy and trust were much more significant predictors of acceptance than concerns about the crime should be considered while advocating innovative technology implementation.

1.4.4 Predictive Policing

By now different applications for predictive policing technologies are developed, and while some predict crime location and time, others tend to predict profiles of offenders and victims (Sandhu and Fussey 2021). Their goal is to provide police and the public with current and accurate data and contribute to higher engagement and empowerment of citizens, increasing their confidence in police (Kounadi et al. 2015). However, the implementation of those technologies raised several issues, from privacy violations over public use of sensitive information to the production of biased predictions (Sandhu and Fussey 2021). Also, those systems require large amounts of data, which POs should supply, and complex algorithmic analysis on which predictions are based. These reduces predictive systems' transparency and understanding.

Predictive systems are becoming a central mechanism for coordinating police work and decision-making processes, producing substantial changes in police work (Lorenz et al. 2021; Vepřek et al. 2020). Due to the lack of tests in which the effectiveness of digital predictive tools is independently replicated (Vepřek et al. 2020 studies that tested the usage of specific predictive digital programs in a specific context provide at least partial insight into their applicability and acceptance.

Tundis et al.'s (2020) assessment of predictive policing app development that enables criminal detection in the real world, and two-way police–citizen communication proved its effectiveness in big cities. After reporting the crime events, the application provides citizens, based on data elaboration and analysis, with a back notification informing them about crime events and criminals' whereabouts. Findings revealed that applications contribute to an average of three minutes of time intervention and time-saving in big cities. App features was assessed by citizens from satisfactory to excellent (content and navigation, functionality, look and feel, response time, and stability). Tundis et al. (2020) concluded that smartphone application is not too invasive to citizens' privacy and uses a minimal data set. Findings from Kounadi et al. (2015) also showed that the public is not aware of the sensitivity to revealing crime locations and that citizens do not consider the revelation of the exact location of burglaries and violent crimes as privacy violation. Citizens believed that data anonymization methods (e.g. street-level data) currently used by the police satisfactorily protect the victims' privacy. They speak in favor of a medium risk protection method – prevention of information disclosure and preference for street-level data, agreeing with the method of sharing crime data on national crime mapping websites in the United Kingdom. Higher disclosure implications were observed for burglaries' locations than for violent crime locations, but reidentification risk modestly impacts the responses. However, most citizens were not aware of crime maps and those methods, nor are they sure how to "read" plot statistics based on those methods. Thus, Kounadi et al. (2015) concluded that when adopting digital tools, it is important to reveal any privacy implications by disclosing data that contain sensitive and confidential information (e.g. location) and give them a clear direction for ethical data use.

Vepřek et al. (2020) found that representatives of the scientific-analytic branches of police use other narratives to legitimize predictive policing while being aware that there is no conclusive support for its effectiveness in crime reduction. Specifically, they pointed to the predictive policing efficiency and transparency within police administration and (partially) toward the public. Also, they were providing contra-arguments of "myths" created in the media and research on predictive policing. Some of them were: keeping POs' autonomy and independence by trying to actively participate in the software development and prediction process, seeking from officials reasons and explanations why a particular decision was made, regarding predictive policing as a merely supportive tool in police work, arguing that humans will stay foremost interpreters of the outcome of the software, and explaining the exclusion of personal data in German predictive policing applications. Interestingly, those representatives did not use a security narrative.

Lorenz et al. (2021) findings indicated that the predictive policing system, used to display geographical distribution of the potential high-risk areas, resulted in the following transforms of the police organization and professionals' work: standardization of decisions and actions, need for POs' specialization, centralization of decision-making, lower probability of rejecting the system prediction (due to an experienced lower level of risk and personal responsibility for system-based decision), automation of police nonroutine tasks relying on algorithmic data analysis, and setting new standards regarding the decision-making (e.g. under which circumstances, algorithmic system's automation of advice could be disregarded). Sandhu and Fussey (2021) study revealed an optimistic view toward predictive policing as a system that emphasized objectification of POs' decisions based on big data and algorithms and reduced the flawed decision due to human bias and subjectivity. However, POs are aware of the limitations of predictive technologies (e.g. biased and flawed predictions due to the low quality or limited data, software potential to reproduce existing and obvious knowledge sometimes in a patronizing fashion, need for checking allegedly objective prediction). Awareness of those limitations leads to POs' resistant attitudes and skepticism toward predictive technology, occasional reluctance to follow instructions to use predictive technology and encouragement of the reassertion of subjective police discretion.

1.4.5 Smart Borders

Out of all domains, the importance of technology implementation is, maybe, the most visible and debatable within border control, since, from a security perspective, the protection of the European borders requires the development of systems, equipment, tools, processes, and methods for rapid identification – that is "smart borders" Hayes and Vermeulen (2012), "iBorder/iBordering" (Pötzsch 2018) or "digital borders" (Chouliaraki and Georgiou 2019). Decisions regarding the use of automated border control (ABC) and multiple biometrics are not just scientific or expert but rather political in nature, as they have implications for fundamental human rights (Lehtonen and Aalto 2017). Political stakeholders argue that technology implementation benefits for enhancing border security outweigh privacy, rights, and legal issues (Lehtonen and Aalto 2017). They support stricter border control to prevent potential negative consequences of predicted immigration for European countries but recognize the importance of collecting and retaining only the necessary personal information and its transparent use. They advocate setting up legal instruments and monitoring mechanisms before implementing the ABC system at the European level and argue for national parliaments' approval for any changes that could affect fundamental rights (e.g. concerns regarding the accessibility of ABC for disabled people). Lehtonen and Aalto (2017) concluded that technology should be kept under democratic and public political control to ensure its acceptability to the users.

According to Crockett et al. (2017), most border managers and officers were enthusiastic about adopting new biometric technologies, their adoption could improve their working conditions, shift management, and resource allocation. However, they pointed to several barriers observed in adopting specific digital technologies for ABC (dirty hands – palm vein scanner technology; facial changes/modification – facial recognition technology) and the need for replacement of old with new generation technology.

Birdi et al. (2021) pointed out that adequate technology was reported as the most common obstacle and the facilitator for cross-border knowledge sharing. Therefore, to achieve international cooperation, there is a need for developing standardized and compatible technological systems that will be able to transfer information quickly. In contrast, the development of specific systems could be used for specific types of collaboration (e.g. preventing human trafficking).

Vrăbiescu's (2020) study findings revealed a gap between declared "controlled" management of the mobility of allegedly irregular mobile EU citizens and actual disorganization in the Schengen border crossing system. Reasons are policy implementation limitations (lack of legislative adjustment to digital demands), poor administration (training of border agents and allocating resources), and political decisions (harmonization or competing narratives). Despite the availability of sophisticated digital tools and preference among officers for using them (more straightforward to use and more efficient than paper-mediated documentation), regulations tend to either make them unusable or limit their practical use. So, police use them selectively. It was observed how each member state acquires other border security and how technologies acquired by them face different stages of implementation while traditional techniques and paperwork remained relevant. Vrăbiescu (2020) concluded that one of the crucial prerequisites for harmonizing legislative member state practices against "internally" undesirable EU citizens is securing the same stage of technology implementation by each member state.

1.4.6 Communication Between Police and Citizens

Communication between police and citizens is embedded in the core of policing – and their contact via digital tools and open sources could also help protect citizens and stimulate community policing (see Sučić and Karlović 2017). Those tools provide easily accessible opportunities for police–citizen interaction. They have many potential benefits – providing police with a large amount of information under low costs, promoting transparency of police work, and a positive image while simultaneously strengthening citizen participation (e.g. providing help with investigations, volunteering). However, current studies revealed many factors that add to the attenuation of assumed positive effects of digitally mediated police – citizen communication.

Zhang et al.'s (2020) findings show that there is established communication between police and citizens through social media and websites, but it is limited to certain roles due to perception of legitimacy and data protection regulations. Citizens' reports (e.g. videos and photos) may have limited value due to the potential to cause data overload and because police can use them only partially while protecting personal privacy. POs experience barriers in accessing data and technology and identify operational challenges associated with using certain technologies in the field (e.g. difficulty typing). It was concluded that technologies facilitate the reporting process for citizens who are afraid of bureaucracy or who are reporting someone they know.

Natarajan's (2016) findings revealed that supplying victims with mobile phones programmed to link directly to police reduced the domestic violence victims' fears and repeated victimization and increased their self-confidence in reaching for help from police. Also, police response to calls commonly resulted in perpetrator arrest. However, there was also the present potential inconvenience of carrying it along with their mobile phones, and a significant proportion of the activations were accidental, producing extra costs for police and reducing their capacity to deal with other emergencies.

Rønn et al.'s (2020) analysis not only showed that Scandinavian police investigators perceived social media information as an important source for investigative work but also expressed fear related to personal and operational security (exposing specific investigations) and the risk of exposing oneself as a private person. Also, police investigators expressed more general fear of making mistakes while using social media, searching it, leaving traces, etc., which is related to the uncertainty about how the algorithms used on social media platforms work. This concern produces anxiety among investigators about not knowing when they are crossing the line for acceptable professional behavior as an investigator. Furthermore, the vague legal framework governing police work in the digital domain and lack of adequate support by police management adds to the feeling of potential illegitimacy of investigators' engagement in social media. This study indicated that additional sources that will make digital investigations easier, more explicit guidelines and procedures, and adaptation of police law and the procedural codes to the digital domain would make POs feel safer and more confident in using social media for investigative work.

On the other side, Grimmelikhuijsen and Meijer's (2015) research on a nationally representative sample showed that a very small percentage of Swedish citizens engage online with the police – 3.5% use social media to receive information from police, and 0.1% for interaction with police. It is concluded that the reach of communication using Twitter is limited and not valid for communication with a broad audience. So, the focus should be placed on better involvement of citizens to assure a better potential for long-term monitoring of police behavior. Due to the level of online interaction, informative use of Twitter (transparency), and not interactive use (participation), was associated with a higher level of perceived effectiveness. While enhancing participation in Twitter does not increase perceived police legitimacy, enhancing transparency on Twitter does increase it, albeit to a limited extent. This led to increased perceived police effectiveness (effectiveness is communicated through social media) and legitimacy (the police demonstrate that they are in touch with society and "modern"). Only perceived effectiveness contributed significantly to legitimacy.

Bullock et al.'s (2021) analysis of the perception of communication experts – POs (comm officers) showed that police as the organization is supporting the use of social media to promote citizen engagement and to assure police visibility (online presence) in communities in a more efficient and less costly way. Comm officers think that this visibility will add to the transparency of police work and improve citizen perceptions of the police, but since there is a lack of objective measures, the size of the visibility impact on citizens' perceptions and behaviors is missing. Although POs are generally familiar with social media use, their willingness to communicate with citizens through social media is not strong. Like in the Rønn et al. (2020) study, some of the comm officers mentioned that it could be linked to worrying about the security and control issues of posted messages, awareness of harm to reputation potential messages may cause, and not feeling confident of generating engaging content. Also, they are aware that the organization cannot control the content on all the accounts, which might lead to reputational damage posted by POs and control citizens' reactions to the messages. Comm officers commented that creating appropriate and engaging content for citizens is not always straightforward and can be challenging – the solution to boosting their user confidence and the quality of messages they see in training and support. Promotion of greater social media uses they see in larger communication teams within police and availability of adequate equipment on which officers can have appropriate apps, use different platforms, and upload engaging content easily. The potential of social media for police to get into contact with groups of people traditionally seldom engaging with police (e.g. younger and minorities) is hard to achieve and keep up with what platforms are being used and by whom. They pointed out how social media afford citizens an ability to access information and ensure better interaction between police and communities, but that there is a need to find out more about the nature of engagement and experiences citizens have with the materials posted by police.

Another exploratory study with communication experts – POs (comm officers) revealed that the primary purposes of social media are: publicizing important messages to citizens (e.g. missing or wanted persons), promotion of police work (e.g. specific successful operations), crime prevention messaging and encouraging crime reporting (Fielding 2021). Comm officers primarily produce the most engaging materials (e.g. personal officers' stories, photography, and video, not only for dramatic events). The content on crime prevention and advice on keeping them safe officers consider important, but they are aware that only a small proportion of people pay attention to it. That is why they tie that advice to incidents happening in their neighborhood. It is highlighted that special attention should be given to advice style and tone, e.g. cartoon-like short videos to reach specific audiences, and coordinated messaging on different social networks. Comm officers suggested that while informal tone/style and greater account activity affect the likelihood of forwarding police tweets, providing links and hashtags create diffusion. However, message attractiveness is topic-sensitive. Social networks are used for informing citizens, and it is common to post different campaigns in which police are collaborating with other organizations and promoting humanitarian actions. Comm officers most commonly use Twitter to warn the public – about routine imminent and "live" events, while speed is the most important in creating warnings. Social media can provide POs with the knowledge of immediate value. So, they often also use it to send appeals, especially exploiting "fun stuff" to increase the audience for appeals. Every social media format has its potential that can be used to achieve the common goal – public engagement that requires accommodating local interests. Similar to Bullock et al. (2021) findings, in Fielding's (2021) study, comm officers again expressed their worries about how to measure the actual impact their presence has on social media – they use different types of statistics, surveys, and analytic tools. However, actual citizens' behavior is hard to capture. Communication challenges include reaching particular populations or locals and making contact when time is critical. So, they often used information that facilitates targeting and tailoring (assessing the target audience's social context), now at lower costs. It is essential to build trust while communicating through social media – so special efforts should be placed on technical aspects of specific accounts, appropriate directness, and honesty while communicating with citizens. Organizational problems in police SM communications included technical and human aspects (Fielding 2021). Comm officers criticize senior officers for waiting too long with police to start using social media and inadequate assessment of the initial choices that platforms/networks use. They also comment on their ignorance of the role of social media, upholding the information (controlling and inhibiting it), and poor adjustment in using this type of reporting. Also they find problematic technology adoption. Social media is perceived just as a tool to pursue strategically, and not a personal objective. Thus, training and encouragement to adopt social media among POs are needed. Currently, comm officers found challenging the effects of their increasing news (agency) function and the need for timely response and reaching more citizens (through, e.g. 24/7 availability and responsiveness to out-of-hours contacts) to enable direct citizen participation.

1.5 Discussion

The review of studies conducted in Europe over the last seven years clearly states a wide-option innovative technology implementation into LEAs. Nevertheless, the road toward it has many turns and several bulges – at the individual, technology, organization, and social level (Bullock 2018; Venkatesh and Bala 2008). There are substantive differences in the level of technology implementation and acceptance within and across European jurisdictions. Those differences reflect the differences in the states' wealth, the general level of societal digitalization, and (inter)national regulations, and are less related to specific LEAs' willingness to adopt technologies (Miró-Llinares 2020). Specific societal processes (e.g. widening of European Union), crisis (e.g. migration/refugee crisis, Brexit), and unexpected events (e.g. terrorist attacks and COVID pandemic) strongly influence the course and speed of specific technologies' implementation in LEAs. Some of the technologies (e.g. social media) represent not just technological but also an organizational and cultural revolution (Bullock 2018). Technology use in LE organizations is an obligation among officers regardless of their skills, knowledge, preferences, or attitudes (e.g. Kashefi 2014). Thus, it is not surprising that we get a very complex interplay of inhibiting and promoting factors of technology that must be negotiated by organizations and individuals (Bullock 2018).

Although technology potential and its benefits go beyond crime prevention (e.g. post-crisis stabilization and mediation), the research speaks in favor of considering algorithmic technologies, information systems, and biometrics as supportive rather than "revolutionary" tools in police work that will provide "absolute security" (Ceyhan 2008; Vepřek et al. 2020). According to POs, specific innovations just reproduce existing and evident knowledge, sometimes in a patronizing fashion (Sandhu and Fussey 2021). Although the advance in digital technologies has modified aspects of the role of POs, much remains the same (Bullock 2018). Consequently, promoting "the great expectations of technology potential" (e.g. Wilson-Kovacs 2021) should be toned down. Also, the operational adoption of some of the most powerful social control technologies is very controversial and produces significant concerns among citizens and the scientific community (Fussey et al. 2021; Gogov 2017). Thus, emerging technologies may cause uncertainty in society, which "results in a growing gap between citizens, technology, and politics," especially concerning the balance between individual privacy and its trade-off with security (Friedewald et al. 2010).

By making it possible to document, inform, and assess policy decision-making, technology increased objectivity and reduced inappropriate decision making enabled by subjective police discretion (Sandhu and Fussey 2021, p. 70). However, questions arise around the neutrality of biometrics technology (Lyon 2008), and the legality of police actions guided by automated policing – algorithms (Rajamäki et al. 2018; Sandhu and Fussey 2021). Concerns were also raised on inconclusive and misguided evidence. However, since they are "science-driven," they can convey the idea that biases, discrimination, and unjustified actions are objectively grounded (Miró-Llinares 2020; Miranda 2015; Mittelstadt et al. 2016; Peeters and Schuilenburg 2018). Also, some researchers raised questions about the consequence of automated systems on human's (POs') reduced and even diminished responsibility (Miranda 2015).

There is no doubt that technology provides easily accessible, cost-efficient, better-quality, and more relevant information for investigative work. It makes it possible to get immediate insight into a police-citizen encounter and communities' behavior, contributing to better crime prediction and early interventions (Bartlett et al. 2013; Omand et al. 2012; Trottier 2017). But constant acquiring of knowledge and information gathering added requirements on an officer to assure a large amount of data, accompanied by records' competition and maintenance. Thus, no substantial increase is gained in expected POs' visibility due to time out of police stations or bureaucracy reduction (Koper et al. 2014; Home Office 2017). Also, it is interesting that a greater amount of ahead-known information did not contribute to POs' situational awareness, and that constant information influx proved to be a disturbing factor in their frontline work (Engelbrecht et al. 2019). Technology's promoted "data hoarding" also raises issues related to its transfer, storage, access, management, data prioritization, protection, and security (Gottschalk 2010; Home Office 2017). There are also present doubts about data accuracy, completion, and integrity (Allen et al. 2016), as well as the ethics of handling information collected through specific sources (e.g. "data scraping," Rajamäki et al. 2018).

Innovative technology implementation is also a product of the "political conception of technologically based modernization" (Frois 2013, p. 4). It helps build a picture of the police as a modern organization in touch with society to highlight police successes (Bekkers and Vincent 2007; Schneider 2016). Police organization reputation management and branding contribute to police legitimacy (Ernst et al. 2021), transparency of police work, and accountability (Miranda 2021) while trying to restore confidence in the police and strengthen citizen participation (Bertot et al. 2010; Zhang et al. 2020).

While at the European level and specific jurisdiction level it is needed to standardize the legal framework for innovative technology employment, citizens' needs regarding technology implementation into LEAs could be summarized under the requirement for police transparency and accountability. Citizens are generally supportive toward police use of new technology, and the main predictors of this support are trust (perception of police performance, privacy concern, and police procedural justice) and legitimacy (Bradford et al. 2020; Grimmelikhuijsen and Meijer 2015). However, the lack of two-sided communication between citizens and police (Grimmelikhuijsen and Meijer 2015; Kounadi et al. 2015) raises questions about the actual level of awareness of privacy threats among citizens. While POs are keeping data containing sensitive and confidential information safe and using them according to legal and ethical standards, the threat should be kept at the minimum.

Police's needs regarding technology implementation are mainly related to acquiring IT knowledge, adequate digital tools, and budgets and assuring technology transparency and accountability (Sandhu and Fussey 2021, p. 70). Digital tool acceptance is needed to produce technology usage benefits (Abbas and Policek 2021; Sandhu and Fussey 2021; Sumuer and Yildirim 2015). Thus, to avoid POs' dissatisfaction and resistance, training should fulfill certain requirements: to be continuous, and consider POs' initial IT skills and preferences (Abbas and Policek 2021); to provide hands-on experience before full system implementation; and to promote efficient utilization of the various digital tools' features (Kashefi 2014), especially targeting and tailoring training for POs' with longer working experience. It is crucial to give POs' insight into available technology (Ernst et al. 2021) and align, as much as possible, new digital tools with their traditional way of working (Engelbrecht et al. 2019). Also, continuous support and assistance in performing on the job are required. Those recommendations will potentially trigger better compliance with technology usage in organizations and comply with the usage protocols (Lapointe and Beaudry 2014; Rivard and Lapointe 2012), thus improving performance and efficiency. Higher transparency of software/algorithms beneath the specific tools and how they reach decisions should increase POs' confidence in technology usage and higher reliability of suggested actions.

1.6 Instead of Conclusion

For adequate innovative technology implementation, everything matters – the way agencies mobilize knowledge, select technologies, adopt practices, and endorse "technological solutions" (Martins and Jumbert 2020). While some of the challenges and obstacles to technology implementation are unpredictable and/or hard to overcome, others are relatively easily solvable. Technology should become more transparent and assure higher professional efficiency and better responsiveness to citizens' needs. Maladaptive technology adoption could be avoided by using an end user-driven approach during its creation, and technology should align with POs' traditional way of working. It should be considered that trust in technology by officers and citizens is one of the most important factors in its perceived usefulness and adoption. Also, technological systems should be standardized and integrated across organizations to promote their coordinated utilization. Finally, to make a more comprehensive decision, there is a need for more contextual knowledge about the technology adoption, the practical effect of policing technologies on police work, and a more rigorous and continuous evaluation of the effectiveness of currently employed technologies.

1.A Appendix

Table 1.A.1 Basic information about analyzed studies, sorted alphabetically by the researched digital tool.

Authors	Publication year	Country	Digital tool	Participants	Study design/data collection	Sample size	Study objective
Miranda	2021	UK	BWC	POs	Interviews	26	BWC use in their professional practice
Henstock and Ariel	2017	UK	BWC	POs	Field randomized controlled trial	46–215 treatment shifts and 215 control shifts	Conditions related to the effectiveness of body-worn-cameras
Lukosch et al.	2018	Netherlands	Crime mapping	POs	Two real-life experiments	39	Experiences and obstacles encountered with the usage of POI crime mapping application
Engelbrecht et al.	2019	Netherlands	Crime mapping	POs	Experiment, survey	53	Effect of a location-based notification system on their situational awareness and task-load
Kounadi et al.	2015	UK	Crime mapping	Public	Survey	201	Police sharing crime data with the public
Miranda	2015	Portugal	Diverse technologies	POs	Interviews	14	The course of (biometric identification) technologies' implementation and its role for police and police work

Author	Year	Country	Technology	Participants	Methods	Sample	Focus
Allen et al.	2016	UK	Diverse technologies	Representatives of forces IT service	Survey, interviews, Delphi studies	45	Experiences and obstacles encountered with current technology, future needs, and preferences
Custers and Vergouw	2015	Australia, Bulgaria, Czech Republic, Finland, France, Hungary, Poland, Romania, Slovakia, Spain, Sweden + Australia	Diverse technologies	LEAs representatives from police forces	Survey	46	Experiences and obstacles encountered with current technology, future needs, and preferences among users
Wilson-Kovacs	2021	UK	Diverse technologies	Digital media experts employed by police	Ethnography, interviews	270 hours of ethnographic observations, 67 (in interviews)	Experiences of digital media experts employed by police and their perception on how digital technologies impact the police organization
Zhan et al.	2020	UK	Diverse technologies	POs and public	Interviews	13	Experience with technology usage
Bradford et al.	2020	UK	Face recognition	Public	Survey	1092 (representative sample)	Police trust and legitimacy as predictors of using live face recognition

(Continued)

Table 1.A.1 (Continued)

Authors	Publication year	Country	Digital tool	Participants	Study design/ data collection	Sample size	Study objective
Natarajan	2016	UK	Mobile devices	Victims and POs	Case study	1093 handset holders; 46 victims	Interaction of the public with police through mobile phones
Abbas and Policek	2020	UK	Mobile devices	POs	Focus groups, survey	57 (in focus groups), 132 (in a survey)	Factors and obstacles related to using mobile devices
Summer and Yildirim	2015	Turkey	Performance support system	POs	Survey; interviews	209 (in a survey); 15 (in interviews)	Factors related to police acceptance of an information technology
Tundis et al.	2020	Germany	Predictive policing (smartphone crime-reporting application)	Public	Interviews	30	Usability of the smartphone app for reporting crime
Vepřek et al.	2020	Germany	Predictive policing	Chief analysts and representatives of the scientific-analytic departments	Interviews	3	Implementation of predictive policing

Author	Year	Country	Field	Participants	Method	N	Focus
Lorenz et al.	2021	Germany	Predictive policing	POs	Interviews	12	How the use of the algorithmic system impacts the police work and organization
Sandhu and Fussey	2021	UK	Predictive policing	POs	Interviews	40	Predictive policing usage – experience, benefits, limitations
Lehtonen and Aalto	2017	Finland, Romania, Spain, UK	Smart borders	Political stakeholders – members of national and EU Parliament	Q sorting experiments	44	Factors related to acceptability in introducing smart borders
Crockett et al.	2017	Hungary, Greece, Latvia	Smart borders	Border guard managers and officers (e.g. passport control officers and document/vehicle experts)	Site surveys, workshops, questionnaires, interviews	N/A	Benefits and obstacles in introducing smart borders
Birdi et al.	2021	Belgium, Czech Republic, France, Germany, Italy, Netherlands, North Macedonia, Romania, Spain, UK	Smart borders	POs	Case study	10 (case studies)	Role of technology in international knowledge sharing

(Continued)

Table 1.A.1 (Continued)

Authors	Publication year	Country	Digital tool	Participants	Study design/ data collection	Sample size	Study objective
Vrăbiescu	2020	France, Romania	Smart borders	Police liaison officers and the border POs, police representatives, civil servants, high-ranked officers in the Ministry for the interior and police organizations	Interviews focus groups, participant observations	22 (in interviews), N/A (in focus groups)	Implementation of smart borders
Feilding	2021	UK	Social media	Communication experts – POs	Interviews	5	Factors influencing the use of social media
Bullock et al.	2021	UK	Social media	Communications experts – police staff	Interviews	23	Factors influencing the use of social media
Bullock	2018	UK	Social media	POs and police staff – users of social media, relevant police managerial roles, communications professionals	Interviews	32	Factors influencing the use of social media

Author	Year	Country	Technology	Sample	Method	N	Aim
Rønn et al.	2020	Denmark, Norway, Sweden	Social media	POs	Interviews	49	Factors and obstacles related to using social media in investigative work
Grimmelikhuijsen and Meijer	2015	Netherlands	Social media	Public	Survey	4492 (representative sample)	Perception of police effectiveness and legitimacy through the use of social media
Saunders et al.	2019	UK	Virtual reality	POs	Experiment – training exercises	80	Assessment of the effectiveness of using virtual reality in POs' training

References

Abbas, N. and Policek, N. (2021). Don't be the same, be better: an exploratory study on police mobile technology resistance. *Police Practice and Research* 22 (1): 849–868.

Allen, D.K., Norman, A., Williams, S.C. et al. (2016). Policing, information and technology in the UK: a national survey leeds university business school: leeds. file:///C:/Users/Ines%20Su%C4%8Di%C4%87/Downloads/Policing_Information_ and_Technology_in_the_UK.pdf (accessed 04 March 2022).

Ariel, B. (2016). Increasing cooperation with the police using body worn cameras. *Police Quarterly* 19 (3): 326–362.

Ariel, B., Farrar, W.A., and Sutherland, A. (2015). The effect of police body-worn cameras on use of force and citizens' complaints against the police: a randomized controlled trial. *Journal of Quantitative Criminology* 31 (3): 509–535.

Ariel, B., Sutherland, A., Henstock, D. et al. (2018). Paradoxical effects of self-awareness of being observed: testing the effect of police body-worn cameras on assaults and aggression against officers. *Journal of Experimental Criminology* 14 (1): 19–47.

Bartlett, J., Miller, C., Crump, J. et al. (2013). Policing in an information age. https://indianstrategicknowledgeonline.com/web/DEMOS_Policing_in_an_Information_ Age_v1.pdf (accessed 04 March 2022).

Bekkers, V. and Vincent, H. (2007). The myths of e-government: looking beyond the assumptions of a new and better government. *Information Society* 23 (5): 373–382.

Bertot, J.C., Jaeger, P.T., and Grimes, J.M. (2010). Using ICTs to create a culture of transparency: E-government and social media as openness and anti-corruption tools for societies. *Government Information Quarterly* 27 (3): 264–271.

Birdi, K., Griffiths, K., Turgoose, C. et al. (2021). Factors influencing cross-border knowledge sharing by police organisations: an integration of ten European case studies. *Police Practice and Research* 22 (1): 3–22.

Bradford, B., Yesberg, J.A., Jackson, J. et al. (2020). Live facial recognition: trust and legitimacy as predictors of public support for police use of new technology. *The British Journal of Criminology* 60 (6): 1502–1522.

Buckingham, S.A., Williams, A.J., Morrissey, K. et al. (2019). Mobile health interventions to promote physical activity and reduce sedentary behaviour in the workplace: a systematic review. *Digital health* 5: 2055–2076.

Bullock, K. (2018). The police use of social media: transformation or normalisation? *Social Policy and Society* 17 (2): 245–258.

Bullock, K., Garland, J., and Coupar, F. (2021). Police-community engagement and the affordances and constraints of social media. *Policing and Society* 31 (4): 373–385.

Ceyhan, A. (2008). Technologization of security: management of uncertainty and risk in the age of biometrics. *Surveillance and Society* 5 (2): 102–123.

Chouliaraki, L. and Georgiou, M. (2019). The digital border: mobility beyond territorial and symbolic divides. *European Journal of Communication* 34 (6): 594–605.

Clavell, G.G. (2018). Exploring the ethical, organisational and technological challenges of crime mapping: a critical approach to urban safety technologies. *Ethics and Information Technology* 20 (4): 265–277.

Crockett, K.A., O'Shea, J., Szekely, Z. et al. (2017). Do Europe's borders need multi-faceted biometric protection. *Biometric Technology Today* 7: 5–8.

Custers, B. and Vergouw, B. (2015). Promising policing technologies: experiences, obstacles and police needs regarding law enforcement technologies. *Computer Law and Security Review* 31 (4): 518–526.

Degenhardt, T. and Bourne, M. (2020). When risks meet: the dance of experience, professional expertise and science in border security technology development. *Criminology and Criminal Justice* 20 (2): 207–225.

Edwards, M., Rashid, A., and Rayson, P. (2015). A systematic survey of online data mining technology intended for law enforcement. *ACM Computing Surveys (CSUR)* 48 (1): 1–54.

Engelbrecht, H., Lukosch, S.G., and Datcu, D. (2019). Evaluating the impact of technology assisted hot-spot policing on situational awareness and task-load. *Proceedings of the ACM on Interactive, Mobile, Wearable and Ubiquitous Technologies* 3 (1): 1–18.

Ernst, S., ter Veen, H., and Kop, N. (2021). Technological innovation in a police organization: lessons learned from the National Police of the Netherlands. *Policing: A Journal of Policy and Practice* 15 (3): 1818–1831.

European Commission (2016). Stronger and smarter information systems for borders and security. Communication from the commission to the European parliament and council. COM(2016) 205 final, Brussels, 6.4.2016. http://www.eulisa.europa.eu/Newsroom/News/Documents/SB-EES/communication_on_stronger_and_smart_borders_20160406_en.pdf (accessed 4 March 2022).

Fielding, N.G. (2021). Police communications and social media. *European Journal of Criminology* 1–19. https://journals.sagepub.com/doi/pdf/10.1177/1477370821998969 (accessed 17 June 2022).

Friedewald, M., Wright, D., Gutwirth, S. et al. (2010). Privacy, data protection and emerging sciences and technologies: towards a common framework. *Innovation–The European Journal of Social Science Research* 23 (1): 61–67.

Frois, C. (2013). *Peripheral Vision: Politics, Technology, and Surveillance*, vol. 22. New York, USA: Berghahn Books.

Fussey, P., Davies, B., and Innes, M. (2021). 'Assisted'facial recognition and the reinvention of suspicion and discretion in digital policing. *The British Journal of Criminology* 61 (2): 325–344.

Gogov, B. (2017). Challenges of using information technologies in policing. *Bezbednosni dijalozi 8* (2): 27–37.

Gottschalk, P. (2010). Crime-based survey instrument for police integrity measurement. *Policing: An International Journal of Police Strategies and Management* 33 (1): 52–68.

Grimmelikhuijsen, S.G. and Meijer, A.J. (2015). Does Twitter increase perceived police legitimacy? *Public Administration Review* 75 (4): 598–607.

Hayes, B. and Vermeulen, M. (2012). Borderline. The EU's new border surveillance initiatives. Assessing the costs and fundamental rights implications of EUROSUR and the "Smart Borders" proposals. A study by the Heinrich Böll Fundation. https://www.tni.org/files/download/borderline.pdf (accessed 04 March 2022).

Heaton, R., Bryant, R., and Tong, S. (2019). Operational risk, omissions, and liability in policing. *The Police Journal* 92 (2): 150–166.

Henstock, D. and Ariel, B. (2017). Testing the effects of police body-worn cameras on use of force during arrests: a randomised controlled trial in a large British police force. *European Journal of Criminology* 14 (6): 720–750.

Home Office (2017). Fact sheet: Police funding for 2018/2019 explained. https://homeofficemedia.blog.gov.uk/2017/12/19/fact-sheet-police-funding-for-2018-19-explained/ (accessed 04 March 2022).

Horsman, G. (2017). Can we continue to effectively police digital crime? *Science and Justice* 57 (6): 448–454.

Kashefi, A. (2014). Investigating the link between users' IT adaptation behaviours and individual-level IT use outcomes using the coping model of user adaptation: A Case study of a work system computerisation project. Doctoral dissertation. Brunel University. https://citeseerx.ist.psu.edu/viewdoc/download?doi=10.1.1.1008.1432&rep=rep1&type=pdf (accessed 04 March 2022).

Koper, C.S., Lum, C., and Willis, J.J. (2014). Optimizing the use of technology in policing: Results and implications from a multi-site study of the social, organizational, and behavioural aspects of implementing police technologies. *Policing: A Journal of Policy and Practice 8* (2): 212–221.

Kounadi, O., Bowers, K., and Leitner, M. (2015). Crime mapping on-line: public perception of privacy issues. *European Journal on Criminal Policy and Research* 21 (1): 167–190.

Lapointe, L. and Beaudry, A. (2014). Identifying IT user mindsets: acceptance, resistance and ambivalence. *2014 47th Hawaii International Conference on System Sciences,* Waikoloa, HI, USA (6–9 January 2014). IEEE. pp. 4619–4628.

Lehtonen, P. and Aalto, P. (2017). Smart and secure borders through automated border control systems in the EU? The views of political stakeholders in the member states. *European Security* 26 (2): 207–225.

Lodge, J. (2004). EU homeland security: citizens or suspects? *Journal of European Integration* 26 (3): 253–279.

Lorenz, L., Meijer, A., and Schuppan, T. (2021). The algocracy as a new ideal type for government organizations: predictive policing in Berlin as an empirical case. *Information Polity* 26 (1): 71–86.

Lukosch, S.G., den Hengst-Bruggeling, M., Horsch, C.H.G. et al. (2018). Exploratory study of a mobile location-based real-time notification system for front-line police officers. *Journal of Universal Computer Science* 24 (7): 916–934.

Lyon, D. (2008). Biometrics, identification and surveillance. *Bioethics* 22 (9): 499–508.

Martins, B.O. and Ahmad, N. (2020). The security politics of innovation: Dual-use technology in the EU's security research programme. In: *Emerging Security Technologies and EU Governance* (ed. A. Calcara, R. Csernatoni and C. Lavallée). London: Routledge.

Martins, O.B. and Jumbert, M.G. (2020). EU Border technologies and the co-production of security 'problems' and 'solutions'. *Journal of Ethnic and Migration Studies* 48 (6): 1430–1447.

Maskaly, J., Donner, C., Jennings, W.G. et al. (2017). The effects of body-worn cameras (BWCs) on police and citizen outcomes: a state-of-the-art review. *Policing: An International Journal of Police Strategies and Management* 40 (4): 672–688.

Miranda, D. (2015). Criminal investigation through the eye of the detective: technological innovation and tradition. *Surveillance and Society* 13 (3/4): 422–436.

Miranda, D. (2021). Body-worn cameras 'on the move': exploring the contextual, technical and ethical challenges in policing practice. *Policing and Society* 32 (1): 18–34.

Miró-Llinares, F. (2020). Predictive policing: Utopia or Dystopia? On attitudes towards the use of Big Data algorithms for law enforcement. https://www.researchgate.net/profile/Fernando-Miro-Llinares/publication/338567228_Predictive_policing_Utopia_or_dystopia_On_attitudes_towards_the_use_of_big_data_algorithms_for_law_enforcement/links/5e4ab39f92851c7f7f43c020/Predictive-policing-Utopia-or-dystopia-On-attitudes-towards-the-use-of-big-data-algorithms-for-law-enforcement.pdf (accessed 04 March 2022).

Mittelstadt, B.D., Allo, P., Taddeo, M. et al. (2016). The ethics of algorithms: Mapping the debate. *Big Data and Society* 3 (2): 1–21.

Müller, M.M. (2011). *Public Security in the Negotiated State: Policing in Latin America and Beyond*. New York: Springer.

Natarajan, M. (2016). Police response to domestic violence: a case study of TecSOS mobile phone use in the London Metropolitan Police Service. *Policing: A Journal of Policy and Practice* 10 (4): 378–390.

Omand, D., Bartlett, J., and Miller, C. (2012). Introducing social media intelligence (SOCMINT). *Intelligence and National Security* 27 (6): 801–823.

Peeters, R. and Schuilenburg, M. (2018). Machine justice: governing security through the bureaucracy of algorithms. *Information Polity* 23 (3): 267–280.

Pötzsch, H. (2018). iBorder/ing. In: *Routledge Handbook of Interdisciplinary Research Methods* (ed. C. Lury and E. Uprichard), 99–103. London: Routledge.

Rajamäki, J., Sarlio-Siintola, S., and Simola, J. (2018). Ethics of open source intelligence applied by maritime law enforcement authorities. In: *Proceedings of the 17th European Conference on Cyber Warfare and Security ECCWS* (ed. A. Josang), 424–431. Oslo: Academic Conferences and Publishing International Limited.

Ratcliffe, J.H. (2016). *Intelligence-Led Policing*. London: Routledge.

Rivard, S. and Lapointe, L. (2012). Information technology implementers' responses to user resistance: nature and effects. *MIS Quarterly* 36 (3): 897–920.

Rønn, K.V., Rasmussen, B.K., Skou Roer, T. et al. (2020). On the perception and use of information from social media in investigative police work: findings from a scandinavian study. *Policing: A Journal of Policy and Practice* 15 (2): 1262–1273.

Sandhu, A. and Fussey, P. (2021). The 'uberization of policing'? How police negotiate and operationalise predictive policing technology. *Policing and Society* 31 (1): 66–81.

Saunders, J., Davey, S., Bayerl, P.S. et al. (2019). Validating virtual reality as an effective training medium in the security domain. *2019 IEEE Conference on Virtual Reality and 3D User Interfaces (VR)* Osaka, Japan (23–27 March 2019). IEEE. pp. 1908–1911.

Schneider, C.J. (2016). Police presentational strategies on Twitter in Canada. *Policing and Society* 26 (2): 129–147.

Skleparis, D. (2016). (In) securitization and illiberal practices on the fringe of the EU. *European Security* 25 (1): 92–111.

Sørensen, C. and Pica, D. (2005). Tales from the police: Rhythms of interaction with mobile technologies. *Information and Organization* 15 (2): 125–149.

Sučić, I. and Karlović, R. (2017). Community policing in support of social cohesion. In: *Community Policing-A European Perspective* (ed. P.S. Bayerl, B. Akhgar, R. Karlović and G. Markarian), 7–19. Cham: Springer.

Sumuer, E. and Yildirim, S. (2015). Exploring user acceptance of an electronic performance support system. *Performance Improvement Quarterly* 27 (4): 29–48.

Trottier, D. (2017). Digital vigilantism as weaponisation of visibility. *Philosophy and Technology* 30 (1): 55–72.

Tundis, A., Kaleem, H., and Mühlhäuser, M. (2020). Detecting and tracking criminals in the real world through an IoT-based system. *Sensors* 20 (3795): 1–27.

Venkatesh, V. and Bala, H. (2008). Technology acceptance model 3 and a research agenda on interventions. *Decision Sciences* 39 (2): 273–315.

Vepřek, L.H., Sibert, L., Sehn, L. et al. (2020). Beyond effectiveness: legitimising predictive policing in Germany. *Kriminologie-Das Online-Journal - Criminology-The Online Journal* 3: 423–443.

Vrăbiescu, I. (2020). Deportation, smart borders and mobile citizens: using digital methods and traditional police activities to deport EU citizens. *Journal of Ethnic and Migration Studies* 48 (8): 1891–1908. http://wrap.warwick.ac.uk/141308/8/WRAP-Deportation-smart-borders-mobile-citizens-digital-Vrabiescu-2020.pdf (accessed 4 March 2022).

Wilson-Kovacs, D. (2021). Digital media investigators: challenges and opportunities in the use of digital forensics in police investigations in England and Wales. *Policing: An International Journal* 44 (4): 669–682. https://ore.exeter.ac.uk/repository/bitstream/handle/10871/125904/Wilson-Kovacs%20March%202021%20DMI.pdf?sequence=4 (accessed 4 March 2022).

Zhang, M., Bandara, A., Price, B. et al. (2020). Designing technologies for community policing. *CHI EA '20: Extended Abstracts of the 2020 CHI Conference on Human Factors in Computing Systems* Honolulu, HI, USA (25–30 April 2020). pp. 1–9.

2

Data Protection Impact Assessments in Law Enforcement: Identifying and Mitigating Risks in Algorithmic Policing

Thomas Marquenie and Katherine Quezada-Tavárez

KU Leuven Centre for IT & IP Law, Leuven, Belgium

2.1 Introduction

Recent technological innovations are reshaping contemporary policing practices around the world as an ever-increasing number of data-driven tools are being introduced in the prevention, detection, and investigation of crime. In the European Union (EU), the myriad of high-tech systems that law enforcement agencies (LEAs) are using include automatic license plate readers, facial recognition, voice identification systems, big data analytics, and predictive policing (Jansen 2018; Spielkamp 2019). In the context of this contribution, the concept of Algorithmic Policing will be used to refer to algorithm-based analytical technologies that allow LEAs to collect and assess large datasets for the purpose of drawing inferences on criminal behavior and making predictions about potentially unlawful activities (Robertson et al. 2020). These novel tools are often expected to contribute to police work in various ways, including increased efficiency and improved operational capacity in the exercise of police duties. At the same time, the development and implementation of advanced analytical systems and Artificial Intelligence (AI) tools have also given rise to new threats that pose serious questions about legal and ethical values and the integrity of police operations.

Since these police technologies are generally data-driven, algorithmic policing practices are typically subject to data protection laws. Within the EU, the Law Enforcement Directive (LED) regulates the processing of personal data in the sphere of policing and criminal justice. Amongst the requirements prescribed by

Security Technologies and Social Implications, First Edition. Edited by Garik Markarian, Ruža Karlović, Holger Nitsch, and Krishna Chandramouli.
Published 2023 by John Wiley & Sons, Inc.

this Directive and the national legislation based thereon is that of a Data Protection Impact Assessment (DPIA). This term refers to a process whereby the agency conducts an analysis of the risks and challenges that may result from the use of technical equipment when processing personal data in order to identify suitable mitigation measures. As further discussed in this contribution, the DPIA is a primary and default way of addressing the concerns associated with policing technologies, as it presents a general standard of examining and addressing these risks.

Despite the relevance of the DPIA as a tool to address such issues, there remains a significant lack of high-level guidance and clear standards regarding the process in a law enforcement context. This contribution attempts to fill this gap by highlighting several of the most pressing issues and exploring concrete technical and organizational solutions. First, it examines the relevant legal provisions and synthesizes existing guidelines regarding DPIAs, which so far mostly concern processing operations under the general and more widely studied General Data Protection Regulation (GDPR) to then highlight the importance of DPIAs in law enforcement. Second, it identifies key legal and ethical issues that are likely to affect the law enforcement's use of modern technologies and explores how they might materialize in practice. Finally, it identifies a number of best practices that contain concrete mitigation measures for law enforcement actors to consider when implementing novel applications. The findings presented in this contribution are based on the research performed in the context of the Horizon 2020 MAGNETO project, concerning the development of advanced analytical tools used to analyze crime data and support law enforcement interventions. The close collaboration with system developers and various European LEAs helped identify the most pressing concerns and promising mitigation strategies that are discussed throughout this contribution.

2.2 Legal Framework and Guidance

2.2.1 The DPIA Requirement

Under data protection law, organizations involved in the processing of personal data are required to **perform a DPIA in certain situations**. Article 27 of the LED sets out the circumstances in which a DPIA is mandatory for LEAs. According to the Directive, a DPIA must be conducted when a processing activity is likely to result in a high risk to the rights and freedoms of natural persons. It does not specify what it means for a processing activity "likely to result in a high risk" nor does it provide an indicative list of situations where a DPIA might be required. This is different from the GDPR that regulates processing general, commercial, and non-security purposes and provides a non-exhaustive list of circumstances that could trigger the DPIA requirement (see GDPR, Article 35(3) and Recital 91). What the LED does specify is that to determine whether there is indeed a high risk, the data controller must take into account the nature, scope, context, and purpose of the processing. The LED also stipulates that the risks vary in likelihood and severity, and provides some relevant elements that may help determine whether a (high) risk exists (Recital 51). It further clarifies that processing operations may turn into a high risk if there exists a particular likelihood of "prejudice to the rights and freedoms" of data subjects (Recital 52).

In addition, national authorities have published **limited guidance** providing a non-exhaustive list of processing operations likely to result in a high risk in law enforcement situations. While not legally binding throughout Europe, these guidelines generally include the use of new technologies such as surveillance systems, the large-scale processing of particularly sensitive categories of data, and the reliance on systematic and extensive data processing activities like profiling and automated decision-making (UK ICO 2019b). While, in general, processing operations meeting two of those criteria would require a DPIA, in some cases, the fulfilment of only one might require the performance of a DPIA (Article 29 Working Party 2017).

As such, it is not required to conduct a DPIA for all processing operations that may result in risks for the rights and freedoms of natural persons, but only for those where **the risks for fundamental rights and freedoms could be high**. For instance, algorithmic policing tools are likely to generate high risks as those systems appear to meet many of the criteria triggering the DPIA requirement. First, they involve the systematic and extensive processing of personal data. Such processing operations may lead to decisions within law enforcement investigations that can ultimately result in actions having significant or adverse effects on the life and rights of an individual. Second, such technologies are used to process large amounts of data related to criminal convictions, offences, and other information regarding sensitive aspects of a person's private life. The possibility for LEAs to identify hidden connections between seemingly unrelated data substantially raises the risk of interfering with citizens' private lives and revealing sensitive details about these individuals. Third, algorithmic policing undoubtedly falls under the category of "new technologies" that Article 27(1) of the LED designates as likely to result in a high risk. As stated above, the deployment of innovative systems and tools is always a risk factor and must therefore be properly and thoroughly assessed.

While DPIAs are required to be conducted in certain cases only, LEAs are nevertheless expected to act with due diligence given the **general obligation of adequate risk management in the LED** (Article 19(1)). Considering the potential negative consequences that might arise in absence of such an assessment, it is advisable to consider carrying out a DPIA even in situations where it is not strictly mandatory, especially so when it involves the adoption of novel technologies. As the following section explains, the DPIA can act as an early warning of the potential legal and ethical risks before they materialize and facilitates the identification of measures to minimize their impact. This is all the more important in the context of public security and criminal justice, where the relevant risks are heightened given the characteristics of the sector and the possible consequences of processing operations in this context (e.g. deprivation of liberty, being accused of a crime, etc.). Therefore, conducting a DPIA is either a strict legal obligation or an established best practice for police agencies.

2.2.2 Elements of a DPIA

Regarding the content of the DPIA, its **minimum features** are set out in Article 27(2) of the LED. This provision states that any such assessment must include: (i) a general description of the processing operations as well as the purpose; (ii) an evaluation of the risks to the rights and freedoms of individuals; (iii) the planned counter-measures; (iv) the safeguards, security measures and mechanisms in place to ensure that personal data is protected; and (v) a demonstration of how the controller complies with the LED provisions, taking into account the rights and legitimate interests of the data subjects and any other people concerned. With that, a DPIA can be defined as a procedure consisting of the systematic description of the envisaged data processing, an evaluation of their necessity and proportionality, an early assessment of the risks attached to those activities, and the identification of adequate mitigation measures to prevent those issues from occurring in practice. This process should be considered an iterative and adaptive endeavor, as it might be the case that the controller needs to revisit certain aspects more than once before finalizing the DPIA (Article 29 Working Party 2017).

As for the elements to be considered in the DPIA, the LED specifies that impact assessments should cover relevant systems and processes of processing operations but not individual cases (Recital 58). Therefore, in a law enforcement context, the DPIA is intended to assess organizational processes and practices instead of specific cases (Schlehahn et al. 2018).

The **mitigation measures** referred to in the Directive are intended to reduce the risks to an acceptable level and will usually be a combination of both technical and organizational actions. As further discussed in Section 2.5, additional technical controls that can contribute to the mitigation of risks in algorithmic policing include encryption, pseudonymization and anonymization, and logging for audit purposes. The accompanying organizational measures may include a policy document outlining how to process the data and manage the system, including regular audits and updates, as well as mandatory data protection training for users of the technology.

2.2.3   State of the Art of DPIA Guidance and Methodology for Law Enforcement

Neither the LED nor the GDPR offer a specific methodology for the DPIA process. Thus, it is up to data controllers to choose an **appropriate assessment framework** or to develop their own approach insofar as it complies with the minimum requirements under data protection law. In this context, various DPIA frameworks and methodologies have been developed over the years. Some of these have been drafted by Data Protection Authorities (DPAs) while others were proposed by scholars and practitioners. Despite the DPIA being a legal requirement both under the GDPR and the LED, existing DPIA guidance and methodologies focus primarily on the needs of private and commercial actors while remaining largely silent on the specificities and needs of law enforcement. The following **review of existing materials** evidently supports that conclusion.

First, the GDPR itself provides more details on the DPIA process than the LED, with equivalent provisions in the former tend to be more detailed than the latter. Second, prominent DPIA guidelines offer little information on the LED framework, both in general (Marquenie 2017) and in relation to DPIAs (Schlehahn et al. 2018; Bas Seyyar and Geradts 2020). To date, the main DPIA guidance in the EU is that produced by the former Article 29 Working Party, which explains the general DPIA requirements under the GPDR, offers an overview of different frameworks and methodologies for DPIAs, and provides a checklist of criteria for an acceptable assessment (Article 29 Working Party 2017). The European Data Protection Supervisor also developed an equivalent methodology, which, while mainly intended for EU institutions, could also serve as a reference source for other organizations (European Data Protection Supervisor 2019).

DPAs across Europe have also issued **DPIA guidelines and templates**. Among the ones considered for this research are those by the Belgian Privacy Commission (Belgium Commissie voor de Bescherming van de Persoonlijke Levenssfeer (CBPL) 2018), the "Privacy Impact Assessment" tools by the French DPA (France Commission Nationale de l'Informatique et des Libertés (CNIL) 2015), the German "Standard Data Protection Model" (Germany Datenschutzkonferenz (DSK) 2016), the guidance note by the DPA in Ireland (Ireland Data Protection Commission 2019), the Spanish "Practical Guide for Impact Assessments under the GDPR" (Spain Agencia Española de Protección de Datos (AEPD) 2018), and the British Information Commissioner's Office's (ICO)'s DPIA guidance and sample template (UK ICO 2018). Various academic publications have also attempted to develop DPIA methodologies, or at least offer a thorough analysis of GDPR provisions to support the successful implementation of the DPIA requirement (e.g. Bieker et al. 2016; Kloza et al. 2020; Friedewald et al. 2022). However, none of the referred guidelines or scholarly works specifically addresses the needs of the law enforcement sector.

When it comes to **DPIAs under the LED, there are no EU-wide guidelines,** methodologies, or frameworks available. Similar results were obtained when attempting to identify such guidance at the national level. The ICO appears to be the only DPA with specific and comprehensive information and guidelines for the law enforcement sector (UK ICO 2019a). It also developed a toolkit for organizations considering using data analytics that could prove useful to identify some of the risks to the rights and freedoms of individuals that may result from the use of data-driven policing technology (UK ICO 2020). While the United Kingdom (UK) is no longer an EU Member State following Brexit, the ICO's resources and support documents could still be useful and relevant for organizations in the security sector. This will continue to be the case insofar as the data protection framework remains equivalent to that of the EU.

Other DPAs have also produced more limited but still relevant resources for law enforcement. Before briefly referring to their content, however, two caveats must be acknowledged. First, most of the guidelines in question concern privacy impact assessments instead of DPIAs. While similar, the latter tends to have a broader scope that also considers the impact on other human rights than privacy alone. Second, these documents are often intended for policymakers in the law enforcement sector rather than for LEAs per se. Still, they could serve as useful reference sources for LEAs when carrying out DPIAs. For instance, the Slovenian DPA published its "Privacy impact assessment guidelines for the introduction of new police powers" in 2014 (Slovenia Information Commissioner of the Republic of Slovenia 2014). In this document, the Slovenian DPA calls for the need to undertake a thorough privacy impact analysis before introducing new legislative proposals regarding police powers, particularly for those with a strong technological component. An equivalent document was developed by the Dutch government, which issued a privacy impact assessment model for draft legislations in 2017 (Netherlands Ministerie van Binnenlandse Zaken en Koninkrijksrelaties, en Ministerie van Veiligheid en Justitie 2017). While somewhat similar to the Slovenian model, the difference between them is that the Dutch one does not only concern legislative initiatives in policing but also in other sectors. Finally, the Belgian DPA for law enforcement published guidelines concerning the role of data protection officers, providing brief details on their involvement in the DPIA process (Belgium Controleorgaan op de Politionele Informatie 2020). While brief and far from comprehensive, this guidance nevertheless provides some details on best practices.

Regarding scholarship, **current literature appears to offer little guidance** on DPIAs under the LED. One of the first and, to date, seemingly most comprehensive publications on this topic appears to be a white paper produced within the EU-funded VALCRI (Visual Analytics for Sense-making in Criminal Intelligence Analysis) project in 2018. The publication consists of a white paper analyzing different DPIA approaches and methodologies at the national level (Schlehahn et al. 2018). That same year, another EU-funded project (VICTORIA – Video Analysis for Investigation of Criminal and Terrorist Activities) contributed to a conference with a presentation on the topic (Naudts 2018). Another relevant work is a 2020 study, comprising a comparative analysis of different privacy impact assessment methodologies toward finding the best fit with the LED requirements (Bas Seyyar and Geradts 2020). Beyond these few sources, however, it appears that limited legal scholarship has been dedicated to the use of DPIAs specifically in the context of policing.

2.3   Importance and Role of DPIAs in Law Enforcement

Conducting a thorough and comprehensive Data Protection Impact Assessment stands to be a critical component in the process of aligning law enforcement practice with data protection norms. Due to the nature of policing and law enforcement's mandate to process data on sensitive and criminal matters, police operations can pose unique risks to the rights and freedoms of citizens. In particular when using novel technologies and powerful algorithmic tools, unintended consequences can arise to the detriment of both societal and individual interests. In this context, the following section examines the particularly important role that DPIAs can play in the field of law enforcement, and further illustrates their significance by examining recent case law.

2.3.1   Significance of DPIAs

Various aspects of law enforcement practice may inevitably affect civil liberties and fundamental rights due to the citizen-state relationship involved. Besides privacy and data protection, concerns have been raised about other fundamental rights that may be impacted, as further explained in Section 2.4. These drawbacks are not based on hypothetical assumptions, but rather on evidence obtained from real-life situations documented in different countries. For example, analyses of heterogeneous databases with foreign law enforcement software in various European countries have illustrated that such technologies are often not developed with data protection in mind and are thus unlikely to meet privacy and data protection by design requirements under national and EU law (Jansen 2018). More concrete examples of possible issues may be found in the United States (US), where flawed facial recognition systems have been associated with wrongful accusations and arrests of individuals (Robertson 2021). While evidence of similar situations within Europe has not been documented to date, it stands to reason that those circumstances could emerge given the uses of similar law enforcement tools as those in the US. If left unaddressed, the legal and ethical risks outlined in this contribution could entail grave and irremediable harm to fundamental rights and values.

Against this backdrop, this section highlights various ways in which a **DPIA is of key importance** for LEAs considering the use of law enforcement AI tools. First, the DPIA urges controllers to look at the processing operations through a **fundamental rights lens** that not only primarily revolves around privacy and data protection but also considers the relevance of other freedoms. In that way, it fosters a better identification, assessment, and mitigation of potential issues at an early stage, thus helping overcome ethical and legal challenges before they materialize. Second, the DPIA can also help **enhance the transparency of processing practices** and decisions to adopt data-driven systems in law enforcement. This is particularly the case if LEAs adopt the practice of making DPIAs available to the public, at least in the form of a redacted and accessible summary (European Data Protection Supervisor 2019) to comply with confidentiality requirements and not to hamper security interests. While not mandatory, enabling access to the DPIA can facilitate a better public understanding of how and why LEAs process (personal) data, and increase awareness of the technologies used, the needs they address, the actual capabilities of the technology (which may at times be misunderstood), and the efforts made to mitigate risks. Improving public awareness of technology-assisted policing to the extent permitted by security interests would not only strengthen the accountability of law enforcement practices but could also foster trust in security-related activities and law enforcement technology. Third, the DPIA serves as a way to **demonstrate compliance with the LED** as it offers a supportive and comprehensive structure to identify, evaluate, and continuously monitor potential risks to fundamental rights and interests when processing personal data.

Considering its positive impact on the prevention and mitigation of risks, the DPIA is gaining ground as the "go-to" mechanism in guidance documents on emerging technologies. An example of this can be found in the Guidelines on Facial Recognition of the Consultative Committee of Convention 108 (Consultative Committee of the Convention for the Protection of Individuals with regard to Automatic Processing of Personal Data, Convention 108 2021), providing detailed recommendations for legislators, developers, and users of the technology in question. The document contains a section devoted to DPIAs, highlighting the importance of system end users like LEAs carrying out DPIAs to tackle the related concerns.

2.3.2 Illustrative Case Law – *Bridges v. South Wales Police*

To illustrate the importance of conducting a DPIA for law enforcement processing, a reference can be made to the Bridges case. This ruling concerns the **use of**

Automated Facial Recognition (AFR) **by the South Wales Police** (SWP) in two instances where they allegedly captured personal data about the claimant, Edward Bridges, a civil liberties campaigner. In the first instance, the court dismissed the action on all grounds, concluding that it was lawful for the police to use AFR software. This ruling, however, was overturned by the UK Court of Appeal. In its decision of 11 August 2020, the appellate court found that the use by SWP of the technology breached privacy rights, data protection laws, and equality laws (*R (on the application of Bridges) vs. Chief Constable of South Wales* 2020). This has been considered a landmark ruling, garnering considerable media and public attention, and praised by some for its positive impact on the regulation of law enforcement technology (Wright 2020).

The Bridges case broke new ground given its finding that this **particular use of AFR was unlawful on the basis of data protection law**. A vital aspect of the ruling revolved around carrying out a DPIA for such processing activities. One of the arguments raised to appeal the first instance decision was that, while the SWP did conduct a DPIA, its assessment did not comply with data protection law as it was alleged to be insufficiently thorough and robust. According to the appellant, the DPIA had three key deficiencies. First, the assessment failed to recognize that while the facial recognition system did not retain personal data of individuals that were not on a watch list, data was nevertheless "processed" within the meaning of data protection law. Second, it was also claimed that the DPIA failed to acknowledge that the processing engaged the rights of individuals under Article 8 of the European Convention on Human Rights. Third, the appellant contended that the DPIA was silent as to other rights that may have been affected by the use of the facial recognition system, such as the right to freedom of expression or freedom of assembly.

Other parties to the case voiced similar concerns about the SWP's DPIA. In particular, the ICO intervened in the proceedings and argued that the assessment did not contain sufficient analysis of "privacy, personal data, and safeguards." Similarly, it contended that the DPIA failed to acknowledge that automatic facial recognition involves the collection of personal data on a "blanket and indiscriminate basis," and that the risk of false positives may, in fact, result in longer retention periods than intended. It also criticized the DPIA for failing to address potential gender and racial bias that could arise from the use of AFR. In light of this, the ICO submitted that the DPIA failed to appropriately assess the risks and mitigation thereof as required under data protection law.

Not all the arguments put forth by the appellant and the intervener regarding the DPIA were accepted by the UK Court of Appeal. For instance, the Court held that the DPIA did recognize the relevance of Article 8 of the Convention. Still, the Court agreed with the argument that the SWP was wrong to decide that there was no interference with that provision. Thus, it ruled that "[t]he inevitable consequence of those deficiencies is that, notwithstanding the attempt of the DPIA to grapple with the Article 8 issues, the DPIA failed properly to assess the risks to the rights and freedoms of data subjects and also failed to address the measures envisaged to address the risks arising from the deficiencies we have found, as required by [data protection law]" (*R (on the application of Bridges) v Chief Constable of South Wales* 2020).

The implications of this ruling go beyond setting a precedent for facial recognition and influencing future policy on this novel and controversial technology in the UK alone. The Bridges case also sends a clear message to LEAs across Europe intending to use advanced law enforcement tools that their deployment of such **technologies must be accompanied by a rigorous and satisfactory assessment** of the risks to the rights and freedoms of individuals and taking all the appropriate measures to mitigate any potentially adverse consequences, which is precisely a key point made throughout this contribution. Moreover, as this landmark ruling shows, a DPIA that does not sufficiently meet the requirements of data protection law may not survive the legal challenge and could result in the relevant law enforcement tools being ruled unlawful.

2.4 Key Legal and Ethical Risks in Algorithmic Policing

The specific circumstances and aspects covered by the DPIA depend on various factors such as the envisaged processing operations and the priorities set by each LEA. Therefore, the necessary steps to assess the legal and ethical risks have to be determined on a case-by-case basis. Yet still, there are some legal and ethical issues that appear to be common in many situations involving the development and implementation of novel police technologies. To provide further guidance on how police agencies might evaluate these challenges, this section explores the most pressing threats to fundamental rights and the broader legal and ethical interests at stake in law enforcement practice. The risks specified in this section have been identified on the basis of widely accepted guidelines and methodologies established by national data protection authorities, using algorithmic policing as a case study.

2.4.1 Fundamental Rights

The implementation of data-driven technologies in law enforcement practice raises various fundamental rights issues. While the use of these tools could adversely affect a considerable number of human liberties, this contribution considers four of these rights to be particularly vulnerable to interference by algorithmic policing.

First, the nature of modern data-driven systems risks infringing upon the **rights to privacy and data protection** (Bas Seyyar and Geradts 2020; Robertson et al. 2020) as they typically involve the processing of large amounts of heterogeneous data obtained from diverse sources. Such data can reveal key information about an individual and contain private or sensitive details. Another risk factor concerns the potential for data breaches, violations of access rights, and overall noncompliance with data protection law. Issues regarding the analysis of large volumes of data while complying with core data protection principles, especially those of data minimization and purpose limitation, are commonplace in algorithmic systems. Similarly, requirements mandating respect for data subject to rights, limits on profiling, restrictions on the use of sensitive data, and general accountability of system processes are bound to raise concerns or legal issues relating to the deployment of these novel tools.

Second, the proliferation of tools with surveillance capabilities threatens to impose chilling effects on the **rights to free speech and assembly** and raises the concern that lawful behavior or the exercise of certain freedoms would be inhibited (Penney 2017). Modern tools amplify the capabilities of LEAs to gather evidence, investigate and combat crime, and analyze data to support their reasoning processes and interventions. As such, they risk increasingly resembling and mimicking some of the features found in large-scale surveillance systems. For instance, algorithmic policing systems can facilitate the collection of open-source intelligence and social media intelligence practices that involve monitoring online activities or tracking persons of interest. Such methods of surveillance risk causing a chilling effect on the exercise of various freedoms as the awareness or perception of government observation may result in people expressing fewer minority views, self-censoring, or being less likely to convene with certain individuals or groups given the fears of potential negative repercussions.

Third, the **right to equality and nondiscrimination** risks are being interfered with as a result of discriminatory and biased policies being exacerbated by AI-powered technologies (Babuta and Oswald 2019). As such, decisions that were made with the assistance of data-driven technologies could result in discriminatory or unfair treatments on the basis of sensitive attributes such as race and religion. Those activities tend to disproportionately affect marginalized and vulnerable groups in society (Eubanks 2018). Thus, the outputs generated by law enforcement technology could lead to unfair scrutiny and excessive policing of minority groups or yield unwarranted conclusions about vulnerable individuals. Moreover, such practices could lead to feedback loops through which persons from historically disadvantaged groups are profiled on the basis of statistical interferences and labeled as a heightened risk given the historic bias toward them and the socioeconomic conditions they were born into (Eubanks 2018).

And fourth, the use of these technologies may violate **due process and fair trial guarantees** (Rich, 2016; Marquenie, 2019; Quezada-Tavárez et al. 2021).

This can happen in a number of ways. For instance, some technologies may distort the general principle of the presumption of innocence or result in wrongful convictions based on faulty computer processes (Rich 2016). Moreover, analytical systems often work in opaque ways and produce results that are hard to explain, which means that individuals affected by those would have fewer meaningful opportunities to challenge any adverse decisions assisted by automated processing. This could violate safeguards related to adversarial hearings, equality of arms, and access to adequate facilities enshrined in fundamental rights instruments (Quezada-Tavárez et al. 2021). Another issue likely to arise is the ability to exercise the right to an effective remedy. The exercise of that right is preceded by the actual knowledge by the affected that his or her rights have been violated, which is not a simple matter in a law enforcement context given that individuals may not even be aware that they are under police surveillance.

2.4.2 Unfairness and Opacity

The **occurrence of bias and inaccuracy in AI** constitutes one of the most pressing concerns associated with algorithmic policing. The algorithms underpinning data-driven tools are trained to interpret and find patterns in complex sets of data. As discussed earlier, research has demonstrated that bias can become engrained in analytical tools. This risk may occur either at the design and development stage or during the deployment of the system itself (Babuta and Oswald 2019). At the design and development stage, bias may stem from skewed training data that risks replicating human biases inherent to the data, as well as from the potentially faulty design of the models. At the deployment stage, the use of the system could result in feedback loops where it perpetually reinforces initially flawed findings. Similarly, the human biases of system operators can play a role as they may disregard important contextual information or could adhere to or deviate from the system's recommendations in a manner that could lead to unfair decisions. For instance, due to the tendency to over-rely on automated outputs (known in the literature as the "risk of automation bias"), there is potential for the human operator to give undue legitimacy to flawed results that could then result in groundless decisions (Citron 2008).

Opacity and unaccountability are similarly acute risk factors in the development and deployment of algorithmic systems. Due to the inherent technical complexities that underline these technologies, difficulties concerning the understanding of their inner workings are common. For this reason, these tools are often considered to resemble veritable "black boxes" with opaque internal operations that preclude operators, auditors, or individuals affected thereby from determining how a certain input resulted in a particular output, or how different values or factors were weighted and considered (Rich 2016). This lack of transparency has numerous ethical and legal implications, such as the inability of end users to provide a justification for the decisions supported by the system or to identify hidden shortcomings. The latter is closely associated with the larger concerns of "mathwashing" (Woods 2016), referring to the mistaken assumption that algorithmic models are free from any subjectivity or bias due to their reliance on statistics and mathematics, and "algocracy" (Danaher 2016), being a situation where algorithmic systems determine the possibilities for humans to participate in public decisions. Mathwashing and algocracy further compound the misconception that algorithms are entirely neutral, unbiased, and objective. If the system produces unreliable or unfair results that are uncritically accepted by human operators who believe the system to be neutral and fair, the harmful and discriminatory consequences might not be identified and addressed as such (Quezada-Tavárez et al. 2021).

To illustrate these concerns, one can consider the example of predictive policing. Research has suggested that, while the models themselves may be free from bias, they nevertheless calculate occurrences of crimes in relevant parts of the territory to which more policing is assigned. However, since the technology is fed with data reflecting existing biases, the locations to which more police officers are assigned generally correspond to already over-policed communities, regardless of the actual levels of criminality (Robertson et al. 2020). Once the data collected through these interventions is ingested back into the system, it can result in a feedback loop through which a greater police presence simply leads to more crimes being recorded in comparison to other areas, thus giving the impression that these communities are inherently more criminal and should be subjected to ever greater police scrutiny (Eubanks 2018).

2.4.3 Police Integrity

The final category of risks involves those that might tarnish the integrity of police operations. If these problems were to occur, they could have severe consequences for the **legitimacy of law enforcement** practice and the public trust therein. Additionally, serious transgressions involving the undue use of these technologies could significantly disrupt police operations in the field and might affect the trustworthiness or admissibility of evidence in court. While several of the earlier mentioned issues could lead to similar consequences, there exist three primary concerns that could directly affect the integrity of algorithmic policing practices.

A first issue is that of **function creep**. This refers to the incremental expansion of the ways in which technology is applied to serve additional goals beyond those for which it was initially intended. A system might be designed or adopted with a specific and narrowly defined objective in mind, only to gradually be used for adjacent yet different purposes over time. In the Netherlands, for example, an initiative requiring citizens to have their fingerprints registered in a database to obtain a passport was originally presented as a measure to combat look-alike fraud with identity documents. The subsequent law, however, granted LEAs extensive access to this information as part of their general mandate of fighting crime (Huissen 2010). Similarly, a situation might arise in which an LEA adopts a tool designed to monitor or profile individuals partaking in organized crime but steadily begins using it as a general-purpose system to evaluate any person of interest for even minor crimes. While not an inherently negative concept (Koops 2021), function creep does raise serious concerns with regard to the privacy of civilians and the legitimacy of police operations. Without sufficient regard for the principle of proportionality, independent oversight, and adequate mitigation measures, important boundaries may become blurred as potent technologies are deployed for progressively broader purposes and police operations might increasingly resemble large-scale surveillance as employed by state intelligence agencies (Joh 2016). Such a scenario could undermine public trust in law enforcement and diminish both the integrity and fairness of police interventions.

A second concern relates to the potential **regression of human autonomy** in key decision-making processes as a result of the growing reliance on algorithmic tools (Lawless and Sofge 2017). As analytics, predictions and risk assessments in the sphere of public policy are frequently outsourced to computer systems (Spielkamp 2019), reality is slowly emerging in which machines are responsible for applying vital rules and informing important decisions. As a result of the earlier mentioned issue of "algocracy," such a scenario poses the risk that human actors gradually lose the ability to interfere and exert meaningful control over computerized processes. Rather than acting as arbitrators who take the context and human values into account, system operators risk being relegated to rubber-stamping the outcomes of increasingly automated processes. In the area of law enforcement and criminal justice, citizens might be further reduced to mere numbers in a system without worthwhile human involvement or discretion (Babuta et al. 2018). As such, police personnel might feel disparaged from challenging the system's recommendations as they could lack the necessary technical capabilities to carefully review the process or could face personal liability for unintended consequences when deviating from the computer's path. By potentially diminishing the social aspects of law enforcement practice and resulting in a **loss of important police skills** (Joh 2019), the use of these technologies could affect the trustworthiness of contemporary police operations.

The final problem relates to the potential occurrence of **system misuse**. In this context, the abuse of IT systems can be defined as the "unauthorized, deliberate, and internally recognizable misuse of assets of the local organizational information system by individuals" (Straub and Nance 1990). For the purposes of this contribution, this includes all misconduct that involves the unintended or unwarranted use of hardware, computer programs, data, and services by both internal and external actors. This poses several concrete concerns. To begin, the **unauthorized use of law enforcement systems** might involve police personnel themselves. On various occasions, police officers have been found to unduly access confidential information (Gurman 2016) or misuse telecommunication systems in violation of internal guidelines (Maass 2015). In these situations, individuals make use of these tools despite not having the required authorization or for a purpose that is unrelated to their mandate. They might retrieve, alter, or delete sensitive data for unwarranted reasons, such as to monitor their acquaintances or serve personal interests.

In addition, these **systems might also be used in an unlawful manner**. Even when an operators act within the boundaries of their direct authorization, the way in which these tools are used can still violate legal norms. In some cases, LEAs have demonstrated a grave lack of care or insufficiently considered the broader legal framework when deploying novel technologies (Garvie 2019), thereby leading international organizations like the Council of Europe to explicitly recognize the risk of "unlawful data processing" as associated with the adoption of analytical tools (Council of Europe (COE) 2018). As the earlier mentioned example of the Bridges Case and similar legal controversy surrounding the acquisition of advanced digital triage systems by the Scottish Police illustrate (Privacy International 2019), the use of novel technologies without careful consideration for the human values and legal framework involved can still constitute unlawful conduct and system misuse despite internal approval. Lastly, **flaws in information and system security** could allow external actors to obtain access to confidential data and make use of classified tools, as several instances have already been documented in which hackers breached police databases containing sensitive information on citizens and informants (Perlroth and Barnes 2021). Similarly, cybersecurity experts have previously identified serious vulnerabilities in forensic tools used by law enforcement to extract data from mobile phones, which has sparked debate on the reliability of the applications and their admissibility in court (Taylor 2021). Thus, cybersecurity and the broader challenge of countering system misuse have become a major point of focus in law enforcement given the sensitivity and importance of its operations (Quinn 2018), especially when they involve the use of analytical tools and large amounts of personal data.

2.5 Best Practices: Mitigation Measures and Safeguards

Identifying and examining the key legal and ethical risks that are introduced by the development and implementation of novel technologies is an important aspect of any DPIA, allowing LEAs to explore concrete mitigation measures and address the likelihood, severity, and impact of the risks described above. **Risk**

mitigation measures and safeguards generally fall into one of two categories. The first kind are those that are **technical in nature**. These are solutions that are built directly into the system at either the software or hardware level. By hardcoding certain processes, fail-safes, or restrictions in the technology and designing it with a proactive and ethical approach in mind, system developers can contribute to the creation of safer and more reliable tools. The second type are measures that are put in place at the **organizational level** of the agency or institution that is responsible for deploying the technology in practice. Rather than making changes to the actual tool or system itself, these measures involve the implementation of practical rules or procedures that frame or limit the use of these applications in order to comply with legal or ethical norms. To achieve the highest standard of risk mitigation with regard to legal and ethical issues is not only a legal obligation per Article 29 of the LED but also a practical recommendation to implement both types of measures.

As described in the introduction, this section highlights various key mitigation measures that were identified in the H2020 MAGNETO Project. It provides an overview of several primary solutions and techniques that should be considered by both LEAs as well as system designers who are developing applications for police practice.

2.5.1 Access Control and Information Security

The first set of mitigation measures relates to access control and information security. Implementing a robust yet flexible access control system is an important safeguard to minimize the impact and likelihood of the abovementioned risks. In the observed use case, such a system proved to be a vital component of responsible and measured system use that allows LEAs to exercise considerable control over how certain data and functionalities can be accessed by police personnel. This is thus an important measure to prevent system misuse and a potent method of facilitating legal compliance by safeguarding the confidentiality of sensitive data.

Generally speaking, there exist two main types of **access control systems** (Ting 2007). Those that involve physical measures that are deployed in a real-world environment and those that concern the use of software-based safeguards and processes in a computer system. The first type, known as Physical Security Access Control Systems, aims to prevent physical intrusion and protect the infrastructure in which the information systems themselves as well as the people who use them and the data they contain are located. The second type, typically referred to as Logical or Information Technology Access Control Systems, seeks to safeguard the data and the proper functioning of the computer systems by employing software-based measures that authenticate users and authorize appropriate system use. To ensure the highest degree of security, it is advisable that LEAs rely on a complementary set of measures from both categories.

First, police forces can take organizational steps to prevent unauthorized access to data or computer systems by means of physical access controls. By implementing **physical barriers to entry and access**, the risk of system misuse and interference with the integrity of police investigations or confidential data can be reduced significantly. Due to the growing capabilities of AI and monitoring applications in law enforcement, it is highly recommended that physical access to these tools is restricted to personnel that is actively involved in their use or maintenance. Thus, these applications might be kept in a separate room that is subject to video surveillance and is only accessible by certain members of the organization. As the use of electronic key cards, scanners, or biometric authentication methods has become commonplace in modern security and access control strategies (Norman 2017), one could rely on such security measures to further protect confidential information systems and improve the accountability of their users.

Second, LEAs or the external developers with whom they might collaborate can implement **logical access controls into the software** itself. This offers a significant degree of flexibility as it allows for a layered approach to how certain data or functionalities are made available to specific types of users. When considering the IT access control measures that are implemented in the software itself, several methods and techniques can be relied on. Generally speaking, logical access control measures are discretionary, mandatory, or role-based in nature (Collins 2014). Within MAGNETO, for example, a role-based system was preferred due to its customizability. By allowing LEAs to create user profiles that match certain roles, responsibilities, or tasks in their organization, access to specific system functionalities or types of data can be reserved for those with the proper access rights and authorization. This plays a significant role in the prevention of several of the earlier mentioned risks, such as system misuse by recording unlawful conduct or denying access to individuals who seek to use the applications and the data therein for unintended purposes. As access control systems can often be tied to extensive logging and recordkeeping protocols, any interactions between the user and the computer can be registered and monitored by administrators to further improve accountability.

The extent to which the logical access controls affect the functioning of the system can vary significantly. On the one hand, they can include straightforward measures such as requiring a login ID and password to sign into the system. Without the correct credentials and authorization, the user will be denied access. On the other, they can be configured to allow for complex restrictions on specific tools and data. For example, a strategic analyst who is tasked with analyzing high-level crime trends might be assigned a profile that does not have access to sensitive details and personal data relating to specific cases, while an operational analyst who is investigating a specific illegal operation might be approved to review this information. Similarly, certain utilities such as those that involve individual and person-based risk assessments could only be made available to investigators working on the most serious types of offenses.

Such an approach to access control and system security thus ties into **compliance with other key data protection principles** in Article 4 of the LED. First, the principle of purpose limitation states that personal data may only be processed for the specified and legitimate purposes for which it was originally obtained (Emanuilov et al. 2020). Second, the data minimization principle requires the processed data to be adequate, relevant, and not excessive with regards to the objective for which it was collected. In other words, data protection law mandates that the storage, use, and analysis of this data by LEAs are limited to what is necessary for a lawful and clearly specified goal. By linking access controls to methods of anonymization and pseudonymization, being the permanent or reversible removal of personal information that allows for an individual to be uniquely identified (Bolognini and Bistolfi 2017), police systems can be configured to only reveal the full details on suspects or victims when a specific operator's assignment requires this, thereby further protecting the privacy interests of citizens. Finally, the principle of security requires that personal data is appropriately secured against unauthorized or unlawful processing by means of appropriate technical or organizational measures. An extensive and configurable access control system can therefore operationalize all of these key legal requirements. Within the same system or database, such a technical measure can ensure that certain data is only accessible to those with the right credentials and that its use is reserved for a specific purpose that minimizes the extent to which personal information is processed, while simultaneously promoting further compliance with the core tenets of information security as reflected in data protection law (Marquenie and Quezada 2019).

As such, it is recommended that extensive and configurable access control measures are integrated into both the organization and the system itself. When utilized to their fullest extent, access controls can play a vital part in improving system security and complying with legal and ethical norms by serving as a backbone for other mitigation measures to be integrated therein.

2.5.2 Value-Sensitive Design

The second category of mitigation measures are those that relate to the concept of value-sensitive design (VSD). This notion refers to a method of system development that considers the importance of **human values as a guiding and systematic principle** during the technical design process. Rather than focusing exclusively or primarily on metrics of performance and efficiency, VSD posits that morality and core values such as human well-being and dignity should be placed at the forefront of system design and translated into software requirements. As the extent to which these principles can be coded into novel technologies remains the subject of debate (van de Poel 2020), this contribution interprets this term broadly and associates it with hardcoded techniques aimed at safeguarding fairness and accountability in algorithmic systems.

In the context of data protection, the notion of VSD contains notable similarities with the legal requirement of **data protection by design and by default**, which mandates that system design considers key values in data protection law (European Network and Information Security Agency (ENISA) 2014). According to Article 20 of the LED, LEAs are required to implement appropriate technical and organizational measures to safeguard data protection principles and protect the rights of individuals when processing personal data. Taking into account the cost of implementation as well as the scope and context of the processing activities, these computer systems are to be designed and constructed in such a way that compliance with human rights and the key principles of fairness and accountability is part of their operation.

To **improve fairness** and avoid system results that are potentially discriminatory, a number of concrete measures should be considered. When machine learning techniques are involved in the process of developing intelligent systems, caution must be exercised to prevent the adoption and replication of human bias by computerized means. Using training data that has been cleaned to ensure that it is accurate, reliable, and represents demographics in a genuine and proportionate manner is an important step toward fairness. To this end, a considerable body of research has explored various methods of cleaning training data (Tae et al. 2019), preserving privacy during the learning stage (Duchi et al. 2014) and detecting bias within algorithmic processes (Turner Lee 2018). System designers and software developers who are active in the sphere of law enforcement should be aware of how certain design choices could result in unintended consequences, and should examine which technical measures are most appropriate and effective for their specific tools.

Technical solutions can thus vary significantly and range from using open-access repositories of vetted training data, such as those that include a diverse set of ethnicities and genders for facial recognition research, to making direct adjustments to the logic or learning process to account for and minimize algorithmic biases. Similarly, it is recommended that additional care is taken when the use of these tools involves the practice of profiling, which is a practice that evaluates or makes predictions about certain personal aspects relating to a natural person such as their behavior, interests, and economic situation, or the processing of sensitive personal data concerning an individual's ethnicity, sexuality, health, or religion. As Articles 10 and 11 of the LED require additional safeguards in these circumstances, LEAs should explore technical measures capable of restricting the use of tools involved in those activities. By, for example, implementing hardcoded limitations that do not allow for these sensitive attributes to be the primary or sole factor in profiling (European Union Agency for Fundamental Rights (FRA) 2018), or designing the machine learning process in such a way that the use of sensitive attributes is limited or excluded altogether (Veale and Binns 2017), LEAs, and system developers can significantly reduce the risk of discriminatory outcomes and improve the overall fairness of the process.

A similar approach should be taken with regard to **algorithmic accountability**. This concept generally refers to the ability of allocating responsibility for the outcomes and decisions that involve the use of algorithmic systems and being able to provide an adequate justification therefor (Reddy et al. 2019). Given that these algorithms can seriously impact the lives of individuals, the topic of accountability has been an important part of debates on AI. Thus, the use of any such system in the context of law enforcement should be subject to potent mitigation measures. At the very least, these applications should be designed with transparency and explainability in mind (Lepri et al. 2017). In this context, transparency refers to the availability of information on the system's processes, while explainability is focused more on being able to make sense of specific system outcomes. LEAs and DPAs should thus be able to audit these tools and understand their design and reasoning.

In addition, the field of **Explainable AI** (XAI) has explored various methods of making computerized learning and decision-making interpretable by human actors (Samek et al. 2019). These solutions can assist in making otherwise opaque processes more transparent and allow system operators to understand how the system analyzed data, balanced different attributes and arrived at a specific outcome. In practice, however, this remains a challenge. While ongoing research continues to develop new techniques for accountability (Barredo Arrieta et al. 2020) and experts have made efforts toward linking the earlier mentioned data protection requirements on explainability to specific solutions, like utilizing a method of counterfactuals to explain algorithmic processes (Wachter et al. 2018), implementing these strategies often presents technical challenges. Nevertheless, LEAs and system designers should take all possible yet reasonable steps toward the development and deployment of technologies that can be understood, audited, and validated as fair and sufficiently transparent.

2.5.3 Human Oversight

The final group of mitigation measures concerns the importance of human oversight and system accountability. In algorithmic policing, a crucial safeguard against the earlier mentioned risks is to ensure that a **human actor maintains**

direct oversight of the use of these technologies in decision-making processes (Zouave and Marquenie 2017). This is recommended for two primary reasons. First, establishing human agency and control over automated or advanced analytical processes is widely considered to be a vital aspect of the ethical use of trustworthy systems (High-Level Expert Group on Artificial Intelligence 2019). As computer systems and AI tools lack a sense of morality and are unable to grasp the context of their use or the impact their actions might have on human beings, it is vital that the autonomy of humans is both protected and promoted in this context. Without such oversight, complex situations and the individuals involved therein could be reduced to mere numbers while systemic issues associated with the deployment of these tools might go unnoticed.

Second, European data protection law has imposed certain **restrictions on the use of automated technologies** that process personal data, and has empowered individuals by awarding them with several rights that they can exercise in this context. Regarding law enforcement, various safeguards must therefore be put in place in order to protect the interests of the data subjects (Marquenie 2017). Following Article 11 and Recital 38 of the LED, the sole use of automated processing technologies, including those that involve the practice of profiling, for the making of decisions that can have significant or adverse effects on individuals must be subject to mitigation measures that include "the right to obtain human intervention" and thus allow citizens to challenge the outcome of the process. In other words, LEAs that rely on these technologies must ensure that a human actor is involved in the procedure by being able to analyze the relevant data and circumstances that led to the outcome presented by a computer system before a final decision is made (UK ICO 2019b).

This can generally be achieved by having a **human in the loop, on the loop, or in command** of the process (High-Level Expert Group on Artificial Intelligence 2019). In the first, a human is capable of intervening in every step of the system's operations. In the second, a human can intervene during the design stage of the system and is able to supervise its general functioning. In the third, a human can monitor the overall activity and use of the system in order to decide upon its use and deployment in specific situations. While it is not always possible or even desirable to combine all three in practice, it is nevertheless clear that a human actor must exercise some degree of control over the use of these tools and have the ability to intervene in key stages of the cycle by reviewing system outcomes and validating the subsequent decisions.

Thus, it is recommended that the system is designed in such a way that it cannot execute or enforce these decisions on its own but instead provides operators with assessments and information to support police personnel. For the **operator to exercise meaningful control** over this process and avoid reducing their role to merely rubberstamping system outputs, they should have the necessary ability and operational authority to challenge and amend the computer-suggested decision. As fairness and reliability cannot simply be automated (Wachter et al. 2021), the operator should have the required skill set and understanding of the system's functionalities and must be able to review the necessary results, data, and reasoning process in a clear and understandable manner. To facilitate this, it is important that LEAs receive **sufficient training** on how to properly utilize these tools. Such training should not only focus on the practical and technical aspects of using the system but should also include the ethical and legal aspects. Every system operator should have an understanding of the risks associated therewith. They must be aware of the technical limitations and capable of recognizing situations in which they should intervene to avoid disparate or harmful consequences.

In addition to these training procedures, it is also paramount that the system is designed with **transparency and accountability** in mind. Without methods in place to review how the system was used and how it processes data to review intelligence or produce assessments, the effectiveness of human supervision is bound to be severely hampered. As such, this approach reflects a combination of both technical and organizational measures. On the one hand, the system prompts end user intervention by implementing technical restrictions on certain functionalities at the software level. On the other, organizational procedures revolving around training and oversight should ensure that the operator is able to meaningfully question the system and intervene in the decision-making process. Thus, the adoption of such mitigation measures is vital to protect human autonomy, safeguard the rights and interests of data subjects, and allow for sufficient accountability when these tools are deployed in police practice.

2.6 Conclusion

This contribution argues that it is paramount that LEAs using algorithmic policing tools take a proactive approach toward addressing legal and ethical risks by identifying and mitigating pressing concerns through concrete measures. In the context of European data protection law, this is a binding legal requirement when these tools or processing activities are likely to result in a high risk to the rights and interests of individuals. Yet despite the importance of this procedure, there exists little guidance and literature on the specifics of DPIAs in law enforcement.

As such, this contribution further examines the DPIA process in policing to highlight some of the most prominent challenges and provide concrete strategies to address outstanding issues. By evaluating recent case law in which insufficiently thorough risk assessments resulted in the use of police tools being ruled unlawful, it illustrates the practical importance of implementing adequate mitigation measures against pressing legal and ethical risks. Without due consideration thereof, law enforcement risks unduly interfering with fundamental freedoms such as the rights to privacy, fair trial, equal treatment, and free speech. Similarly, the use of these tools might tarnish the integrity of police operations and stands to negatively impact their fairness and reliability in absence of certain precautions.

To support efforts toward addressing these risks and enabling compliance with legal and ethical norms, adherence to the earlier mentioned best practices is recommended for the development and implementation of algorithmic tools. Based on the findings of a real-life use case involving the development of novel police technology, a strong emphasis should be placed on access controls, value-sensitive design, and human oversight as key mitigation measures that can be implemented at both the technical and organizational level. While LEAs must remain vigilant and proactive in exploring additional strategies tailored to their own needs and circumstances, close adherence to the proposed strategies can significantly reduce both the likelihood and severity of threats to the integrity and fairness of contemporary policing practice.

Acknowledgments

This work has been performed under the H2020 786629 project MAGNETO, which has received funding from the European Union's Horizon 2020 Programme, and received support from the Cybersecurity Initiative Flanders – Strategic Research Program (CIF). This paper reflects only the authors' views.

References

Article 29 Working Party (2017). Guidelines on Data Protection Impact Assessment (DPIA) and determining whether processing is "likely to result in a high risk" for the purposes of Regulation 2016/679, adopted on 4 April 2017, as last revised and adopted on 4 October 2017. WP 248 rev.01. https://ec.europa.eu/newsroom/article29/items/611236 (accessed 10 March 2020).

Babuta, A. and Oswald, M. (2019). Data analytics and algorithmic bias in policing. Royal United Services Institute for Defence and Security Studies. https://rusi.org/publication/briefing-papers/data-analytics-and-algorithmic-bias-policing (accessed 5 May 2021).

Babuta, A., Oswald, M., and Rinik, C. (2018). *Machine Learning Algorithms and Police Decision-Making Legal, Ethical and Regulatory Challenges*, 45. Royal United Services Institute for Defence and Security Studies.

Barredo Arrieta, A., Díaz-Rodríguez, N., Del Ser, J. et al. (2020) Explainable Artificial Intelligence (XAI): concepts, taxonomies, opportunities and challenges toward responsible AI, *Information Fusion*, 58, pp. 82–115. doi:https://doi.org/10.1016/j.inffus.2019.12.012.

Bas Seyyar, M. and Geradts, Z.J.M.H. (2020) 'Privacy impact assessment in large-scale digital forensic investigations', *Forensic Science International: Digital Investigation*, 33. doi:https://doi.org/10.1016/j.fsidi.2020.200906.

Belgium Commissie voor de Bescherming van de Persoonlijke Levenssfeer (CBPL) (2018). Aanbeveling uit eigen beweging met betrekking tot de gegevensbeschermingseffectbeoordeling en voorafgaande raadpleging (CO- AR-2018-001). Aanbeveling 01/2018. https://www.gegevensbeschermingsautoriteit.be/publications/aanbeveling-nr.-01-2018.pdf (accessed 25 May 2021).

Bieker, F., Friedewald, M., Hansen, M. et al. (2016). A process for data protection impact assessment under the European general data protection regulation. In: *Privacy Technologies and Policy* (ed. S. Schiffner, J. Serna, D. Ikonomou et al.), 21–37. Cham: Springer International Publishing.

Bolognini, L. and Bistolfi, C. (2017) 'Pseudonymization and impacts of Big (personal/anonymous) data processing in the transition from the Directive 95/46/EC to the new EU general data protection regulation', *Computer Law & Security Review*, 33(2), pp. 171–181. doi:https://doi.org/10.1016/j.clsr.2016.11.002.

Citron, D.K. (2008). Technological due process. *Washington University Law Review* 85 (6): 66.

Collins, L. (2014) 'Access controls', in Vacca, J.R. (ed.) Cyber Security and IT Infrastructure Protection. Elsevier, pp. 269–280. doi:https://doi.org/10.1016/B978-0-12-416681-3.00011-2.

Consultative Committee of the Convention for the Protection of Individuals with regard to Automatic Processing of Personal Data, Convention 108 (2021). Guidelines on facial recognition. T-PD(2020)03rev4. https://rm.coe.int/guidelines-on-facial-recognition/1680a134f3 (accessed 29 January 2021).

Controleorgaan op de Politionele Informatie (2020). Advies uit eigen beweging betreffende de invulling van de functionaris voor gegevensbescherming of DPO. DD200018.

Council of Europe (COE) (2018). Practical guide on the use of personal data in the police sector.

Danaher, J. (2016) 'The threat of algocracy: reality, resistance and accommodation', *Philosophy & Technology*, 29(3), pp. 245–268. doi:https://doi.org/10.1007/s13347-015-0211-1.

Duchi, J.C., Jordan, M.I. and Wainwright, M.J. (2014) 'Privacy aware learning', *Journal of the ACM*, 61(6), pp. 1–57. doi:https://doi.org/10.1145/2666468.

Emanuilov, I., Fantin, S., Marquenie, T. and Vogiatzoglou, P., (2020). Purpose limitation by design as a counter to function creep and system insecurity in police artificial intelligence, UNICRI Special Collection on Artificial Intelligence, pp. 26–38.

Eubanks, V. (2018). *Automating Inequality: How High-Tech Tools Profile, Police, and Punish the Poor*. New York: St. Martin's Press.

European Data Protection Supervisor (2019) Accountability on the ground Part II: data protection impact assessments & prior consultation. v1.3. https://edps.europa. eu/sites/edp/files/publication/19-07-17_accountability_on_the_ground_part_ii_ en.pdf (accessed 25 May 2021).

European Network and Information Security Agency (ENISA) (2014). Privacy and data protection by design - from policy to engineering. LU: Publications Office. https://data.europa.eu/doi/10.2824/38623 (accessed 3 June 2021).

European Union Agency for Fundamental Rights (FRA) (2018). Preventing unlawful profiling today and in the future: a guide. Publications Office of the European Union, p. 138. https://fra.europa.eu/en/publication/2018/preventing-unlawful-profiling-today-and-future-guide.

France Commission Nationale de l'Informatique et des Libertés (CNIL) (2015). Privacy Impact Assessment 1 (Methodology), 2 (Templates) and 3 (Knowledge bases). https://www.cnil.fr/en/privacy-impact-assessment-pia (accessed 25 May 2021).

Friedewald, M., Schiering, I., Martin, N. and Hallinan, D. (2022). Data protection impact assessments in practice. In: *Computer Security. ESORICS 2021 International Workshops* (ed. S. Katsikas, C. Lambrinoudakis, N. Cuppens et al.), 424–443. Cham: Springer International Publishing.

Garvie, C. (2019). Garbage in, garbage out: face recognition on flawed data. Georgetown law - center on privacy & technology. https://www.flawedfacedata. com (accessed 8 June 2021).

Germany Datenschutzkonferenz (DSK) (2016). The standard data protection model: A concept for inspection and consultation on the basis of unified protection goals, V.1.0 – Trial version, unanimously and affirmatively acknowledged (under abstention of Bavaria) by the 92. *Conference of the Independent Data Protection Authorities of the Bund and the Länder in Kühlungsborn on 9–10 November 2016.* https://www.datenschutzzentrum.de/uploads/sdm/SDM-Methodology_V1.0.pdf (accessed 25 May 2021).

Gurman, S. (2016). Across US, police officers abuse confidential databases, Associated Press. https://apnews.com/article/699236946e3140659fff8a2362e16f43 (accessed 8 June 2021).

High-Level Expert Group on Artificial Intelligence (2019). *Ethics Guidelines for Trustworthy AI.* European Commission.

Huissen, R. (2010). De rekbare doelen van de vingerafdrukkendatabase, Platform Burgerrechten. https://platformburgerrechten.nl/2010/09/18/de-rekbare-doelen-van-de-vingerafdrukkendatabase/ (accessed 8 June 2021).

Ireland Data Protection Commission (2019). Guidance note: Guide to Data Protection Impact Assessments (DPIAs). https://www.dataprotection.ie/ sites/default/files/uploads/2019-10/Guide%20to%20Data%20Protection%20 Impact%20Assessments%20%28DPIAs%29_Oct19_0.pdf (accessed 25 May 2021).

Jansen, F. (2018). Data Driven Policing in the Context of Europe. Working Paper. Data Justice Lab. https://datajusticeproject.net/wp-content/uploads/ sites/30/2019/05/Report-Data-Driven-Policing-EU.pdf (accessed 25 April 2021).

Joh, E.E. (2016). The new surveillance discretion: automated suspicion, big data, and policing. *Harvard Law & Policy Review* 10: 28.

Joh, E.E. (2019). The consequences of automating and deskilling the police. *UCLA Law Review – Discourse* 67: 34.

Kloza, D., Calvi, A., Casiraghi, S. et al. (2020) 'Data protection impact assessment in the European Union: developing a template for a report from the assessment process', *d.pia.lab Policy Brief*, 1, pp. 1–52. doi:https://doi.org/10.31228/osf.io/7qrfp.

Koops, B.-J. (2021) 'The concept of function creep', *Law, Innovation and Technology*, 13(1), pp. 29–56. doi:https://doi.org/10.1080/17579961.2021.1898299.

Lawless, W.F. and Sofge, D.A. (2017) 'Evaluations: autonomy and artificial intelligence: a threat or savior?', in Lawless, W.F. et al. (eds) Autonomy and Artificial Intelligence: A Threat or Savior? Cham: Springer International Publishing, pp. 295–316. doi:https://doi.org/10.1007/978-3-319-59719-5_13.

Lepri, B., Oliver, N., Letouzé, E. et al. (2017). Fair, transparent, and accountable algorithmic decision-making processes: the premise, the proposed solutions, and the open challenges. *Philosophy & Technology*, 31, pp. 611–627. doi:https://doi. org/10.1007/s13347-017-0279-x.

Maass, D. (2015). Misuse rampant, oversight lacking at California's law enforcement network, Electronic Frontier Foundation. https://www.eff.org/deeplinks/2015/11/ misuse-rampant-oversight-lacking-californias-law-enforcement-network (accessed 8 June 2021).

Marquenie, T. (2017) 'The police and criminal justice authorities directive: data protection standards and impact on the legal framework', *Computer Law & Security Review*, 33(3), pp. 324–340. doi:https://doi.org/10.1016/j.clsr.2017.03.009.

Marquenie, T. (2019). The impact of predictive policing and law enforcement AI on human rights: The right to fair trial under pressure. In: *Rethinking IT and IP Law – Celebrating 30 years of CiTiP* (ed. KU Leuven Centre for IT & IP Law). Intersentia.

Marquenie, T. and Quezada, K. (2019) 'Operationalization of information security through compliance with directive 2016/680 in law enforcement technology and practice', in Vedder, A. et al. (eds) Security and Law. 1. Intersentia, pp. 97–128. doi:https://doi.org/10.1017/9781780688909.005.

Naudts, L. (2018). The Data protection impact assessment for law enforcement agencies. *12th International Conference on Communications*, Bucharest, Romania (15 June). https://lirias.kuleuven.be/retrieve/527499 (accessed 16 March 2021).

Netherlands Ministerie van Binnenlandse Zaken en Koninkrijksrelaties, en Ministerie van Veiligheid en Justitie (2017). Model gegevensbeschermingseffectbeoordeling Rijksdienst (PIA). https://www.rijksoverheid.nl/documenten/rapporten/ 2017/09/29/model-gegevensbeschermingseffectbeoordeling-rijksdienst-pia (accessed 25 May 2021).

Norman, T.L. (2017) 'Foundational security and access control concepts', in Electronic Access Control. Elsevier, pp. 21–42. doi:https://doi.org/10.1016/B978-0 -12-805465-9.00002-6.

Penney, J.W. (2017) 'Internet surveillance, regulation, and chilling effects online: a comparative case study', *Internet Policy Review*, 6(2). doi:https://doi. org/10.14763/2017.2.692.

Perlroth, N. and Barnes, J.E. (2021). D.C. police department data is leaked in a cyberattack. *The New York Times* (27 April). https://www.nytimes. com/2021/04/27/us/dc-police-hack.html (accessed 8 June 2021).

van de Poel, I. (2020) 'Embedding values in Artificial Intelligence (AI) systems', *Minds and Machines*, 30(3), pp. 385–409. doi:https://doi.org/10.1007/ s11023-020-09537-4.

Privacy International (2019). Old law, new tech and continued opacity: police Scotland's use of mobile phone extraction. https://privacyinternational.org/report/3202/ old-law-new-tech-and-continue-opacity-police-scotlands-use-of-mobile-phone-extraction.

Quezada-Tavárez, K., Vogiatzoglou, P. and Royer, S. (2021) 'Legal challenges in bringing AI-evidence to the criminal courtroom', *New Journal of European Criminal Law*, 12(4). doi:https://doi.org/10.1177/20322844211057019.

Quinn, C. (2018). The emerging cyberthreat: cybersecurity for law enforcement. *Police Chief Magazine*. https://www.policechiefmagazine.org/the-emerging-cyberthreat-cybersecurity/ (accessed 8 June 2021).

R (on the application of Bridges) v Chief Constable of South Wales (2020). UK Court of Appeal, EWCA Civ 1058. https://www.judiciary.uk/wp-content/uploads/2020/08/R--Bridges-v-CC-South-Wales-ors-Judgment.pdf (accessed 11 August 2020).

Reddy, E., Cakici, B. and Ballestero, A. (2019) 'Beyond mystery: putting algorithmic accountability in context', *Big Data & Society*, 6(1), p. 2053951719826856. doi:https://doi.org/10.1177/2053951719826856.

Rich, M.L. (2016) 'Machine learning, automated suspicion algorithms, and the fourth amendment', *University of Pennsylvania Law Review*, 164(4), pp. 871–929. https://scholarship.law.upenn.edu/penn_law_review/vol164/iss4/2/ (accessed 22 March 2021).

Robertson, A. (2021). Detroit man sues police for wrongfully arresting him based on facial recognition, The Verge. https://www.theverge.com/2021/4/13/22382398/ robert-williams-detroit-police-department-aclu-lawsuit-facial-recognition-wrongful-arrest (accessed 14 April 2021).

Robertson, K., Khoo, C., and Song, Y. (2020). *To Surveil and Predict: A Human Rights Analysis of Algorithmic Policing in Canada*. The Citizen Lab & University of Toronto Faculty of Law.

Samek, W., Montavon, G., Vedaldi, A. et al. (eds) (2019) Explainable AI: Interpreting, Explaining and Visualizing Deep Learning. Springer International Publishing

(Lecture Notes in Artificial Intelligence, Lect. Notes Computer State-of-the-Art Surveys). doi:https://doi.org/10.1007/978-3-030-28954-6.

Schlehahn, E., Marquenie, T. and Kindt, E. (2018). Data Protection Impact Assessments (DPIAs) in the law enforcement sector according to Directive (EU) 2016/680 - A comparative analysis of methodologies. VALCRI project. http://valcri. org/our-content/uploads/2018/06/VALCRI-DPIA-Guidelines-Methodological-Comparison.pdf (accessed 15 March 2021).

Slovenia Information Commissioner of the Republic of Slovenia (2014). Privacy Impact Assessment (PIA) guidelines for the introduction of new police power. https://www.ip-rs.si/fileadmin/user_upload/Pdf/smernice/PIA_guideliness_for_introduction_of_new_police_powers_english.pdf (accessed 25 May 2021).

Spain Agencia Española de Protección de Datos (AEPD) (2018). Guía práctica para Las Evaluaciones de Impacto en la Protección de los Datos Sujetas al RGPD. https://www.aepd.es/sites/default/files/2019-09/guia-evaluaciones-de-impacto-rgpd.pdf (accessed 25 May 2021).

Spielkamp, M. (2019). Automating Society: Taking Stock of Automated Decision-Making in the EU. Algorithm Watch.

Straub, D. and Nance, W. (1990). Discovering and disciplining computer abuse in organizations: a field study. *MIS Quarterly* 14 (1), pp. 45–61.

Tae, K.H., Roh. Y., Hun Oh, Y. et al. (2019). Data cleaning for accurate, fair, and robust models: A big data - AI integration approach. *Proceedings of the 3rd International Workshop on Data Management for End-to-End Machine Learning - DEEM'19. the 3rd International Workshop*, Amsterdam, Netherlands: ACM Press, pp. 1–4. doi:https://doi.org/10.1145/3329486.3329493.

Taylor, J. (2021). Signal's hack of surveillance tech used by police could undermine Australian criminal cases, The Guardian. http://www.theguardian.com/australia-news/2021/may/02/how-the-hacking-of-surveillance-tech-used-by-police-could-undermine-australian-criminal-cases.

Ting, D. (2007) 'Managing access control – combining physical and logical security', *Card Technology Today*, 19(3), pp. 9–10. doi:https://doi.org/10.1016/S0965-2590(07)70057-9.

Turner Lee, N. (2018) 'Detecting racial bias in algorithms and machine learning', *Journal of Information, Communication and Ethics in Society*, 16(3), pp. 252–260. doi:https://doi.org/10.1108/JICES-06-2018-0056.

UK ICO (2018). Guide to the General Data Protection Regulation (GDPR) - Data Protection Impact Assessments (DPIAs). https://ico.org.uk/for-organisations/guide-to-data-protection/guide-to-the-general-data-protection-regulation-gdpr/data-protection-impact-assessments-dpias/ (accessed 25 May 2021).

UK ICO (2019a). Guide to law enforcement processing - data protection impact assessments. https://ico.org.uk/for-organisations/guide-to-data-protection/

guide-to-law-enforcement-processing/accountability-and-governance/data-protection-impact-assessments/ (accessed 16 March 2021).

UK ICO (2019b). Guide to law enforcement processing (Part 3 of the bill). https://ico.org.uk/media/for-organisations/guide-to-data-protection/guide-to-law-enforcement-processing-1-1.pdf (accessed 16 March 2021).

UK ICO (2020). Toolkit for organisations considering using data analytics. https://ico.org.uk/for-organisations/toolkit-for-organisations-considering-using-data-analytics/ (accessed 16 March 2021).

Veale, M. and Binns, R. (2017) 'Fairer machine learning in the real world: Mitigating discrimination without collecting sensitive data', *Big Data & Society*, 4(2), p. 205395171774353. doi:https://doi.org/10.1177/2053951717743530.

Wachter, S., Mittelstadt, B. and Russell, C. (2018) 'Counterfactual explanations without opening the black box: automated decisions and the GDPR', *Harvard Journal of Law & Technology*, 31(2). doi:https://doi.org/10.2139/ssrn.3063289.

Wachter, S., Mittelstadt, B. and Russell, C. (2021) 'Why fairness cannot be automated: bridging the gap between EU non-discrimination law and AI', *Computer Law & Security Review*, 41, p. 105567. doi:https://doi.org/10.1016/j.clsr.2021.105567.

Woods, T. (2016). "Mathwashing," Facebook and the zeitgeist of data worship, Technical.ly Brooklyn, 6 August. https://technical.ly/brooklyn/2016/06/08/fred-benenson-mathwashing-facebook-data-worship/ (accessed 7 June 2021).

Wright, F. (2020). Bridges V CCSWP: A landmark case in the era of automated facial recognition, Human Rights Pulse. https://www.humanrightspulse.com/mastercontentblog/bridges-v-ccswp-a-landmark-case-in-the-era-of-automated-facial-recognition (accessed 5 May 2021).

Zouave, E.T. and Marquenie, T. (2017). An inconvenient truth: algorithmic transparency accountability in criminal intelligence profiling. *European Intelligence and Security Informatics Conference (EISIC)*. *European Intelligence and Security Informatics Conference (EISIC)*, IEEE, pp. 17–23. doi:https://doi.org/10.1109/EISIC.2017.12.

3

Methods of Stakeholder Engagement for the Co-Design of Security Technologies

Andrea Iannone, Luigi Briguglio, Carmela Occhipinti and Valeria Cesaroni

R&D Department, CyberEthics Lab., Rome, Italy

Acronyms and Abbreviations

COS	Community of Stakeholders
ECB	External Communication Board
FR	First Responder
GDPR	General Data Protection Regulation
H2020	Horizon 2020 (the European Commission financing scheme for research and innovation)
KPI	Key Performance Indicator
LEA	Law Enforcement Agency
SA	Sentiment Analysis
SAT	Social Acceptance of Technology (Methodology)
SIA	SItuational Awareness
UTAUT	Unified Theory of Acceptance and Use of Technology

3.1 Toward a Holistic Approach for Technology Assessment

The increasing complexity of technological developments has pushed their reach into more niches of human life than previously imagined. Invasion of individuals' privacy and other related issues have spurred the creation of regulatory frameworks,

Security Technologies and Social Implications, First Edition. Edited by Garik Markarian, Ruža Karlović, Holger Nitsch, and Krishna Chandramouli.
Published 2023 by John Wiley & Sons, Inc.

such as the European Union's General Data Protection Regulation (GDPR), that safeguard individuals' fundamental and human right to privacy. However, safeguarding citizens' privacy rights does not exhaust ethical concerns: a technocratic form of government could ensure such a standard while repressing many others.

In order to exhaustively mitigate ethical concerns, ex-ante evaluations focusing on such a perspective by measuring the perceptions of technological innovations have assumed critical importance. Law enforcement agencies (LEAs) are not exempt from this requirement. Especially when certain novel technological means are uncritically prescribed as necessary, the exploration of the nexus between security and human rights merits a reflective approach, such as that favored by the proactive involvement of stakeholders in real-world processes of adoption of security technologies. Indeed, traditional functional and nonfunctional requirements risk hiding a plethora of perspectives during the deployment of security technology. However, if these perspectives are otherwise brought to light, LEAs attempting to deploy technological innovations could face lower barriers to adoption.

This chapter aims to provide LEA management personnel or any other interested reader, useful tools and techniques for uncovering similar perspectives by engaging stakeholders[1] and, thus, avoiding or mitigating risks related to them being left unaddressed. In the remainder of the Introduction, we provide a brief overview of the literature regarding assessment methodologies. The main body of the chapter describes the experiences of using specific tools and techniques for engaging stakeholders in two European Union security research projects financed under the Horizon 2020 framework, PERSONA and ASSISTANCE. First, we focus on providing an overview of project management best practices for the identification and subsequent engagement of stakeholders. We then proceed to explain the rationale and results, within the context of the aforementioned projects, of the use of sentiment analysis (SA) and focus groups, two diverse methods for the gathering of feedback and analysis of opinions from stakeholders.

This diversity to implement the method in PERSONA and ASSISTANCE is justified by the heterogeneity and diverse nature of technologies developed by the projects; as well as the different objectives and contexts of their application.

However, the co-creation stakeholder engagement approach makes available different tools and it is flexible enough to be fine-tuned according to the type of stakeholders and the type of research to be developed. In this way, the co-creation process will have a single conceptual core of reference (that of the creative and dialogical activation of the relationship between stakeholders and engagers) but will be able to make polyhedral use of different tools, thus making the co-creation dynamically fruitful.

---

1 A definition of "stakeholder" is provided in the coming sections.

These two projects each touch upon distinct facets of security technology such that they are representative of greater debates in the field. While the latter is concerned with "extraordinary" circumstances during which technology is meant to secure the lives of users (FRs) and citizens, the former was involved with the "ordinary" use case in which technology may have either made more efficient or rendered less carefree the experience of citizens' freedom of movement, a fundamental right. In essence, both projects examined technological deployments that, if poorly executed, could compromise the physical, mental, and social well-being of users and citizens in different ways.

There was and is, therefore, the need to conduct wide-spectrum evaluations such as those previously described. These evaluations require the use of tested and validated methods, which include but are not limited to those that favor stakeholder engagement. To assess the likelihood of adoption of the security technologies they wish to deploy and see adopted, LEAs should consider how socially acceptable stakeholders at large perceive those technologies to be. Social acceptance has been defined as whether "a new technology is accepted – or merely tolerated – by a community" (Taebi 2017).

The evaluation of this type of acceptance implies the need to assess and measure a variety of phenomena that are diverse in nature and that range from economic to ideological. Existing approaches, such as the Unified Theory of Acceptance and Use of Technology (UTAUT), developed by Venkatesh et al. (2003) have attempted to do so. UTAUT posits that four independent variables (gender, age, experience, and voluntariness of use) affect (i) an individual's expectations of performance and use of technology and (ii) the social and technical environments in which that same individuals will use that technology; in other words, exogenous and endogenous factors influence users' intended and thereby effective usage of technology. Despite its great acclaim, there is no shortage of criticisms toward UTAUT. For instance, according to Bagozzi, UTAUT is a baroque "patchwork of many largely unintegrated and uncoordinated abridgements" in which "few of the included predictors are fundamental, generic, or universal" (Bagozzi 2007).

Therefore, as opposed to initiating from the perspective of the potential users, evaluations could commence by examining how a given technology is designed and communicated and how it is linked to the actual social, economic, and political aspects on which it will more or less likely impact. In fact, if we take seriously the concept of socio-technical systems, one must consider that technology and society are co-implied and shape one another. Originating in organizational studies in Post-War Britain, the concept of the socio-technical system indicates that, in society as inside public- or private-sector organizations, "technical and social systems are independent of each other in the sense that the former follows the laws of the natural sciences while the latter follows the laws of human sciences and is a purposeful system. Yet they are correlative in that one requires the other for the transformation of an input into an output" (Trist 1981). Since then, as technologies have become more omnipresent in everyday life outside of work, the definition of the socio-technical system has evolved to encompass aspects tied to the relations between subsystem components that in earlier work were not considered to be relevant (Haavik 2011).

Against this backdrop, there are three key elements to consider in order to evaluate technology from a socio-technical point of view; these are presented in the following paragraph together with guiding questions.

First, the factual and the stated impacts on the economic and organizational spheres: will technology disrupt existing relationships in the industry adopting it? Are potential disruptions connoted in a generally positive or negative light by media and policy players? Second, the co-implications between technology and the socio-political sphere: how will values likely change? Are there privacy, ethical, or other types of impacts on different categories of stakeholders? Third, individuals' perception of the consequences of their use of the technology: how is their user experience shaped? Do they express trust in the provider of the technology?

Deeply intertwined, these three elements constitute the main pillars of an assessment methodology called Social Acceptance of Technology (SAT), which provides a new integrated and holistic approach to understanding the implication of technological innovation on the social sphere. SAT's research model, which is modular and scalable, disentangles the three elements previously described by structuring them into the following four, fundamental conceptual constructs – called "bubbles" – that represent distinct and complementary facets of social acceptance.

- **User-Experience Acceptance:** The first bubble aims to understand how users balance the risks and benefits they perceive to be associated with technology with the expectations that the technology's specification, communication, and marketing material convey.
- **Social Disruptiveness Acceptance:** The second bubble investigates how and to what extent the technology under consideration reframes societal relations, from the perspective of impact both on production and socio-political processes.
- **Value Impact Acceptance:** The third bubble evaluates the extent to which, in a given social context, the technology concerned complies with values common to different classes of stakeholders. Values include but are not limited to those connected with perceptions of stronger social justice, such as antidiscrimination, equality of opportunity, attention to human rights, and comprehension of intersectionality.
- **Trust Acceptance:** The fourth and final bubble evaluates the extent to which the technological tool is considered reliable according to the individual user and society as a whole. Since reliability is influenced by elements included in other bubbles, the trust bubble takes into account evaluation elements from the first three bubbles.

Throughout the entire evaluation process, analysts perform stakeholder engagement by: (i) identifying and mapping stakeholders; (ii) adhering to good communication practices; (iii) conducting sentiment analyses, focus groups interviews, and surveys to gather data on stakeholders' perceptions. In the following sections, we will illustrate SAT's tools and techniques for stakeholder engagement by referencing two concrete use cases.

3.2 Methods of Stakeholder Engagement

The definition of terms and conditions (i.e. scope, time, cost, and quality) for properly executing and managing activities aimed at innovating processes and technological solutions, usually involves two main counterparts, i.e. the customers in whose interest the innovation is ideated and the providers of the innovative solution.

However, this dichotomy does not take into account the surrounding crowd of other actors whose perspectives should be considered. These other actors might have a stake or an interest in the specific technological development, or in any strategy involving its deployment in view of achieving certain objectives. The totality of actors, including customers and solution providers, are commonly called **stakeholders**.

Based on their interest, role, and power, stakeholders might influence technology development and its deployment. So, if stakeholders perceive they can benefit from the technology, they are more likely to be supportive and positive about it. However, if stakeholders perceive that the technology may damage their interests or, more generally, have a negative outcome for them, they are more likely to oppose it and depict it in a bad light.

For this reason, as per project management's best practices (PMBOK Guide 2017), it is definitely important at the beginning of the project to identify all stakeholders and classify them through mapping tools. This classification will allow those managing the innovation project to take the appropriate measures to manage stakeholders and their engagement.

3.2.1 Stakeholder Identification and Mapping

Indeed, the "**Identification of Stakeholders**" is the preliminary process of regularly **identifying** project stakeholders and of analyzing relevant information regarding their interests, attitudes, expectations, involvement, interdependencies, influence, and potential impact on project success. This process allows project managers to **map** stakeholders, being aware of stakeholders who are less than enthusiastic or opposed to the project, in order to define suitable approaches and techniques for their management and engagement.

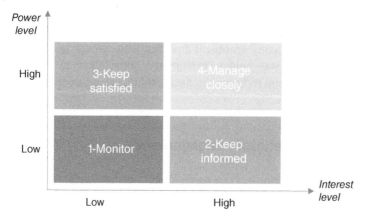

Figure 3.1 Stakeholders' mapping matrix: interest vs. power.

This process is usually performed by analyzing use case scenarios, potential impacts on business operation, submitting questionnaires and surveys, and employing sentiment analyses. Data resulting from these analyses are documented by representation tools such as the **stakeholder-mapping matrix**, which is based on interests and power of influence (Figure 3.1).

Each of the four identified areas considers a specific group of stakeholders, and according to specific strategies suggested by the communication management theory, it is possible to define suitable strategies to be applied (i.e. monitor, keep informed, keep satisfied, and manage closely). For instance, stakeholders characterized by low power and low interest can be constantly monitored to identify any potential change in power and/or interest, while stakeholders characterized by low power but high interest have to be constantly informed. As a consequence of this, stakeholder management and engagement require accurate planning, management, and monitoring of the way to communicate for each group of stakeholders. This last requirement underlines how strictly related communication and stakeholders' management are.

After the identification and mapping of the stakeholders, it is necessary to **"Plan stakeholders' engagement,"** i.e. carry out the process of developing approaches to involve project stakeholders based on their needs, expectations, interests, and potential impacts on the project.

This process can be supported by tools and techniques such as the prioritization of needs and expectations, mind mapping, and **stakeholder engagement assessment matrix**. The latter allows to plan the current and desired level of engagement, as well as to monitor and assess it, for each stakeholder or groups of them (Figure 3.2).

These two first processes, i.e. identification and planning, favor the setup of the methodological framework for properly managing, engaging, and monitoring stakeholders.

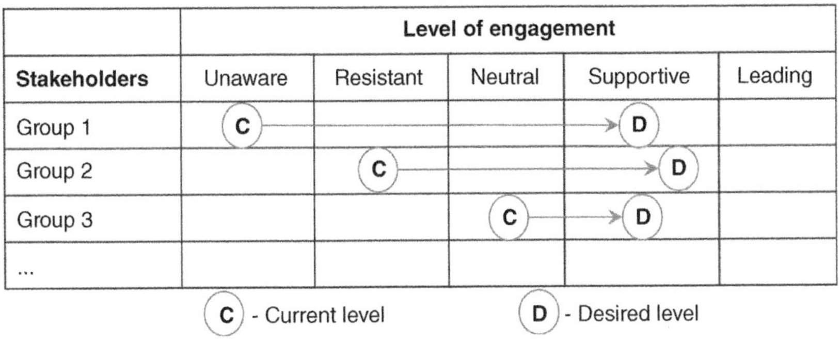

Stakeholders	Level of engagement				
	Unaware	Resistant	Neutral	Supportive	Leading
Group 1	C			D	
Group 2		C		D	
Group 3			C	D	
...					

C - Current level   D - Desired level

Figure 3.2 Stakeholder engagement assessment matrix.

An instance of these processes has been carried out in the PERSONA project for the identification and recruitment of external "interested" members, who were invited to join the "Community of Stakeholders" (CoS). In accordance with the specificities of the project, which addressed developments in the field of border-crossing solutions and related privacy concerns, CoS members were divided into three macro areas corresponding to each of their converging interests (Figure 3.3).

3.2.2 Stakeholder Engagement and Co-Design

Essentially, stakeholder engagement is communicating and working with stakeholders, with the objective of addressing their needs, expectations, and issues. Communication regards explaining and promoting a choice to target groups, rather than influencing a target group's behavior (i.e. marketing).

For this reason, as mentioned earlier, most of the best practices related to engagement are strictly related to communication. Without entering into details about communication theories, for the sake of clarity, this chapter reports communication ground rules to be applied for contributing to the success of stakeholder engagement initiatives.

Communication assumes that counterparts are using a common language, with well-known terms from shared dictionaries, for facilitating comprehension and understanding of information. This assumption may seem obvious, however, when dealing with challenging objectives and disruptive technologies, it is quite usual to witness unideal communication behaviors such as – inter alia – spin,

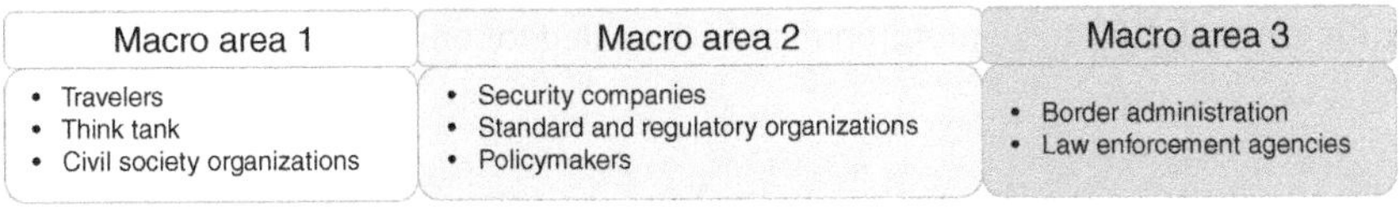

Macro area 1	Macro area 2	Macro area 3
• Travelers • Think tank • Civil society organizations	• Security companies • Standard and regulatory organizations • Policymakers	• Border administration • Law enforcement agencies

Figure 3.3 PERSONA stakeholders' identification and mapping.

dissimulation, corporate or technical jargon, or even worse, silence in front of press or external audience.

These approaches may cause a negative perception of technical outcomes and the project itself, impacting (i) the trust toward research activities and (ii) the social acceptance of the project's outcomes.

Citizens, but in general any stakeholder, may be particularly concerned with regard to projects' challenging objectives and disruptive technologies due to the fact that these might be **perceived** as having a potential impact on their fundamental rights (i.e. privacy, human rights, or other civil liberties). In light of this, being aware of such a risk, it is important to devote a special commitment to dealing with the communication of information, press, or more in general, with critiques addressed to the project activities and outcomes.

In order to mitigate this risk, LEAs might consider adopting the best practice in the security sector and this is known as **"crisis communication."**[2] The main idea is to appoint an "External Communication Board" (ECB) composed of multidisciplinary experts. The ECB should provide **judgment** regarding the information transmitted by the project team and evaluate the comprehensibility and potential risks related to its communication. Furthermore, experts can suggest refinements to terms used in the communication for improving the comprehension of a specific **target audience** while maintaining accuracy.

As a matter of principle, the communication has to use specific terms for each target group of stakeholders just because each target group might be characterized by its own dictionary with specific terms as well. So, the preparation of communication material has to be done after the identification and mapping of the different stakeholder groups, addressing their specific needs and expectations as well.

Another relevant principle to be considered is that stakeholders may not have all the details of the project team and that they do not want to hear long presentations full of technicalities, but, on the other hand, they expect to receive a brief explanation of the current issues and how these are overcome with the new technological solution. This means that external audiences should never be overloaded with long documents to be read and obligated to attend long presentations. Instead, it is definitely necessary to distil technical documentation with the objective of informing the audience, and this **"informative material"** can be realized – inter alia – in the form of infographics, case study sheets, and videos (whether animated or in live action). Together with the preparation of informative material that aims to properly explain the benefits and risks associated with the usage of the new technology, it is important to define a set of **Key Performance Indicators (KPIs)** to be monitored and controlled for ensuring the success of the

---

2 https://www.efsa.europa.eu/sites/default/files/crisis_manual_160315.pdf

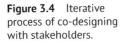

Figure 3.4 Iterative process of co-designing with stakeholders.

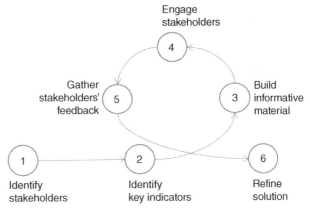

project outcome. Managers can measure KPIs by running surveys and focus groups. Both allow the **gathering of feedback** and the assessment of the assonance among transmitted messages by the informative material and the perceptions of the engaged stakeholders.

This process of informing stakeholders and assessing their perceptions cannot be performed in a single, step-wise process. Rather, it is itself an iterative and incremental process to be integrated within the development process, making it possible to recursively use stakeholders' feedback for the refinement process, and potentially enabling the collaboration among stakeholders and project team, i.e. co-design (Figure 3.4). Indeed, outcomes details improve with the development process. As a matter of fact, stakeholder engagement should follow agile methodologies[3] as well.

This iterative process of engagement and co-design with stakeholders was adopted, in different ways, in both the PERSONA and ASSISTANCE projects.

The co-creation approach needs a certain degree of malleability in the use of its tools (questionnaires, focus groups, working groups, etc.) as the objective is to stimulate the active and creative component of the stakeholders. For this reason, given the dynamic and creative nature of the engagement process through co-creation, it is necessary to modulate and select the best tools to conduct this process each time, calibrating them both on the type of stakeholders involved and on the type of context on which the research is to be carried out. Stakeholders were invited to participate in events and workshops in order to openly debate issues emerging from the project's developments. Furthermore, they were offered access to the online tool, PERSONA STAR,[4] which functioned both as a repository of the

---

3 For a deeper dive into agile methodology, visit http://agilemanifesto.org/

4 https://persona-star.cyberethicslab.com

informative material based on more than 300 pages of technical documents and as a means of gathering feedback through questionnaires regarding each phase of the project. PERSONA STAR was one of the most relevant and exciting activities in the project since it allowed the external audience to capture the key messages of the project and provide valuable insights for its improvement.

In the following sections, we explain in greater detail the methods and results of specific stakeholder engagement strategies adopted by PERSONA and another H2020 research project, **ASSISTANCE**, which aims to enhance the ability of first responders to operate safely in very different disaster scenarios.

3.2.3 Sentiment Analysis

There may be cases in which stakeholders are difficult or impossible to identify and map. In such cases, indirect techniques of stakeholder analysis are called for. One such technique is known as SA. It is a relatively novel method whose purpose is to provide analysts with a "snapshot" of the view of the public at large on a specific term (e.g. "face recognition") in a more or less defined place (e.g. a specific airport) during a set period of time (e.g. 2019). The means used to reach this end are derived from various disciplines and techniques, such as natural language processing, text analysis, and computational linguistics. Such techniques measure people's emotions based on, for example, their online activity;[5] these emotions range from negative and are considered harbingers of social acceptance.

The results of SA provide decision makers with additional information that they can use to determine whether policies they plan to implement are more or less likely to be successful. Thanks to the vastness and the variety of data online on any given day, appropriate statistical techniques for regularly sampling, approximating trends, and modeling the data can be applied to generate reliable results.

SA's accuracy has been well documented despite its relative novelty. While the frequency of both social media mentions and search activity may increase given contingencies (e.g. the sudden usage of facial recognition by an LEA in conjunction with a specific event may spur Google users to learn more about the technology), the sentiments associated with those technologies by social media and web users have been demonstrated to remain stable over time. For example, in Wang (2012), SA proved to give useful information during the 2012 US Election; in Wilson (2005) and Liu (2015), theoretical arguments are given to support its validity. Finally, the excellent book by Pozzi et al. (2016) presents a comprehensive study on the use of SA in the field of social media.

---

5 SA must occur within the boundaries dictated by the law and in compliance with applicable contractual conditions and privacy regulations, such as Twitter's own privacy policy and, more importantly, the European Union's General Data Protection Regulation (GDPR) 2016/679.

Within the context of PERSONA, the authors of the present chapter proposed SA as a way to understand travellers' sentiments toward these technologies. This proposal was necessarily given COVID-19-related restrictions, which made in-person questionnaires impossible.

In the framework applied, SA was aimed at evaluating the responses of web and social media users by automatically analyzing data from Google Trends, i.e. the free service that Google provides to showcase the popularity of a given search query across various regions and languages, and from Twitter. The analysis was conducted on the following technologies, which are the most well-known among those used in biometric border crossings and, thus, the most likely to be referenced in Google searches[6] and Tweets:

- Artificial intelligence
- Automated border control gates
- e-passport
- Facial recognition
- Fingerprint enrolment
- Iris enrolment and ID
- Sensors

As shown in Figure 3.5, Google Trends analyses consisted in plotting the frequency of searches (results are indexed to the maximum at 100) – taken as a proxy for the Internet user interest in the technology – in specific countries over a five-year period to see whether there was an increase. Analyses of Twitter data (Figure 3.6), instead, consisted in comparing the textual contents of Tweets to an

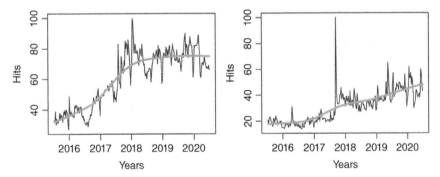

Figure 3.5 Global Google Trends lines for artificial intelligence (left) and facial recognition (right).

6 Especially in Europe, Google search queries are a good proxy for overall internet searches, since Google has a volume market share for searches of over 90%. https://gs.statcounter.com/search-engine-market-share/all/europe

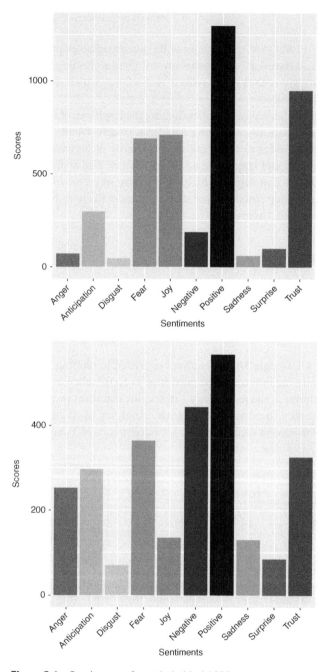

Figure 3.6 Sentiments of people behind 1000 tweets away from airports mentioning "artificial intelligence" (left) and 1000 tweets mentioning "facial recognition" (right). While positive sentiments are dominant for the former term, negative sentiments and fear and anger seem to be crowding out lower scoring of positive sentiments in the case of the latter term.

open-source thesaurus that associates a word's semantics to one of eight emotional states and two sentiments described later. The thesaurus used was the National Research Council of Canada's Emotion Lexicon.[7] The text was sourced from Tweets geotagged both at and far from airports in multiple two-week periods.

Despite cultural differences, it has been shown that a majority of affective norms are stable across languages, therefore non-English sentences can be translated automatically (Balahur and Turchi 2012), and the words subsequently compared to the lexicon, with respect to (i) the states of anger, fear, anticipation, trust, surprise, sadness, joy, or disgust and (ii) negative or positive sentiments.

The trends shown in Figure 3.5 were identified using a SARIMA model for analysis of the large data set characterized by a seasonal, nonstationary nature. While Google searches for artificial intelligence appear to have flattened after a peak in 2018, those for facial recognition increased and are close to matching search volumes for the prior term.

Conceptually, the main conclusion drawn from the SA undertaken in PERSONA was that, out of the eight technologies mentioned earlier, the two that seemed to have the best chances of being deemed "acceptable" overall by the general public were "e-passport" and "artificial intelligence." Interpreting this conclusion from a socio-technical perspective, relational aspects of subsystem components would seem to explain this supposed aversion, something that by focusing solely on ordinary business efficiency and effectiveness targets would otherwise be overlooked. Interpreting this conclusion through the SAT model, it can be said that technologies such as biometric border controls, which separate users (travellers) from beneficiaries (border control authorities), seem to instil a greater sense of fear than those that, upon use, allow users to feel "more in the loop." To put it differently, travelers' current expressions of their user experience seem to indicate that they perceive that the potential risks of newer, more privacy-invasive biometric technologies such as facial recognition outweigh their potential benefits. Hence, older, more familiar technologies such as "e-passport" and "artificial intelligence" seem to be more positively perceived.

Methodologically, the key result for PERSONA was that SA delivered only a partial picture of the likelihood of social acceptance of the given technologies. It would have been necessary to include, for validation purposes, surveys of intended end users. In other words, as methods for stakeholder consultation, SA and surveys can complement each other; if the results of either are vague, the other can be used to favor more precise interpretations.

---

7 https://nrc.canada.ca/en/research-development/products-services/technical-advisory-services/sentiment-emotion-lexicons

SA's strength lies in the fact that it offers a cost- and time-effective way of gathering opinions; furthermore, as a data-gathering technique of which users are unaware, it is spontaneous, as opposed to surveys, whose necessary pre-explanatory process could compromise the authenticity of responses. However, SA results could favor ingrained biases, for example by excluding those who do not access the given online services or by relying too heavily on the personal motivations of those users who have stronger interests in expressing their perspectives online (e.g. those who are professional of a specific field).

Despite the fact that the development of our SAT methodology had not started at the time of the PERSONA project, SA now is one of the techniques used in SAT to engage stakeholders. In conclusion, our experience in PERSONA has underlined how SA, as a tool for public consultation, has two main strengths and a slight weakness, of which LEA decision makers should be aware if they decide to adopt SA as a method of stakeholder engagement.

3.2.4 Focus Groups

Given the specificities of the other H2020 security project analyzed in this chapter, ASSISTANCE, our approach to involving stakeholders was different. As opposed to PERSONA, whose purpose was to develop an assessment method of certain technologies, ASSISTANCE aims to develop the technologies themselves. The purpose of ASSISTANCE's technologies, which will be tested in three field pilots, is twofold: (i) to help and protect different kinds of FR organizations involved in the mitigation of large natural or human-made disasters; (ii) to enhance first responders' capabilities and skills for facing complex situations related to different types of incidents.

The technologies developed in the project are of different types, from embodied and wearable technologies, which enhance human sensory capabilities, to autonomous technologies such as drones, UAVs, and robots equipped with specific sensors that allow to monitor different elements of the emergency context.

The ASSISTANCE project also aims to create a training network for First Responders based on tools such as virtual reality, mixed reality, and augmented reality to increase and develop the skills and capabilities of the first responder.

Therefore, the peculiarity of this project lies in the delicate balance that is established between individuals and technology in the context of emergency and vulnerability.

Within the extraordinary security context of disaster management, it is evident that the engagement of FRs themselves, as primary stakeholders and early adopters of technologies, is quite relevant, especially as far as the second expression of the project's purpose is concerned. Operational success in complex situations, in fact, entails a high-enough level of situational awareness, which, in the first instance, following Endsley's definition, can be defined as the understanding that an individual or team has of a situation (Endsley 2011). Said awareness can involve information related to the natural environment (e.g. the quantity of a certain toxic gas in the atmosphere after an explosion) and to the sociocultural one (e.g. the habitual male–female relationship in a given context).

However, the notion of situational awareness, henceforth SIA, turns out to be extremely stratified and complex since it includes within it several aspects that are closely interdependent, which have been outlined in the literature as *states, systems,* and *processes* of awareness (Lundberg 2015) where *states* of SIA refers to the awareness of the situation at a given time, *systems* refers to the distribution of SIA between members of a team and between people and objects and the exchange that takes place between these parts of a system, and *processes* refers to changes in SIA due to changes in information.

In fact, the subject's awareness of the context and environment derives from a dynamic balance between several aspects: the subject's ability to interact with the environment (where interaction means the ability to analyze and understand information through a cognitive ability to organize information and concepts); an integrated and developed sense of self such that one can perceive oneself as an active subject in relation to the environment.

Situational awareness is therefore configured both as a process and as the result of an active and dynamic relationship of information exchange and processing between subjects, objects, and environments.

As Endsley states: "*Situation awareness can be thought of as an internalized mental model of the current state of the operators' environment. All of the incoming data from the many systems, the outside environment, fellow crew members and others must be all brought together into an integrated whole. This integrated picture forms the central organizing feature from which all decision making and action takes place.*" (Endsley 2001, p. 3).

The technologies developed by ASSISTANCE significantly mediate the individual's relationship with reality, affecting both his ability to interpret the context and his capacity to act and coordinate operations. This hybridization between human and nonhuman actors in the context of the scenarios outlined by ASSISTANCE creates a condition of *interoperability* between subjects and technological objects, namely "mutual connections between two or more systems or entities to enable systems and entities to exchange and share information in order to further act, function, or produce on the principles of that information" (Lier and Hardjono 2011, p. 2).

For this reason, the very concept of SIA, although always referring to the human subject, is strongly determined and influenced by the relationship between subjects and technological objects, which must be understood as parts of an interdependent system.

FRs' increased situation awareness has been shown to be correlated with better field performance. In a global context in which "pressure from consumers for better public services, fiscal concerns, and the threat of terror increase, there is likely to be greater demand on disaster management agencies to improve their effectiveness" (Heinrich 2002, p. 5). ASSISTANCE technologies aim to provide FR with both kinds of information listed earlier so that their effectiveness can indeed improve. As we have noted, if the perception and awareness of FRs are mediated by different technologies, it becomes crucial to understand the point of view of the operators involved. For this reason, to assess whether FRs in the project possess a sufficient level of situation awareness, we have planned three focus groups with them.

A focus group is an ensemble of individuals interacting in the presence of a moderator, who – by stimulating the group through a set of action prompts or questions – uses the group's interaction to gain information about a specific issue (Litosseliti 2003).

Although there are different methods for conducting a focus group (Wilkinson 1998), the main idea is to involve participants – selected according to the needs of the research – in the discussion based on certain themes proposed by the moderator. The moderator can utilize one or more of the different validated questionnaires and techniques such as those reviewed in Jane (2019). Another approach is to simulate a scenario or recall an experience.

During the ASSISTANCE project, three focus groups will be held with the FRs immediately after an exercise with the technologies developed by the project in three realistic scenarios of different emergency and disaster situations: an earthquake in an urban context, a fire in an industrial site, a terrorist attack in a public place.

Currently, we have carried out the first focus group with the FRs following the realization of the first disaster scenario, set in Turkey.

The objective we pursued in conducting the first focus group was to investigate the perception of the FRs regarding the technologies used in the exercise, in order to understand to what extent and in what way the use of these technologies impacted the situational awareness of the rescuers.

To assess the situational awareness of first responders, some questions were proposed, such as:

- How do you think the embodied technologies affect your perception of yourself, your abilities, and your limits?
- Regarding technologies such as drones and robots, do you think these can increase your awareness of the situation?
- Does the autonomy of these technologies make you feel that you are no longer in control of the situation?

These questions helped us develop a dialogue among the FRs and between the FRs and the moderator that allowed us to focus on the dynamics of co-construction of situational awareness within a team.

The responses of the FRs were recorded and analyzed following the laddering interviewing technique. Through laddering, an interviewer elicits responses from one or more interviewees about an element, possibly a person, an object, a situation, an event, etc. The way in which the elicitation occurs favors "modeling people's belief structures in a simple, systematic way, establishing individual's superordinate personal constructs" (Veludo-de-Oliveira et al. 2006, p. 626). Having originated in psychology studies in the 1960s, laddering was later applied to consumer research upon the development of the means–end chain theory, which hierarchically connects (as shown abstractly in Figure 3.7) "attributes (A) of products with particular consequences (C), and how these consequences satisfy their [consumers'] values (V)" (Kaciak and Cullen 2006, p. 142).

Means–end models of responses will serve us in forming interpretations of the FRs' perception as primary stakeholders of the ASSISTANCE technologies through the lens of a socio-technical outlook and of our Value-Impact bubble in SAT. Value-based motivations of actions impact the way in which different stakeholder groups interact in a disaster context through technology.

As noted earlier, in fact, in this project, SIA emerges in a context of interoperability between subjects and objects in a given context. The responses of the FRs during the focus group emphasized that the technologies developed by ASSISTANCE provide crucial information for the coordination of operations and allow it to be exchanged within the team smoothly and efficiently, thus increasing the awareness of the emergency situation.

At the same time, however, many of the FRs noted a sense of loss of autonomy and reduced awareness of self and situation due to the pervasiveness of the technologies used. In particular, the constant use of cameras and, more importantly, the impossibility of being able to turn them off, lead to a feeling of control and, consequently, distraction and discomfort with the situation and with themselves. Some FRs have therefore stressed an out-of-the-loop dynamic generated by ASSISTANCE technologies, that might lead to lower SA in emergency contexts.

These elements allowed us to build, together with the FRs, the path to be followed in outlining new research paths to be investigated in the next focus groups, with the aim of assessing the risks and potentialities of the technologies developed by ASSISTANCE.

Figure 3.7 Means–end chain.

Some ways of minimizing these risks are in fact easily achievable, such as developing ways of using technology that involve active control by the rescuer, thus increasing their active involvement in the situation and enhancing their situational awareness.

The focus group therefore makes it possible to develop a research and analysis methodology that makes active participation its strong point, and collaboration between research teams and primary stakeholders its fundamental dynamic.

Through this stakeholder engagement methodology, an excessive conceptual focus on the performativity of technological tools is avoided, in order to emphasize the interactive dynamics and shared construction of a sense of awareness in emergency dynamics.

3.3 Conclusions

Throughout the course of a project in which potentially controversial technologies are deployed in public spaces, public consultations should occur iteratively so that problematic issues of the chosen system can be identified and addressed. Upon identification of such issues, innovation managers can then choose to redesign part or all of the technology in question. The process of involving stakeholders is, therefore, clearly fundamental to the process of participatory co-design of technology deployment.

For these reasons, we highly encourage and recommend LEA personnel tasked with deploying technological innovations employ some or all of the tools and techniques described in this chapter. By conducting focus groups in conjunction with SA, as suggested in, innovation managers may find that the strengths of the former help interpret the results of the latter. Conversely, the large data sets that SA allows technicians to analyze in a timely manner make up for the time-intensity and small sample sizes of focus groups.

However, these consultations should not be considered the sole means to determine that system's acceptability. Other means include the appointment of independent panels of experts, operating with autonomy outside the control of the public authority in charge of the deployment, and tasked with issuing a qualified and balanced opinion regarding the technology at hand. What matters is to elaborate an understanding that anticipates the benefits and risks perceived by stakeholders. Perceptions vary according to stakeholders' levels of prerequisite knowledge of technology and their concern over negative impacts in the social, health, political, economic, or even technical fields. Depending on the stakeholder mix and the specificities of their perception, technology developers and deployers should propose certain technological solutions and not others.

In security, stakeholders' diverse nature implies the need to conform, to a greater or lesser degree, the technology adoption process to their needs. This is why the results of the assessment of the social acceptance of security technologies should be reviewed by policy makers, innovators, and the general public, to ensure that there are appropriate mitigation or avoidance strategies for any risks uncovered during the process.

Stakeholders expect technology to have a given impact on their user experience and values; these expectations consequently shape their perception of the technology. Since generally negative perceptions could invalidate the technology adoption process, engaging stakeholders through sentiment analyses and focus groups can help anticipate some of the more problematic issues.

3.4 Recommendations

Following the experience gained through the work on the co-creation approach of stakeholder engagement on the PERSONA and ASSISTANCE projects, we would like to briefly conclude by providing some recommendations on the stakeholder engagement:

- **Mapping:** Make an in-depth analysis of the type of stakeholders to be involved in the co-creation process and through which modalities. As we have seen, the selection of stakeholders to be involved is crucial in conducting an analysis that can lead to meaningful results.
- **Planning:** Select, depending on the context of the survey to be conducted, the most appropriate tools and techniques with which to conduct the analysis (informative material, questionnaires, focus groups, and SA). Based on mapped stakeholders and identified tools and techniques, plan the cycles, in terms of objectives and duration, to be carried out in the co-creation iterative process.
- **Communication focus:** Since communication is a crucial factor in the engagement perspective, it is advisable in advance to have a clear picture of the type of communication to be adopted. As we have stated in the document, it is preferable to rely on an ECB composed of multidisciplinary experts, in order to monitor and control communication channels and avoid any misunderstandings, criticisms (e.g. due to incomprehensible messages and/or technical jargons) and barriers in pursuing the co-creation process of stakeholder's engagement.
- **Analyze:** To correctly analyze the results obtained, it is necessary to first have a theoretical framework. The SAT methodology is the theoretical framework that provided the conceptual background for the tools used. Without a clear conceptual architecture outlining the research questions and objectives, it is not possible to evaluate data and information in a coherent manner.

- **Defining control factors:** Establishing KPIs in advance or, in the case of focus groups, adopting a semantic analysis method (consistent with the type of survey to be developed) are some of the effective strategies to understand the results obtained.

Acknowledgments

- The writing of this chapter has been made possible thanks to funding received from the European Union's Horizon 2020 research and innovation program under grant agreements no. 832576 (ASSISTANCE) and no. 787123 (PERSONA).
- The writers wish to express their thanks to Dr. Antonio Carnevale, Dr. Piercosma Bisconti Lucidi, Dr. Emanuela Tangari, and the rest of the team at CyberEthics Lab. for their ongoing help in the development of the SAT methodology.

References

Bagozzi, R. P. (2007). The legacy of the technology acceptance model and a proposal for a paradigm shift. *Journal of the Association for Information Systems* 8 (4). doi:https://doi.org/10.17705/1jais.00122.

Balahur, A. and Turchi, M. (2012). Multilingual sentiment analysis using machine translation? *Proceedings of the 3rd Workshop in Computational Approaches to Subjectivity and Sentiment Analysis*, Jeju, Korea, 52–60.

Endsley, M.R. (2001). Designing for situation awareness in complex systems. *Second International Workshop on Symbiosis of Humans Artifacts and Environment*, Kyoto, Japan, 1–14.

Endsley, M.R. (2011). Towards a theory of situation awareness in dynamic systems. In: *Situational Awareness*, 1e (ed. E. Salas and A.S. Dietz), 34. London: Routledge.

Haavik, T. K. (2011). On components and relations in sociotechnical systems. *Journal of Contingencies & Crisis Management* 12 (2), 99–109. doi:https://doi.org/10.1111/j.11468-5973.2011.00638.x

Heinrich, C.J. (2002). Outcomes-based performance management in the public sector: implications for government, accountability and effectiveness. *Public Administration Review* 62 (6): 712–725.

Jane, G.V. (2019). *Human Performance and Situation Awareness Misures*. CRC Press.

Kaciak, E. and Cullen, C.W. (2006). Analysis of means-end chain data in marketing research. *Journal of Targeting, Measurement and Analysis for Marketing* 15 (1): 12–20.

Lier, B. and Hardjono, T.W. (2011). Luhmann meets the matrix: exchanging and sharing information in network-centric environments. *Journal of Systemics Cybernetics and Informatics* 9 (3): 66–70.

Litosseliti, L. (2003). *Using Focus Groups in Research*. A&C Black.

Liu, B. (2015). *Sentiment Analysis: Mining Opinions, Sentiments, and Emotions* 1 Cambridge: Cambridge University Press. doi:https://doi.org/10.1017/CBO9781139084789.

Lundberg, J. (2015). Situation Awareness Systems, states and processes: a holistic framework. *Theoretical Issues in Ergonomics Science 16* (5), 447–473. doi:https://doi.org/10.1080/1463922X.2015.1008601.

PMI (2017). *A Guide to the Project Management Body of Knowledge*, 6e. Newton Square, PA: Project Management Institute.

Pozzi, F., Fersini, E., Messina, E., and Bing, L. (2016). *Sentiment Analysis in Social Networks*. Morgan Kaufmann.

Taebi, B. (2017). Bridging the gap between social acceptance and ethical acceptability. *Risk Analysis, 37*(10), 1817–1827. doi:https://doi.org/10.1111/risa.12734

Trist, E.L. (1981). *The Evolution of Socio-Technical Systems*, vol. 2. Toronto: Ontario Quality of Working Life Center.

Veludo-de-Oliveira, T.M., Ikeda, A.A., and Campomar, M.C. (2006). Discussing laddering application by the means-end chain theory. *The Qualitative Report 11* (4): 626–642.

Venkatesh, V., Morris, M.G., Davis, G.B., and Davis, F.D. (2003). User acceptance of information technology: toward a unified view. *MIS Quarterly* 425–478.

Wang, H., Can, D., Kazemzadeh, A. et al. (2012). A system for real-time twitter sentiment analysis of 2012 US Presidential Election Cycle. *Proceedings of the ACL 2012 System Demonstrations*, Los Angeles, CA, 115–120.

Wilkinson, S. (1998). Focus group methodology: a review. *International Journal of Social Research Methodology* 1 (3): 181–203.

Wilson, T., Wiebe, J., & Hoffmann, P. (2005). Recognizing contextual polarity in phrase-level sentiment analysis. *Proceedings of HLT/EMNLP* doi:https://doi.org/10.3115/1220575.1260619

4

Performance Assessment of Soft Biometrics Technologies for Border Crossing

Bilal Hassan[1,2], Ebroul Izquierdo[1,3], and Krishna Chandramouli[1,3]

[1] *Multimedia and Vision Research Group, School of Electronic Engineering and Computer Science, Queen Mary University of London, London, UK*
[2] *Faculty of Engineering & Environment, Northumbria University London Campus, London, UK*
[3] *Venaka Media Limited, London, UK*

4.1 Introduction

The field of biometrics research encompasses the need to associate an identity with an individual based on the person's physiological or behavior traits (Hassan et al. 2021). While the use of intrusive techniques (Dantcheva et al. 2015) such as retina scans and fingerprint identification has resulted in highly accurate systems, the scalability of such systems in real-world applications like surveillance and border security has been limited (Hassan and Izquierdo 2021). As a branch of biometrics research, the origin of Soft Biometrics could be traced back to the need for nonintrusive solutions for extracting physiological traits of a person (Nixon et al. 2015). Following the high number of research outcomes reported in the literature on Soft Biometrics, this chapter aims to consolidate the scope of Soft Biometrics research across the following five thematic schemes:

- a review on Soft Biometrics research, evaluating data sets, proposing annotation strategies, and building the largest context-aware bag of Soft Biometrics
- an evaluation of anthropometric Soft Biometrics using landmark localization tools
- an assessment of 4-factor metrics affecting individual Soft Biometrics

Security Technologies and Social Implications, First Edition. Edited by Garik Markarian, Ruža Karlović, Holger Nitsch, and Krishna Chandramouli.
© 2023 The Institute of Electrical and Electronics Engineers, Inc.
Published 2023 by John Wiley & Sons, Inc.

- proposing and testing of partial human silhouette-based feature estimation
- to showcase significant performance of prototype transfer learning model working with limited instances relevant to border control

As per the definition, "Soft Biometrics traits are physical, behavioral, or adhered human characteristics, classifiable in predefined human compliant categories. These categories are, unlike in the classical biometric case, established and time-proven by humans with the aim of differentiating individuals. In simple words, the Soft Biometrics traits instances are created in a natural way, used by humans to distinguish their peers" (Dantcheva et al. 2011).

One of the main reasons to adopt Soft Biometrics is seamless authentication as depicted in (Prakash and Mukesh 2014). A significant example is an authentication during online sessions or exams (Niinuma et al. 2010), etc., in a seamless manner. On the other hand, the set of Soft Biometrics is increasing day by day as more features are being introduced. This is another motivation for a standalone Soft Biometrics recognition or retrieval system development (Dantcheva et al. 2015). There are many different application areas like surveillance (Reid et al. 2013a; Semertzidis et al. 2016), social robotics (De Carolis et al. 2019), IoT (Tomičić et al. 2018), social media and mobile authentication (Geng et al. 2017; Neal and Woodard 2019), where standalone Soft Biometrics-based recognition or retrieval is performed at an experimental level. These are some of the strong motivations behind using Soft Biometrics. The experimental level success of Soft Biometrics across different application domains highlight its importance, more specifically, for enhanced security and border control. A conceptual framework for the implementation of Soft Biometrics-based recognition system in a border control scenario is presented in Figure 4.1. A list of candidate Soft Biometrics like height, spectacles, ethnicity, gender, age, etc., are demonstrated. Some of these are permanent while others are temporary.

Overall, a comprehensive analysis of Soft Biometrics systems development opens a key area of work, i.e. anthropometric and geometric Soft Biometrics. The anthropometric and geometric features are measurements, ratios, and proportions of the human body. In our case, these features will be estimated from a 2D image. The experimental techniques developed to estimate anthropometric and geometric features use human body pose estimation tools (Kocabas et al. 2020) as baseline architecture. Although, the goal is not to find the pose, rather these tools localize landmarks of the human face and body. To understand this, we explored and listed 10 different open-source pose estimation tools too. These tools provide landmark coordinates of various joints of the human body and detection confidence for each landmark. There are certain hybrid methods, which combine landmark localization tools with a human silhouette (Sharif et al. 2020).

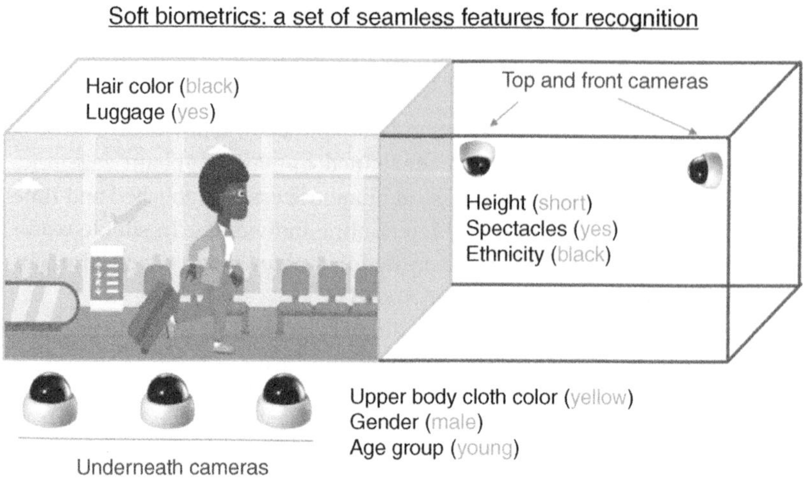

<u>Soft biometrics: a set of seamless features for recognition</u>

Figure 4.1 A conceptual framework for seamless recognition. *Source:* Courtesy of Hassan et al. (2021), Springer Nature, CC BY 4.0.

So, human silhouette combined with landmark localization proved to be a candidate for person recognition over time, which is a bit challenging task as compared to reidentification in a multi-camera environment. Usually, people appear after a certain time period at public places like airports, carrying accessories, changing of clothes, etc. In this chapter, we are going to discuss a new recognition framework using two types of images, e.g. whole and upper body silhouettes. A customized version of DeepLabv3 was used for human body semantic segmentation. Later, a generic Fourier descriptor (GFD)-based feature set is fed to the One-Vs-Rest schema in the ensemble of K-Nearest Neighbor (KNN) and Random Forest (RF) classifiers (Iqbal et al. 2016). The experiments were carried out on Front-View Gait (FVG) dataset recorded in the year 2017 and 2018, respectively. An overall recognition accuracy using both classifiers on the whole body and upper half of human silhouette images is discussed in detail.

On the other hand, deep learning (Zhang et al. 2020) methods are gaining more attention for feature extraction and classification in recent years. However, a large amount of data is required to train a deep network either for feature extraction or classification. Most of the time, the required amount of data is not available for the training of the deep network. To overcome this challenge, pretrained deep networks are an alternate. These pretrained networks are usually trained and validated on large-scale benchmark datasets, e.g. ImageNet, etc. These pretrained models are then used to retrain on new datasets of smaller size, and the task of feature extraction along with classification is performed later, termed as "Transfer Learning" (Zhuang et al. 2020). In this chapter, we analyzed 26 different pretrained available in KERAS API are listed. These models are trained on ImageNet dataset and evaluated on several other common datasets.

The rest of the chapter is organized as follows. In Section 4.2, a comprehensive review of Soft Biometrics ranging from dataset development to quantitative feature estimation and recognition using a temporary modality of the human body like clothing, etc., is presented. The section also introduces tools for human body keypoint localization. Subsequently, Section 4.3 describes techniques related to anthropometric Soft Biometrics and the outcome of our work using tools like OpenPose. In Section 4.4, existing limitations in terms of Soft Biometrics datasets and recommendations including the context-aware bag of Soft Biometrics dataset is presented. Section 4.5 outlines an insight into four influential factors related to individual Soft Biometrics including the significance of Soft Biometrics fusion. In Section 4.6, to overcome the limitation of data, the effectiveness of transfer learning models is discussed. Later, Section 4.7 presents an evaluation of partial human silhouette and transfer learning-based techniques along with a comparison with a benchmark. Finally, a discussion of obtained results and the conclusion of the chapter is presented in Sections 4.8 and 4.9, respectively.

4.2 Literature Review

In the recent era, Soft Biometrics is becoming one of the leading solutions for seamless recognition and a replacement for traditional biometrics (Bolle et al. 2013). There are certain reasons behind adopting Soft Biometrics, i.e. they are nonintrusive features (Dantcheva et al. 2015), offer feature and modality-level independence (Sundararajan et al. 2019) and provide a semantic description for each individual feature (Denman et al. 2015). Overall, it is a seamless approach for recognition or retrieval (Dantcheva et al. 2011). Usually, Soft Biometrics is a set of all types of facial, body, behavioral, and material features highly suitable for the identification of individuals (Nixon et al. 2015) and (Jain et al. 2006). Their application is broad ranging from recognition at public places to retrieval of the probe from the gallery (Flynn et al. 2008) or database (Dantcheva et al. 2015).

Generally, a large number of nonintrusive features are part of the whole human body. They are normally categorized as demographic, global, anthropometric, material, behavioral, medical features, etc. (Dantcheva et al. 2015; Sundararajan et al. 2019). They are not just limited to the face or body, rather they are estimated using various other temporary or permanent modalities of a human body (Nixon et al. 2015). The origin of Soft Biometrics goes back to the eighteenth century, e.g. Bertillon system, where the purpose was criminal identification. The Bertillon system provides the description of a suspect's physical attributes (Nixon et al. 2017)

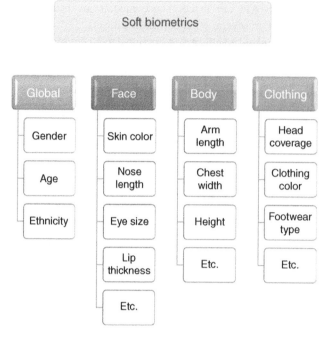

Figure 4.2 Soft Biometrics taxonomy.

and they are referred to as anthropometric features. So, the key idea behind using Soft Biometrics only is seamless recognition and retrieval.

Soft Biometrics is actually a set of features, which are extracted from the whole human body using all temporary or permanent modalities (Garg et al. 2018). Generally, the face, its appearance, structure, and body with limbs are referred to as permanent modality (Zhang et al. 2015), while any other type of material to cover comes under the temporary modality class (Nixon et al. 2017). To showcase the classification, a taxonomy of Soft Biometrics is presented in Figure 4.2. Indeed, the amount of features present in each modality is infinite in number while this number depends upon the identification scenario. Later, an extensive collection of Soft Biometrics is also presented (Hassan et al. 2014c).

As discussed earlier, each modality of the human body contains a rich set of Soft Biometrics. Now, it is of utmost importance to provide a semantic description for each Soft Biometrics feature. The semantic description is actually a real-world definition of a soft biometric feature, mostly depending upon a scenario, e.g. recognition or retrieval (Denman et al. 2015). For example, a person may have gender specification as male, height as short, face as thin, and he is wearing a black coat. This is a semantic description of an individual against the following Soft Biometrics: (i) gender, (ii) height, (iii) face type, and (iv) clothing using the categorical method of annotation. By using categorical annotation, an individual can be retrieved from a larger group of people more easily (Nixon et al. 2017). On the other hand, comparative semantic description is another method of annotation where two individuals are compared against a similar set of soft biometric features. In Soft Biometrics, both categorical and comparative methods of semantic description are common and as a whole referred to as qualitative methods (Reid et al. 2013b).

Overall, qualitative methods of the semantic description presented promising results. However, they are not scalable. Despite the scenario, e.g. probe-gallery matching or identification in surveillance (Shoaib Farooq et al. 2014), there is a significant need for a quantitative description scheme for Soft Biometrics annotation. In the recent past, annotation was mostly done using qualitative methods. This creates room for the development of quantitative methods like anthropometrics and geometry, though the estimation becomes a hard problem in the real world. Fortunately, several experimental models presented significant success in recent years (Hasan and Babaguchi 2016). In fact, quantitative methods may prove more reliable, if the Soft Biometrics estimation process improves.

For instance, in (Martinho-Corbishley et al. 2018), a new method called super fine attribute annotation is proposed using crowdsourcing. The Soft Biometrics of gender, age, and ethnicity are reannotated from the famous PEdesTrian Attribute (PETA) dataset (Deng et al. 2014) of images. This large-scale dataset is a combination of 10 reidentification datasets. Each time respondents were given an image and a 5-scale visual prototype for each trait. The respondents were advised to perform the matching of an image with a visual prototype. The 5-scale annotation type was categorical. This is perhaps the largest and most reliable annotation performed till date.

Although, crowdsourcing is considered a more reliable way of annotating a dataset but for very large datasets, it is not feasible. The time and effort increase as dataset volume increases. Before crowdsourcing, expert opinion has been a way to annotate datasets. It is done for a lesser number of soft traits and on small datasets by an expert. Like in Tome et al. (2014, 2015) and Vera-Rodriguez et al. (2017), expert experience is exploited for soft traits-based dataset annotation. It is evident in research that in all the expert opinion-based annotation scenarios, the number of distinct individuals and their images are in few hundreds except (Tome et al. 2014) where it is about 1700. That is why, it consumed a lot of time and effort too. Moreover, in expert opinion, only absolute and categorical annotations are performed. The expert opinion method reflects human perception actually. They describe an individual in qualitative or quantitative way. There is only one recognition scenario (Gonzalez-Sosa et al. 2018) using the Labelled Faces in the Wild (LFW) dataset, where we have a larger dataset of images from daily life but the number of features to be annotated is very small, i.e. 6.

Saying one way or the other, crowdsourcing has been the most dominant way of annotating datasets. The annotations are performed in both types, categorical and comparative. We have several datasets like Southampton Multibiometric Tunnel DB (Tome et al. 2014; Martinho-Corbishley et al. 2015), Soton Gait DB (Shutler et al. 2004), LFW-MS4 (Huang and Learned-Miller 2014), and their subsets and modified versions (Samangooei 2010), which have been annotated using both categorical and comparative annotations. However, the annotation method, number of respondents, amount of responses received, and the number of Soft Biometrics annotated are changing. It is important to note that most of these datasets cover whole human body modalities, i.e. face, body including limbs and clothing, etc. (Hassan et al. 2014a).

Generally, it has been observed that many researchers declare gender, age, and ethnicity as derivative Soft Biometrics (Lin et al. 2020). They put them in a new category called global traits. In recent years, there is a large number of research experiments performed to estimate these global Soft Biometrics from constrained or unconstrained image or video scenes (Phillips et al. 2000; Terhorst et al. 2020). That is why, we decided to explore and summarize recent successful outcomes of research for global traits estimation. Our analysis includes both types of approaches, e.g. hybrid and independent.

To recognize individuals in constrained or unconstrained scenes, the three global traits were used in combination usually. The task of recognition was performed on image or video datasets (Kanade et al. 2000; Bainbridge et al. 2013). The hybrid recognition model of gender, age, and ethnicity was used for recognition in multiple research experiments (Martinho-Corbishley et al. 2018; Boutros et al. 2019; El-Samak and Alhanjouri 2019). A large number of datasets and various feature estimation, classification, and deep learning methods were used for this purpose. The hybrid recognition models are of two types, i.e. gender-age-ethnicity and gender-age. One of the most common hybrid models for global traits estimation is composed of gender, age, and ethnicity (Wan et al. 2018). There is a large number of models developed to estimate these three features using different datasets over the years (Srinivas et al. 2017). The feature estimation techniques included face and body landmarks-based measurements to color features. For the purpose of classification or retrieval, support vector machine and deep learning-based methods like VGG-16 were used. The second common hybrid model for global traits estimation includes gender and age. It is missing ethnicity information and there is no reason provided for it. Usually, ethnicity is used to distinguish populations actually while gender and age are specific to every distinct individual. The gender- and age-based models developed over the years are versatile in nature. There are so many different kinds of feature estimation and classification or retrieval methods used for this purpose (Wan et al. 2018). The most common feature estimation techniques include raw pixel-based processing, Haar-like features, local binary patterns, texture and biologically inspired features, etc. (Fang et al. 2019). The classification again includes simple classifiers like variants of a support vector machine and many different deep learning methods like ML-Net, CNN-ELM, Attention Networks, Deep-CNN, etc. (Shin et al. 2017; Duan et al. 2018; Gurnani et al. 2019).

In contrast to hybrid approaches discussed earlier, the three global traits, e.g. gender, age, and ethnicity were used independently as well (Xia et al. 2020). The goal was to perform recognition or retrieval using each of these global Soft Biometrics. We already discussed that there can be a scenario where a global trait is used independently for recognition or retrieval (Pei et al. 2020). That is why, it is important to analyze each global trait individually in different research experiments. The list of feature estimation and classification techniques tested was rich too. It includes landmark localization using OpenPose, local binary patterns, histogram of gradients, aesthetic (Nam et al. 2020), intensity-based (Xie and Pun 2020), and texture features (Dornaika et al. 2019). For classification or retrieval, variants of support vector machine, clustering techniques like K-NN and deep learning-based methods like CNN, ResNet, etc. were used (Angeloni et al. 2019; Ouafi et al. 2019). Similarly, gender and age were estimated from unconstrained image or video scenes separately. Age is the only global trait among a group of three which is used for recognition more (Pei et al. 2020; Xia et al. 2020). The outcome of age estimation can be of two types. It can be presented as overall accuracy or in the form of age group categorization. Moreover, raw pixels, appearance features, landmarks, local binary patterns, etc., were used for feature estimation. The classification was again performed using a variant of the support vector machine and different deep learning methods (Xie and Pun 2020). The third global trait called ethnicity was used a lesser number of times for recognition or retrieval as compared to gender and age (Dornaika et al. 2019). One reason is application at a higher abstraction level, i.e., to distinguish populations, rather individuals (Ouloul et al. 2019). Also, there is not any specialized list of ethnicity datasets. It is really hard to collect a multi-ethnicity dataset. Like gender and age, ethnicity was also computed using techniques like raw pixel, landmark localization, and local binary patterns. The classification was performed using deep learning methods like VGG-16, etc. (Huri et al. 2018).

4.3 Human Body Anthropometrics

Overall, a comprehensive analysis of Soft Biometrics systems development opens up a key area of work, e.g. anthropometric and geometric Soft Biometrics. The anthropometric and geometric features are measurements, ratios, and proportions of the human body. In our case, these features will be estimated from a 2D image. The experimental techniques developed to estimate anthropometric and geometric features use human body pose estimation tools (Kocabas et al. 2020) as baseline architecture. Although, the goal is not to find the pose, rather these tools localize landmarks of the human face and body. To understand this, we explored and analyzed 10 different open-source pose estimation tools. These tools provide landmark coordinates of various joints of a human body and detection confidence for each landmark. There are certain hybrid methods, which combine landmark localization tools with a human silhouette (Sharif et al. 2020).

4.3.1 Human Body Keypoints Estimation

Generally, it has been observed that anthropometric and geometric features of a human body are difficult to estimate more accurately from 2D images. However, there are more discriminating features too. Moreover, to estimate anthropometric and geometric features, the human body landmark localization has been a critical step. The process of landmark localization is not new to 2D images. It is being performed as an initial step in many human body pose estimation tools. So, taking the advantage of existing open-source tools, we decided to implement and evaluate the accuracy of landmark localization provided by these tools. By using more accurate landmark localization, the goal of anthropometric features estimation can be achieved more accurately. Overall, we studied the following nine different open-source tools for landmark localization, which is actually keypoints estimation – a complete review of these tools is presented in (Hassan et al. 2021).

- CMU-OpenPose
- AlphaPose
- OpenPifPaf
- DensePose
- Real-Time Multi-Person Pose Estimation
- DeepPose
- HyperFace
- Wrench AI
- Multi-Person Pose Estimation in the Wild

4.3.2 Anthropometric Features Estimation Using Landmark Localization Tools

As discussed earlier, the quantitative method of dataset annotation is a strong candidate for more accurate recognition (Fosdick 1915; Sadhya et al. 2017). However, the detection accuracy of anthropometric features is a big challenge.

It is also studied in the literature review that anthropometric features estimation depends upon landmark localization using 2D images or videos. To localize landmarks of the human body including limbs and face, we decided to use open-source pose estimation tools (Li and Deng 2020). The landmark localization is a preliminary step in pose estimation tools. In the previous section, we mentioned nine different open-source pose estimation tools. We decided to present output from two benchmark tools for estimating anthropometric features.

4.3.2.1 OpenPose for Anthropometric Features Estimation

OpenPose (Cao et al. 2019) is a real-time multi-person open-source API to detect 135 keypoints from a single image and from the face, hand, foot, and body. The objective of OpenPose is to detect the pose of the human body from a 2D image. The API achieves real-time performance and high accuracy regardless of the number of people present in a 2D image (Simon et al. 2017). In our case, OpenPose is very useful to extract and store body landmark locations from a 2D image along with detection confidence for each landmark. OpenPose provides a total of 25 body landmarks including the foot (Wei et al. 2016). OpenPose takes an image or video as input; after processing, it provides an output image with landmarks localized for each individual in the image along with a JSON file containing landmark information stored for each individual. In our developed framework, we customized the output of OpenPose, accessed and stored only the required 25 landmarks from the face and body including limbs and foot as shown in Figure 4.3. The landmark information contains x and y coordinates along with detection confidence for that particular landmark. This information is stored in a data frame of 25×3, where each row points to a particular landmark.

The anthropometric features estimation process involves measurements and ratios of the human body to use as a feature. For example, the length of the right and left arms can be measured using Euclidean distance (Danielsson 1980). In our experiment, we measured the length of the right and left arms by measuring the Euclidean distance between the wrist and shoulder landmarks of that particular arm. The outcome of our developed model is a feature vector containing measurements and ratios between the human body. This feature set is built for classification. To extract

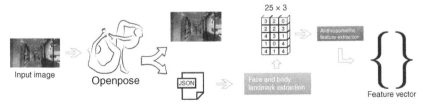

Figure 4.3 OpenPose framework for anthropometric features estimation.

Input: OpenPose Output Json File

Output: DataFrame: 25 X 3

$N \leftarrow NumberofPeopleInJsonFile;$

for $PeopleCounter \leftarrow 0$ **to** $N - 1$ **do**

    $KeyPoints \leftarrow people[PeopleCounter];$

    $DataFrame[0] \leftarrow KeyPoints;$

end

Algorithm 4.1 Customizing OpenPose output – accessing and storing required landmarks for each individual.

or estimate anthropometric features using OpenPose, we first decided to customize and store the output of OpenPose. The objective of customization was to access and store only required landmarks while ignoring the rest. We accessed and stored a set of 25 landmarks from the face and body including limbs and foot. To customize the output of OpenPose, a python script was developed as shown in Algorithm 4.1.

The data frame generated for every single image or a frame from a video contains 25 keypoints for each individual in the image. Each individual is stored as a row in the data frame. The number of columns is 75 for each individual object as each landmark has x and y coordinate values along with detection confidence. The maximum value of detection confidence provided by OpenPose for any landmark can be 1. To extract features using, we set a minimum threshold of 0.7, any landmark with detection confidence below the threshold is ignored. So, the arm's length feature is computed using the mathematical formulation of Euclidean distance as shown in Algorithm 4.2.

4.3.2.2 AlphaPose for Anthropometric Features Estimation

An initial experiment in our work revealed that the accuracy of anthropometric features extracted from 2D images is affected by several factors like, distance and occlusions, etc. For example, lengths and widths of a particular body organ change with respect to changes in distance from the camera. An image sequence or video of the same individual measurement taken as a feature changes according to distance from the camera. This factor is hard to manage but certain parameters like camera calibration are useful to interpolate features like lengths, widths, etc. On the other hand, ratios between upper and lower bodies presented better results than straight-line measurements like lengths and widths. Moreover, landmark localization is the preliminary step in the pose estimation tools like, some of these tools like AlphaPose (Fang et al. 2017) provide a pose tracker (Xiu et al. 2018). The pose tracker tracks the same individual across multiple views. This is indeed a very useful functionality to

Input: DataFrame[Index]

Output: AttributeValue

$W \leftarrow WristDetectionConfidence$;

$S \leftarrow ShoulderDetectionConfidence$;

$X \leftarrow ShoulderCoordinates$;

$Y \leftarrow WristCoordinates$;

if $W \geq 0.7 \& S \geq 0.7$ **then**

  | $AttributeValue \leftarrow EuclideanDistance(X, Y)$;

else

  | $AttributeValue \leftarrow -1$;

end

Algorithm 4.2 Feature estimation – arm's length.

be exploited. In our opinion, the outcome of recognition experiments can be improved by using them with some other techniques while performing recognition in task-uncontrolled environments. There could be several techniques to work with, like human silhouette (Chen and Wang 2019), etc. In Table 4.1, the outcome of left shoulder–elbow length is measured using Euclidean distance. The left shoulder–elbow length is an anthropometric feature extracted for each individual in the MMV pedestrian dataset. We took the output feature value for three individuals and the same number of images for each. These three images appear one after the other in the evaluation dataset. It is evident from the outcome that shoulder–elbow length for first person is similar in frames 2 and 3, while it is lesser in frame 1. In the case of persons 2 and 3, the lengths measured in each frame are different. It is clear from the output that the straight line measurements are highly affected by the increasing or decreasing distance from the camera.

Table 4.1 Length measurement across frames of the same individual.

	Left shoulder elbow length		
Person no.	Image 1	Image 2	Image 3
1	27.179 581 030 619 24	43.014 038 138 728 65	42.719 920 142 715 61
2	42.040 042 269 246 09	60.949 660 573 296 05	35.311 764 399 417 93
3	35.134 080 918 675 004	62.989 584 004 024 02	16.193 923 922 261 686

4.4 Working on Dataset for Soft Biometrics

One of the biggest challenges toward the evaluation of a standalone Soft Biometrics system is the availability of a benchmark dataset. More specifically, it should be designed for the same purpose. In previous sections, this problem is pointed out in particular. In order to design or develop a benchmark dataset for standalone Soft Biometrics system evaluation, we started to find out datasets recorded in the same session from multiple views. More specifically, if datasets were recorded in multiple sessions for the same individuals with a certain time gap, there is a very long list of datasets recorded in a single session with multiple camera views like CASIA (Zheng et al. 2011). The CASIA-B version is recorded from 11 different angles for 124 distinct individuals. Indeed, it is a challenging dataset. However, there are three datasets recorded with a certain time gap, i.e. FVG (Zhang et al. 2019a, b), ILRW (Lee et al. 2018), and Motion Re-ID (Zhang et al. 2018). These three datasets are not available publicly for commercial use. However, the FVG dataset can be used for academic purpose after the consent from authors. In our experimental work, we planned to evaluate our model on FVG datasets. We also decided to record the dataset for the evaluation of our proposed standalone Soft Biometrics application as a challenge. The objective was to record the same individual at different distances, involving face or head and body including limbs and clothing, etc. Moreover, one of the biggest challenges was to record the same individuals with a certain time gap with a change in physical structure and appearance. We have already recorded the first session for 50 individuals in early 2020 and plan to record the second session later. We also plan to evaluate our model on this developed dataset. The detail of this dataset called MMV Pedestrian is presented ahead.

4.4.1 Front-View Gait Dataset

One of the major requirements in the dataset design or development process we faced was the time gap in the recording of sessions for the same individuals. This is a bit challenging task to develop such kind of dataset, as access to the same people after a certain time gap is a really hard problem. Usually, a small number of people are available for repeated sessions. The FVG is a unique image or video dataset recorded with one-year time gap for the same individuals (Zhang et al. 2019b). There are a total of 12 people recorded again with a gap of one year. The dataset was recorded in the years 2017 and 2018, respectively, including significant variations like three different viewing angles, three different walking speeds, carrying bags, changing clothes, etc. In 2017, 147 people were recorded while, in 2018, 91 people were recorded. There were only 12 people recorded in both years covering all the variations. The details of the camera used for recording, camera height, resolution, the total number of videos recorded, etc., can be found in (Zhang

Table 4.2 Information about a subset of the dataset used from FVG.

	Recording year	
Image type	**2017**	**2018**
Sessions	1	2
–45°	✓	✓
0°	✓	✓
45°	✓	✓
Normal walking	✓	✓
Fast walking	✓	✓
Slow walking	✓	✓
Carrying bag/hat	✓	
Changing clothes		✓
Multiple persons		
Total frames count	5563	4973

et al. 2019a). The FVG dataset is actually a walking people dataset, originally developed for gait recognition. However, the dataset covers the whole human body, i.e. face or head, body including limbs and clothing, etc. It also recorded using carrying some luggage and changing of clothes in the second year. In our case, we selected following images for different individuals from FVG dataset as shown in Table 4.2.

In our work, we have taken images of only 12 individuals recorded in both years. We selected images with three different angles, three different walking speeds, and carrying bags or wearing a hat from the year 2017. Similarly, from the year 2018, we selected images of three different angles, three different walking speeds, and changing of clothes. The selected images contain only one person. A sample set of selected images from the years 2017 and 2018 is shown in Figure 4.4. There were a total of 5563 images selected for all 12 individuals from the year 2017 and 4973 from the year 2018. We used data from the year 2017 for training while from the year 2018, for testing.

4.4.2 MMV Pedestrian Dataset

The Multimedia and Vision (MMV) Pedestrian dataset is recorded in the MMV lab at Queen Mary University of London, UK. It consists of frontal video sessions of 50 distinct individuals having 38 males and 12 females from 19 different nationalities and at four different distances from the camera as shown in Figure 4.5.

(a)   (b)

(c)   (d)

(e)   (f)

Figure 4.4 Images used from FVG. (a) Normal walking – 2017. (b) Fast walking – 2017. (c) Slow walking – 2017. (d) Images/normal walking – 2018. (e) Fast walking – 2018. (f) Changing clothes – 2017/carrying bag – 2018.

The age range for individuals was 21 years old to 55 years old. The dataset consists of a series of more than 300 frames for each individual. The video from these frames can be reproduced by defining a fixed frame per second rate. Each of the 50 individuals was advised to walk in the corridor while continuously looking toward the camera. The python script to capture the video at 30 FPS was used to record the video. The resolution was 1280×720 and images were stored in the .jpg format. The same script was used to split the video into frames.

The view from the MMV corridor set up for the recording of the dataset is also shown in the pedestrian images. This was around a 20 m-long corridor and proved to be sufficient for the recording of at least 300 frames for each individual. The corridor also reflects the view like a real-time environment, i.e. a normal corridor

(a) (b) (c) (d)

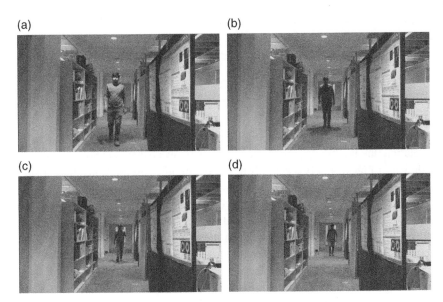

Figure 4.5 Images from MMV pedestrian dataset – frames at four different distances: (a) 4 m, (b) 6 m, (c) 8 m, and (d) 10 m.

at the entrance of a building or critical infrastructure, etc. The objective of recording in such an environment was to build a dataset, which is very close to reality. The dataset contains several different types of information about individuals like gender, age nationality, and number frames for each individual.

One of the most exciting aspects of a dataset is the capturing of frames at four different distances from the camera. The four distances from the camera are 4, 6, 8, and 10 m. For this purpose, green color markings were placed on the surface. In our literature review part (Guo et al. 2018), we already inspected that distance has a higher impact on the recognition process. The face has a higher recognition accuracy at a close distance from the camera while the body including limbs is opposite it. That is why, we decided to place the markings on the floor and separate a subset of frames for each individual at these four different distances. They are very useful while training or evaluating the proposed system performance.

4.5 Some Influential Factors for Soft Biometrics

To make the recognition process robust, we also analyzed four different parameters, which directly influence the performance of any Soft Biometrics system at the feature level. A partial representation of the content related to those four factors from the original research (Hassan et al. 2021) is presented ahead. These four factors include:

- Attribute correlation
- Distance
- Permanence score and stability
- Feature- and modality-level fusion

One of the key factors influencing the individual Soft Biometrics is attribute correlation that is actually pair-wise correlation between different Soft Biometrics as shown in Figure 4.6. It is actually a sign of support and relevance that attributes provide to each other in a recognition framework. Another factor is the distance that shows level of estimation for different modalities of human body at different distances from the camera, and it is evident that face is always more difficult to recognize at far distance from the camera than body and clothing as shown in Figure 4.7. Similarly, permanence score and discrimination power as presented in Figure 4.8 are two correlated factors to be used for measuring inter- and intra-class variation as shown in Figure 4.8. Finally, feature and modality level fusion produced more accurate recognition than individual modality as shown in Figure 4.9.

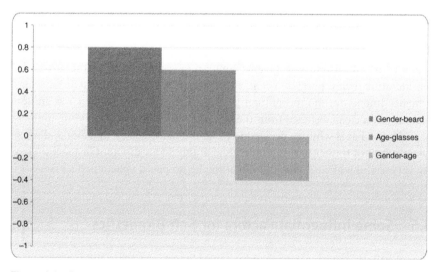

Figure 4.6 Pearson correlation by Gonzalez et al. *Source:* Adapted from Gonzalez-Sosa et al. (2018).

Year	Work	Modality	Traits	Close	Medium	For
2019	[106]	Face (F)	10	Acc – 99.2	Acc – 99.0	Acc – 49.3
		Body (B)	10	Acc – 99.3	Acc – 98.4	Acc – 96.6
		Clothing (C)	10	Acc – 98.5	Acc – 95.8	Acc – 95.9
		F–B–C	30	Acc – 98.5	Acc – 92.5	Acc – 82.6
2018	[95]	Face/head (F/H)	10	Acc – 95.7	Acc – 62.7	Acc – 13.1
		Body (B)	10	Acc – 85.4	Acc – 57.4	Acc – 55.4
		Clothing (C)	10	Acc – 82.5	Acc – 69.4	Acc – 67.0

Figure 4.7 Impact of distance on Soft Biometrics. *Source:* Adapted from Hassan et al. (2021).

Year	Work	Name	An	Features	Subjects	Img/sub	Sessions	Total	Method	Range	Method	Range
2018	[93]	LFW-MS4	Com (vis)	24	430	4	1	1720	Pear	0.41–0.80	—	—
			Com (sem)	24	430	4	1	1720		0.35–0.95	—	—
2015	[4]	ATVS	Cor	32	50	8	2	400	Mean	0.45–0.90	Ratio	0.34–1.0
		DB	Dis	24	50	8	2	400	Mode	0.46–0.78		0.25–1.0
		MORPH	Cor	32	130	6	6	780	Mean	0.61–0.94		0.35–1.0
		DB	Dis	24	130	6	6	780	Mode	0.45–0.94		0.30–1.0

Figure 4.8 Computing permanence score and stability. *Source:* Adapted from Hassan et al. (2021).

Year	Author	Modality	Features	Single/Fusion	Performance (%)
2019	[106]	Face (F)	10	Single modality	Acc: 97.0
		Body (B)	10	Single modality	98.0
		Clothing (C)	10	Single modality	83.0
		F–B–C	30	Rank score-sum	98.5
2019	[112]	Face/clothing	256/256	F-score sum	EER: 0.007

Figure 4.9 Comparing feature and modality-level fusion. *Source:* Adapted from Hassan et al. (2021).

4.6 Working with Limited Data Using Transfer Learning

In recent years, deep learning (Zhang et al. 2020) methods are gaining more attention for feature extraction and classification. However, a huge amount of data is required to train a deep network either for feature extraction or classification. Most of the time, the required amount of data is not available for the training of the deep network. To overcome this challenge, pretrained deep networks are proposed. These pretrained networks are usually trained and validated on large-scale benchmark datasets, i.e. ImageNet, etc. These pretrained models are then used to retrain new datasets of smaller size and the task of feature extraction and classification is performed. This approach is called Transfer Learning (Zhuang et al. 2020). In our original work, we are focused on 26 pretrained models available in KERAS API (Hassan et al. 2021). These models are trained on the ImageNet dataset and evaluated on several other common datasets.

4.6.1 Transfer Learning for Feature Extraction and Classification

As discussed earlier, deep learning models (Goodfellow et al. 2015) have obtained sufficient attention in the recent past. We also decided to use deep learning for feature estimation and classification. One of the major requirements deep learning models put is a very large amount of datasets like ImageNet (Deng et al. 2009). In our case, we do not have sufficient data to train deep convolution networks. So, we decided to use pretrained deep convolution models to overcome insufficient data requirements (Tan et al. 2018).

To accomplish this task, KERAS API (Gulli and Pal 2017) provide 26 pretrained models using the ImageNet dataset. These models can be used for feature extraction and classification. Moreover, by removing a full convolution layer, only features may be extracted and classification tasks can be performed using any linear classifier like support vector machine or k-nearest neighbor, etc. Moreover, these pretrained models can be retrained using any small datasets too. In Figure 4.10, we presented a pictorial view of the proposed framework. The input image will be fed to the network. It is important to mention here that each model takes different size

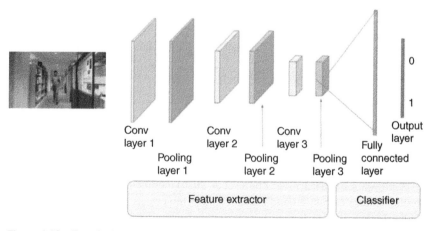

Figure 4.10 Transfer learning framework for feature extraction and classification. *Source:* Courtesy of Learn OpenCV, Keras Tutorial (2018).

images as input. The deep model can be one of the 26. In our experiment, we tested a single image using all 26 models by removing the full convolution layer from the model first. Later, we extracted the features only. Each model provided a feature set of different sizes (Hassan et al. 2014b). This feature set can be provided as input to any linear classifier for label assignment. The second experiment we did was classification using the same network, i.e. using softmax, and obtained the class label for each input image. The full convolution layer provides a defined number of predictions for each input image. In our case, we obtained the top three predictions from each model and a single prediction provided by each model was in the format of three components set. The first component is the class name, the second is the class description, and the last one is the prediction score. The outcome of our experiments using 26 different pretrained models is presented ahead.

4.6.2 Initial Outcome of Transfer Learning-Based Feature Estimation and Classification

As discussed earlier, transfer learning (Tan et al. 2018) models have been very useful for feature extraction and classification where limited data was available for training, etc. The classification, however, can be performed using a full convolution layer of the same model or any linear classifier. We used pretrained models available in KERAS as discussed in the previous section. At this point, we did a very simple experiment of predicting image class by feeding input to the pretrained model on the ImageNet (Deng et al. 2009) dataset. We provided the same image as shown in Figure 4.11 as input to all the 26 models. The required input

Figure 4.11 Input image for pretrained convolution networks.

shape is different for each model. Each model is implemented as a feature extractor and classifier both. The output feature shape has been different from each model too and the top three predictions from each model were reported in Table 4.3.

In our experiment as shown in Table 4.3, the input shape of the image, output feature shape, and top three predictions were shown. The input image shapes for most of the models were 224×224 and 299×299. Similarly, the output feature shape $(1, 7, 7, 2048)$ has been the most common feature shape type. The feature set output by each model can be used as input to any linear classifier at this stage. The most interesting are the top three predictions by each model using a full convolution layer. The reason for getting the top three predictions is setting the number of labels obtained in our experiment (Shoaib Farooq et al. 2014). The pretrained models in KERAS are trained on ImageNet datasets, that is why we obtained some very close outcomes. The original image is of the corridor in the laboratory environment, i.e. educational environment. That is why, we obtained a library, a bookshop, a sliding_door, etc. There is a door at the back of the person walking in

Table 4.3 Predicting outcome of pretrained models on input image from MMV pedestrian dataset.

Model	I/P shape	Feature shape	Classification Outcome		
			First	Second	Third
Xception	299×299	$(1, 7, 7, 512)$	library	sliding_door	passenger_car
VGG16	224×224	$(1, 10, 10, 2048)$	book_shop	library	book_case
VGG19	224×224	$(1, 7, 7, 512)$	gas_pump	passenger_car	sliding_door
ResNet50	224×224	$(1, 7, 7, 2048)$	prison	streetcar	passenger_car
ResNet101	224×224	$(1, 7, 7, 2048)$	library	bookshop	washer
ResNet152	224×224	$(1, 7, 7, 2048)$	bookshop	prison	library
ResNet50V2	224×224	$(1, 7, 7, 2048)$	library	streetcar	passenger_car
ResNet101V2	224×224	$(1, 7, 7, 2048)$	passenger_car	Streetcar	bookshop
ResNet152V2	224×224	$(1, 7, 7, 2048)$	streetcar	library	passenger_car
InceptionV3	299×299	$(1, 8, 8, 2048)$	library	bookshop	sliding_door
IncepResNetV2	299×299	$(1, 8, 8, 1536)$	library	bookshop	bookcase

Table 4.3 (Continued)

Model	I/P shape	Feature shape	Classification Outcome		
			First	Second	Third
MobileNet	224×224	(1, 7, 7, 1024)	barbershop	vend_machine	turnstile
MobileNetV2	224×224	(1, 7, 7, 1280)	library	file	doormat
DenseNet121	224×224	(1, 7, 7, 1024)	library	cash_machine	vend_machine
DenseNet169	224×224	(1, 7, 7, 1664)	vend_machine	prison	barbershop
DenseNet201	224×224	(1, 7, 7, 1920)	library	bookshop	prison
NaseNetMobile	224×224	(1, 7, 7, 1056)	gas_pump	machine	library
NaseNetLarge	331×331	(1, 11, 11, 4032)	library	bookshop	bookcase
EfficientNetB0	224×224	(1, 7, 7, 1280)	library	prison	sliding_door
EfficientNetB1	240×240	(1, 7, 7, 1280)	library	cash_machine	bookshop
EfficientNetB2	260×260	(1, 8, 8, 1408)	library	bookshop	cash_machine
EfficientNetB3	300×300	(1, 9, 9, 1536)	library	prison	bookshop
EfficientNetB4	380×380	(1, 11, 11, 1792)	library	bookshop	bookcase
EfficientNetB5	456×456	(1, 14, 14, 2048)	library	bookshop	bookcase
EfficientNetB6	528×528	(1, 16, 16, 2304)	library	bookshop	bookcase
EfficientNetB7	600×600	(1, 18, 18, 2560)	library	bookshop	cash_machine

the corridor. Moreover, there are several outcomes, which are true outputs of the classifier like gas_pump, street_car, etc.

4.7 Experimental Result

As discussed earlier, person recognition over time is challenging. That is why, we decided to propose and develop a new framework based on human silhouette using the FVG dataset. This framework comprised of multiple components as shown in Figure 4.12. To extract silhouettes from an RGB image, we used DeepLabv3, a benchmark tool developed by Google for semantic segmentation. DeepLabv3 segments 20 different objects, i.e. car, human, sheep, train, etc., in an image along with background subtraction. In our work, semantic segmentation was performed using

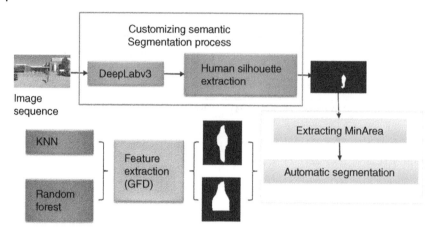

Figure 4.12 Our proposed framework for person verification.

Figure 4.13 The outcome of the segmentation process.

DeepLabv3 with a custom output on RGB images from the FVG dataset. The customized output contains a human silhouette as a foreground component while the remaining part of the image as a background. The foreground also contains a few unknown smaller regions as a foreground. So, all the connected components were found in the image by drawing contours, only the biggest contour area is drawn as shown in Figure 4.13, considered to be a human object.

The single best silhouette image contains a human object as a foreground component while a large amount of pixels as the background. In contrast to (Alsedais and Guest 2017), we used the RotatedRectangle property from OpenCV to draw a minimum area box around the silhouette. It avoids any silhouette parts from cropping than StraightBoundingRectangle used in (Alsedais and Guest 2017). However, the output image can be horizontally rotated. We addressed this problem by developing a rotation formulation based on width and height ratio as shown in Figure 4.13.

In the next step, the process of automated segmentation was performed and eight different segments were cropped including the full silhouette image. The upper regions of the human silhouette depicted the best reidentification rate. That is why, we selected only the full silhouette image obtained in the last step and upper half, which was the result of halving the height of the full minimum area silhouette image. The upper silhouette is obtained by making half of full silhouette image as shown in Figure 4.14.

Later, feature extraction was a bit challenging task while the human silhouette was in motion. However, to compute a fixed-size feature vector on silhouette images having decreasing distance from the camera, a GFD (Zhang and Lu 2002) is used by (Alsedais and Guest 2017). We reused the same technique and a feature vector of 52×1 is obtained for each full and upper half silhouette images of every person.

$$\text{UpperHalf} = I\left(w, h/2\right) \tag{4.1}$$

A common limitation in most of the classifiers is to struggle while distinguishing well between a larger number of classes in the dataset (Fernandez et al. 2017). To cope with this challenge, an ensemble of binary classifiers is a handful solution – commonly known as One-vs-Rest schema. In this schema, one classifier is fitted against each class. Moreover, it is computationally efficient too and it is always easier to obtain knowledge about each class. To tackle multiclass problems, this is a widely used approach. An abstract view of One-vs-Rest schema is presented in Figure 4.15, where we have samples or data points from three classes to distinguish, present in the training set. The diagram depicts how all three classes are in one single space. However, when we train one specific classifier for each class, the feature set for each class is acquired by one single classifier and stored in a separate space. So, each time features of test data are matched with the

Figure 4.14 Minimum area silhouette segments.

(a)　　　　　(b)

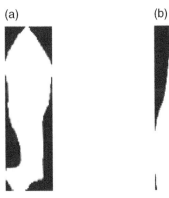

One-vs-all (one-vs-rest)

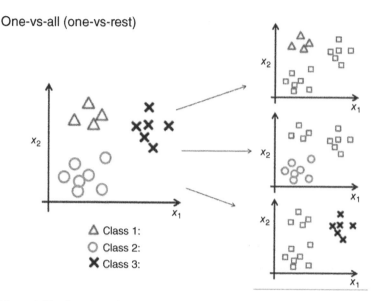

Figure 4.15 Overview of One-Vs-Rest classification schema. *Source:* Courtesy: medium.com.

features of all the classes one by one and test data is assigned with the label of class having minimum distance.

In our work, KNN and RF classifiers in One-Vs-Rest schema were used. The data was split into training and test sets randomly, i.e. 80 and 20%, respectively. The KNN classifier was used with five neighbors having uniform weights and with Minkowski metric for distance measurement. On the other hand, the RF classifier was used with default depth till all the nodes were expanded. The Receiver Operating Characteristic (ROC) curve for each class in One-Vs-Rest settings was computed along with the mean Area Under the Curve (AUC). The ROC curve for each class was plotted in One-Vs-Rest-Schema on a single graph and it provides a comparative recognition rate for each class and highlights the distinct cases where the recognition rate is lower.

As discussed earlier, we selected the FVG dataset for experimentation. It contains images recorded from three different viewing angles and, more specifically, in multiple sessions having the accessory and appearance variation. There were three different experiments using images recorded in multiple sessions, and the accessory and appearance variation. Moreover, in all the experiments, three different angle variations were used. So, we have whole-body and upper-half human silhouette images. In case of a whole-body human silhouette, 6K+ images from appearance change, and 8K+ images from multi-session and accessory categories

Table 4.4 The outcome of whole body human silhouette experiments.

Subset information	Angle variation (°)	No. of images	KNN	RF
Multi-session	−45, 0, 45	8165	0.93	0.94
Accessories	−45, 0, 45	8102	0.95	0.95
Appearance	−45, 0, 45	6817	0.93	0.94

AUC, area under the curve.

were used and minimum recognition accuracy of more than 90% was achieved, as shown in Table 4.4.

An additional set of experiments was designed for upper-half human silhouette images similar to whole-body human silhouette images. Again, three experiments, i.e. verification using multiple sessions, and accessory and appearance images were performed, having all three angle variations in each case. There were more than 8K+ images used in the first two experiments while nearly 7K images were used in the last experiments and recognition accuracy of more than 90% was provided by the RF classifier, while nearly 89% by KNN, as shown in Table 4.5.

In our work, we are using the One-vs-Rest classification schema. In this schema, usually a single image from each class is selected as a probe. Later, it is compared with the rest of the classes. In this situation, all the images from all the 12 classes from our dataset were used as gallery images and the recognition accuracy was computed against gallery. The experiment was carried out by selecting probe images from each class and comparing them with gallery images. As the outcome of these experiments, there are 12 ROC curves, one for each class was plotted on a single graph which depicts accuracy measure. Also, a single graph containing 12 curves better compares the recognition rate among distinct individuals. Moreover, we have two different classifiers and three different types of experiments, which resulted in six graphs in total.

Table 4.5 The outcome of upper-half human silhouette experiments.

Subset information	Angle variation (°)	No. of images	KNN	RF
Multi-session	−45, 0, 45	8170	0.88	0.92
Accessories	−45, 0, 45	8105	0.88	0.91
Appearance	−45, 0, 45	6821	0.89	0.91

AUC, area under the curve.

The true classification rate using KNN and RF for the whole-body human and upper silhouettes is shown in Figures 4.16 and 4.17, respectively. The curves shown actually reflect the best match of the probe with the gallery images. For instance, in Figure 4.16a, the probe image has been taken from each class of the

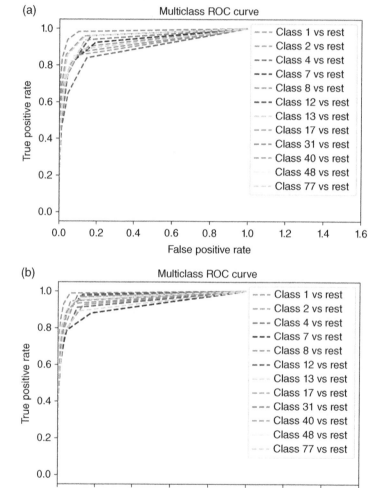

Figure 4.16 ROC curve for the whole-body human silhouette experiments. (a) 2017 and 2018-KNN. (b) 2017 and carrying accessories-KNN. (c) 2017 and changing clothes-KNN. (d) 2017 and 2018-RF. (e) 2017 and carrying accessories-RF. (f) 2017 and changing clothes-RF.

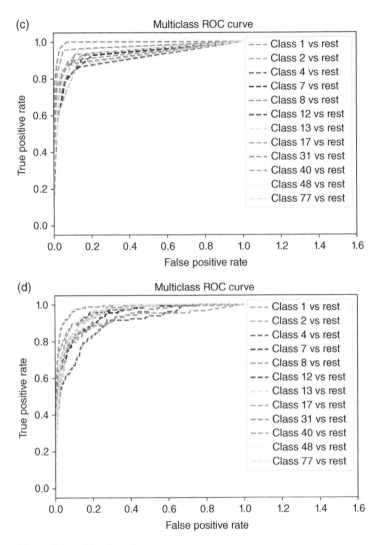

Figure 4.16 (Continued)

2017 dataset as a probe and, later on, it is compared for the highest match probability with the rest of the image classes in the gallery, e.g. the 2018 dataset. The
highest match probability actually reflects verification.

Additionally, an essential requirement of any recognition system is to evaluate
its performance against similar systems. To the best of our knowledge, there is no

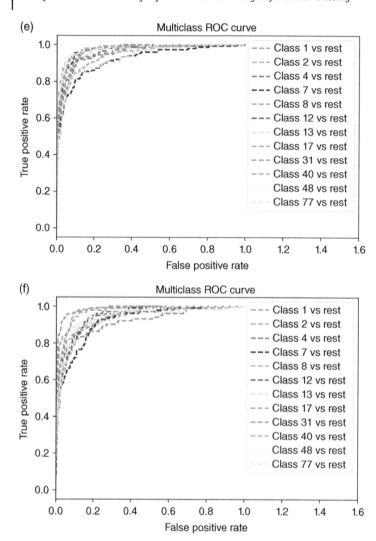

Figure 4.16 (Continued)

system which has been tested on a dataset of the same people captured over a one-year gap. However, there are certain key systems which are developed to work on appearance features, i.e. clothing change as shown in Table 4.6. In our work, we performed recognition based upon accessory information too. This is another contribution to our work. Table 4.6 clearly indicates that our system outperforms recent benchmarks.

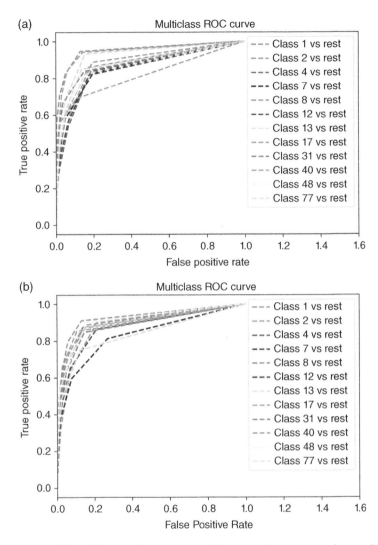

Figure 4.17 ROC curve for the upper-half human silhouette experiments. (a) 2017 and 2018-KNN. (b) 2017 and carrying accessories-KNN. (c) 2017 and changing clothes-KNN. (d) 2017 and 2018-RF. (e) 2017 and carrying accessories-RF. (f) 2017 and changing clothes-RF.

4.8 Discussion

The content presented in this chapter covers a detailed review of Soft Biometrics including the evaluation of different techniques related to anthropometric Soft Biometrics and auxiliary attachment properties of the human body. One of the

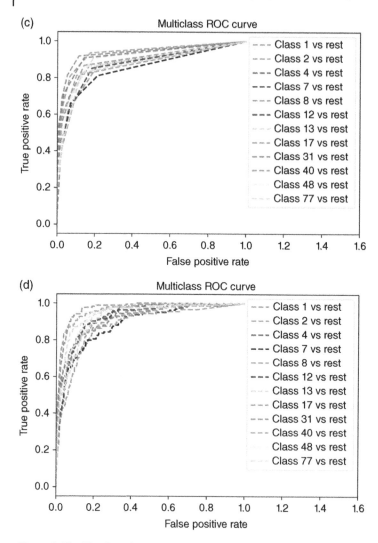

Figure 4.17 (Continued)

main objectives was to propose and develop a method for seamless verification at border crossing points. It also requires that the method meets security standards and provides fast verification in a seamless manner. In finding a solution to the stated problem, it has been observed that anthropometrics is one of the leading areas in Soft Biometrics to explore. In addition to this, the information about the auxiliary attachment of the human body is another valuable factor to support the overall verification process as auxiliary attachments usually reflect significant

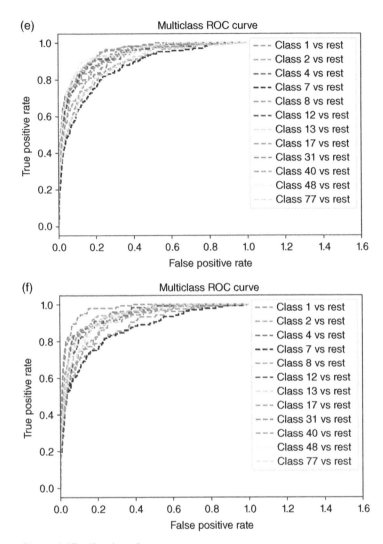

Figure 4.17 (Continued)

information about culture, traditions, etc. In general, we identified and presented several critical research areas for improvement in Soft Biometrics research. It includes the use of transfer learning for verification and development of federated learning architectures to maintain the privacy of the data, etc., more specifically where the scenario is border crossing and we are dealing with limited data and not available completely at one place. To accomplish the stated challenges, we evaluated multiple different pretrained deep learning models and reported significant

Table 4.6 Annotation methods and types.

Methods	Accuracy (%)
Baseline-ResNet50	65.0
Multi-scale DL architectures	73.5
Part-based conv baseline	72.9
Part-aligned representations	84.5
Ours (accessories) – whole body	95.0 and 95.0
Ours (appearance) – whole body	93.0 and 94.0
Ours (accessories) – upper half	88.0 and 91.0
Ours (appearance) – upper half	89.0 and 91.0

success in terms of recognition. To the best of our understanding, following are the key areas for improvement in Soft Biometrics for verification:

- development of benchmark dataset
- quantitative annotations for Soft Biometrics
- proof of concept for automated estimation
- evaluating multi-modality fusion framework
- proposing federated learning architecture for global Soft Biometrics estimation

4.9 Conclusion

It is concluded from the discussion that Soft Biometrics is getting wider attention from the research community working for seamless and secure border crossing solutions. In this chapter, we presented a comprehensive review of Soft Biometrics research ranging from datasets to a bag of context-aware Soft Biometrics features. Initially, we tested different landmark localization tools for anthropometric features estimation. The anthropometrics are actually human body measurements including ratios, proportions, etc. They are promising features of the human body and they can be estimated successfully from 2D images. However, the first step includes accurate estimation or extraction from the CCTV, later matching in case of verification and retrieval for reidentification. We also provided a collection of candidate Soft Biometrics from which a good number of anthropometric features may be extracted more easily and accurately. To estimate these features, there are open-source tools, which perform landmark localization using images of the human body. Additionally, a general understanding of anthropometric datasets and features is another dimension to consider. This is helpful in selecting the features, which are possible to estimate first and in an easier manner.

Later, a proof of concept using transfer learning techniques is presented in this chapter. In our case, we are dealing with the problem of limited data as we have images for only 12 individuals available recorded in the years 2017 and 2018, respectively. The reason for using such kind of data with a long gap is to address the issue of verification in border crossing scenarios where people usually appear after a gap of weeks, months, or, sometimes, years. In order to perform verification using such kind of data transfer learning is a key solution, which is actually a design approach. To perform this task, we initially tested 26 different transfer learning models available in KERAS API on the MMV Pedestrian dataset. These models are trained on the ImageNet dataset. The initial outcome of different models is presented and they are used in their original form and their first three classification outcomes are shown.

Finally, clothing or material Soft Biometrics are used to evaluate the performance of the seamless recognition framework. We presented a model that aims to evaluate the recognition performance on multi-session and multi-exemplar images, e.g. images of the same individuals recorded over time, carrying luggage, or change in appearance, etc. To accomplish the recognition task in such kind of scenario, human silhouette information is exploited. The original human silhouette in full and segmented, e.g. upper half showed promising results on the given dataset. Moreover, the images of individuals include angle variation too. The experiments were carried out on the FVG dataset where the ensemble of classifiers was proposed. It was noticed that model may face scalability issues. As a future course of action, we plan to extend the dataset by recording the same individuals again and with appearance changes.

References

Alsedais, R. and Guest, R. (2017). Person re-identification from CCTV silhouettes using generic fourier descriptor. *2017 International Carnahan Conference on Security Technology (ICCST)*, 1–6, Madrid, Spain (23–26 October 2017). IEEE.

Angeloni, M., de Freitas Pereira, R. and Pedrini, H. (2019). Age estimation from facial parts using compact multi-stream convolutional neural networks. *Proceedings of the IEEE International Conference on Computer Vision Workshops*, Seoul Korea (27 October–2 November 2010).

Bainbridge, W.A., Isola, P., and Oliva, A. (2013). The intrinsic memorability of face photographs. *Journal of Experimental Psychology: General* 142 (4): 1323.

Bolle, R.M. et al. (2013). *Guide to Biometrics*. Springer Science & Business Media.

Boutros, F. et al. (2019). Exploring the channels of multiple color spaces for age and gender estimation from face images. *22nd International Conference on Information Fusion, FUSION*, 2–5, Ottawa, ON (2–5 July 2019).

Cao, Z. et al. (2019). OpenPose: realtime multi-person 2D pose estimation using part affinity fields. *IEEE Transactions on Pattern Analysis and Machine Intelligence* https://ieeexplore.ieee.org/document/8765346.

Chen, Y. and Wang, Y. (2019). An anthropometric dimensions measurement method using multi-pose human images with complex background. *Journal of Physics: Conference Series* 1335 (1) IOP Publishing: 012005.

Danielsson, P.-E. (1980). Euclidean distance mapping. *Computer Graphics and Image Processing* 14 (3): 227–248.

Dantcheva, A., Velardo, C. et al. (2011). Bag of soft biometrics for person identification. *Multimedia Tools and Applications* 51 (2): 739–777.

Dantcheva, A., Elia, P., and Ross, A. (2015). What else does your biometric data reveal? A survey on soft biometrics. *IEEE Transactions on Information Forensics and Security* 11 (3): 441–467.

De Carolis, B., Macchiarulo, N. and Palestra, P. (2019). Soft biometrics for social adaptive robots. *International Conference on Industrial, Engineering and Other Applications of Applied Intelligent Systems*, 687–699, Graz, Austria (9–11 July 2019). Springer.

Deng, J. et al. (2009). *Construction and Analysis of a Large Scale Image Ontology*. Vision Sciences Society.

Deng, Y. et al. (2014). Pedestrian attribute recognition at far distance. *Proceedings of the 22nd ACM International Conference on Multimedia*, 789–792, Orlando, FL (3–7 November 2014). ACM.

Denman, S. et al. (2015). Searching for people using semantic soft biometric descriptions. *Pattern Recognition Letters* 68: 306–315.

Dornaika, F., Arganda-Carreras, I., and Belver, C. (2019). Age estimation in facial images through transfer learning. *Machine Vision and Applications* 30 (1): 177–187.

Duan, M. et al. (2018). A hybrid deep learning CNN-ELM for age and gender classification. *Neurocomputing* 275: 448–461.

El-Samak, A.F. and Alhanjouri, M. (2019). Soft biometrics estimation using shearlet and waveatom transforms with three different classifiers. *2019 IEEE 7th Palestinian International Conference on Electrical and Computer Engineering (PICECE)*, 1–8. IEEE. https://library.iugaza.edu.ps/thesis/124208.pdf.

Fang, H.S. et al. (2017). RMPE: regional multi-person pose estimation. *Proceedings of the IEEE International Conference on Computer Vision*, Venice, Italy (22–29 October 2017).

Fang, J. et al. (2019). Muti-stage learning for gender and age prediction. *Neurocomputing* 334: 114–124.

Fernandez, A. et al. (2017). An insight into imbalanced big data classification: outcomes and challenges. *Complex & Intelligent Systems* 3 (2): 105–120.

Flynn, P.J., Jain, A.K., and Ross, A.A. (2008). *Handbook of Biometrics*. Springer.

Fosdick, R.B. (1915). Passing of the bertillon system of identification. *Journal of the American Institute of Criminal Law and Criminology* 6: 363.

Garg, R. et al. (2018). Biometric authentication using soft biometric traits. *2018 Fifth International Conference on Parallel, Distributed and Grid Computing (PDGC)*, 259–264, Solan, India (20–22 December 2018). IEEE.

Geng, L. et al. (2017). Soft biometrics in online social networks: a case study on twitter user gender recognition. *2017 IEEE Winter Applications of Computer Vision Workshops (WACVW)*, 1–8, Santa Rosa, CA (24–31 March 2017). IEEE.

Gonzalez-Sosa, E. et al. (2018). Facial soft biometrics for recognition in the wild: recent works, annotation, and COTS evaluation. *IEEE Transactions on Information Forensics and Security* 13 (8): 2001–2014.

Goodfellow, I.J. et al. (2015). Challenges in representation learning: a report on three machine learning contests. *Neural Networks* 64: 59–63.

Gulli, A. and Pal, S. (2017). *Deep Learning with Keras*. Packt Publishing Ltd.

Guo, B.H, Nixon, M.S. and Carter, J.N. (2018). Fusion analysis of soft biometrics for recognition at a distance. *2018 IEEE 4th International Conference on Identity, Security, and Behavior Analysis (ISBA)*, 1–8, Singapore (11–12 January 2018). IEEE.

Gurnani, A. et al. (2019). SAF-BAGE: salient approach for facial soft-biometric classification-age, gender, and facial expression. *2019 IEEE Winter Conference on Applications of Computer Vision (WACV)*, 839–847, Waikoloa, HI (7–11 January 2019). IEEE.

Hasan, M. and Babaguchi, N. (2016). Long-term people reidentification using anthropometric signature. *2016 IEEE 8th International Conference on Biometrics Theory, Applications and Systems (BTAS)*, 1–6, Niagara Falls, NY (6–9 September 2016). IEEE.

Hassan, B. and Izquierdo, E. (2021). Person recognition across multi-session and multi-exemplar images using ensemble of classifiers. In: *Thirteenth International Conference on Digital Image Processing (ICDIP 2021)*, vol. 11878, 1187807. International Society for Optics and Photonics.

Hassan, B., Akram, M.U. et al. (2014a). A study on re process models for offshore software development. *Journal of Basic and Applied Scientific Research* 4: 114–119.

Hassan, B., Akram, U. et al. (2014b). A publicly available RGB-D data set of Muslim prayer postures recorded using microsoft kinect for windows. *Journal of Applied Environmental and Biological Sciences* 4: 115–125.

Hassan, B., Shoaib Farooq, M. et al. (2014c). Requirement engineering practices in Pakistan software industry: major problems. *Journal of Applied Environmental and Biological Sciences* 4: 391–397.

Hassan, B., Izquierdo, E., and Piatrik, T. (2021). Soft biometrics: a survey. *Multimedia Tools and Applications* Special Issue: 1–44.

Huang, G.B. and Learned-Miller, E. (2014). Labeled Faces in the Wild: Updates and New Reporting Procedures. *Dept. Comput. Sci., Univ. Massachusetts Amherst, Amherst, MA, USA, Tech. Rep*, 14–003.

Huri, K., David, E.O. and Netanyahu, N.S. (2018). DeepEthnic: multi-label ethnic classification from face images. *International Conference on Artificial Neural Networks*, 604–612, Rhodes, Greece (4–7 October 2018). Springer.

Iqbal, R. et al. (2016). Evaluation of low power mobile devices in intelligent transportation systems. *Journal of Applied Environmental and Biological Sciences* 6 (3S): 152–158.

Jain, A.K., Bolle, R., and Pankanti, S. (2006). *Biometrics: Personal Identification in Networked Society*, vol. 479. Springer Science & Business Media.

Kanade, T., Cohn, J.F. and Tian, Y. (2000). Comprehensive database for facial expression analysis. *Proceedings Fourth IEEE International Conference on Automatic Face and Gesture Recognition (Cat. No. PR00580)*, 46–53, Grenoble, France (28–30 March 2000). IEEE.

Keras Tutorial (2018). Transfer learning using pre-trained models j learn openCV. https://www.learnopencv.com/keras-tutorial-transfer-learning-using-pre-trained-models (accessed 24 September 2020).

Kocabas, M., Athanasiou, N. and Black, M.J. (2020). VIBE: video inference for human body pose and shape estimation. *Proceedings of the IEEE/CVF Conference on Computer Vision and Pattern Recognition*, 5253–5263, Virtual (14–19 June 2020).

Lee, K.W. et al. (2018). Wardrobe model for long term re-identification and appearance prediction. *2018 15th IEEE International Conference on Advanced Video and Signal Based Surveillance (AVSS)*, 1–6, Auckland, New Zealand (27–30 November 2018). IEEE.

Li, S. and Deng, W. (2020). Deep facial expression recognition: a survey. *IEEE Transactions on Affective Computing* Early Access: 1.

Lin, X. et al. (2020). Task-oriented feature-fused network with multivariate dataset for joint face analysis. *IEEE Transactions on Cybernetics* 50: 1292–1305.

Martinho-Corbishley, D., Nixon, M.S. and Carter, J.N. (2015). Soft biometric recognition from comparative crowdsourced annotations. London (15–17 July 2015). https://ieeexplore.ieee.org/abstract/document/7317969

Martinho-Corbishley, D., Nixon, M.S., and Carter, J.N. (2018). Super-fine attributes with crowd prototyping. *IEEE Transactions on Pattern Analysis and Machine Intelligence* 41 (6): 1486–1500.

Nam, S.H. et al. (2020). Age estimation by super-resolution reconstruction based on adversarial networks. *IEEE Access* 8: 17103–17120.

Neal, T.J. and Woodard, D.L. (2019). You are not acting like yourself: a study on soft biometric classification, person identification, and mobile device use. *IEEE Transactions on Biometrics, Behavior, and Identity Science* 1 (2): 109–122.

Niinuma, K., Park, U., and Jain, A.K. (2010). Soft biometric traits for continuous user authentication. *IEEE Transactions on Information Forensics and Security* 5 (4): 771–780.

Nixon, M.S., Correia, P.L. et al. (2015). On soft biometrics. *Pattern Recognition Letters* 68: 218–230.

Nixon, M.S., Guo, B.H. et al. (2017). Towards automated eyewitness descriptions: describing the face, body and clothing for recognition. *Visual Cognition* 25 (4–6): 524–538.

Ouafi, A. et al. (2019). Two-stages based facial demographic attributes combination for age estimation. *Journal of Visual Communication and Image Representation* 61: 236–249.

Ouloul, I.M. et al. (2019). Improvement of age estimation using an efficient wrinkles descriptor. *Multimedia Tools and Applications* 78 (2): 1913–1947.

Pei, W. et al. (2020). Attended end-to-end architecture for age estimation from facial expression videos. *IEEE Transactions on Image Processing* 29: 1972–1984.

Phillips, P.J. et al. (2000). The FERET evaluation methodology for face-recognition algorithms. *IEEE Transactions on Pattern Analysis and Machine Intelligence* 22 (10): 1090–1104.

Prakash, A. and Mukesh, R. (2014). A biometric approach for continuous user authentication by fusing hard and soft traits. *International Journal of Network Security* 16 (1): 65–70.

Reid, D.A. et al. (2013a). Soft biometrics for surveillance: an overview. In: *Handbook of Statistics*, vol. 31, 327–352. Elsevier.

Reid, D.A., Nixon, M.S., and Stevenage, S.V. (2013b). Soft biometrics; human identification using comparative descriptions. *IEEE Transactions on Pattern Analysis and Machine Intelligence* 36 (6): 1216–1228.

Sadhya, D. et al. (2017). BioSoft-a multimodal biometric database incorporating soft traits. *2017 IEEE International Conference on Identity, Security and Behavior Analysis (ISBA)*, 1–6, New Delhi, India (22–24 February 2017). IEEE.

Samangooei, S. (2010). Semantic biometrics. PhD thesis. University of Southampton.

Semertzidis, T. et al. (2016). Soft biometrics in low resolution and low quality CCTV videos. Madrid, Spain (23–25 November 2016). https://ieeexplore.ieee.org/abstract/document/8267352.

Sharif, M. et al. (2020). Human action recognition: a framework of statistical weighted segmentation and rank correlation-based selection. *Pattern Analysis and Applications* 23 (1): 281–294.

Shin, M., Seo, J.H. and Kwon, D.S. (2017). Face image-based age and gender estimation with consideration of ethnic difference. *2017 26th IEEE International Symposium on Robot and Human Interactive Communication (RO-MAN)*, 567–572, Lisbon, Portugal (28 August–1 September 2017). IEEE.

Shoaib Farooq, M. et al. (2014). Studio applications and software development kits for microsoft kinect: a survey, 398–402. http://escholar.umt.edu.pk:8080/jspui/handle/123456789/1448.

Shutler, J.D. et al. (2004). On a large sequence-based human gait database. In: *Applications and Science in Soft Computing* (ed. A. Lotfi and J.M. Garibaldi), 339–346. Springer.

Simon, T. et al. (2017). Hand keypoint detection in single images using multiview bootstrapping. *Proceedings of the IEEE conference on Computer Vision and Pattern Recognition*, Honolulu, HI (21–26 July 2017).

Srinivas, N. et al. (2017). Age, gender, and fine-grained ethnicity prediction using convolutional neural networks for the East Asian face dataset. *2017 12th IEEE International Conference on Automatic Face & Gesture Recognition (FG 2017)*, 953–960, Washington, DC (30 May 2017–3 June 2017). IEEE.

Sundararajan, A., Sarwat, A.I., and Pons, A. (2019). A survey on modality characteristics, performance evaluation metrics, and security for traditional and wearable biometric systems. *ACM Computing Surveys (CSUR)* 52 (2): 39.

Tan, C. et al. (2018). A survey on deep transfer learning. *International Conference on Artificial Neural Networks*, 270–279, Rhodes, Greece (4–7 October 2018). Springer.

Terhorst, P. et al. (2020). Unsupervised enhancement of soft-biometric privacy with negative face recognition. arXiv preprint. arXiv: 2002.09181.

Tome, P., Fierrez, J. et al. (2014). Soft biometrics and their application in person recognition at a distance. *IEEE Transactions on Information Forensics and Security* 9 (3): 464–475.

Tome, P., Vera-Rodriguez, R. et al. (2015). Facial soft biometric features for forensic face recognition. *Forensic Science International* 257: 271–284.

Tomičić, I., Grd, P., and Bača, M. (2018). A review of soft biometrics for IoT. *2018 41st International Convention on Information and Communication Technology, Electronics and Microelectronics (MIPRO)*, 1115–1120, Opatija, Croatia (21–25 May 2018). IEEE.

Vera-Rodriguez, R. et al. (2017). Exploring automatic extraction of body-based soft biometrics. *2017 International Carnahan Conference on Security Technology (ICCST)*, 1–6, Madrid, Spain (23–26 October 2017). IEEE.

Wan, L. et al. (2018). Fine-grained multi-attribute adversarial learning for face generation of age, gender and ethnicity. *2018 International Conference on Biometrics (ICB)*, 98–103, Gold Coast, QLD (20–23 February 2018). IEEE.

Wei, S.E. et al. (2016). Convolutional pose machines. *Proceedings of the IEEE conference on Computer Vision and Pattern Recognition*, 4724–4732, Las Vegas, NV (1 July 2016).

Xia, M. et al. (2020). Multi-stage feature constraints learning for age estimation. *IEEE Transactions on Information Forensics and Security* 15: 2417–2428.

Xie, J.-C. and Pun, C.-M. (2020). Deep and ordinal ensemble learning for human age estimation from facial images. *IEEE Transactions on Information Forensics and Security* 15: 2361–2374.

Xiu, Y. et al. (2018). Pose flow: efficient online pose tracking. arXiv preprint. arXiv: 1802.00977.

Zhang, D. and Lu, G. (2002). Shape-based image retrieval using generic Fourier descriptor. *Signal Processing: Image Communication* 17 (10): 825–848.

Zhang, H. et al. (2015). On the effectiveness of soft biometrics for increasing face verification rates. *Computer Vision and Image Understanding* 137: 50–62.

Zhang, P. et al. (2018). Long-term person re-identification using true motion from videos. *2018 IEEE Winter Conference on Applications of Computer Vision (WACV)*, 494–502, Lake Tahoe, NV (12–15 March 2018). IEEE.

Zhang, Z., Tran, L., Liu, F., et al. (2019a). On learning disentangled representations for gait recognition. arXiv preprint. arXiv: 1909.03051.

Zhang, Z., Tran, L., Yin, X. et al. (2019b). Gait recognition via disentangled representation learning. *Proceedings of the IEEE Conference on Computer Vision and Pattern Recognition,* 4710–4719, Long Beach, CA (16–19 June 2019).

Zhang, Z., Cui, P., and Zhu, W. (2020). Deep learning on graphs: a survey. *IEEE Transactions on Knowledge and Data Engineering* https://ieeexplore.ieee.org/abstract/document/9039675.

Zheng, S. et al. (2011). Robust view transformation model for gait recognition. *2011 18th IEEE International Conference on Image Processing*, 2073–2076, Brussels, Belgium (11–14 September 2011). IEEE.

Zhuang, F. et al. (2020). A comprehensive survey on transfer learning. *Proceedings of the IEEE* 109 (1): 43–76.

5

Counter-Unmanned Aerial Vehicle Systems: Technical, Training, and Regulatory Challenges

David Fortune[1], Holger Nitsch[2], Garik Markarian[3], Damir Osterman[4], and Andrew Staniforth[1]

[1] SAHER (Europe), Harju maakond, Estonia
[2] Department of Policing (CEPOLIS), University of Applied Sciences for Public Service in Bavaria, Fürstenfeldbruck, Germany
[3] Emeritus Professor, University of Lancaster and CEO of Rinicom Intelligent Solutions Riverway House, Morecambe Road Lancaster LA1 2RX, UK
[4] Ministry of Interior Research and Innovation, Zagreb, Croatia

5.1 Introduction

Unmanned aerial vehicles (UAVs), or drones, have earned their status as a contemporary disruptive technology, proving themselves to be an innovative development that has significantly altered the way that consumers, industries, and businesses across the world operate (Smith and Scott 2020). As a disruptive technology, drones have swept away systems and traditional operating practices because they have a diverse range of attributes that are recognizably superior. It is clear to see why drones offer a new and exciting opportunity across all sectors as they can be operated remotely; they present little or no risk to their operators; they can be acquired easily; their operation can be mastered simply and safely; and their environmental impact on reducing emissions and carbon footprints when compared to other traditional forms of transport is impressive. But the major factor critical to the success of the proliferation of drones remains the cost-effectiveness of commercial UAVs. As the average unit price of drones has decreased with their proliferation and reliability, drone use has accelerated to be successfully deployed as a crucial link in supply chain logistics for the pharmaceutical industry, enabling delivery of fresh blood plasma and essential drugs to remote regions inaccessible to other forms of transport.

Security Technologies and Social Implications, First Edition. Edited by Garik Markarian, Ruža Karlović, Holger Nitsch, and Krishna Chandramouli.
© 2023 The Institute of Electrical and Electronics Engineers, Inc.
Published 2023 by John Wiley & Sons, Inc.

UAVs have also proven their value as reconnaissance and delivery agents in the health care and emergency services sectors, supporting fire and rescue operations. In agriculture, drones are being used to chart patterns and success rates for irrigation, and to monitor the health of growing crops via infrared and other technologies. But the greatest impact on the day-to-day operation of the business will be the increasing use of drones for parcel delivery. With large retail and logistics companies investing in delivery drones with the aim of achieving increased efficiency, lower costs, and increased customer satisfaction, they are becoming an increasingly familiar aspect of life and work across the world today as industry forecasters suggest that delivery drones could become business as usual by 2030 (Whyte et al. 2018). During a time when all organizations and governments across the world are under pressure to be more efficient, environmentally friendly, innovative, and ambitious in how they deliver services, drones offer a unique lens on the world below, gathering data quickly and accurately from hard-to-reach places, creating a unique record in near real time.

The sudden and dramatic rise of the use of commercial drones, from hobby enthusiasts to a ubiquitous business tool, remains in its infancy. The proliferation of UAVs represents a disruptive technological innovation that continues to develop at exponential speed, and on a global scale. Autonomously piloted systems have the potential to revolutionize how people and goods are transported and to support entirely new and disbursed economic societies with profound implications. At the same time, this new technology is being hijacked by those with hostile intentions, adopting and adapting the use of drones for their own nefarious purposes, thereby creating a new counter-drone and drone-detection industry to prevent harm. Unfortunately, in the wrong hands, drones have the capacity to damage, destroy, and disrupt, and when used as a terrorist tactic, they have the capability to conduct deadly and determined attacks. This chapter shall therefore first examine the drone terrorist threat landscape and explore drone and counter-drone technologies to highlight the operational challenges of security forces to understand and implement effective countermeasures to safeguard public security from new and emerging drone technology threat vectors.

5.2   Drone Terror Threat Landscape

The security threats from the UAVs exist for a long time and the use of drones by terrorists were reported since the early 90s of the last century. Table 5.1 summarizes some of the earlier terrorist attacks where perpetrators employed different types of UAVs with various degrees of sophistication (Staniforth 2020; Ajay and Mishra 2009).

These were very dangerous but isolated cases with effects restricted by limitations of technologies available to terrorists. Most recently, during the early hours of Sunday, 27 June 2021, two consecutive explosions occurred at the high-security Jammu Air

Table 5.1 Terrorist attack using unmanned aerial vehicles.

Date	Name of Organization/ individual	Nature of threat	Preparation level	Support base	Source of information
1995	Aum Shinrikyo, the Japanese Terrorist Group	Attacked the Tokyo subway	Planned to use remote-control helicopters to spray sarin gas (dangerous chemicals from air)	Japanese Terrorist Group	Literature available on this subject
2001	Osama bin Laden	Planned to kill George W. Bush and other heads of state at the G-8 Summit in Genoa, Italy	Considered using remote-control airplanes packed with explosives	Al-Qaeda	Intelligence inputs
June 2002	Al-Qaeda	Planned to attack passenger aircraft	Considered using model airplanes	Al-Qaeda	Reuters news agency
August 2002	Revolutionary Armed Forces of Colombia or FARC	Exact target not known	Possession of nine remote-controlled unmanned aircraft	FARC	Colombian Army Unit
December 2002	Palestinian Terrorist Group	Attacked built-up Israeli area	Model planes for conversion into miniature air bombers with explosive payloads	Palestinian Extremist Group	Counter terror report
November 2003	A British National held at Camp Delta, Guantanamo Bay, Cuba	Attack the house of commons	Acquire a drone to attack with anthrax	Al-Qaeda	London independent newspaper
March, 2004	A Palestinian Extremist Group	Attack a Jewish settlement in Gaza sector	Use of a UAV loaded with explosives	Palestinian Extremist Group	Israeli intelligence

Force station in India (Chhina and Singh 2021). Located 15 km from the border of Pakistan, the military base had suffered a suspected terrorist drone attack, which caused minor injuries to two Indian Air Force (IAF) personnel. Following an analysis of the threat from drones and an assessment of the intelligence landscape, security authorities have raised concerns of a possible "drone jihad" by Pakistan-based terror groups plotting to attack New Delhi celebrations during Independence Day on 15 August. To mitigate the threat, Delhi Police Commissioner Balaji Srivastava sanctioned a ban on the use of drones and other aircraft in specified areas which came into force on 16 July, and remained in place for a period of 32 days up to 16 August, 2021. The successful delivery of numerous drone attacks worldwide by terrorists raised concerns amongst national security policymakers across the world, serving to reinforce what they already knew: that drones present a clear and present danger to the public, which police and security authorities remain poorly prepared to prevent.

The utility and attractiveness of UAVs are further evidenced through their adoption of terrorist groups in theaters of conflict. Islamic State (IS) first used drones to film suicide car bomb attacks, posted online by militants as part of their propaganda campaigns to raise awareness of their cause and to recruit and radicalize others to their ranks. As their use of drone technology advanced, American and Iraqi military commanders revealed that IS drones were employed to support direct action on the battlefield. When Kurdish forces fighting IS in northern Iraq shot down a small drone the size of a model airplane during 2016, they believed it was like the dozens of drones the terrorist organization had been flying for reconnaissance in the area (Rassler 2016). Seizing the drone and transporting it back to their outpost for further examination, the captured drone was thought to be able to provide intelligence on IS drone operations. But as they were taking it apart, the small Improvised Explosive Device (IED) contained inside detonated, killing two Kurdish fighters in what is believed to be the first time IS has successfully used a drone with explosives to kill troops on the battlefield. The drone IED attack has been recently followed by further IS drone operations, prompting American commanders in Iraq to issue a warning to forces fighting the group to treat any type of small flying aircraft as a potential explosive device. For some American military analysts and drone experts, the incidents confirmed their view that military authorities were slow to anticipate the terrorist adaption of drones as weapons. Based on the experiences of coalition military leaders in Iraq and Syria, it was right to believe that drones would continue to present a security challenge in theaters of conflict, as well as an attack planning option for domestic terrorist groups. On 4 August, 2018, as Venezuelan President Nicolás Maduro addressed a military parade in Caracas on Avenida Bolívar, one of the capital's main thoroughfares, the sound of an explosion suddenly scattered civilians and soldiers alike (Watson 2018). State news cameras and social media at the event captured fragmented images of mass confusion – smoke rising above the city, a formation of soldiers scattering and bodyguards leaping to shield the president. Only later would the story be pieced together: two small drones flying over the event had exploded. Neither was close enough to deliver lethal damage, though seven members of the Venezuelan National Guard were injured. In the aftermath of the attack, dozens of people were arrested as Venezuelan officials launched an investigation to work out, who had orchestrated the apparent assassination, the police and security force operation identifying the group, which included defectors from the Venezuelan military, whose aim was to kill the President. The plan was believed to have been foiled by the presidential security guards, who caused the drones to explode prematurely by activating the cell phone signal blockers that protect the president causing the blasts. The failed assassination attempt was alarmingly ambitious. The attack instantly made protecting heads of state even more complex; so varied are government leaders' schedules and public appearances. Not only did the assassination attack plan provide evidence that drones could be preprogrammed to swoop in from almost any direction, but they could also be used by anyone with the means to buy them. The attack also showed that threats from the sky were no longer the exclusive domain of nation-states, with weaponized drones now being firmly in the hands of non-state actors.

For terrorists, the accelerated development of drone technologies presents a unique opportunity to support ever more sophisticated surveillance activities, being used to conduct hostile reconnaissance on a target location, for ongoing mission support during an operation providing increased situational awareness, or as a rudimentary cyber-surveillance platform to collect local electronic communications that are not well encrypted. The adoption of drones for terrorist purposes is a significant security concern for governments across the world. Reinforcing the concern of this new threat, in August 2019, European Union Security Commissioner, Julian King warned that drones could be used for acts of terrorism stating that: "Drones are becoming more and more powerful and smarter which makes them more and more attractive for legitimate use, but also for hostile acts" (Doffman 2019). The warning followed the publication of a leaked secret report in December 2018 from France's Anti-Terrorism Unit (UCLAT) to the country's Special Committee on Terrorism. The report warned of "a possible terrorist attack on a football stadium by means of an unmanned drone that could be equipped with biological warfare agents" ("European Union Terrorism Situation and Trend Report 2019" 2019). The terrorist use of UAVs has already materialized in theaters of conflict with devastating impact, confirmed by Assistant Commissioner Neil Basu, head of Counter Terrorism Command at the Metropolitan Police stating that "Drones have been used on the battlefield and what's used on the battlefield will eventually be adapted to be used on domestic soil" (Tarallo 2020). Moreover, Catherine De Bolle, Executive Director of Europol has stated that a major security concern for Europe, and other nations across the world, remains the return of Foreign Terrorist Fighters (FTFs) from theaters of conflict with combat and technical expertise ("European Union Terrorism Situation and Trend Report 2019" 2019). Europol also reveals that terrorist attacks across Europe have shown a recurrent targeting of public spaces and as terrorist organizations innovate their techniques, Europol and Interpol have stated the response needs to be as equally innovative to mitigate emerging homeland security threats, which includes those posed by the terrorist use of UAVs. While the threat landscape from UAVs is diverse, the greatest concern amongst the international security community is the expectation that terrorists and terrorist groups will flirt with new technologies in an attempt to harness the power of drones to attack crowded public spaces. The UAV terrorist threat vector reveals a set of challenges that are required to be addressed by the security forces, including police and partner emergency agencies in order to improve their response to a variety of drone related incidents. But central to effectively managing and mitigating the new and emerging terrorist drone threat vectors is a thorough understanding and appreciation by security forces and public authorities of the current and future capacity and capability of drone and counter-drone technologies.

5.3   UAV Configurations and Categories of UAVs

In the context of this book, we will refer to a drone as an UAV or remotely piloted aircraft (RPA), which itself is a component of a larger unmanned aerial system (UAS), consisting of a (number) of UAVs, a ground station (GS), and various communication links between the UAVs and GS. UAVs can operate in a controlled mode piloted by a pilot, or in autonomous mode, utilizing onboard computers and navigation equipment. A typical UAS configuration is shown in Figure 5.1.

Recently, the use of UAV swarms is becoming more and more prevalent (Hambling 2015), stimulated by the introduction of Low-Cost UAV Swarming Technology (LOCUST) developed with the support of the US Navy (Rohrlich 2019). This technology is replacing the small number of expensive piloted UAVs with a large number of cheap but similarly capable UAVs flying in swarm formations in autonomous mode guided by onboard artificial intelligence (AI) and predefined flight plan. A typical UAV swarm configuration is shown in Figure 5.2.

The main advantage of a swarm is the ability to operate as a unit with a shared objective. To achieve this, the swarm must be intelligent and self-configuring, capable to change formation and behavior as per the overall mission goal and the specifics of the operational scenario. A typical swarm will include elements of AI and mesh networking allowing UAVs to be aware of each other's movements and autonomously create flying formations as required by the overall mission objective.

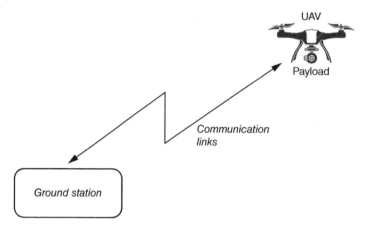

Figure 5.1 Typical single UAV configuration.

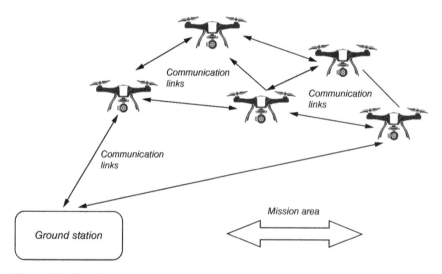

Figure 5.2 Typical swarm configuration.

Piloting the swarm brings additional challenges for the coordinator as instead of piloting a single drone, the operator must manage the whole swarm simultaneously. This is a particular advantage in military applications as due to low flight altitude and small size, swarms are invisible to antiaircraft batteries and even if detected, these batteries often do not have enough ammunition to stop them, as was proven in the attack on Saudi oil refineries in 2020 (Rohrlich 2019). These advantages of swarms create additional challenges for the developers of C-UAV systems and law enforcement agencies (LEAs) as the simultaneous detection, tracking, and classification of a large number of UAVs attacking a target could lead to a high percentage of false positive and false negative errors. At the same time, if all the UAVs in the swarm are detected and classified by the C-UAS systems, it may not be able to neutralize all the UAVs due to lack of time or shortage of ammunition (Staniforth 2020).

Unfortunately, there is no single standard for the classification of UAVs today. Defence agencies, as early adopters of UAVs, have their own classifications, which vary from country to country and even within a country from force to force. For example, the US Air Force and the US Marine Corps have their own independent and noncompatible classification systems (Staniforth 2020). In these classification systems, UAVs are categorized as:

- VTOL (Vertical Takeoff and Landing),
- LASE (Low Altitude, Short Endurance),
- LALE (Low Altitude, Long Endurance),
- MALE (Medium Altitude, Long Endurance),
- HALE (High Altitude, Long Endurance).

One of the most comprehensive reviews of various UAV classification systems is presented in (Hassanalian and Abdelkefi 2017), which includes the classification of categories of drones, as shown in Figure 5.3, where each group may include the same types of UAVs, such as:

- *HTOL – Horizontal takeoff and landing.* HTOL are tail plane-aft, tail plane-forward, tail-aft on booms, and tailless or flying wing UAVs (Stevanovic et al. 2012). These UAVs may have propulsion systems at the rear of the fuselage or at the front side of the UAV.
- *VTOL – Vertical takeoff and landing.* VTOL UAVs can take off and land vertically and do not need a runway for takeoff.
- *Hybrid – Tilt-wing, tiltrotor, tilt-body, and ducted fan.* These UAVs combine the capability of both VTOL and HTOL types (Wikipedia 2019).
- *Helicopter* – There are four types of helicopter UAVs, namely single rotor, coaxial rotor, tandem rotor, and quadrotor (Austin 2011).
- *Heliwing* – Heliwing UAVs are types of drones which use a rotating wing as their blade. They can fly like a helicopter vertically and also fly like a fixed-wing UAV.
- *Various unconventional types* – These are UAVs that cannot be placed in previously defined categories. Usually, bio-inspired flying machines are assigned to this group.

There is also a new category of rapidly emerging UAVs, called Small Dust (SD) (Ajay and Mishra 2009), which due to their very small size and swarm formation could become the most challenging type of UAVs from the point of C-UAV system developers. Categories of UAVs are shown in Figure 5.3.

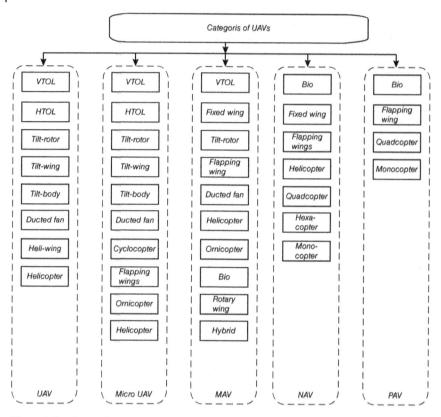

Figure 5.3 Categories of UAVs.

UAVs are also classified by weight and flight range as shown in Table 5.2.

Another widely accepted classification is the classification proposed by the US Department of Defence (DoD), where UAVs are classified into five categories, according to their size, maximum gross takeoff weight (MGTW), operating altitude, and airspeed as shown in Table 5.3 ("U.S. Army Roadmap for Unmanned Systems 2010–2035" 2010; Hassanalian and Abdelkefi 2017):

5.4 Counter-Drone Technology

Government agencies, armed forces, and the leading industry around the world are looking for ways to counter the threat from the unlawfully flying UAVs. Every stakeholder in this challenge acknowledges that this is a complex problem, which cannot be resolved by one solution suitable for all possible security threats.

Table 5.2 Classification of UAVs by weight and flight range.

S. No.	Designation	Weight range	Flight range
1.	Micro and mini UAVs – close range	W ≤ 5 kg	25 km ≤ R ≤ 40 km
2.	Lightweight UAVs – small range	5 kg < W ≤ 50 kg	10 km ≤ R ≤ 70 km
3.	Lightweight UAVs – medium range	50 kg < W ≤ 100 kg	70 km ≤ R ≤ 250 km
4.	Average UAVs	100 kg < W ≤ 300 kg	150 km ≤ R ≤ 1000 km
5.	Medium heavy UAVs	300 kg < W ≤ 500 kg	70 km ≤ R ≤ 300 km
6.	Heavy medium-range UAVs	500 kg ≤ W	70 km ≤ R ≤ 300 km
7.	Heavy UAVs – large endurance	1500 kg ≤ W	R ≤ 1500 km
8.	Unmanned combat aircraft	500 kg < W	R ≤ 1500 km

Table 5.3 UAS classification according to the US DoD.

Category	Size	Maximum gross takeoff weight (MGTW) (lbs)	Normal operating altitude (ft)	Airspeed (knots)
Group 1	Small	0–20	<1200 AGL[a]	<100
Group 2	Medium	21–55	<3500	<250
Group 3	Large	<1320	<18 000 MSL[b]	<250
Group 4	Larger	>1320	<18 000 MSL[b]	Any airspeed
Group 5	Largest	>1320	>18 000 MSL[b]	Any airspeed

[a] AGL = Above Ground Level
[b] MSL = Mean Sea Level
Note: If the UAS has even one characteristic of the next level, it is classified in that level.
Source: Adapted from U.S. Army Roadmap for Unmanned Systems 2010–2035" 2010; Hassanalian and Abdelkefi (2017).

Furthermore, there is a common understanding that only a comprehensive solution scalable for various scenarios could produce the required level of counter-UAV protection. Although there is a wide variety of views on the details of this comprehensive solution and how this problem should be addressed and solved, there is a generic agreement that the solution should be a combination of two approaches: regulatory and technological (Staniforth 2020) and the generic classification of C-UAV systems is presented in Table 5.4 (Michel 2019).

There are different technologies available for both monitoring (i.e. detection, tracking, and classification) and neutralization of drones. Detection, tracking, and

Table 5.4 Generic classification of C-UAV systems.

Type of C-UAV system	Description
Ground-based: fixed	Systems developed for installations in fixed or nomadic applications
Ground-based: mobile	Systems developed for installations on vehicles and to be operated on the move
Hand-held	Systems developed to be operated by a single individual by hand. Most of these systems look like rifles or small arms
UAV-based	Systems developed to be installed on UAVs

Source: Adapted from Michel (2019).

Table 5.5 Types of sensors used in C-UAV systems.

Type of sensor	Description
Radar	Detects and tracks UAVs by their radar signature
Radio frequency (RF)	Detects, tracks, and identifies both the UAV and the pilot by monitoring radio frequencies used by UAVs
Electro-optical (EO)	Detects, tracks, and classifies UAVs utilizing EO cameras
Infrared (IR)	Detects, tracks, and classifies UAVs utilizing IR cameras
Acoustic	Detects and tracks UAVs utilizing acoustic sensors
Visual monitoring by humans	Relies on security personnel visually monitoring the skies with binoculars
Combined sensors	Multiple sensors fused together to provide more reliable detection, tracking, and classification of UAVs

classification are allowed and recommended as the key step in the countering UAV process. Neutralization of drones is still (in most countries) not legally permitted and currently is subject to numerous regulatory and legal discussions. Typical monitoring technologies are summarized in Table 5.5.

Each of these technologies has its individual advantages and limitations and it is a common agreement of all stakeholders that a C-UAV system should incorporate integration of various sensors to compensate for the shortcomings of induvial sensors. The advantages and limitations of various sensors are summarized in Table 5.6 (Staniforth 2020; Michel 2019).

Ideally, civil, security, and military authorities will need a C-UAV system to detect, identify, classify, track, and neutralize any type of hostile UAV in any

Table 5.6 Comparison table for various detection sensors.

Type of sensor	Detection range	Position accuracy	Identification and classification	Auto mode	Detection of pilot	Multiple targets	Low visibility/ night	Passive system	Price
Radar	++++	++++	+	−	−	++++	++++	−	−
RF	++++	++++	++	−	+++	++++	++++	++++	+
EO/IR	++	++++	++++	++++	−	++++	++	++++	++++
Acoustic	−	−	+	−	−	+	++++	++++	++++
Human	−	−	+++	−	−	−	−	++++	+
Thermal imaging	−	+	++	++	−	+++	++++	++++	−

Source: Adapted from Staniforth 2020 and Michel (2019).

setting. Differences between civilian and military C-UAV solutions are mainly in the detection ranges and the implementation of the C2 and neutralization tools. In most civilian applications, there are no neutralization measures and these systems act primarily as an alerting system when a UAV is detected (this is due to the complex regulatory situation and for minimization of collateral damages).

It is now a common practice to use a comprehensive analytical approach to the C-UAV operations (Ltd. n.d.). A schematic diagram of this system, presented in Figure 5.4, consists of:

- An engine to consume incoming data and ensure it is correct and consistent.
- A database to handle analysis.
- A user interface which can be accessed from any user-friendly device.

This solution eliminates the need for continuous 24/7 human monitoring by engaging human operators ONLY when AI/ML Module classifies detected objects as UAVs. Operationally, this allows the integration of C-UAV monitoring into the existing surveillance monitoring process without additional operational expenditure. The solution already is accepted for installation on numerous high-profile critical infrastructure sites in the United Kingdom and abroad and is becoming a de-facto standard for future C-UAV systems.

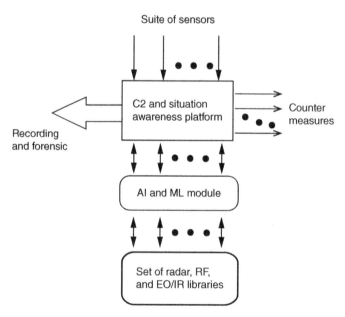

Figure 5.4 A schematic diagram of comprehensive C-UAV system with AI and ML.

5.5   Programming Rogue Drone Countermeasures

C-UAV systems are developed and installed in order to provide a technological foundation for countering drones which is a complex multistep process involving interaction between several distinct systems and between those systems and the human operator(s) and typical neutralization techniques are summarized in Table 5.7 (Michel 2019).

Table 5.7   Countermeasures used in C-UAV systems.

Countermeasure	Description
RF jamming	Disrupts UAVs data and video data links
GNSS jamming	Disrupts UAV GNSS link, GPS or GLONAS. Without synchronization with the GNSS system, a UAV will hover, land, or "return to home"
Spoofing	Allows C-UAV system operator to take control of or misdirect the targeted UAV by creating a "virtual" GNSS channel with wrong navigation information
Hacking	Interception of the UAV navigation system and reading its flight plan and flight data
Dazzling	Implementation of high-power laser beam(s) to blind the camera(s) on the UAV
Laser	Burns critical part of UAVs frame and components using direct energy, causing a crash of the UAV
High-power microwave	Send pulses of high-power microwave signals, destroying UAVs electronics components
Shooting nets	Entangles drones and/or their propellers
Projectiles	Employs regular or custom-designed ammunition to destroy incoming UAV
Water canons	Directs high-pressure water toward incoming UAV, causing a crash
Interceptor drones	A drone designed to intercept the target drone and bring it "back to base"
Collision drones	A drone designed to collide with the target UAVs
Falcons	Specially trained falcon birds who catch UAVs as prey
Missiles	Conventional missiles used for destroying large UAVs
Guns	Conventional riffles used by snipers to shoot down the UAV
Combined effectors	Several different and complementary neutralization techniques used in the same C-UAV system for increased reliability of neutralization.

Source: Adapted from Michel (2019).

However, like UAV detection sensors, there is no single solution, which will be ideal for all possible threat scenarios. Therefore, when considering the selection of countermeasure, the following factors need to be considered:

- Disturbing communication systems in the surrounding area
- Disturbing navigation and other electronic systems in the protected area
- Collateral damage created by the selected countermeasure
- Range
- Time to reload
- Accuracy
- Ease of use
- Organization fit
- A-symmetric warfare
- Compliance with the law and regulations

Furthermore, the selection of the most appropriate neutralization tool for a specific security threat caused by a UAV is only one part of the solution. To ensure that the installed C-UAV system delivers the required levels of protection once a drone is detected, a clearly defined counter-drone neutralization chain must be established.

5.5.1 The Counter-UAV Neutralization Chain

In (Staniforth 2020), a comprehensive solution to ensure that both security and safety threats from rogue UAVs will be reliably mitigated if and/or when it happens is proposed. The block diagram of this technique, called Counter-UAV (C-UAV)M Neutralization Chain C-UAV Neutralization Chain, is illustrated in Figure 5.5.

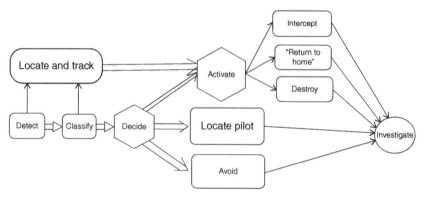

Figure 5.5 C-UAV neutralization chain.

As it follows from this diagram, the chain starts with the detection and location of the UAV, utilizing sensors, which are integrated into the C-UAV system. The detection could be achieved by a single sensor (for example, radar or RF detection) or multiple sensors fused together in the C2 platform. The benefits of the multisensor comprehensive approach were explained in the previous section, but it is worth emphasizing that as different sensors provide different information, their fusion usually produces a more comprehensive picture. For example, an RF sensor may detect the pilot while an optical sensor may help identify if a UAV is carrying a payload, etc. Once a UAV is detected, it needs to be classified, usually with EO/IR sensors and the embedded AI module, and as soon as a UAV is classified and identified as a rogue UAV, it needs to be tracked continuously.

Once a drone is identified as a rogue drone, an alarm is raised a decision must be made on how to respond to the alarm. In most of the C-UAV systems currently installed around the globe, this decision is made by a human operator who usually has a variety of options on how to respond with the help of supporting information from the C2 and situation awareness platforms. C-UAV system operators usually have a very short time to choose the most appropriate neutralization measure. For example, if a DJI INSPIRE drone is detected at around a 2 km range and classified as a UAV at around a 1.5 km range, it could reach the object in less than 50 seconds (if travelling full speed of 94 km/h). As at least half of this time needs to be allocated to the activation of neutralization measures, this means that C-UAV operator will have less than 30 seconds to make a potentially life-critical decision. Furthermore, it is expected that drone velocity will be constantly increasing building up pressure on C-UAV operators.

Typically, the C-UAV operator will choose one of the following options:

- **Activate one or few neutralization tools** – These include jamming, spoofing, kinetic, interceptor drones, laser guns, snipers, eagles, water cannons, etc. It must be emphasized that particularly in civilian environments, mitigation should be considered as a "last resort" measure as C-UAV teams may have a very limited window of time to make this decision.
- **Locate the pilot and stop the flight** – This is feasible ONLY with an RF detection sensor and is usually applied in scenarios where a drone is perceived as not dangerous or life-threatening (for example, illegally flying paparazzi, TV or amateur drones trying to get exclusive pictures).
- **Do nothing with the drone** – In some cases, it will be safer to do nothing with the drone and instead focus security efforts on actions of possible targets. For example, if a yacht with celebrities on board detects a paparazzi drone, it is easier to ask everyone just to leave the deck, and put clothes on (or maybe even to take them off, depending on individual preferences and agenda) than trying to jam or shut the drones, which, depending on country of location, could open legal problems for the operators of the C-UAV system.

Even though a drone is destroyed, the job of the C-UAV operator is not complete. In all cases, the drone or remains of the drone will be landing on the ground. Depending on the neutralization technique used, this could result in a wide range of effects, there the intercepted UAV needs to be retrieved and isolated. If the drone is potentially armed, an explosive ordnance disposal team may be called in to assess and, if needed, disable the device (Michel 2019). Unarmed drones must likewise be treated with caution as they may carry chemical or biological compounds. Furthermore, even if the UAV is not armed, its lithium-ion battery may pose a risk of combustion. Once the drone is neutralized and safe to approach, the C-UAV operator must engage with forensic investigators, who should follow internal procedures to ensure that the integrity of the system and the potentially valuable data it carries are not compromised (Staniforth 2020; Michel 2019).

5.6 Training End Users of C-UAV Systems

Threat assessments analyzing the attack planning potential for terrorists to use drones are amplified by the increasing availability of drones and their decreasing costs, making them readily accessible to lone actors and organized terrorist groups with hostile intentions. Combining the increasing sophistication of drones to carry larger payloads, now capable of being operated beyond the line of sight of the pilot and providing a platform to launch cyberattacks, makes commercially available drones excellent tools for terrorists. Moreover, the number of high-profile rogue drone incidents have exposed critical fault lines in the protection of critical infrastructures from drone attacks. The response to these major incidents, and other rogue drone incursions that continue to occur with alarming regularity, unwittingly reveal attractive vulnerabilities, which terrorists are now seeking to exploit (A Staniforth 2021). Most concerning of all is that each drone event has revealed the need for all first-responder agencies and public authorities to improve their collective knowledge and response to such incidents. What is becoming increasingly clear to homeland security policymakers is the first step in countering the threat is the provision of training to inform safety and security personnel in drone and drone-detection technology. This is now recognized by homeland security policymakers as a fundamental step toward delivering a safe and effective incident response to the drone threat vector. It is also acknowledged that such training should be designed, developed, and delivered to the relevant authorities are able to recognize specific drone attributes such as type and payload, serving to improve the initial sighting and detailed reporting of drone incidents.

Recognizing these security challenges that advancements in UAV technology have delivered, a consortium of first-responder practitioners, academic security professionals and private industry drone and drone detection partners, joined forces to progress project DroneWISE, a research and innovation action funded under the auspices of the European Commission Internal Security Fund for Policing (ISF-P) ("DroneWISE First-Responder Agency Operational Briefing 2021"). Combining their expertise, the multidisciplinary approach of DroneWISE has delivered a series of practical end user-focused measures designed to amplify and augment the response to terrorist attacks on public spaces using a drone. The research outputs from project DroneWISE conducted by consortium partners confirmed that many first-responder agencies had not fully developed the capacity or capability to effectively respond to a drone-related incident, including a potential terrorist attack on public space (Andrew Staniforth 2020b). The interoperability challenges of multiple emergency service agencies effectively responding to major terrorist incidents are well documented, and developing and implementing coordinated plans to respond to a drone-related terrorist event adds greater layers of complexity. Project DroneWISE key learnings included the need for all first-responder agencies to be alert to the terrorist use of drones, including their adoption in theaters of conflict by insurgent groups not only to conduct hostile reconnaissance for attack planning but also be adapted to carry explosives. Furthermore, as outlined in a DroneWISE First-Responder Operational Briefing, published during the project to regularly inform and update all LEAs during the research of key lessons learned, stated that "drone terrorist incidents highlight just some of the security concerns when responding to the terrorist use of drones, which includes important post-incident forensic recovery and analysis as drones may hold vital information for police investigations" (Andrew Staniforth 2020a). The purpose of project DroneWISE was therefore to provide protective measures for first-responders so they can support the prevention of such attacks and that they were better prepared and equipped to respond when attacks do occur.

The learning from DroneWISE research, which examined drone and counter-drone tools, techniques, and technologies, signaled the urgent operational need to develop an educational program to upskill and increase the knowledge and awareness of all first-responder agency personnel in the nefarious misuse of disruptive drone technology. Responding to this critically identified need, the DroneWISE Counter-UAV Training Programme Framework was created, with the aim of providing first-responder practitioners with a detailed and holistic understanding of the threat posed by rogue drone activity and the effective measures required to manage and mitigate risk and effectively respond to a terrorist attack by use of a drone at a public place. A major aspect of this training was the need to better understand drone and counter-drone technology, which being incorporated into the strategic aim of the training, at the conclusion of which all students completing the DroneWISE Counter-UAV Training Programme Framework will be able to:

1) Demonstrate a comprehensive understanding of the drone threat landscape and the capacity and capability of drones and related technologies.
2) Explain the relevant law, rules, and regulations relating to the illegal use of drones.
3) Demonstrate a comprehensive understanding of drone detection technologies and the measures required to counter the threat from rogue drone activities.
4) Design and develop a robust threat assessment to manage and mitigate the risks from rogue drone activity.
5) Demonstrate a practical knowledge of drone detection investigative techniques to identify rogue drone activity.
6) Devise a comprehensive strategic response to drone threats demonstrating an ability to develop drone security policy, practice, and procedure.

The purpose of the DroneWISE Counter-UAV Training curriculum is to provide a set of modules that present a menu of options in order for all first-responder agencies to design and tailor training provision, which is required to meet their identified operational training needs and requirements. The initial vision of the DroneWISE Counter-UAV Training was to design a series of modules that could be practically delivered to first-responder agency personnel to directly meet their operational demands and constraints of time, budget, resource, and resilience implications. Furthermore, the suite of modules could be considered either being delivered in a traditional face-to-face classroom setting or, alternatively, can be delivered entirely online or a blended online and offline delivery approach. The core curriculum modular elements of the DroneWISE Counter-UAV Training are illustrated in Table 5.8.

To support and underpin the training programme for first-responders, project DroneWISE has also developed automated self-assessment questions, which warry from not only from module to module but are different if the same module is being tested multiple times. A snapshot of this section is shown in Figure 5.6.

In addition, DroneWISE also delivered tactical options and decision-making frameworks for operational key-decision makers and commanders of major incidents, supported by a Counter-UAV Command Training Handbook providing authoritative guidance for first-responders. To address the immediate and short-term vulnerabilities, the DroneWISE project training will be delivered to first-responder practitioners across Europe during the project. The short-term needs of first responder agencies will further benefit from the delivery of a Counter-UAV Command, Control, and Coordination Strategy, providing a multiagency

Table 5.8 DroneWISE counter-UAV training programme framework.

Module	Aim	Learning outcomes
Module 1: Introduction to DroneWISE Counter-UAV Training	To provide introduction and overview of the DroneWISE Counter-UAV Training Programme Framework	• To provide an overview of the DroneWISE Counter-UAV Training aim, objective, and student outcomes. • To explain the DroneWISE project end user research and captured evidence base, which has been assessed and analyzed to inform the training programme. • To explain the operational requirement for all first-responder agencies to develop skills, knowledge and expertise to prevent and protect public spaces from a terrorist attack using a UAV. • To identify student expectations of attending and completing the DroneWISE Counter-UAV Training. • To identify and capture drone, counter-drone, terrorism and crisis management knowledge and expertise of the first-responder students attending to ensure an appropriate level of training delivery to meet their needs and requirements.
Module 2: Terrorism and attacks on public spaces	To provide an introduction to terrorism and the terrorist tactic of attacking public spaces	• To provide a first-responder agency operational understanding of terrorism including definition, classification, and key characteristics. • To provide an understanding of the terrorist tactic to attack places, including methodology, key motivations and intended outcomes. • To examine a series of case studies assessing terrorist attacks on public spaces. • To introduce and explain protective security methods and measures to protect public spaces from a terrorist attack.

(Continued)

Table 5.8 (Continued)

Module	Aim	Learning outcomes
Module 3: UAV threat landscape	To provide a comprehensive understanding of the drone threat landscape	• To examine the terrorist use of drones in theaters of conflict. • To explore the organized criminal use of drones. • To examine the threat from drones by political and environmental activists. • To examine the threat of the use of drones for smuggling drugs and weapons into prisons. • To explore the threat of rogue drone incursions at airports and other restricted aviation sites. • To examine the hostile reconnaissance threat of rogue drone activity at critical infrastructure sites and sectors. • To explain the threat of rogues drone activity for purposes of industrial espionage and sabotage. • To explore the threat of rogue drone incursions and the impact and intrusion on the right to privacy of citizens from the media, paparazzi, private investigators or state actors.
Module 4: UAV technology	To provide an introduction to understanding UAV and related technologies	• To explain the development and proliferation of drone technologies from off-the-shelf toys to fully autonomous high-capacity professional drones • To examine the use of drone technologies across public and private industry • To explore the classification and categorization of drones and the impact on the threat assessment process • To examine the capacity and capabilities of drones and associated technologies in relation to illicit use cases

Module		
Module 5: Counter-Unmanned Aerial Systems (C-UAS) technology	To provide an introduction to understanding Counter-Unmanned Aerial Systems (C-UAS) and related technologies	• To explain the development of drone detection technologies including various technologies such as radar, radio frequency, acoustics, and video analytics • To examine the different types of drone detection techniques and the importance of data fusion and data flow • To explore the technical challenges of drone detection in challenging operational environments
Module 6: UAV legislation and regulation	To provide an introduction to the relevant law, rules and regulations relating to the illegal use of drones	• To examine the relevant international and national laws for the use of drones • To explore the local, regional, and national rules and regulations governing the use of drones • To explore the governance, guidance, and oversight of drone use and ownership
Module 7: Crisis management – command and control of UAV terrorist incidents	To provide an introduction to crisis management key principles theory and practice, offering operational decision-making considerations for the effective command and control of UAV terrorist incidents	• To examine the key principles, including theory and practice, of crisis management • To explore operational decision-making models and processes • To examine command and control key considerations and consequences for managing a UAV terrorist incident
Module 8: Forensic recovery of UAV	To provide an introduction to the forensic recovery and digital investigation of drones	• To examine the best practices for the effective recovery of drones. • To explore the digital investigative opportunities for the gathering of intelligence and capturing of evidence from a drone. • To examine the health and safety considerations and consequences of responding and recovering a drone following a terrorist incident.

(Continued)

Table 5.8 (Continued)

Module	Aim	Learning outcomes
Module 9: Threat and risk assessment – reporting suspicious sightings of UAVs	To provide attendees with practical working knowledge of designing and developing threat assessments to manage and mitigate the risks from rogue drone activity	• To explain the methodology of developing risk assessment processes. • To examine the need for a threat assessment process to cover the full diversity of rogue drone threats. • To explore the theory and practice of decision-making models to support threat and risk assessment processes. • To practically apply threat and risk assessment methodology to effectively manage rogue drone activity.
Module 10: Counter-UAV security strategy	To provide first-responder agency personnel with the capability to design and deliver a comprehensive strategic response to drone threats by developing and implementing drone security policy, practice, and procedure	• To explain the value of preparedness in managing the threat and risk from rogue drone incursions. • To examine the purpose and priority of developing a strategic response to rogue drone threats. • To explore the design and development of drone security policy, practice, and procedure.

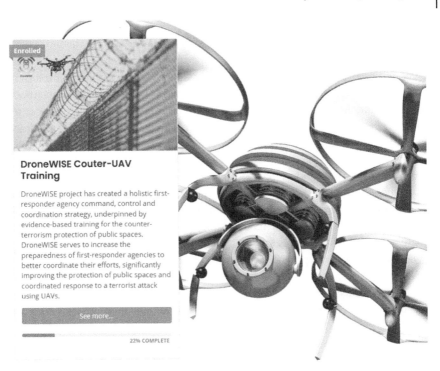

Figure 5.6 Snapshot of DroneWISE self-assessment page.

command policy with decision-making models and a threat and risk matrix. To meet the medium and long-term needs of first-responder agencies, project DroneWISE delivered a Counter-UAV Train-the-Trainers Programme to upskill and amplify first-responder training, and all training support materials will be made readily accessible via a Counter-UAV Online Training Portal. The combination of DroneWISE measures will serve to significantly improve the coordinated emergency response to better protect public spaces from drone terrorist attacks. Moreover, the DroneWISE project partners recognize that technology alone cannot solve the threats from the terrorist use of drones without an increased understanding, awareness, and integration of operational plans and procedures of multiple emergency services and authorities responsible for protecting public spaces. To mitigate rogue drone risks, DroneWISE learning outputs reinforce the notion that all in authority would be wise to learn that responding to the threat of drones is largely ineffective without fully understanding the threat landscape through increasing knowledge of drone and counter-drone technologies, alongside assessing motivations from hostile actors and specific risks and vulnerabilities of their intended target.

5.7 Conclusions

In a world of startling change, the first duty of government remains to protect the safety and security of its citizens. Governments know, for example, that international terrorist groups are determined to exploit their increasing levels of openness to attack, plot, and kill innocent citizens, or inflict mass disruption to services to destabilize a nation's economy to progress their political, ideological, or religious motivations. Given the persistent severity of the terrorist threat, and the instability and uncertainty of Afghanistan returning to a haven for terrorist groups following the withdrawal of coalition forces engaged in the so-called "War on Terror," the governments across the world no longer accept that they should simply prepare to respond to the types of terrorist attacks already encountered. All in authority now recognize, given advancements in new technologies as tools for terrorists, that this reactive posture will not preserve their national security and so an increasingly proactive and creative approach has been implemented, dedicated to identifying new and emerging terrorist threat vectors, founded upon the security principles of preparedness and assessing risk and managing the consequence of past, present, and future terrorist events. This new proactive posture now forms an essential part of tackling international contemporary terrorism. One such emerging threat is the adoption of drones as a tactical attack planning option for terrorists to cause mass disruption, damage economic stability, and threaten security.

Drones are becoming increasingly sophisticated, which makes them more attractive not only for legitimate use but also for hostile acts. The possible terrorist attack on a public place by means of an unmanned drone that could be equipped with biological warfare agents presents a clear and present danger. The terrorist use of UAVs, which has already materialized in theaters of conflict with devastating impact, are tactics and techniques that could be used as part of domestic terrorist events that give rise to grave concerns amongst national security policymakers across the world as the new era of global international terrorism reveals with alarming regularity that terrorist plotters achieve their intended objectives, defeating all of the state's security measures put in place at the time. Unfortunately, this pattern is not set to change, governments across the world will prevent further terrorist atrocities, but there is a very strong likelihood that they will not stop them all. In the light of that conclusion, all in authority must dedicate themselves to increasing their knowledge and understanding of counterterrorism and the new threat vector of the deadly and determined terrorist use of drones to attack public spaces (Wellig et al. 2018).

The multiagency first-responder Counter-UAV Training Programme designed by project DroneWISE provides a model approach to responding to the terrorist use of drones to attack public places. As key takeaways from the DroneWISE project have illustrated, all first-responder agencies must now examine their capacity and capability to effectively respond to a UAV terrorist attack on public space and take positive steps to develop a coherent and coordinated multiagency plan to implement in response to a UAV terrorist attack. Moreover, lessons from the DroneWISE research recommend that this plan must be developed in collaboration with multiple first-responder agencies and other civil departments engaged in crisis response, and made subject to rigorous review and regular testing and exercising to ensure the joint response keeps pace with the developing UAV terrorist threat landscape. The DroneWISE model of integrated programming, including the development of training, policy, practice, and procedure, to raise knowledge and awareness of technological advancements offers a blueprint for governments to effectively manage and mitigate risks, not only from drones but also from other disruptive technologies in the security domain including the adoption and adaption of AI and big data analytics.

In conclusion, the proliferation of drones provides further evidence that social and technical innovations continue to occur at an ever-increasing speed, causing fast and drastic changes to society. These changes, driven by the possibilities offered by new and emerging technologies, affect citizens, governments, and all public and private industry sectors. Drones are democratizing the sky and enabling new participants in aviation, quickly evolving beyond their military origin to become powerful business tools (Hambling 2015). To mitigate rogue drone risks, all in authority would be wise to learn that responding to the threat of drones is wholly ineffective without fully understanding the threat landscape through increasing knowledge of drone and counter-drone technologies, alongside assessing motivations from hostile actors and specific risks and vulnerabilities of their intended target. In conclusion, to defeat all manner of rogue drone terrorist threat vectors, the procurement and deployment of appropriate equipment are required, combined with the integration of that equipment into a comprehensive and coherent counter-drone strategy that is synchronized with existing security operations, and embedded within the very culture of managing risk and improving resilience.

References

Ajay, L and Mishra, A. (2009). Aerial terrorism and the threat from unmanned aerial vehicles. *Journal of Defence Studies* 3 (3): 54–65.

Chhina, A.S. and Singh, M.A. (2021). A new kind of terror: Two bombs fall on Indian Air Force base in Jammu. *The Indian Express.*

Doffman, Z. (2019). Warning over terrorist attacks using Drones given by EU security chief. Forbes. https://www.forbes.com/sites/zakdoffman/2019/08/04/europes-security-chief-issues-dire-warning-on-terrorist-threat-from-drones/#4bcb380d7ae4.

DroneWISE First-Responder Agency Operational Briefing (2021). European Commission. https://dronewise-project.eu/wp-content/uploads/2021/01/DroneWISE-First-Responder-Agency-Operational-Briefing.pdf.

European Union Terrorism Situation and Trend Report (2019). Europol. https://doi. org/10.2813/788404.

Hambling, D. (2015). *Swarm Troopers: How Small Drones Will Conquer the World*. Venice: Archangel Inc.

Hassanalian, M. and Abdelkefi, A. (2017). Classifications, applications, and design challenges of Drones: a review. *Progress in Aerospace Sciences* 91: 99–131. https:// doi.org/https://doi.org/10.1016/j.paerosci.2017.04.003.

Ltd, Operational Solutions (n.d.) FACE, (2022). https://osldronedetect.co.uk/osl-face (accessed 27 March 2022).

Michel, A.H. (2019). *Eyes In The Sky: The Secret Rise of Gorgon Stare and How It Will Watch Us All*. Mariner Books.

Rassler, D. (2016). *Remotley Piloted Innovation: Terrorism, Drones and Supportive Technologies*. West Point: Combating Terrorism Center.

Rohrlich, J. (2019). Drones just attacked the World's largest oil refinery. Quartz. https://qz.com/1709290/drones-attack-worlds-largest-oil-refinery-in-saudi-arabia/.

Smith, T. and Scott, G. (2020). Disruptive technology: What is disruptive technology. Investopedia. https://www.investopedia.com/terms/d/disruptive-technology.asp.

Staniforth, A. (2020a). Countering the use of drones for terrorism. *Crisis Response Journal* 15 (3): 94–95.

Staniforth, A. (2020b). Disruptive technology: the Drone threat landscape. *Crisis Response Journal* 15 (3): 94–96. https://blog.artechhouse.com/wp-content/uploads/ sites/7/2020/10/Disruptive-technology-The-drone-threat-landscape-Crisis- Respone-Journal-.pdf.

Staniforth, A. (2021). Rogue drone detection: Countering the terrorist use of drones to attack public spaces. Policing Insight.

Staniforth, G.M.;.A. (2020). *Countermeasures for Aerial Drones*. ARTECH House.

Stevanovic, J., Stanimirovic, Z., Lakic, Nada., et al. (2012). Stimulating effect of sugar dusting on honey bee grooming behaviour. Available online: https://www.scielo.br/j/ aabc/a/3LVbdvP3yryBBbG85g3R43G/? lang=en&format=html

Tarallo, M. (2020). Fatalities from terror attacks continue to decrease. ASIS Security Management Magazine. https://www.asisonline.org/security-management- magazine/articles/2020/03/fatalities-from-terror-attacks-continue-to-decrease/.

U.S. Army Roadmap for Unmanned Systems (2010–2035). US Department of Army. https://irp.fas.org/program/collect/uas-army.pdf.

Watson, K. (2018). Venezuela president maduro survives 'Drone Assassination' attempt. *BBC News*.

Wellig, P., Speirs, P., Christof Schuepbach et al. (2018). Radar systems and challenges for C-UAV. *2018 19th International Radar Symposium (IRS)*, 1–8. https://doi. org/10.23919/IRS.2018.8448071.

Whyte, E., Frances, J., Gillham, J., and Murray, J. (2018). Skies without Limits: Drones – taking the UK's economy to new heights. PWC. https://www.pwc.co.uk/ intelligent-digital/drones/Drones-impact-on-the-UK-economy-FINAL.pdf.

6

Critical Infrastructure Security Using Computer Vision Technologies

Xindi Zhang[1], Ebroul Izquierdo[1], and Krishna Chandramouli[1,2]

[1] Multimedia and Vision Research Group, School of Electronic Engineering and Computer Science, Queen Mary University of London, London, UK
[2] Venaka Media Limited, London, UK

6.1 Introduction

Modern critical infrastructures (CI) are increasingly turned into distributed, complex cyber-physical systems that require proactive protection and fast restoration against physical or cyber incidents or attacks. In complementary to the cyber threats, the nature of physical threats faced by CI operators is compounded by the use of drones in addition to the human intrusion against the infrastructure with malicious intent. Unmanned aerial vehicles (UAV), also known as drones, have been developed rapidly in recent years. Nowadays, companies such as Amazon, Alibaba, and even pizza chains are pushing forward to use drones, for service provision such as package and food delivery. However, the high-speed mobility and behavior dynamics of UAVs need to be monitored to detect and subsequently, to deal with rogue drones piloted with malicious intent. The misuse of drones can be a huge threat not only to the safety of property but also human lives. Because of the increasing number of drones terrorism, malicious and illicit activities, it is necessary to detect the drone before it getting close to people or buildings (Brust et al. 2018).

An example of the region to be protected against intruders is presented in Figure 6.1. The region surrounding the CI is categorized into (i) safe zone; (ii) alert zone; and (iii) mitigate zone. The safe zone corresponds to the region perimeter in which the presence of any object does not present a danger to the operation of the critical zone and is in legal compliance with the appearance of the object. The region between the safe and alert zone represents an increase in the threat level and has

Security Technologies and Social Implications, First Edition. Edited by Garik Markarian, Ruža Karlović, Holger Nitsch, and Krishna Chandramouli.

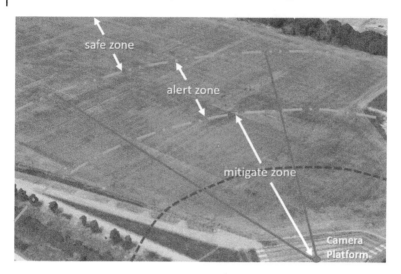

Figure 6.1 The critical infrastructure security perimeter.

breached the legal limit of safety within the operational perimeter of the CI. Any object penetrating the perimeter of the safe zone should be alerted of its presence in the infrastructure command center. Subsequently, the violation of the alert zone is considered to pose an imminent threat to the infrastructure and thus mitigation action should be executed to neutralize the threat before the perimeter of the critical region is penetrated. The distance of these zones varies depending on the CI, the nature of the threat, and the national regulations governing the operations of the CI.

Among the several modalities of information processing, the recent advances in the ability to process visual data have gained prominence since the introduction of deep-learning architectures. Traditionally, the task of object detection is to classify a region for any predefined objects from the training data set. Early attempts at drone detection also adopted a similar approach for the detection of an image region to be consisting of a drone or not. In this context, the application of computer vision was applied for the selection of suitable representations of objects using handcrafted features. The most successful approaches using handcrafted features require a Bag of Visual Words (BoVW) was reported in Sivic and Zisserman (2003) that includes representations of the objects with the help of local feature descriptors such as Scale Invariant Feature Transform (SIFT) (Lowe 1999), Speeded-Up Robust Features (SURF) (Bay et al. 2008), and histogram of oriented gradients (HOG) (Dalal and Triggs 2005). After training a discriminative machine learning (ML) model, e.g. Support Vector Machines (SVM) (Cortes and Vapnik 1995), with such representations, the images are scanned for the occurrence of learned objects with the sliding window technique. These reported methods have two crucial drawbacks. The first one is that the features have to be crafted well for the problem domain to highlight and describe the important information in the image. The second one is the computational burden of the exhaustive search done by the sliding window technique.

Among the general categorization of object detection, in the context of the H2020 research project DEFENDER funded by the EU and protection against physical intrusion to critical infrastructure, the literature on people detection plays a crucial part. With formidable progress achieved in the field of deep learning algorithms within image classification tasks, similar approaches have started to be used for attacking the object detection problem. These techniques can be divided into two simple categories – region proposal-based and single-shot methods. The approaches in the first category differ from the traditional methods by using features learned from data with Convolutional Neural Networks (CNNs) and selective search or region proposal networks to decrease the number of possible regions as reported in Girshick et al. (2014), Girshick (2015) and Ren et al. (2017). In the single-shot approach, the objective is to compute the bounding boxes of the objects in the image directly instead of dealing with regions in the image. A method for this is extracting multi-scale features using CNNs and combining them to predict bounding boxes as presented in He et al. (2015b) and Liu et al. (2016a). Another approach reported in the literature, named You Only Look Once (YOLO) divides the final feature map into a 2D grid and predicts a bounding box using each grid cell (Redmon et al. 2016).

Despite the success of computer vision technologies in addressing real-world applications, the deployment of such solutions within an operational environment requires technical innovation to protect the citizen rights and also to integrate organizational policies on threat identification and monitoring. Addressing these crucial requirements, the chapter presents the activities carried out in DEFENDER project for the development of an intelligent situational awareness framework that integrates the output of key computer vision technologies. The intruder detection algorithm has been applied for monitoring the security perimeter of a CI based on the implementation of spatial rules that identify the malicious perpetrator (either a drone or a person). While the presence of a UAV penetrating the alert zone is considered an imminent security risk, the presence of a human is subsequently analyzed using a person reidentification framework to identify malicious events carried out by perpetrators including infrastructure reconnaissance. In addition, to protect the identity of non-malicious users, the use of privacy-preserving technologies and encrypted media repositories has been integrated. Finally, the rule-based knowledge model is used to analyze the threat severity and provide actionable intelligence to the command center.

The research contributions of the chapter include:

- design and implementation of a situational awareness module that can monitor the horizon for intruder appearance;
- to develop a hardware signalling module that temporally synchronizes the situation awareness module and the object detection component;

- to identify the intruder object based on a multi-class deep-learning network using RFCN; and
- to estimate the distance of the intruder object and alert the command center for implementing countermeasures to neutralize the threat of intruder objects.

The rest of the chapter is structured as follows. In Section 6.2, a detailed review of various person- and drone-detection systems reported in the literature is presented. The review includes the analysis of the long-range radar systems for completeness. However, as the scope of the research presented in the paper relates to the application of computer vision technologies, a detailed analysis of the shortcomings of the techniques reported in the literature is further analyzed. Subsequently, in Section 6.3, an overview of the proposed dual-camera system for autonomous long-range drone detection is presented. The section outlines the various software components that are designed to interface with the underlying hardware equipment. Section 6.5 presents in detail the performance evaluation of the proposed system carried out in support of critical infrastructure operators. The discussion on the distance estimate approaches is considered in Section 6.6. The conclusion and future work are presented in Section 6.7.

6.2   Literature Review

The recent advances in the field of computer vision and deep learning can be summarized into two main categories: (i) methods based on a region proposal; and (ii) methods based on a single shot. The first class of algorithms differs from traditional methods in that it uses CNNs to learn the features of regions extracted through selective search or region proposal networks, as reported in Girshick et al. (2014), Girshick (2015) and Ren et al. (2015). In the single-shot approach, the goal is to directly compute the bounding boxes of objects in the image, rather than processing the regions of the image. One approach uses CNNs to extract multi-scale features and combine them to predict the bounding box as proposed in He et al. (2015b) and Liu et al. (2016b). Another approach, called YOLO, reported in the literature (Redmon et al. 2016), divides the final feature map into a two-dimensional grid and uses each grid cell to predict a bounding box. The techniques mentioned originate from the overall goal of object detection and are not explicitly qualified to tackle drone classification. A large number of datasets that are trained on well-known objects that are frequently encountered in real-life are used to develop a framework for detection.

Within the computer vision community, the research of person detection has attracted studies from interdisciplinary teams, ranging from the design of autonomous vehicles to intelligent surveillance (Jiang and Huynh 2018), person reidentification (Liu et al. 2017; Xu et al. 2017), and robot navigation (Geiger et al. 2013; Khan et al. 2018). Prior to the recent progress in DCNN-based methods (Tian et al. 2015), some researchers combined boosted decision forests with hand-crafted features to obtain pedestrian detectors (Zhang et al. 2015). At the same time, to explicitly model the deformation and occlusion, part-based models and explicit occlusion handling (Zhang et al. 2016) are of concern. Intelligent video surveillance has been one of the most active research areas in computer vision (Wang 2013). Most of the work has been done for single-camera multi-object tracking (MOT). Several existing Multi-Target Multi-Camera Tracking (MTMCT) algorithms reported in the literature are based on an off-line method, which requires considering before and after frames to merge tracklets and do post-processing to merge the trajectory. In the literature, hierarchical clustering (Zhang et al. 2017) and correlation clustering (Ristani and Tomasi 2018) are reported for merging the bounding box into tracklets from neighbor frames. In that case, the tracking is hysteresis (delay in outputting final results), which cannot track the person in time and get the current exact location.

The remotely piloted autonomous systems (RPAS) and the UAVs undertake unpredictable computer-controlled movements that vary in speed and exploit the maneuvering capabilities of the physical object. Their resemblance to other aerial objects such as birds, aeroplanes, result in challenges attributed to automatic detection, identification and most importantly accurate localization in the 3D space. In order to solve this problem, several types of sensors (RF, GPS, radio waves, radar, acoustic, etc.) have been proposed in the literature and subsequently been deployed for drone detection (Taha and Shoufan 2019). While the deployed sensors can identify all the objects, it is important to recognize the specific malicious drone that might be approaching the CI with the intention of creating harm. In this regard, the application of computer vision techniques has resulted in improved performance as reported in Gökçe et al. (2015). While the previously reported approaches considered the use of features extracted from a single-frame appearance of drones, the use of motion and spatiotemporal features has also been studied. In particular, the approach that first creates spatiotemporal cubes using the sliding window method at different scales applies motion compensation to stabilize ST cubes and finally utilizes boosted tree and CNN-based regressors for bounding box detection (Rozantsev et al. 2017). In addition, multi-frame representation of a drone is learnt by convolutional long short-term memory (ConvLSTM) in Yoshihashi et al. (2017). The cross-correlation layer helps generate search windows and localize the drone. Earlier approaches reported in the literature, have focused on detection accuracy with existing datasets. However, those approaches have failed to specify the detection range of distance and the operation speed, which are important in practical applications. Vision-based approaches depend on the appearance feature of the interest target. For long-range targets, the pixels shown in the video are too less to offer enough features. The target is too small to be detected by the algorithm. In this paper, a real-time holistic system is demonstrated to detect intruder drones appearing on the horizon from a far distance against a security area with the help of a dual-camera corporation.

6.3 Critical Infrastructure Security Using Computer Vision Technologies

In this section, individual components developed for the detection of different forms of intruders threatening the operations of the CI are presented. The four components are categorized into (i) detection of drone intruders; and (ii) detection of malicious persons. Both of these components are presented in the following two subsections.

6.3.1 Framework for Detecting Drone Intruders

As presented in Figure 6.1, the functional specification of the system requires the installation of the drone detector at the perimeter of the critical infrastructure able to protect against imminent attacks exploiting the vulnerable pathways, through which the malicious drone could be piloted. Addressing the real-world needs of the operational environment, the conceptual design of the proposed solution is presented in Figure 6.2.

The system implementation contains four components, namely (i) situation awareness module; (ii) pan-tilt-zoom (PTZ) platform; (iii) multi-class drone classifier using deep learning; and (iv) alert command center. In the beginning, there are two cameras, a static camera and a PTZ camera, streaming their video to the system and being aligned at first. The situation awareness module is operating based on static camera videos to monitor intruders. The PTZ platform consists of a pan-tilt platform with a camera that supports programmatic control of the focal length of the lens.

The Raspberry Pi processes the PTZ signals to enable the appropriate binary bits that are interfaced with the servo motors to position the platform precisely. The continuous media stream captured by the camera is transmitted to the analytical component, where the media is processed using the deep-learning network framework for drone detection, and the intruders on the horizon are then identified. When the intruder is identified as a drone, the identification situation and intrusion proof will be reported by the command center. Figure 6.3 shows the various operating states involved in the drone detection platform. The installation phase involves the installation of the detector at the infrastructure perimeter. The next step is to configure the operating environment of the detector, which includes aligning two cameras to identify the region of attack against the background. Subsequently, the analytics component was considered to be two operating states

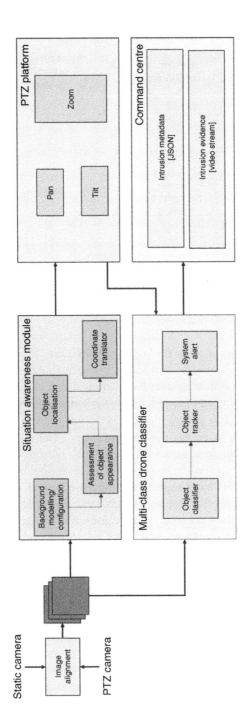

Figure 6.2 Proposed dual-camera system.

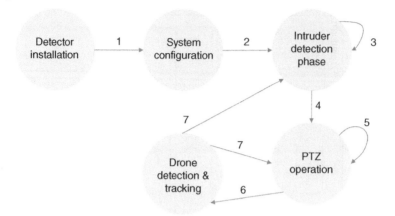

Figure 6.3 Operational states of the proposed system.

and a third state for signalling Raspberry Pi with instructions for PTZ. The rest of the section provides a detailed outline of the various state transitions that were implemented for the proposed system to operate.

6.3.1.1   System Configuration for the Region of Protection

The equipment configuration is a critical step in ensuring the successful operation of the proposed system against a malicious drone attack. It involves the modelling of foreground and ground objects against which the malicious drone could not be piloted. Such foreground objects include trees, grass, and any manmade structure (such as energy distribution poles). The rationale for such a premise is based on the fact that CI are operated away from the urban population due to safety regulations in farmlands. Therefore, the number of intruder objects that could create harm to infrastructures are limited. In most cases, the appearance of birds, aeroplanes, helicopters, and people is a common sight. Therefore, to model the background, the captured video stream is structured into a 20×20 grid as presented in Figure 6.4. The grid offers the security personnel to identify the regions containing the foreground and natural objects, through which the drone could not be piloted. The marked regions are ignored through the use of the binary mask. The binary mask is a black and white image, the grids selected by security personnel are drawn in black, and the remaining regions are drawn in white. After multiplying the binary mask with the frame, any movement in the foreground regions will be ignored. The unfiltered region that presents the vulnerability through the point of attack from the drone is further processed by the analytics component. For the dual-camera system, the intruder detection and zoom into the region are operated by two different cameras. To use the static camera to guide the PTZ operation to reach a certain grid,

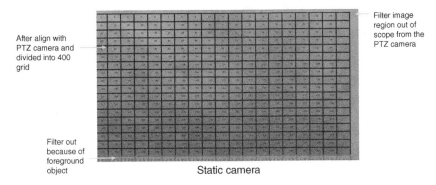

After align with PTZ camera and divided into 400 grid

Filter image region out of scope from the PTZ camera

Filter out because of foreground object

Static camera

Figure 6.4 Detector configuration of the background objects.

the scene they captured should be aligned at the beginning. The method used is the Brute-force matcher, which matches the feature point of two different images and localizes the matched region. Based on the matched region, the area is divided into 400 grids for further detection and guidance. An example is shown in Figure 6.4. The view of the static camera is aligned with the PTZ camera and divided into 400 grids. The area does not align and the grids containing foreground objects are filtered out by the binary mask.

6.3.1.2 Situation Awareness Module

Following the configuration, the static camera enters the intruder detection phase in which the detector continues to scan the horizon for any potential intruder objects. As the objective of the detector is to provide security for the maximum field of view, the focal length of the camera is maintained at a minimum. Therefore, the amount of pixel variations captured by the camera is limited to a small region in the image, with effectively few pixel changes. With such a level of low quantity of information available, the deep-learning networks are not able to successfully process the video resulting in the detection. Therefore, the proposed system uses one of the classical vision-based techniques for edge detection, namely the Canny algorithm to identify the potential objects appearing on the horizon. The operation of the algorithm is summarized in Eq. (6.1), which uses a Gaussian filter to smooth the image and remove noise.

$$H_{ij} = \frac{1}{2\pi\sigma^2} \exp\left(-\frac{\left(i-(k+1)\right)^2 + \left(j-(k+1)\right)^2}{2\sigma^2}\right); \tag{6.1}$$

$$1 \le i, \ j \le (2k+1). \tag{6.2}$$

The equation corresponds to a $(2k+1)\times(2k+1)$ Gaussian filter kernel. The kernel size used in this paper is 5×5 with $\sigma = 1$. The kernel is convoluted with the image to remove high-frequency variations. Subsequently, the image is processed with a Sobel kernel across both vertical and horizontal directions. The derivative in the vertical direction (G_y) and the horizontal direction (G_x) results in the determination of the edge gradient for each pixel:

$$\text{EdgeGradient}(G) = \sqrt{G_x^2 + G_y^2} \tag{6.3}$$

$$\text{Angle}(\theta) = \tan^{-1}\left(\frac{G_y}{G_x}\right) \tag{6.4}$$

Following the assignment of the intensity gradient at each pixel in the video sequence, a threshold is applied to distinguish pixels that appear to be a part of the edge. The value of the threshold is empirically selected to preserve the connectivity of continuous pixel sequences against noise introduced by spatial objects such as clouds. The pixel gradient values below the threshold are ignored as noise and are not considered in subsequent processing of the image sequences.

Further to the computation of the edge gradient, the dilation is operated by Eq. (6.5). The maximizing operation enlarges the edges to be an entire foreground. The dilation kernel used is 3×3.

$$\text{dst}(x,y) = \max_{(x',y'):\text{element}(x',y')\neq 0} \text{src}(x+x', y+y') \tag{6.5}$$

The bounding box is generated by finding the contour of the foreground. The outcome is presented in Figure 6.5. In this example, there are two intruders detected in the view of the static camera. The bigger size of the bounding box means the intruder is closer to the infrastructure which has priority to identify. So, the biggest bounding box is drawn in blue with a red trajectory. The red trajectory is the connection of the center points of previous bounding boxes. The thickness of the trajectory decays with the increasing number of frames. Other objects are drawn in a green box waiting for the next round of operation.

The bounding box of the intruder object to a specific grid in the image captured with the fixed focal length of the static camera facilitates the analytics component to single the Raspberry Pi and the camera to gather additional information from the respective grid through the pan-tilt and zoom operation.

6.3.1.3 PTZ Platform Signalling and Control

The objective of the PTZ operation is to focus on the grid where the intruder has been detected from the static camera and gather additional visual information

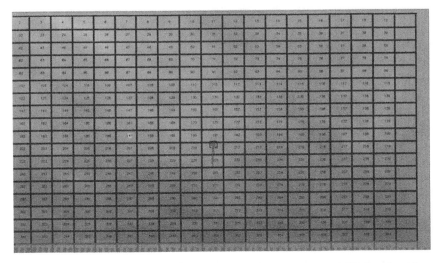

Figure 6.5 Intruder object localization using the edge detection and dilation algorithm.

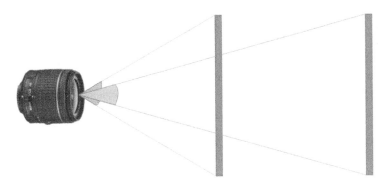

Figure 6.6 The impact of focal length variation on the camera FoV.

to be processed by the deep-learning algorithm. To achieve this objective, the following premise has been adopted. The video stream resolution supported by the camera is full HD resolution (1980×1080 at 30 FPS) and despite the changes in the focal length, the output of the camera remains the same. The variation of the focal length changes to the Field of View (FoV) is presented in Figure 6.6. As the camera is pointed toward the intruder object by progressing increasing the focal length, the FoV narrows which limits the ability to scan large regions.

Considering the neutral state of the camera position is at 90 degrees for both pan and tilt, a look-up table has been created with pre-encoded values that correspond to the estimated changes to be signalled for each of the grid positions as configured in Figure 6.4. To reach a certain block, the platform should pan and tilt in relative degree according to specific values (59, 62, 65, 68, 70, 73, 77, 79, 82, 86, 90, 94, 98, 101, 104, 107, 111, 114, 117, 120) for pan and (108, 106, 104, 102, 101, 100, 99, 97, 95, 92, 90, 88, 87, 85, 83, 82, 79, 77, 75, 73) toward tilt. In the operational environment, pan to 65 degrees and tilt to 106 degrees will reach block 23, pan to 111° and tilt to 77° will reach block 337.

Besides, the ratio of the intruder object bounding box to the overall video frame has been considered in determining the level of zoom to be used for acquiring additional visual information based on which the drone detection can be operated. The relationship between the size of the intruder object and the correspondent signalling of the focal length variations is presented in Table 6.1. The ratio is computed between the width of the video sequence and the width of the bounding box marked at the periphery of the intruder object. The signalling parameter to control the focal length of the camera is determined based on the object ratio as identified by the intrusion detection from the static camera.

The focal length variation will influence the FoV of the camera as shown in Figure 6.6 and Table 6.2. Following the focal length changes, the video stream obtained is further processed by drone detection (as presented in Section 6.3.1.4). It is also important to note that, the signalling received from the analytics component is processed by the Raspberry Pi, and further triggers the servo motor actions, it is important to note that any change to the camera position results in an unfocused image with a video stream containing blurry vision until the camera hardware is re-adjusted using the in build auto-focus functionality. Therefore, the PTZ operation inherently includes a time delay before transitioning to the drone detection phase of operation. During the time of zoom in and re-adjust, the target may change its position which will be out of view for the PTZ camera. So the static camera keeps scanning the horizon and guides the PTZ platform pointing to the latest grid position.

Table 6.1 Mapping of intruder detection size to the zoom level.

Size ratio	Zoom level
>200	15
>150	14
>100	10
>75	9
>50	8
>10	7
>5	4
≤5	0

Table 6.2 The mapping of FoV against camera focal length.

Signalling zoom level	FoV	Camera focal length (mm)
0	54.94	5.27
1	46.53	6.42
2	41.89	7.24
3	36.91	8.34
4	32.21	9.67
5	27.44	11.46
6	22.92	13.83
7	18.05	17.68
8	14.09	22.74
9	10.81	29.73
10	7.66	42.03
11	5.39	59.79
12	4.53	71.16
13	3.78	85.30
14	3.41	94.57

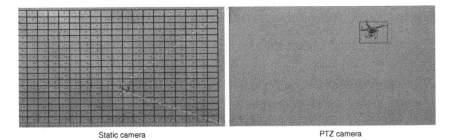

Static camera   PTZ camera

Figure 6.7 The result of the drone detection following the PTZ operation using the RFCN network.

6.3.1.4 Multi-Class Drone Classification using Deep-Learning

After the PTZ platform zooms into the region, the view is large enough for operating object detection as outlined in Figure 6.7. The training model used in the paper is based on an extension of the architecture proposed by Dai et al. (2016). Generally, the region-based object detection can be divided into three sub-networks that perform feature extraction, provide bounding boxes based on the region-proposal network, and perform final classification and bounding box regression. The feature extractor used by this paper is ResNet 101, as proposed in He et al. (2015a).

The RFCN places 100 layers in the shared subnetwork to transfer the time-consuming CNN to the first two shared subnetworks and uses only one convolution layer to calculate predictions. For dimensionality reduction purposes, the last 1000 class fully connected layer in ResNet101 is replaced by a 1 * 1 convolution layer with a depth of 1024. The $K^2(C+1)$-channel convolutional layer is then used to present the position-sensitive score map. RFCN has proposed the position-sensitive score map to improve the accuracy. The region of interest (RoI) is divided into grids of $K*K$ with a depth of $(C+1)$ (1 corresponds to the background) after getting region proposals. Every grid has its own scores. Finally, the grid scores are combined to obtain the final output. The combined vote of the scores for each grid contributes to the determination in the respective RoI of the final scores of the $C+1$ classes. C is the number of classes. Since object detection is trained to identify drones, compared to other objects that may appear in the sky (e.g. birds, aeroplanes, etc.). In this paper, C is set to 3, representing drones, birds, and airplanes, respectively.

RFCN's loss function is as follows, which includes loss of classification and loss of regression. As balance weight, the λ equals 1.

$$L\left(s, t_{x,y,w,h}\right) = L_{cls}\left(s_{c^*}\right) + \lambda\left[c^* > 0\right]L_{reg}\left(t, t^*\right) \tag{6.6}$$

In this equation, c^* is the RoI ground truth label ($c^* = 0$ for background). lambda is the balanced weight that is set to 1. Classification uses the cross-entropy loss of $L_{cls}\left(s_{c^*}\right) = -\log\left(s_{c^*}\right)$. The bounding box coordinates are tx, y, w, h. L_{reg} is a bounding box regression. To train the model, we used annotated images of drones, airplanes, and birds, each with 5000 images of each type. The model is exported in order to make predictions after 200000 training steps.

If the target is detected as a drone, the system will send an alarm based on the estimated distance between the target and the camera platform and keep tracking the drone until the system mitigates the intruder drone. Otherwise, the system will ignore this target and start searching for a new target.

6.3.1.5 Tracking Interface with Sensing Equipment

To achieve accurate and real-time visual tracking of UAVs, three main challenges need to be addressed, namely (i) computation time; (ii) motion blur, changes in the appearance of the UAV and changes in lighting due to environmental effects; and (iii) drifting between the object and the boundary frame. To address these challenges, the novelty of the proposed framework is the integration of the object detection component described in Section 6.3.1.4 with an object-tracking algorithm, called Kernelized Correlation Filters (KCF), as presented in Henriques et al. (2014). The implementation of the algorithm is outlined in Algorithm 6.1. The tracker will update the local area of the UAV based on the previous frame

Input: PTZ_video_frame I_i, Static_video_frame I_{si}

Result: Drone detected in the horizon B

create_tracker;

init_detector;

camera_alignment(I_0, I_{s0});

do in parallel

> **while** *true* **do**
>
>> Grid_ID=intruder_detection(I_{si});
>>
>> initiate_servo_position($Grid\_ID$);
>
> **end**

end

do in parallel

> **if** *if $i == 1$* **then**
>
>> $B = detection\_algorithm(I_i)$;
>>
>> $start\_tracker = false$;;
>>
>> $previous\_frame = I_i$;
>
> **else**
>
>> **while** *true* **do**
>>
>>> read_current_frame (I_i);
>>>
>>> **if** $start\_tracker = true$ **then**
>>>
>>>> reinitialise_tracker(I_{i-1}, B_{i-1});
>>>>
>>>> $B = calculate\_drone\_position(I_i)$;
>>>
>>> **else**
>>>
>>>> $B = update\_drone\_position(I_i)$;
>>>
>>> **end**
>>>
>>> **if** $i\%5 == 0$ **then**
>>>
>>>> $B = detection\_algorithm(I_i)$;
>>>>
>>>> $start\_tracker = true$;
>>>
>>> **end**
>>>
>>> initiate_servo_position(B)
>>
>> **end**
>
> **end**

end

Algorithm 6.1 Pseudocode for the video analytics algorithm for drone detection.

(I_{i-1}) and the bounding box (B) of the previously detected UAV. However, if the detection algorithm identifies the UAV in each fifth frame (k) will reinitialize the tracker in the next frame ($k+1$), based on this frame (k). If the drone is not detected by the detection algorithm, the tracker will be updated continuously based on the previous frame, which is further based on the previous tracking feature. The empirical choice to update the tracker every five frames is to balance the detection algorithm's computational complexity with the need to correct for drift caused by the UAV's rapid motion. If the update interval is more than five frames, the drift introduced by the KCF could lead to an inability to track the UAV accurately. On the other hand, if the update interval is less than five frames, then the detector's computational complexity is too high to enable the UAV to be visually locked in real time.

The results of the detection and tracking algorithm are input to the sensing platform, which controls the movement of the PTZ parameters of the PTZ platform. The relative PTZ parameters are calculated via the initiate_servo_position function to trigger the servo motor controller. Based on the captured video footage, the position is determined by the coordinates of the center point of the detected drone B. If the ratio of x coordinates is less than 0.4 or more than 0.6, the platform is triggered to turn left or right. If the ratio of y coordinates is less than 0.3 or greater than 0.7, the platform will be tilted up or down. The scaling parameter is determined by dividing the frame width by the box width. Whether the parameter is greater than 7 or less than 4, this will cause the camera to zoom in or out.

6.3.1.6 Alert Component

The final component of the proposed framework includes the alarm system to record the drone detection event into the centralized command center deployed in the cloud for enabling the human operator to trigger a suitable mitigation action. The report metadata contains two key data elements, namely (i) event log; and (ii) media log. The event log is a JavaScript Object Notation (JSON) structure consisting of detector deployment specification in terms of the orientation of the camera, geolocation of the detector deployment, the associated reference to the critical infrastructure, and the coordinate translation of the detected drone from 2D visual plane to the 3D world coordinate. In addition, to the event log, it is vital to transmit the associated media element to ensure the human operator is provided with associated evidence prior to the deployment of the respective intruder drone mitigation strategy. While there exist several techniques to transmit continuous media streams through the Internet Protocol (IP) network, the proposed framework adopts the event-emitter design to optimize the data stream transmitted through the network. This is achieved using the event message protocol supported by Apache Kafka (Narkhede et al. 2017). The detector is configured to generate an event for each media timestamp in which the intruder drone is detected. Upon such an event being received, the media bitstream is encoded as a JPEG image and the data is posted to the predetermined message queue. The cloud-hosted Apache Kafka is interfaced with a consumer, which is hosted upon the Flask server (Grinberg 2014). The consumer end-point is accessed via the web browser to facilitate the visualization of the media evidence that is associated with the event log. The Uniform Resource Locator (URL) for accessing the media log is also included in the event log for visualising the media object obtained from the Kafka message queues.

6.4 Intelligent Situational Awareness Framework for Intruder Detection

The proposed intelligent situational awareness framework interfaces directly with the three detectors developed in the project and enables the construction of high-level surveillance events such as intrusion, loitering and access control authentication for early-stage identification of malicious actions against critical infrastructure. The proposed framework is presented in Figure 6.8 and consists of three stages, namely (i) video sequence, captured from the sensor deployed at the perimeter of the infrastructure; (ii) computer vision technologies, capable of processing multiple video streams using the deep-learning network; and (iii) the situational awareness components, in which the organizational policies and practices are encoded to ensure the security restrictions are not violated by malicious actors. In order to protect the privacy and rights of non-malicious actors, the proposed framework incorporates the use of privacy-preserving technologies as outlined in Section 6.4.3. The processed outcome from the situational awareness component

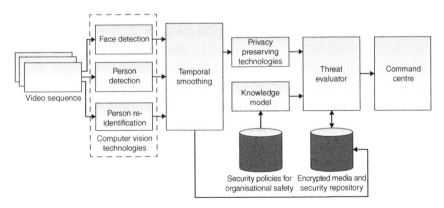

Figure 6.8 Framework.

is then integrated into the command center to categorize the threat and also the severity with which the mitigation actions should be carried out according to the organizational policies. Additional details on the video analytics components integrated within the platform can be found in Arachchilage and Izquierdo (2019).

6.4.1 Temporal Smoothing

The computation of media streams captured from the detectors is often subjected to frame-level processing as supported by the specification of the camera. One of the challenges in performing a frame-level analysis results in the lack of ability to model the global situational awareness of the environment. To address this challenge, the proposed situational awareness component implements a stream analytics solution with the use of latency processing that allows for buffering the input media stream for a few seconds prior to the deployment of the computational module. The stream analytics platform allows for the construction of global situational awareness through the consolidation of the media sources collected in the buffer. The initial latency period of the detector does not affect the performance of the detector, but rather enhances the reliability and severity measure of the alerts generated.

6.4.2 Encrypted Media Repository

Following the implementation of the General Data Protection Regulation (GDPR) across Europe, data privacy and protection have become an inherent necessity to protect against malicious use of the computational systems capable of extracting semantic metadata from the detectors deployed at the perimeter of the critical infrastructure. Despite the ongoing debate between the data privacy and security requirements, the DEFENDER project has adopted the use of a privacy-by-design system, in which all the media data captured from the detectors are stored as encrypted media data. An overview of the system adopted within the project has been presented in Figure 6.9. The encryption is carried out using AES 256 Crypt specification.[1] All the media data extracted from the computational units are encrypted using a predetermined password as adopted by the organizational policies.

6.4.3 Privacy-Preserving Technologies

There are seven privacy-preserving techniques reported in the literature including blur, pixelating, emboss, solid silhouette, skeleton, 3D avatar, and invisibility (Padilla-López et al. 2015). The new capabilities of such systems provide the

---

1 https://www.aescrypt.com/.

Figure 6.9 Encrypted media repository.

computational tools with the ability to collect and index a huge amount of private information about each individual, approaching the perimeter of the critical infrastructure. However, between the balance between privacy and security, the project has adopted the rationale that no personal data should be processed or made available to the command center until a threat has been identified, which requires neutralization. To this end, the use of privacy-by-design methodology incorporated within the media processing framework adopts the use of Gaussian blur to mask the identity of the person against the extraction of usable features. For the person reidentification component, the use of a feature extraction module based on AlexNet protects the identity of the person without compromising the computational ability of the platform. The complementarity between the encrypted media repository and the privacy-preserving technology has will lead to the user acceptance metric evaluation for the deployment of the DEFENDER media processing components for infrastructure security.

6.4.4 Knowledge Model

The knowledge model represents a set of high-level business rules that encodes the notion of abnormal behaviour at the perimeter of critical infrastructure. The syntax adopted for the rule definition is based on JSON representation that systematically formalizes the attributes of the detector, for anomaly detection. The rules encoded for media-based physical security detectors relate to the spatial coordinates which are deemed restricted against public pathways. In addition, the high-level event representation syntax for event detection such as loitering and reconnaissance are also encoded in the JSON format based on the timestamps. The detector outcomes following the media processing are also exported in JSON format as specified in the knowledge base. The threat-level severity is predetermined based on the proximity of the threat against breaching the perimeter of the critical infrastructure.

6.4.5 Threat Evaluator

The threat evaluator module receives input from privacy-preserving technology output and the organizational guidelines on the threat models and severity. In addition, the module will also interact with the encrypted media repository to present the decrypted media data to the command center upon the detection of the threat. The module evaluates the spatial constraints configured within the platform to determine the threat level. For an instance, the intruder detector has two levels of severity based on the proximity of the threat to the critical infrastructure. The severity levels are appropriately identified and the evolution of the threat in time will be continuously monitored through alerts shared with the command center. The spatial configuration of the infrastructure environment has been presented in Figure 6.10. For the determination of high-level threat analyzers such as reconnaissance or loitering, specification of temporal rules have been defined within specific time windows to identify malicious perpetrators. These rules are quantified through a JSON syntax as outlined in Section 6.4.4. The anonymous identity labels assigned to the individual extracted from the detectors are used to visually cluster and enable correlation between the repeated appearance of the same individual near the vicinity of the critical infrastructure. The command center provides a unified interface for the collection of media captured from distributed availability of the detectors. The web interface allows for easy navigation for the selection of different detector outputs that are spatiotemporally indexed.

Figure 6.10 Intrusion detection.

6.4.6 Command Center

The command center is a central interface that interfaces with each of the detectors and integrates the different modules within the proposed framework. Upon the installation of the detector at the perimeter, the detector is configured with the command center through the specification of the IP address through which the detector will communicate with the command center. The detector installation at the Erchie trial site for intruder detection is presented in Figure 6.11. The registration of the detector installation is carried out using a RESTFul interface and JSON metadata consumed by the command center. Subsequently, the evidence collected from the detector both raw data and the processed output are both transmitted to the threat evaluator module, which upon the determination of the data sources, decides to present the privacy-protected results or the raw data based on the severity of the threat level.

One of the challenges of MTMCT framework presented in the literature is the inability of the framework to anchor against a specific Person of Interest (POI) for modelling threat events such as loitering. In this regard, the MTMCT component has been further developed to include "unsupervised multi-camera person reidentification" framework. The overall framework design of the proposed framework is presented in Figure 6.12. The implementation of the person detection component relies on the use of Region-based Fully Convolutional Networks (R-FCN), followed by the feature extraction of the detected person with a set of deep-learning features. The deep-learning features extracted from the identified bounding boxes are then subjected to the application of an unsupervised algorithm for clustering the

Figure 6.11 Detector installation for intruder detection.

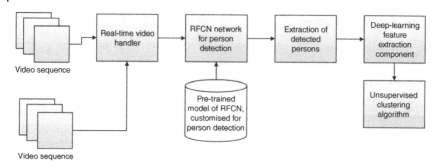

Figure 6.12 Person reidentification.

people. The processing of the deep-learning features is further exploited to ensure the infrastructure operators can provide an anchor image of a POI, to retrieve the appearance of the person across several surveillance cameras.

6.5 Experimental Result

To evaluate the performance of the whole system, each component tests separately. The algorithm part was tested on record videos with ground truth labels to evaluate their performance via average precision (AP) (Everingham et al. 2010) and Central Distance Curve Metric (Cehovin et al. 2015; Wu et al. 2013). The system part was tested by field trials in the real world to evaluate the capability of (i) maximum distance for intruder monitor distance by the static camera, (ii) the overall drone detection performance of the dual-camera system and (iii) the performance of the alert component. Those tests are implemented in Olympic Park, London, with DJI Phantom 3, which offers a ground truth trajectory with a time stamp for evaluating the system.

In the algorithmic part, the proposed security framework for targeting drone attacks is experimentally evaluated using visual analysis techniques in two phases, namely (i) the accuracy of the detection algorithm implemented using RFCN; and (ii) the efficiency of the proposed approach in tracking the flight path of the drone. The experimental results are based on a set of video footage in an urban environment taken within 450 m from the attack point, using the DJI Phantom 3 Standard as a pilot. A total of 39 attack simulations were created, with the duration of each attack ranging from 6 to 117 seconds, resulting in a total of 12.36 minutes of drone flight.

For the system part, the autonomous drone detection system is installed. The static camera and PTZ camera have the same focal length and imitate the situation of attaching from the horizon. The system is placed on the perimeter of the infrastructure and points to the direction outside. When the intruder moves toward the infrastructure, the object will be captured by the monitor camera. The long-range distance against which the PTZ operation is triggered. These aspects have been presented in the rest of the section along with the hyperparameters used in the experimental evaluation. The attack against the infrastructure was simulated using DJI Mavic Pro[2] and Phantom 3[3] drones, both of which belong to the class of mini-drones.

6.5.1 Drone Detection Accuracy

The evaluation protocol used for drone detection is AP (Everingham et al. 2010), which is the summary of the shape of the precision/recall curve.

The experimental results are based on a set of video clips piloted from the point of attack, taken by a standard DJI Phantom 3 drone in an urban environment. A total of 39 simulations of attacks were made, with the length of each attack varying from 6 to 117 seconds, resulting in a total flight time of 12.36 minutes for the drone. The performance of the proposed RFCN Resnet101 network was compared with three other models of the deep learning network, namely SSD Mobilenet (Liu et al. 2015), SSD Inception v2 (Szegedy et al. 2015) and Faster RCNN Resnet101 (Ren et al. 2015). They have been trained and tested on the same dataset. Result pairs are shown in Table 6.3.

6.5.2 Tracking Accuracy

The performance of the proposed detection and tracking framework is quantified according to Cehovin et al. (2015) and Wu et al. (2013) using the performance evaluation of the central distance curve metric for object tracking. The central distance curve metric measures the distance between the center of the tracking bounding box and the center of the ground truth box and summarizes the ratio at different thresholds. The test results of the system shown in Figure 6.13 represent the metrics of the central distance curve for different UAV

Table 6.3 Drone detection accuracy.

Method	AP (%)
SSD Mobilenet (Howard et al. 2017; Liu et al. 2015)	30.39
SSD Inception v2 (Szegedy et al. 2015)	7.78
Faster RCNN Resnet101 (Ren et al. 2015)	69.49
RFCN Resnet101	81.16

2 https://www.dji.com/uk/mavic.
3 https://www.dji.com/uk/phantom-3-pro.

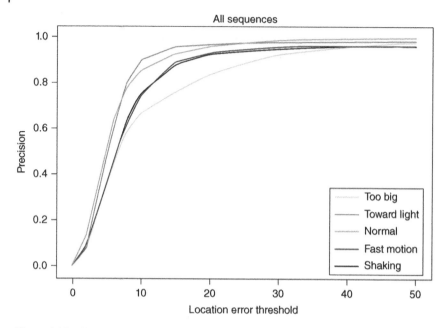

Figure 6.13 Central pixel distance curve of different situations.

flight paths. The various curves describe the different scenarios in which the UAV flight paths occur. Such scenarios include (i) the drone appearing in front of the sensing platform; (ii) the drone passing in front of the sun; (iii) the drone flight occurring at the horizon; (iv) the drone speed and acceleration exceeding the approved specification due to environmental reality; and (v) the motion aspect added by the sensing equipment while the drone video is being filmed.

A frame is considered to be tracked correctly if the predicted center of the target is within the distance threshold of the ground truth. At lower thresholds, higher accuracy means that the tracker is more accurate, and missing the target will prevent it from achieving perfect accuracy over a very large threshold range. When a representative accuracy score was required, a threshold of 20 pixels was selected. In the five scenarios defined for the framework evaluation, the overall average accuracy score of 95.2% for all footages was achieved and is shown in Figure 6.13.

6.5.3 Intruder Detection Capability

The capacity of the system depends on the static camera, which operates for intruder detection. The wider and higher resolution camera can cover more area and long distance. The static camera used in this experiment has the same focal length as the PTZ camera.

Table 6.4 The capability regards the method.

Method	Max distance (m)	Ratio
Motion detection	80	58
Canny (30 100)	160	116
Canny + sharpen	200	146
Canny (15 300) + sharpen	250	166

The maximum distance between the camera with the drone (Phantom 3) that the intruder detection can detect is shown in Table 6.4. The ratio is the frame width divided by the bounding box width of the intruder object. The motion detector can also be used for intruder detection, which considers the moving object in the scene. However, the maximum distance is too small for attack precaution. Canny with minimum threshold 30 and maximum threshold 100 increases the distance twice as the distance in motion detection. Adding some image-processing methods for prepossessing helps improve the capability. The frame is sharpened before Canny makes the edge much clearer to detect. After adjusting the threshold of Canny, the maximum distance was further extended.

6.5.4 System Detection and Tracking Performance

The overall functionality of the dual-camera system has two phases: first, detect the intruder drone from the horizon, then keep tracking the trajectory of the drone's movement. The detection performance is related to Sections 6.5.1 and 6.5.3. Since the PTZ camera can zoom into the grid with regard to the guidance of the static camera, the overall detection part performance has 81.16AP with a maximum distance of 250 m.

Since the goal of the tracking phase is to have the object at the center of the video and we do not have ground truth values in the actual test, we can rate each frame's output and measure the average score of the total frames. The evaluation method used is shown in Figure 6.14. If the bounding box center point is in the red zone, the precision of detection and tracking is 100%. However, if the center point is inside the yellow zone, it is given an accuracy score of 75%. Similarly, if the center is in the blue zone, the frame will be given a 50% accuracy score. Finally, if the region does not contain the drone's presence, a 0% accuracy score is given, resulting in the drone's loss, either through a visual analysis module software implementation or through a camera-controlled delay phase.

The overall PTZ functionality is shown in Figure 6.15, which maps the overall flight path performed by the UAV. In the sense of real-time drone monitoring, one of the main challenges that need to be tackled is ensuring that the drone is large

Figure 6.14 Performance calculation.

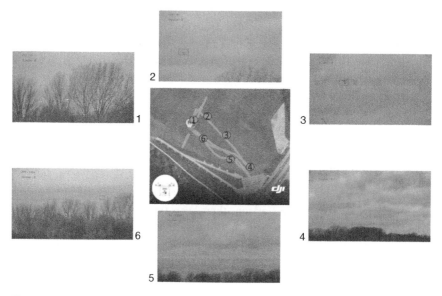

Figure 6.15 The trajectory of a drone flight with tracking by PTZ camera.

enough for the video analytics feature to be properly detected. In this regard, it is critical to control and trigger the camera's zoom parameters to check the horizon prior to drone intrusion. In addition, since the momentum and direction of the UAV are heavily influenced by environmental parameters such as wind speed and direction (both headwind and tailwind), the accuracy of the tracking algorithm depends on the latency of the control hardware platform. Thus, three parameters are controlled in the proposed framework, called pan, tilt, and zoom to ensure tracking of the performance of the UAV. To quantify the sensing platform's performance objectively, it is crucial to consider the feedback received from the component of the analysis. The input given to the analytics component, however, depends on the visual information obtained from the horizon.

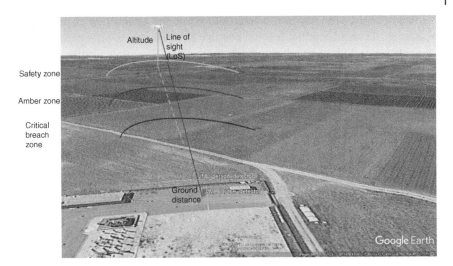

Figure 6.16 Protection area.

6.5.5 Evaluation of System Latency Against Geographical Perimeter

The region is divided into several zones depending on the distance between the object with the location of the camera system as shown in Figure 6.16. A distance larger than 250 m is a safe zone. The object inside this region is ignored which cannot cause any threat to the infrastructure. A distance between 250 and 150 m is an alert zone. Even if the distance is still long enough, the object may approach the infrastructure at a fast speed. So, the system pays attention and sends an alarm to the system. A distance lesser than 150 m is a mitigate zone. The intruder is close enough and can cause damage or attack the infrastructure. So, the system sends a strong alarm and triggers other neutralized system to prevent the attack. The field of view is shown in the blue line, which depends on the focal length of the static camera. The angle in our experiments is 54.94°.

In our experiment, the distance estimation is realized by searching in a distance Look-Up-Table (LUT) with regard to the size of the detection bounding box and the zoom level of the PTZ camera. We build this LUT every 10 m. After getting the estimated distance regarding the protection area definition, the system will send an alarm to show the situation.

6.6 Distance Estimation

The proposed system has performed sufficiently well-detecting drones from 80 to 220 m for the attacks simulated by mini-drones, one of the key operational requirements that have been considered out of scope in the paper relates to the distance estimation of the drone upon the detection. While the localization of the drone position in 3D world coordinate is not possible to be computed without the use of triangulation technique or other suitable approaches, the distance estimation is a vital parameter for the infrastructure operators to be able to develop strategies for the deployment of mitigation protocols. Thus, a brief review of how the visual information captured from the camera could be translated into the distance estimation is presented.

In order to locate the intruder drone, the distance between the drone and the camera in the real world should be calculated. The proposed distance computation considers the camera focal length measure as outlined in Figure 6.17.

According to the trigonometric relationship between the angle and the edge, the relationship between the real width and the real distance in the world coordinate system can be shown as follows:

$$\text{real width} = 2\tan\frac{\alpha}{2}\cdot\text{real distance}$$

$$(6.7)$$

α is the horizontal field of view according to the zoom level, which can be found in Table 6.2.

The ratio of the real width of the field and the width of the real drone is equal to the ratio of the frame width and the drone width in the frame. So, the equation is:

$$\frac{\text{real width}}{\text{real drone width}} = \frac{\text{frame width}}{\text{frame drone width}}$$

$$(6.8)$$

And the equation can be transformed into:

$$\text{real width} = \frac{\text{frame width}}{\text{frame drone width}}\cdot\text{real drone width}$$

$$(6.9)$$

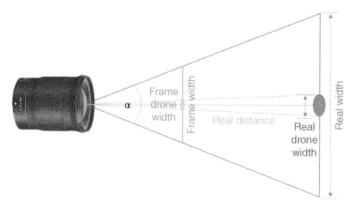

Figure 6.17 The relation between the frame and the real world.

Then putting the equation into Eq. (6.7) will get:

$$\text{real distance} = \frac{\left(\text{frame width} / \text{drone width in frame}\right) \cdot \text{real drone width}}{2\tan\left(\alpha_{zoom} / 2\right)} \qquad (6.10)$$

The frame width equals the resolution of the HD video captured by the camera. The width of the drone detected within the frame is to be obtained by the area of the detected bounding box. The appearance of the drone in the real world is dependent upon the physical dimensions of different drones as specified by the manufacturers. Following the level of focal length parameter of the camera, the distance between the camera and the detected drone can be estimated by Eq. (6.10). The validation of this mathematical analysis is to be carried out against different sizes of the drone.

6.7 Conclusion

In this paper, an operational prototype of a long-range drone detection system is presented equipped to protect CI against drone attacks. The system presents a seamless operation between the deep-learning algorithm signalling low-cost hardware. The novelty of the paper lies in the ability of the system to detect intruder objects flying at the perimeter of infrastructure with minimal visual information and subsequently attain more visual data to detect malicious drones. The mechanism helps to enlarge the distance of protection. The design of the dual-camera system helps to minimize the latency between the intruder object monitor phase and the deep-learning-based drone detection phase so that is capable to run in real-time. The combination between RFCN and KCF helps improve the drone detection accuracy and as outlined in the experimental results an overall 95.2% AP score against drone attacks was achieved by the platform. The future work will continue to investigate approaches to compute the distance which can be used to deploy mitigating strategies for infrastructure security.

References

Arachchilage, S.W. and Izquierdo, E. (2019). A framework for real-time face-recognition. *2019 IEEE Visual Communications and Image Processing (VCIP)*, Sydney, NSW, Australia (December 2019), 1–4. https://doi.org/10.1109/VCIP47243.2019.8965805.

Bay, H., Tuytelaars, T., Van Gool, L. et al. (2008). Speeded-up robust features (SURF). In: *Computer Vision – ECCV 2006. ECCV 2006. Lecture Notes in Computer Science*, vol. 3951 (ed. A. Leonardis, H. Bischof and A. Pinz). Berlin, Heidelberg: Springer. https://doi.org/10.1007/11744023_32.

Brust, M.R. Danoy, G., Bouvry, P. et al. (2018). Defending against intrusion of malicious UAVs with networked UAV defense swarms. *CoRR* abs/1808.06900. arXiv: 1808.06900. http://arxiv.org/abs/1808.06900.

Cehovin, L., Leonardis, A., and Kristan, M. (2015). Visual object tracking performance measures revisited. *CoRR* abs/1502.05803. arXiv: 1502.05803. http://arxiv.org/abs/1502.05803.

Cortes, Corinna and Vladimir Vapnik (1995). Support-vector networks. *Machine Learning*. https://doi.org/10.1023/A:1022627411411.

Dai, J., Li, Y., He, K. et al. (2016). R-FCN: object detection via region-based fully convolutional networks. *CoRR* abs/1605.06409. arXiv: 1605.06409. http://arxiv.org/abs/1605.06409.

Dalal, N. and Triggs, B. (2005). Histograms of oriented gradients for human detection. *Proceedings – 2005 IEEE Computer Society Conference on Computer Vision and Pattern Recognition, CVPR 2005*. ISBN: 0769523722. https://doi. org/10.1109/CVPR.2005.177.

Everingham, M., van Gool, L., Williams, C. K. I. et al. (2010). The pascal visual object classes (VOC) challenge. *International Journal of Computer Vision* 88 (2): 303–338.

Geiger, A., Lenz, P., Stiller, C. et al. (2013). "Vision meets robotics: the KITTI dataset". *International Journal of Robotics Research*. https://doi.org/10.1177/0278364913491297.

Girshick, R. (2015). Fast R-CNN. *Proceedings of the IEEE International Conference on Computer Vision*. arXiv: 1504.08083. ISBN: 9781467383912. https://doi. org/10.1109/ICCV.2015.169.

Girshick, R., Donahue, J., Darrell, T. et al. (2014). Rich feature hierarchies for accurate object detection and semantic segmentation. *Proceedings of the IEEE Computer Society Conference on Computer Vision and Pattern Recognition*, 1440–1448. arXiv: 1311.2524. ISBN: 9781479951178. https://doi.org/10.1109/CVPR.2014.81.

Gökçe, F., Üçoluk, G., Şahin, E. et al. (2015). Vision-based detection and distance estimation of micro unmanned aerial vehicles. *Sensors* 15 (9): 23805–23846.

Grinberg, M. (2014). *Flask Web Development: Developing Web Applications with Python*, 1e. O'Reilly Media, Inc. ISBN: 1449372627, 9781449372620.

He, K., Zhang, X., Ren, S. et al. (2015a). Deep residual learning for image recognition. *CoRR* abs/1512.03385. arXiv: 1512.03385. http://arxiv.org/abs/1512.03385.

He, K., Zhang, X., Ren, S. et al. (2015b). Spatial pyramid pooling in deep convolutional networks for visual recognition. *IEEE Transactions on Pattern Analysis and Machine Intelligence* 37 (9): 1904–1916. https://doi.org/10.1109/ TPAMI.2015.2389824.

Henriques, J. F., Caseiro, R., Martins, P. et al. (2014). High-speed tracking with kernelized correlation filters. *CoRR* abs/1404.7584. arXiv: 1404.7584. http:// arxiv.org/abs/1404.7584.

Howard, A. G., Zhu, M., Chen, B. et al. (2017). MobileNets: efficient convolutional neural networks for mobile vision applications. *CoRR* abs/1704.04861. arXiv: 1704.04861. http://arxiv.org/abs/1704.04861.

Jiang, Z. and Huynh, D.Q. (2018). Multiple pedestrian tracking from monocular videos in an interacting multiple model framework. *IEEE Transactions on Image Processing.* https://doi.org/10.1109/TIP.2017.2779856.

Khan, Asif, Bernhard Rinner, and Andrea Cavallaro (2018). Cooperative robots to observe moving targets. *IEEE Transactions on Cybernetics.* https://doi.org/10.1109/ TCYB.2016.2628161.

Liu, W., Anguelov, D., Erhan, D. et al. (2015). SSD: single shot multiBox detector. *CoRR* abs/1512.02325. arXiv: 1512.02325. http://arxiv.org/abs/1512.02325.

Liu, W., Anguelov, D., Erhan, D. et al. (2016a). SSD: single shot multibox detector. *Lecture Notes in Computer Science (including subseries Lecture Notes in Artificial Intelligence and Lecture Notes in Bioinformatics).* ISBN: 9783319464473. https://doi. org/10.1007/978-3-319-46448-0_2.

Liu, W., Anguelov, D., Erhan, D. et al. (2016b). SSD: single shot multibox detector. *European Conference on Computer Vision*, Amsterdam, The Netherlands (8–16 October 2016), 21–37. Springer. http://www.eccv2016.org/.

Liu, Z., Wang, D., and Lu, H. (2017). Stepwise metric promotion for unsupervised video person reidentification. *Proceedings of the IEEE International Conference on Computer Vision.* ISBN: 9781538610329. https://doi.org/10.1109/ICCV.2017.266.

Lowe, D.G. (1999). Object recognition from local scale-invariant features. *Proceedings of the IEEE Internationa, Conference on Computer Vision.* https://doi.org/10.1109/ ICCV.1999.790410.

Narkhede, N., Shapira, G., and Palino, T. (2017). *Kafka: The Definitive Guide Real-Time Data and Stream Processing at Scale*, 1e. O'Reilly Media, Inc. ISBN: 1491936169, 9781491936160.

Padilla-López, J.R., Chaaraoui, A.A., and Flórez-Revuelta, F. (2015). *Visual privacy protection methods: a survey. Expert Systems with Applications* 42: 4177–4195. https://doi.org/10.1016/j.eswa.2015.01.041.

Redmon, J., Divvala, S., Girshick, R. et al. (2016). You only look once: unified, real-time object detection. *Proceedings of the IEEE Computer Society Conference on Computer Vision and Pattern Recognition,* 779–788. ISBN: 9781467388504. https://doi.org/10.1109/CVPR.2016.91.

Ren, S., He, K., Girshick, R. et al. (2015). Faster R-CNN: towards real-time object detection with region proposal networks. *CoRR* abs/1506.01497. arXiv: 1506.01497. http://arxiv.org/abs/1506.01497.

Ren, S., He, K., Girshick, R. et al. (2017). Faster R-CNN: towards real-time object detection with region proposal networks. *IEEE Transactions on Pattern Analysis and Machine Intelligence. arXiv: 1506.01497. issn: 01628828.* https://doi.org/ 10.1109/TPAMI.2016.2577031.

Ristani, E. and Tomasi, C. (2018). Features for multi-target multi-camera tracking and re-identification. *Proceedings of the IEEE Computer Society Conference on Computer Vision and Pattern Recognition*. arXiv: 1803.10859. ISBN: 9781538664209. https://doi.org/10.1109/CVPR.2018.00632.

Rozantsev, A., Lepetit, V., and Fua, R. (2017). Detecting flying objects using a single moving camera. *IEEE Transactions on Pattern Analysis and Machine Intelligence* 39 (5): 879–892. https://doi.org/10.1109/TPAMI.2016.2564408.

Sivic, J. and Zisserman, A. (2003). Video google: a text retrieval approach to object matching in videos. *Proceedings of the IEEE International Conference on Computer Vision*. https://doi.org/10.1109/ICCV.2003.1238663.

Szegedy, C., Vanhoucke, V., Ioffe, S. et al. (2015). Rethinking the inception architecture for computer vision. *CoRR* abs/1512.00567. arXiv: 1512.00567. http://arxiv.org/abs/1512.00567.

Taha, B. and Shoufan, A. (2019). Machine learning-based drone detection and classification: state-of-the-art in research. *IEEE Access* 7: 138669–138682. https://doi.org/10.1109/ACCESS.2019.2942944.

Tian, Y., Luo, P., Wang, X. et al. (2015). Deep learning strong parts for pedestrian detection. *Proceedings of the IEEE International Conference on Computer Vision*. ISBN: 9781467383912. https://doi.org/10.1109/ICCV.2015.221.

Wang, X. (2013). Intelligent multi-camera video surveillance: a review. *Pattern Recognition Letters* https://doi.org/10.1016/j.patrec.2012.07.005.

Wu, Y., Lim, J., and Yang, M. (2013). Online object tracking: a benchmark. *2013 IEEE Conference on Computer Vision and Pattern Recognition*, 2411–2418. https://doi.org/10.1109/CVPR.2013.312.

Xu, S., Cheng, Y., Gu, K., et al. (2017). Jointly attentive spatial-temporal pooling networks for video-based person reidentification. *Proceedings of the IEEE International Conference on Computer Vision*. arXiv: 1708.02286. ISBN: 9781538610329. 10.1109/ICCV.2017.507.

Yoshihashi, R., Trinh, T. T., Kawakami, R. et al. (2017). Learning multi-frame visual representation for joint detection and tracking of small objects. *CoRR* abs/1709.04666. arXiv: 1709.04666. http://arxiv.org/abs/1709.04666.

Zhang, S., Benenson, R., and Schiele, B. (2015). Filtered channel features for pedestrian detection. *Proceedings of the IEEE Computer Society Conference on Computer Vision and Pattern Recognition*. https://doi.org/10.1109/CVPR.2015.7298784.

Zhang, L., Lin, L., Liang, X. et al. (2016). Is faster R-CNN doing well for pedestrian detection? *Lecture Notes in Computer Science (including subseries Lecture Notes in Artificial Intelligence and Lecture Notes in Bioinformatics)*. https://doi.org/10.1007/978-3-319-46475-6_28. arXiv: 1607.07032.

Zhang, Z., Wu, J., Zhang, W. et al. (2017). Multi-target, multi-camera tracking by hierarchical clustering: recent progress on dukeMTMC project. *CoRR* abs/1712.09531. arXiv: 1712.09531. http://arxiv.org/abs/1712.09531.

7

Evaluation of Content Fusion Algorithms for Large and Heterogeneous Datasets

Theodoros Alexakis, Nikolaos Peppes, Evgenia Adamopoulou,
Konstantinos Demestichas, and Konstantina Remoundou

Institute of Communication and Computer Systems, National Technical University of Athens, Athens, Greece

7.1 Introduction

In the last few decades, there is a shift in human activities from person-to-person communication to online interaction. Information and Communication Technologies (ICTs) are integrated more than ever in today's society and crime just followed the same path. The boundaries of technology exploitation by criminals are only limited by their capabilities and expertise. So, it consists quite a challenge for LEAs and security practitioners to answer effectively to their methods. In this direction, one of the most common challenges faced in almost every aspect of the technological world is how to handle heterogeneous, big data streams. This does not seem to differ for crime investigation processes where vast amounts of heterogeneous data referring to people, places, events, actions, and so on are involved. Thus, state-of-the-art methods and tools of knowledge representation and information extraction are needed to be adapted to the complex and dynamic crime investigation domain (Dzemydiene and Kazemikaitiene 2005).

Till today, LEAs engaged systems that consist of basically Relational Database Management Systems (RDBMS) or physical copies. In systems like these, it is not possible to correlate information in an automatic and fast way so as to decrease the investigation time. Furthermore, data originating from different data sources might contain instances related, for example, to the same persons that cannot be easily identified in RDBMS systems or physical copies without the human effort. Thus, LEAs and security investigators and practitioners are willing to replace their

Security Technologies and Social Implications, First Edition. Edited by Garik Markarian,
Ruža Karlović, Holger Nitsch, and Krishna Chandramouli.
© 2023 The Institute of Electrical and Electronics Engineers, Inc.
Published 2023 by John Wiley & Sons, Inc.

outdated tools with a new technical infrastructure that can speed up their investigations. The detection of duplicate instances is such an example of a process than can be highly accelerated when knowledge extraction methods are applied.

The procedure for merging duplicate instances is often called data fusion. Data fusion according to Hall and Llinas (1997) is the combination of data from multiple sources and associated databases in order to achieve improved accuracy and more specific inferences than could be achieved by the use of a single source alone.

The person fusion methodology described in this chapter calculates a similarity degree between pairs of different person instances using different algorithms in three different-sized datasets so as to provide useful insight into their performance. Nevertheless, in crime investigations, the decision of the fusion/merger of any kind of data is up to authorized personnel of the LEAs (e.g. investigators, officers, etc.) in order to avoid any useful information loss. The data that can be used as input to a person fusion tool can be stored in an ontology, which creates a common communication language and understanding among different cooperating tools such as the person fusion one (Masita et al. 2017).

7.2 Data Preprocessing and Similarity Calculation Techniques

The duplicated or misspelled person attributes such as last name, first name, middle name, and place of birth. are quite a common problem in vast data streams from numerous heterogeneous sources. Thus, there is the need to establish a mechanism which firstly would gather and prepare the data (preprocessing) and then via specific algorithms and methods would calculate similarity metrics for each pair of person instances based on their declared attribute. More specifically, Elmagarmid et al. (Elmagarmid et al. 2006) mention that there are two distinct stages of the process; (i) the data preparation; and (ii) the calculation of similarity metrics. So, the data preparation or preprocessing or, as it is widely known as the Extraction, Transform, and Loading (ETL) procedure contains different stages the main of which are: parsing, data transformation, and data standardization (Elmagarmid et al. 2006; Vassiliadis 2009). Parsing mainly refers to the identification and isolation of specific data pieces such as person attributes in vast volumes of raw data and aims at focusing only on the data needed for a specific task or process. Thus, it is easier to process and compare specific data samples than complex and irrelevant data. Following that, the transformation process of the data practically transforms data into specific data types and formats suitable for the corresponding application. Data transformation is directly connected to data standardization. It is of utmost importance to convert the data, which in our case refers to the personal attributes, which are parsed through various sources in a common unified format for interoperability purposes.

After the steps described earlier for the data preprocessing and standardization, the similarity algorithms/methods can be applied so as to detect similar person instances based on their declared attributes found in the various data sources. There are various methods to calculate the similarity between two different pieces of information, which can be classified into five main categories according to Felix Naumann (Naumann 2013): (i) Edit-based similarity; (ii) Token-based similarity; (iii) Hybrid; (iv) Phonetic or sound-based similarity; and (v) Domain-dependent. In Table 7.1, the classification of several different methods of similarity calculation in the five main categories mentioned earlier is depicted.

The edit-based similarity methods as well as token-based and hybrid methods focus mainly on textual similarity. Thus, these types of similarity metrics are designed to handle typographical errors well. Also, as is often the case, typographical conventions lead to rearrangement of words (e.g. "John Doe" versus "Doe, John"). In such cases, token-based metrics perform better. In addition to the textual files, during investigations, LEAs also gather audio testimonies, which require

Table 7.1 Similarity metrics categorization.

Category	Method
Edit-based	Jaro
	Jaro-Winkler
	Hamming
	Levenshtein
	Damerau-Levenshtein
	Smith-Waterman
	Smith-Waterman-Gotoh
Token-based	Words/n-grams
	Cosine similarity
	Dice
	Jaccard
Hybrid	Monge-Elakn
	Soft TF-IDF
Phonetic	Metaphone
	Double metaphone
	New York State Identification and Intelligence System (NYSIIS)
	Kolner Phonetik
	Soundex
Domain-dependent	Rules
	Numeric attributes
	Dates

phonetic similarity metrics. Textual similarity metrics focus on the string-based representation of the database records. However, strings may be phonetically similar even if they are not similar in a character or token level. The phonetic similarity metrics are trying to address such issues and match such strings. The earlier mentioned categories are a general approach to similarity metrics and for the purposes of this study, we mainly focus on textual files and the corresponding features.

7.3 Description of the Algorithms Used

The person fusion methodology presented in this chapter engages textual data that can be processed using several different algorithms among those presented in the Table 7.1. Thus, selected algorithms for experimentation in the scope of this study include Jaro, Jaro-Winkler, Levenshtein, Cosine similarity and Jaccard similarity. The aforementioned selection was performed in order to test the efficiency and the behavior of both edit-based and token-based algorithms for the task of person instances comparison. The exclusive choice of edit-based and token-based algorithms was underpinned by their appropriateness for textual analysis. Further details on these algorithms and the way they are implemented for the considered person fusion tool are provided in the following paragraphs.

7.3.1 Jaro Similarity and Distance

The Jaro similarity was introduced by Mathew Jaro in 1989 (Jaro 1989). The Jaro similarity metric basically calculates the similarity between two given strings. The result of this calculation is from 0 to 1. 1 means that the two strings are exactly the same whereas 0 indicates that the two strings are totally different. The Jaro similarity can be calculated using equation (7.1) as seen below:

$$\text{Jaro similarity} = \begin{cases} 0, for\, m = 0 \\ \frac{1}{3}\left(\frac{m}{|s_1|} + \frac{m}{|s_1|} + \frac{m-t}{m}\right), for\, m! = 0 \end{cases} \tag{7.1}$$

where:
- m is the number of matching characters. As matching characters are considered the characters that their distance is not bigger than the result of the equation (7.2):

$$\left\lfloor \frac{\max(|s_1|,|s_2|)}{2} \right\rfloor - 1 \tag{7.2}$$

- *t* is half the number of transpositions. A transposition is considered to occur when two characters are the same but not in the same place in the two strings examined. Thus, the number of transpositions is half the number of the matched misplaced characters.

$|s_1|$, $|s_2|$ are the lengths of strings s_1 and s_2, respectively

In addition to the Jaro similarity metric, the Jaro distance metric calculates how distant two strings are. Thus, as shown in equation (7.3), Jaro distance is the difference of the Jaro similarity value from 1.

$$\text{Jaro distance} = 1 - \text{Jaro similarity} \tag{7.3}$$

7.3.2 Jaro-Winkler Similarity and Distance

As an evolution to the Jaro similarity metric, William Winkler, in 1990 (Winkler 1990), introduced his own variant named as Jaro-Winkler similarity. The main differentiation between these two approaches is that the Jaro-Winkler similarity engages a prefix with length *l*. The use of this prefix enables the algorithm to favor strings that match from the beginning for a set prefix of length *l* characters. In practice, that means that this method emphasizes more on strings that have the first *l* characters similar. The Jaro-Winkler similarity can be calculated, then, as depicted, in equation (7.4):

$$\text{Jaro} - \text{Winkler similarity} = \text{sim}_{\text{Jaro}} + lp\left(1 - \text{sim}_{\text{Jaro}}\right) \tag{7.4}$$

where:

- sim_{Jaro} is the Jaro similarity as calculated by equation (7.1)
- *l* is the length of the prefix at the start of the string
- *p* is a constant scaling factor. The value of *p* is calculated as shown in equation (7.5)

$$p \le \frac{1}{L} \tag{7.5}$$

L is the maximum value (number of characters) of the length *l*. Thus, the Jaro-Winkler similarity is always equal or less to the value 1.

The Jaro-Winkler distance is similar to the Jaro distance metric and is calculated as shown in equation (7.6).

$$\text{Jaro} - \text{Winkler distance} = 1 - \text{Jaro} - \text{Winkler similarity} \tag{7.6}$$

7.3.3 Levenshtein Distance and Similarity

Vladimir Levenshtein presented its distance metric regarding two strings in 1965 for the first time in the Russian language while later the same year, the English version of his article appeared (Levenshtein 1965). Levenshtein distance is the smallest number of character-edit operations needed in order to transform one string so as to be identical to another. The edit operation contains insertion, deletion, and substitution. The Levenshtein distance between two strings can be calculated as depicted in equation (7.7):

$$
\text{lev}_{s_1,s_2} =
\begin{cases}
\max(i,j) & \text{if} \min(i,j) = 0 \\
\min
\begin{cases}
\text{lev}_{s_1,s_2}(i-1,j)+1 \\
\text{lev}_{s_1,s_2}(i,j-1)+1 \\
\text{lev}_{s_1,s_2}(i-1,j-1)+1_{\left(s_{1i} \neq s_{2j}\right)}
\end{cases}
& \text{otherwise}
\end{cases}
\tag{7.7}
$$

where:
- lev_{s_1,s_2} is the Levenshtein distance between string s_1 and string s_2
- i is the index of each character of string s_1
- j is the index of each character of string s_2

In equation (7.7) the first branch denotes the number of insertion or deletion operations needed to transform a string into an empty string while the second branch is practically a recursive expression, where the first subbranch represents the deletion operation, the second the insertion and the third the substitution operation.

The Levenshtein distance is often used so as to calculate a normalized metric called Levenshtein similarity or normalized Levenshtein distance and is calculated as shown in equation (7.8).

$$
\text{Levenshtein similarity} = 1 - \frac{\text{lev}_{s_1,s_2}}{\max\left(|s_1|,|s_2|\right)}
\tag{7.8}
$$

where:
- lev_{s_1,s_2} is the Levenshtein distance between string s_1 and string s_2
- $|s_1|$ is the length of string s_1
- $|s_2|$ is the length of string s_2

7.3.4 Cosine Similarity

The cosine similarity is a metric that calculates how similar two non-zero vectors of an inner product space are (Gomaa and Fahmy 2013)." Basically, it is equal to the cosine of the angles between those two vectors. The cosine similarity calculation formula is depicted in equation (7.9).

$$\text{Cosine similarity} = \cos(\theta) = \frac{\sum_{i=1}^{n} s_{1_i} s_{2_i}}{\sqrt{\sum_{i=1}^{n} s_{1_i}^2} \sqrt{\sum_{i=1}^{n} s_{2_i}^2}} \tag{7.9}$$

where:
- s_1 is the first string
- s_2 is the second string
- θ is the angle between the vectors of the strings s_1 and s_2

In general, cosine similarity ranges from −1 to 1 but for textual comparison this range is limited from 0 to 1. Thus, when two strings are completely different the cosine similarity is 0 and when the two strings are identical the cosine similarity is equal to 1.

7.3.5 Jaccard Similarity

Jaccard similarity or Jaccard index, as is also known, was introduced and developed by Paul Jaccard in 1901 (Jaccard 1901) and till today is a widely used similarity metric for different sample sets. As far as the textual similarity is concerned, Jaccard similarity is used to define the similarity between two texts. This similarity is the intersection of the two texts divided by the union of them. Thus, the Jaccard similarity is calculated using equation (7.10).

$$\text{Jaccard similarity} = \frac{s_1 \cap s_2}{s_1 \cup s_2} \tag{7.10}$$

where:
- s_1 is the first string
- s_2 is the second string

7.4 Proposed Methodology and Data Used

The current study provides a benchmarking of different algorithms for the string-based similarity between distinct data person instances. Data fusion is generally considered the integration of raw data (Castanedo 2013) and knowledge from multivariate sources. In this study, the term "fusion" is actually detailed to the identification and merging of similar person instances. The comparison of person instances herein was conducted on first name and surname data entries using the algorithms presented in Section 7.3. The comparison results of different algorithms are elaborated in Section 7.5.

For the purpose of this study, three different datasets were created with random names, i.e. a dataset with 100 random names, a dataset with 1000 random names and finally a 10 000 random names dataset. The three different-sized datasets were created in order to study the behavior of the considered algorithms in terms of computational efficiency while the dataset grows bigger in terms of its size.

The person instances are compared in pairs. So, every person instance is compared with every other person instance. Thus, in order to gain a better insight into the comparisons required for each dataset, Table 7.2 depicts the number of comparisons needed for 100, 1000, and 10 000 names.

The datasets provided as input were randomly generated names with each dataset containing approximately 20% of similar person instances. For example, in the 10 000 random names dataset, 2000 of them were similar. The predefined percentage of similar names enabled a better insight into the functionality of the algorithms evaluated as it enabled the calculation of the exact similarity threshold of each algorithm. Moreover, as obvious from Table 7.2, the number of comparisons increases radically as the volume of names in the dataset increases. For example, approximately 50 million comparisons are required for a 10 000 names dataset, regardless of the algorithm used. Therefore, it is of utmost importance to study the computational efficiency of each algorithm in order to find a feasible and practical solution for the needs of LEAs' personnel given the large volume of the dataset used in criminal investigations. In this light, the following steps were followed during the implementation and testing processes for each dataset and algorithm tested:

- **Name normalization:** This step deals with Unicode quirks, converts to lower case, removes irrelevant symbols, collapses whitespaces, splits the resulting string by whitespace, and converts each word to a double metaphone. Appropriate libraries are used to normalize, to implement miscellaneous processes, such as the detachment of umlauts, rare letters, accents and/or other nontypical Unicode-based normalizations. Moreover, duplicates are removed with possible issues of multiple common name instances.

Table 7.2 Number of comparisons needed and similar person instances per dataset.

Dataset	Number of comparisons	Number of similar person instances
100	4950	20
1000	499 500	200
10 000	49 995 000	2000

- **Definition of the name's fingerprint:** The definition of the name's fingerprint as a set of all possible combinations of involved metaphones is carried out in this step. The distance between two names is set to 0 if their fingerprint sets have an intersection and 1 otherwise. A total (calculated) number of combinations is used for evaluation purposes of the studied algorithms during the implementation processes.
- **Greed matching of the pairs:** At this stage, possible multiple matches are ignored, duplicates are removed, and subsequently the rest pairs of person instances are sorted and concatenated.

The similarity score (confidence level) is calculated by comparing person instances using string-based similarity measurements. For the string-based similarity, several approaches and algorithms from those mentioned in Table 7.1 are deployed including Jaro, Jaro-Winkler, Levenshtein, cosine similarity, and Jaccard similarity. All, these algorithms were tested and evaluated using the same dataset so as to compare their performance.

The accuracy metric, i.e. the percentage of instances "matched" correctly, was used for benchmarking purposes. To evaluate the results forced from the aforementioned algorithm implementations, on the selected, unique dataset, the similarity degree metric was calculated and used in order to retrieve the exact number (20% of the whole dataset) of the person instances "matched" correctly. This threshold that develops on each distinct size of dataset actually trades the recall for precision metric.

To summarize, a distance metric is used as a threshold in our computations; if the estimated distance between two distinct person instances is greater than this threshold value, the algorithm concludes that there is no match on the specific pair, therefore the recall is reduced but the precision is being improved.

In a nutshell, the sequence of steps deployed in the current study is as follows:

- Problem definition of fuzzy people instances matching
- Dataset definition
- Algorithms selection for the implementation and comparison processes during the current study
- Accuracy evaluation of the selected dataset
- Apply the previous steps to retrieve the appropriate threshold, to ensure high precision in calculations.

7.5 Results

The testbed used for the algorithms' performance evaluation was an Arch Linux OS system with i9-9900k CPU, 2080ti GPU, and 32 GB or RAM, equipped with a 500 GB SSD drive. The five different algorithms were evaluated separately for

Table 7.3 Execution time in seconds and threshold of each algorithm for the three given datasets.

Dataset	Algorithm	Execution time (seconds)	Similarity threshold
100 random names	Jaro	0.0166	0.7700
	Jaro-Winkler	1.3278	0.8820
	Levenshtein	0.4023	0.6000
	Cosine similarity	0.3215	0.5900
	Jaccard similarity	0.3064	0.3890
1000 random names	Jaro	1.5392	0.8675
	Jaro-Winkler	37.3244	0.9465
	Levenshtein	132.3366	0.7695
	Cosine similarity	31.8852	0.7395
	Jaccard similarity	30.0023	0.5850
10 000 random names	Jaro	158.4162	0.8935
	Jaro-Winkler	3812.9781	0.9145
	Levenshtein	11919.2141	0.7155
	Cosine similarity	3257.3214	0.7694
	Jaccard similarity	3064.9685	0.6150

each of the three datasets deployed for the purposes of this study. Table 7.3 includes the results for each algorithm in terms of execution time and the similarity threshold.

As obvious from Table 7.3 and as was well expected, the execution time increases as the size of the dataset increases. In order to further highlight results regarding the execution time, Figures 7.1–7.3 depict the time needed for each algorithm per dataset.

Figures 7.1–7.3 indicate that for the 100 random datasets, the fastest algorithm is the Jaro, the slowest is the Jaro-Winkler and the rest of them are very close concerning the execution time. Regarding the medium-sized dataset, the fastest algorithm is again the Jaro, the slowest is the Levenshtein algorithm while the rest of them require almost equal execution times. Last but not least, for the large dataset, the Jaro algorithm is once again the fastest algorithm, the slowest is again the Levenshtein algorithm while all the others continue to perform similarly. Comparing all the above results, it is worth mentioning that the Jaro similarity algorithm is by far the fastest in all datasets. What is more, the Levenshtein similarity algorithm's execution time increased significantly compared to the rest of

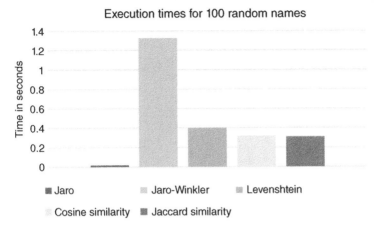

Figure 7.1 Execution times for 100 random names.

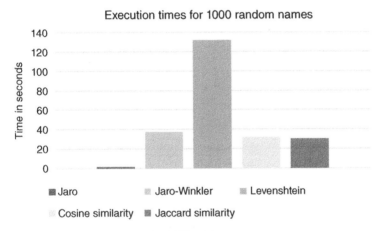

Figure 7.2 Execution times for 1000 random names.

the algorithms. Figure 7.4 features execution time results for all the three datasets and all the algorithms tested.

As far as the similarity threshold is concerned, Figure 7.5 presents a relevant overview of the results of all algorithms and datasets. As can be seen in Figure 7.5, the average similarity threshold for all algorithms increased alongside with the number of names. Also, as the number of names increases, the average threshold trend flattens. It is worth mentioning that the Jaro and Jaro-Winkler algorithms have significant higher threshold values compared to the rest of the algorithms. Except for the Levenshtein and the Jaro-Winkler algorithm, the rest of them

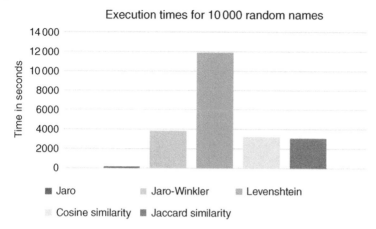

Figure 7.3 Execution times for 10 000 random names.

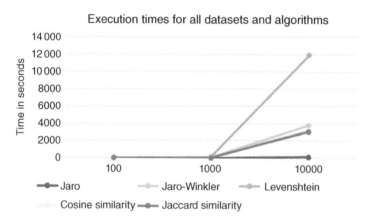

Figure 7.4 Execution times for all datasets and algorithms.

follow an upward stabilizing trend as the size of the dataset increases. All the aforementioned information is featured in Table 7.3 and depicted in Figure 7.5.

7.6 Person Fusion Toolset Design for Future Development

A person fusion tool could provide an estimation on whether two persons refer to the same instance and the respective degree of confidence (similarity degree) will be based on both the numeric and the string-based features of the person as those

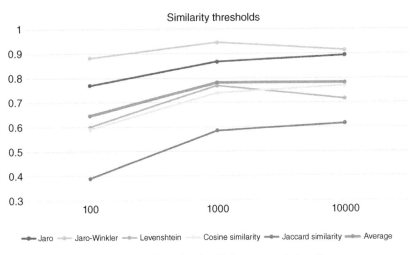

Figure 7.5 — Similarity threshold results for all datasets and algorithms.

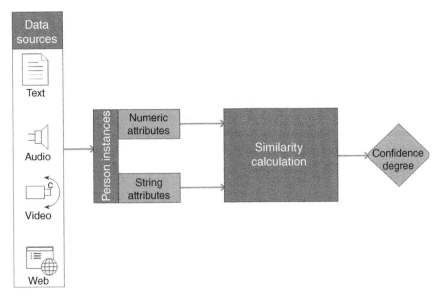

Figure 7.6 Person fusion tool flow diagram.

are asserted into the knowledge base. A high-level architecture scheme of a proposed person fusion tool is presented in Figure 7.6.

A possible design of a person fusion tool can be based on a variation of the k-Nearest Neighbor (KNN) algorithm (Hechenbichler and Schliep 2004). Specifically, appropriate weights can be applied to the contribution of each feature to the calculation of a total score or a similarity degree between two person instances. The idea of weighting features when using the KNN algorithm is applied to provide greater importance to features that typically are more unique in each person such as first name, surname, and date of birth. The person instances in a knowledge base, for example, are compared in pairs. So, every person is directly compared with every other different person. Based on the textual analysis both for string and numeric characters of each attribute, a total score is calculated in order to provide an insight into how similar these two persons are. Assuming that a person p can be characterized by n features $f(i)$, $i = 1, \ldots n$, the similarity of two persons p_i and p_j can be expressed as shown in equation (7.11):

$$\text{Similarity}\left(p_i, p_j\right) = \sum_{k=1}^{n} w_k \times \text{Similarity}\left(f_i(k), f_j(k)\right) \tag{7.11}$$

where:
- w_k is the weight of attribute k
- $f_i(k)$ is the value of the k attribute of person instance i
- $f_j(k)$ is the value of the k attribute of person instance j

The person fusion tool will utilize a string-based similarity module which is responsible for examining both the numeric and the string features of person attributes. This approach is considered the most appropriate for features expected in LEAs' databases in order to cope with the typographical variations in data gathered from several heterogeneous sources. For instance, the difference between two birth dates "06/05/2021" and "05/06/2021" may be major if we assume that both data entries are read as dd/mm/yyyy but in case the structure of these dates is different and the first one is dd/mm/yyyy and the second one mm/dd/yyyy, then it is actually exactly the same information despite the fact that they differ in one character. As a result, metrics are used for all the features with different weights so to conclude an overall score (confidence) between each pair of persons.

A major consideration is the multiple possible instances of a given entity over the available diverse information sources. This can be a person detected by various different sensors, or any information tied to an event. This leads to fusion tools which will be critical in assisting the LEAs.

7.7 Discussion

In this chapter, a comparative study between different textual edit-based and token-based similarity algorithms was performed. For benchmarking purposes, three different sized datasets with a predefined percentage of similar persons were used as input. Then, three edit-based and two token-based similarity algorithms were engaged so as to evaluate their performance in terms of execution time and the similarity threshold needed in order to detect the 20% of similar names.

The comparative study conducted in this chapter showed that person fusion even in large datasets is a feasible process for LEA investigators, provided that suitable algorithms are used. Thus, the person fusion tool proposed in Section 7.6 as a future direction of this study, aims the elimination of the duplicated information obtained from various sources, as well as the accuracy and better representation of the results. The study presented was focused on the similarity functions and algorithms that can return the similarity between two string inputs (attributes of persons) in order to decide whether those inputs need to be fused or actually refer to a different instance.

Based on this approach, the presented methodology evaluates both the pair of matched and non-matched persons. More specifically, the third step of the proposed methodology, namely "Algorithms selection for the implementation and the comparison processes during the current study" is actually based on the dataset cleaning and preprocessing stage, where the initial, raw dataset is transformed into one with an understandable format, for further processing. Afterward, the initially known similar and nonsimilar pair of persons are identified in order to properly perform the evaluation using the suggested algorithms and define the precise threshold for the model to approximately detect the predeclared number of the matched pair of persons. The methodology was designed and implemented focusing on the detection of nonmatched cases as well. As long as the model receives as input more elaborate datasets (with common and uncommon pairs of persons), the extracted model will provide more accurate results; thus, it will eliminate the possibility of false-positive, matched pairs of persons that will be characterized as unmatched. Again, the computed threshold will be the point where the "matched" as well as the "unmatched" pairs will be handled based on the needs of using the specific methodology.

Moreover, the method engaged to compare the results of different algorithms indicated that textual and token-based similarity algorithms had very promising results. These algorithms are mature and widely tested and seem to behave efficiently when it comes to small datasets and a limited feature selection. However, with datasets containing a large number of entries, e.g. 10 000 names, the efficiency of these algorithms decreases as the required computational time increases dramatically. This indicates that even if these algorithms feature high accuracy and classification rates, the time needed for their execution increases as the dataset grows larger. Taking into account the fact that in the real world, person instances contain many different attributes in addition to the first name and last name such as gender, age, residence address, and identification document, it is obvious that these algorithms alone require a lot of time to produce results and this could lead to less fast investigation processes. In this light, the system proposed in Section 7.6 engages different attributes by assigning different weights to each attribute based on its significance, as the latter is defined by the LEA personnel. In addition to different attributes and in order to make the system more efficient in terms of computational time, Machine Learning or/and Deep Learning methods must be adopted. Machine Learning and Deep Learning techniques require a significant amount of time for the training process while the algorithms used in this study can be engaged for labeling processes. After the completion of the training process, a well-trained system can produce prediction results regarding the similarity of two person instances almost instantly. This could lift the time restrictions and aid LEA officers in their investigation processes when it comes to person instances similarity calculation.

The European Union is a multilinguistic environment and thus each tool offered to European Legislation offices should take into account the harmonization rules and principles that are advised to exist in the European Union Legislation offices (Taylor 2011). In order to overcome the multilingual datasets problem when LEAs do not provide datasets, which contain person instances written in the English alphabet, the system could engage a translation mechanism, where each input dataset will be converted into English. It is worth mentioning that across Europe, most countries' identification documents contain the properties of a person both in their country language and in English, thus it would be wise to adopt the English language as default for comparison operations and training of Machine Learning or Deep Learning processes.

References

Castanedo, F. (2013). A review of data fusion techniques. *The Scientific World Journal* 2013: 704504–704522.

Dzemydiene, D. and Kazemikaitiene, E. (2005). *Ontology-Based Decision Support System for Crime Investigation Processes*, 427–438. Boston: MA, Springer.

Elmagarmid, A., Ipeirotis, P., and Verykios, V. (2006). Duplicate record detection: a survey. *IEEE Transactions on Knowledge and Data Engineering* 19 (1): 1–16.

Gomaa, W. and Fahmy, A. (2013). A survey of text similarity approaches. *International Journal of Computer Applications* 68 (13): 13–18.

Hall, D. and Llinas, J. (1997). *An Introduction to Multisensor Data Fusion*, 6–23. IEEE.

Hechenbichler, K. and Schliep, K. (2004). Weighted k-nearest-neighbor techniques and ordinal classification. http://epub.ub.uni-muenchen.de/

Jaccard, P. (1901). Distribution de la Flore Alpine dans le Bassin des Dranses et dans quelques régions voisines. *Bulletin de la Societe Vaudoise des Sciences Naturelles* 37 (140): 241–272.

Jaro, M.A. (1989). Advances in record-linkage methodology as applied to matching the 1985 census of Tampa, Florida. *Journal of the American Statistical Association* 84 (406): 414–420.

Levenshtein, V.I. (1965). Binary codes capable of correcting deletions, insertions and reversals. *Doklady Akademii Nauk SSR* 163 (4): 707–710.

Masita, J., Pui, L.C., Maizura, N.N., and Fatihah, M. (2017). Knowledge representation model for crime analysis. *Procedia Computer Science* 116: 484–491.

Naumann, F. (2013). *Similarity Measures*. Postdam: HPI.

Taylor, S. (2011). The European Union and National Legal languages: an awkward partnership? *Revue française de linguistique appliquée* 16: 105–118.

Vassiliadis, P. (2009). A survey of extract-transform-load technology. *International Journal of Data Warehousing and Mining* 5: 1–27.

Winkler, W.E. (1990). String comparator metrics and enhanced decision rules in the fellegi-sunter model of record linkage. In: *JSM Proceedings, Survey Research Methods*, 354–359. Alexandria, VA: American Statistical Association http://www.asasrms.org/Proceedings/y1990f.html.

8

Stakeholder Engagement Model to Facilitate the Uptake by End Users of Crisis Communication Systems

Grigore M. Havârneanu[1], Laura Petersen[1], and Natasha McCrone[2]

[1] Security Division, International Union of Railways (UIC), Paris, France
[2] RiniSoft Ltd, Sliven, Bulgaria

8.1 Introduction

Chemical, Biological, Radiological, Nuclear, and explosive (CBRNe) incidents, whether accidental or terrorist-based, can have a high impact on society. Recent history has demonstrated that both military and civilian populations could be exposed to highly hazardous CBRNe agents following conflicts, natural outbreaks, industrial incidents, or terrorist attacks resulting in severe consequences including serious mass injury and death.

For example, the ongoing COVID-19 pandemic has revealed the impact of a natural outbreak on everyday life activities, such as how we travel, work, interact, and communicate with our peers. People have learned to use new safety measures and protocols such as hand hygiene, face masks, or physical distancing. These measures have also revealed some of the challenges related to how people manage uncertainty, interact remotely, keep safe distances, and communicate with more difficulty when wearing protective equipment such as face masks.

However, this is just a small glimpse into the chaos of a more serious CBRNe incident, be it an unfortunate accident or a willful attack.

CBRNe risks or threats are very challenging because they are hard to detect, the consequences of exposure are often unknown, and there is the possibility of delayed effects of contamination. As a result, CBRNe risks are typical of the so-called "dread" risks – defined by lack of perceived control, catastrophic potential, and fatal consequences (Slovic 2002; Slovic et al. 2004). There are numerous past disasters to

Security Technologies and Social Implications, First Edition. Edited by Garik Markarian, Ruža Karlović, Holger Nitsch, and Krishna Chandramouli.

illustrate this such as the iconic Chernobyl or Fukushima accidents, or smaller-scale accidents involving the release of toxic substances (e.g. derailment of trains transporting dangerous goods in the vicinity of densely populated areas). Also, the willful use of CBRNe agents or nonconventional weapons with malicious intentions in public spaces is not an isolated case. EUROPOL (2019) reported an increase in the use of pyrotechnic mixtures to produce improvised explosive devices (IEDs) in jihadist plots. Three terrorist plots involving CBRN materials were disrupted in 2018 in the EU. A general increase in CBRN terrorist propaganda, tutorials, and threats was also observed. Based on historic evidence, such attacks or failed attempts have already been carried out on public transport premises and today is a growing threat in various parts of the world (e.g. Havârneanu and Petersen 2021).

An example can be a "dirty bomb," which is an IED acting also as a chemical, biological, or radioactive dispersal device during detonation. In this case, the explosion would not only kill and injure the people close to the deflagration point, but would also allow – for example – toxic chemical vapors, biotoxins, spores, bacteria, viruses, or radiological isotopes to spread over a large area and be inhaled by a much larger number of victims. This *modus operandi* would be more harmful and lethal than "conventional attacks." A mass-casualty CBRNe attack can be classified as a low-likelihood-high-impact and evolving threat (European Commission 2017). As this threat continues to develop, there is the need for an improved European Union (EU) Action plan on CBRN preparedness (European Commission 2017).

The illegal use of CBRNe material to carry out a serious criminal or terrorist attack is an enormous challenge for practitioners, both in regards to preparedness and planning as well as in terms of crisis response. The required response is a "whole community issue" as the impact of such an incident often extends beyond national boundaries and beyond decontamination (DHS 2014). Indeed, response to and recovery from these incidents can also require action from the private sector (e.g. emergency medical service providers, health care facilities, chemical companies, and transportation companies) as well as from multiple levels of government and may necessitate requesting resources from surrounding jurisdictions through mutual aid. Communication and coordination among these groups are essential, yet evidence from past incidents suggests that improvements are needed (DHS 2014).

Thus, for the challenge of CBRNe's effective response to be met, two important elements should be taken into account. First, one must consider effective cooperation between all first responder categories that need to coordinate their response actions (e.g. firefighters, emergency medical services, civil protection, police and military units, etc.) as well as other practitioners, who are not highly specialized in CBRNe's response, but who are very likely to be affected in case of an incident (e.g. transport practitioners, security experts of rail, public transport operators, etc.). This would require cooperation arrangements between stakeholders at all levels, civil-military and cross-border cooperation, specialized training, joint multidisciplinary exercises, common or compatible procedures, and other actions, which can stimulate collaboration and cooperation between practitioners with various levels of expertise in the CBRNe area (European Commission 2017; EUROPOL 2019; NATO 2008).

Second, the specialized response must take into account the expectations, circumstances, and special needs of the general population with all its diverse and vulnerable groups (e.g. Eid et al. 2019). This would require performing psychological and human factor (HF) research, studying human behavior, and analyzing what governments, local authorities, and practitioners can learn from the civil society. These learnings can then be used to optimize how practitioners prepare themselves before a major incident and how they respond during and after the incident. CBRNe preparedness and response must therefore include a better understanding of civilian responses to such events and how to better communicate with both victims and witnesses. Indeed, the way in which emergency responders manage a CBRNe incident will affect the way in which citizens behave, in terms of their compliance and cooperation with recommended actions, thus potentially affecting the outcomes of the incident (Carter and Amlôt 2016).

All the above-mentioned challenges as well as the observations that citizens will not only take action to defend themselves but that they will also work together and with the authorities to try to overcome a threat and help others were highlighted during the initial research stages of the EU-funded Horizon 2020 project PROACTIVE (PReparedness against CBRNe threats through cOmmon Approaches between security praCTItioners and the VulnerablE civil society). From this perspective, the citizen is the "ultimate end user," who is already on the field when the incident occurs and who can act effectively (e.g. demonstrate good reflexes) in the initial stages until the first responders arrive on site. Once the specialized practitioners and other end users begin deploying the first response measures, the citizen can act as a reliable partner in emergency response by cooperating with the first responders, facilitating their job, and by assisting or helping their peers.

The project conducted two systematic literature reviews, one on academic literature (Hall et al. 2019) and one on grey literature (Davidson et al. 2019). The reviews revealed a number of practice gaps and provided recommendations to fill them, among which communication with the public emerged as one of the most important and sensitive topics.

8.2 Risk and Crisis Communication Challenges for CBRNe

During CBRNe incidents, citizens interact with practitioners in ways that are unique and react depending on how first responders communicate instructions to the public. This is very challenging because of the particular CBRNe context: establishment of a "hotzone" and other distance perimeters, the particular pieces of equipment that first responders are wearing or using, specific procedures which are put in place, immediate or delayed effects of the toxic substances on the human body, etc. The majority of the public are almost totally unaware of the practicalities involved in these kinds of incidents, including the processes or procedures that practitioners use to deal with them. In these instances, citizens depend more than ever on the type of communication, tactics, techniques, and technology employed by practitioners. For instance, seeing practitioners arrive in hazmat suits while waiting to begin decontamination, a process which often involves disrobing, is considered further fear-inducing (Carbon et al. 2021). In this context, risk communication (pre-incident public communication) is essential to help the public know basic information about a CBRNe scenario. It can raise public awareness before a crisis, contributing to an overall improved preparedness and response.

The ways in which practitioners manage an incident also affect the ways in which citizens behave in terms of their cooperation and compliance. In order to enhance appropriate behaviors from citizens, effective communication strategies should be prioritized over control strategies (e.g. Carter et al. 2014). Another key aspect of compliance during CBRNe incidents is trust level (e.g. Hall et al. 2020; Hughes and Chauhan 2015). Where there are higher levels of trust in practitioners from citizens, the level of legitimacy and institutional authority of the police or other emergency organizations are higher. Thus, trust level and associated legitimacy, in turn, have an impact on the public's consequent preparedness to obey, comply, and respond to first responders' and emergency services' directions during a critical incident. Such public compliance with the directions of first responders can also clearly be enhanced through the use of "clear," unambiguous messages and the way in which these messages are delivered to the audience. Therefore, when it comes to CBRNe events, communication during the response phase can be even more challenging than pre-incident communication. When performed appropriately and through the right tools, it can help responders better manage diverse and vulnerable groups of people, contributing to an overall improved response.

The PROACTIVE literature analysis identified four main communication-related recommendations with a focus on vulnerable groups and their communication needs (Hall et al. 2020): (i) The public should be provided with sufficient information (information should be easily understandable; the message short, simple, clear, and easy to recall) with regular updates; (ii) Trust should be developed by delivering messages via a credible source (e.g. a spokesperson taking into account local risk cultures); (iii) The message should be accessible and inclusive, disseminated in a consistent manner across multiple communication channels, and in multiple language formats (text, pictographs, audio description, sign language, braille, easy-to-read, etc.); (iv) Crisis communication should incorporate psychological constructs, which reduce anxiety and increase behavioral efficacy for the public by e.g. providing details of effective protective actions, which can be taken during an emergency, and how to undertake these.

The tools and procedures that are currently used by first responders need to be adapted to meet the needs of vulnerable groups and facilitate real-time communication during the actual incident. By following these recommendations and utilizing effective and inclusive communication tools, CBRNe practitioners should be able to facilitate public compliance with protective measures in a real-life situation and also ensure that the communicated messages reach the whole society, including vulnerable groups.

8.3 CBRNe Disaster Crisis Communication Systems, Especially Disaster Apps

When practitioners communicate with citizens during a crisis, they need not only think about overcoming the earlier mentioned communication challenges but also about the technological means with which they communicate (Steelman et al. 2015). While a plethora of smartphone applications for disaster preparedness and response are currently available on various app stores (Bachmann et al. 2015; Tan et al. 2017), very few have been developed for CBRNe. In fact, a search on the Google Play app store in June 2021 for the keyword "CBRN" returned only 14 relevant results, none of which was geared toward crisis communication with the public. Similarly, a search on the Apple App Store revealed only six available apps. In both cases, these tended to be glossary/reference apps or apps which are part of a larger training system.

Disaster apps have been shown to be a successful means of crisis communication despite their limitations. Some critical issues for developing a successful disaster app include ensuring low battery usage (Pylvas et al. 2018; Tan et al. 2020) or including sound for warnings (Tan et al. 2020), but addressing these types of concerns is relatively easy from a technological standpoint. What is harder to ensure is the interest and continued use of a given disaster app. Indeed, apps are based on an "opt-in" system, whereby a smartphone owner must download the app. A recent study of German citizens found that only 16% have downloaded a disaster app (Kaufhold et al. 2020). However, having downloaded the app is not enough as users should familiarize themselves with the app before the crisis hits so as to be able to use it well under stressful crisis conditions (Nilsson and Stølen 2011; Tan et al. 2017). Once the app has been downloaded, there is still the issue of getting the users to actually use the app. Data from 2018 showed that 21% of users abandon an app after just one use (Upland 2021a) and 71% of apps do not last past 90 days (Upland 2021b).

This begs the question – how can an app be made useful and attractive enough to get a smartphone owner to download, keep installed, and use it, knowing that

CBRNe incidents are rare occurrences? Research has shown that for apps in general and also disaster apps specifically, involving users in development is key to ensuring app sustainability (Kouadio 2016; Pylvas et al. 2018; Tan et al. 2017). Therefore, project PROACTIVE has created a Stakeholder Engagement Model for the implementation of the research and innovation activities with the ultimate goal of developing an innovative CBRNe Crisis Communication System. This system is composed of three tools: the first tool is a Web Collaborative Platform for law enforcement agencies (LEAs) to facilitate daily operations and response to a CBRNe incident. The second tool is a Modular App for Practitioners to facilitate daily operations and the response of LEAs and First Responders to a CBRNe incident. Finally, the third tool is a Mobile App for the members of the public that will enable all the citizens (including those considered vulnerable) to better communicate in real time and according to their needs.

The following sections of this chapter illustrate how this Stakeholder Engagement Model was applied in the development of the PROACTIVE CBRNe Crisis Communication System.

8.4 The PROACTIVE Stakeholder Engagement Model

8.4.1 Two Advisory Boards: PSAB and CSAB

Project PROACTIVE is built around a strong social engagement with end users. This is done through the two project Advisory Boards, which were designed as two independent but interconnected extended networks for experts. Their role and interaction were planned through two dedicated workflows in the project. They provide an extended pool of practitioners and civil society representatives, which were created at the very beginning of the project. The pool of experts is continuously growing since board members are recruited throughout the project's lifetime. These experts are directly involved in the project research, development, and innovation activities and help the project team members collect essential end user requirements as well as test and validate the main project outcomes.

8.4.1.1 The Practitioner Stakeholder Advisory Board (PSAB)

The involvement of CBRNe practitioners is being achieved through the creation and implementation of the PSAB. The PSAB aims to represent an international panel of experts from different areas of knowledge and practice and with diverse levels of experience in emergency management or CBRNe response.

This network of contacts includes law enforcement, fire brigades, medical responders, the military, civil protection, research/academia, government agencies, policy officers, transport practitioners such as rail security experts, and

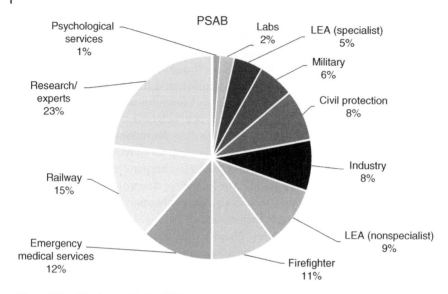

Figure 8.1 Pie chart with the PSAB member category breakdown.

various NGOs who best represent the agencies who would have to respond in the event of a CBRNe incident. At the time of this writing (February 2022), the PSAB has 87 members representing the following categories (Figure 8.1): research (23%), railway security (15%), police (14%), emergency medical services (12%), firefighters (10%), civil protection (8%), industry, (8%), defense (6%), laboratories (2%), and psychological services (1%).

PSAB members span over a large number of countries from Europe and beyond: Belgium, Canada, Croatia, Czech Republic, Estonia, Finland, France, Germany, Greece, Ireland, Israel, Italy, Latvia, Luxemburg, Norway, Poland, Slovenia, Spain, Netherlands, Turkey, the United Kingdom, Ukraine, and the United States.

8.4.1.2 The Civil Society Advisory Board (CSAB)

The involvement of citizens is being achieved through the creation and implementation of the CSAB. The CSAB is made up of a diverse panel of members of the public and civil society organizations, including representatives of vulnerable groups, thus representing human diversity. Members of the CSAB include regular citizens, local representatives, resilience teams, representatives of mental health organizations, associations of the elderly, children, persons with disabilities, independent experts in citizen science, etc. At the time of this writing, the PROACTIVE CSAB has 46 members, from individual experts (on subjects e.g. vulnerability or disability rights) to civil society organizations, and covers a wide range of different groups as shown in Figure 8.2: experts (28%), blind and partially sighted (11%),

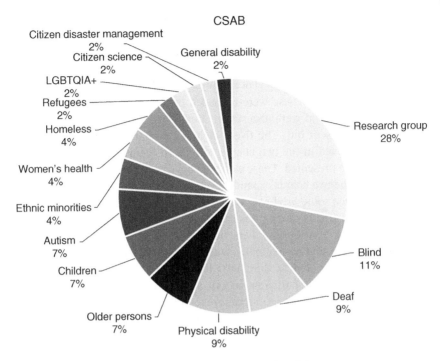

Figure 8.2 Pie chart with the CSAB member category breakdown.

deaf and hard of hearing (9%), physical disability (9%), older persons (7%), children (7%), autism (7%), ethnic minorities (4%), women (4%), homeless (4%), refugees (2%), LGBTQIA+ (2%), citizen science (2%), citizen disaster management (2%), and general disability (2%).

CSAB members currently cover a large number of countries from Europe and beyond: Bangladesh, Belgium, Czech Republic, Finland, Germany, Hungary, Italy, Japan, Lebanon, Montenegro, Poland, Portugal, Romania, Spain, Sweden, the United Kingdom, and the United States.

8.4.2 Recruitment for the Advisory Boards

Recruitment for the advisory boards began before the project was financed, with the signing of Letters of Intent during the proposal stage. Once the project was funded, these organizations were contacted again to reconfirm their interest in being a member of an advisory board and signed a Non-Disclosure Agreement (NDA). Recruitment of new advisory board members began right at the start of the project and will continue throughout the project lifetime. Members have been sought out from all over the world and membership is open to all those who wish to contribute. The project website included from the start an explicit section about the PSAB and the CSAB recruitment. Essential information was posted on the website giving potential candidates the option to express their interest via a contact form.

To further increase the likelihood of accepting to be a part of the advisory board, two flyers were created. These were uploaded on the project website (https:// proactive-h2020.eu/) and were also systematically attached to all the invitation emails which were sent out. The flyers included a chart showing the type of organizations involved in the two boards (similar to Figures 8.1 and 8.2) and a map of countries represented. These elements have been periodically updated in the two flyers as the two boards expanded.

The flyers include some brief text, which clarifies that the board members are expected to participate as much or as little as they can via workshops, surveys, interviews as well as contributions to the field exercises and that the project would expect their feedback and inputs in line with their area of expertise and available resources. They also include a short FAQ list, which explains why one should consider joining and if the participation will cost them anything. In addition, the flyers clarify the official invitation procedure to project events. As of now, the flyers also include some key information about the NDA, specifically that this document is required to secure the confidentiality of project results and that it covers all the members of one organization.

The first six months of the project corresponded to the creation of the PSAB and CSAB and the recruitment of the initial members. Despite the large recruitment efforts, we observed quite low return rates in terms of positive answers and signed NDAs. For example, from a list of 128 experts initially invited by email, only 36 decided to sign up for the PSAB during the first months of the project (Swain and Kelly 2019) corresponding to a 28% positive return ratio. During the next recruitment stage, the list was extended to a total of 152 candidates (i.e. organizations or individual experts who were invited one time or received a one-time follow-up reminder). From this pool of invited candidates as well as others who were independently identified by various consortium partners, 83 have joined the PSAB, which translates into almost a 54% positive return ratio until June 2021.

Recruiting CSAB members turned out to be even more challenging and resulted in a much lower success rate. During the first project months, out of the 11 civil society organizations, which had signed a Letter of Intent at the proposal phase, only three decided to sign an NDA at project month six. Huge efforts were also put in place to involve CSAB members in the countries where the three PROACTIVE field exercises will take place: Germany, Italy, and Belgium. However, the results were sometimes deceiving. For example, out of 33 organizations contacted in Belgium, only one decided to join the CSAB. Consequently, the project team decided to further improve the recruitment process, especially toward the CSAB candidates.

8.4.2.1   Personalized Individual Emails and Follow-Up Process for the CSAB

For the CSAB members, the recruitment process had to be elaborated further. Potential candidates often had concerns and systematically asked several questions in particular with respect to the NDA.

One question concerned the designation of a singular person to the advisory board. The PROACTIVE NDA does indeed ask for a single person to be assigned to the role of "advisor to the advisory board." However, the NDA covers the entire organization and all their members/employees. Another question concerned the inclusion of assistants accompanying disabled people. Similar to the answer to the first question, if the assistant is part of the same organization, then they are covered. However, if they are a third party, it was clarified that they will also need to sign an NDA. Many organizations asked how much participation was expected when joining the CSAB. To answer these questions and other concerns, the project team developed a more detailed information sheet to help them have all the practical information from the start. The main points are listed below:

- **Joining the CSAB is an opportunity to voice the rights and needs of society's various vulnerable groups.** The CSAB is vital to project results. We rely on your knowledge and experience. You will be able to influence project outcomes and ensure they are inclusive and respectful of all members of society.
- **Joining the CSAB does not cost you/your organization anything.** Subject to getting an invitation from the coordinator, the project will reimburse eligible travel and accommodation costs when you attend a physical event organized by project PROACTIVE. Staff costs are not covered by this PROACTIVE budget.
- **After joining the CSAB, your contribution is always optional; you choose where and when you want to participate.** As a CSAB member, you will be invited to contribute input and feedback through several project activities such as surveys, workshops, and webinars.
- **The Non-Disclosure Agreement (NDA) protects the confidentiality of sensitive project outcomes.** While most project outcomes are public, the NDA controls the information flow and progress of project results. It does not require you to contribute to the project. One signed NDA covers all representatives of your organization.
- **Joining the CSAB will bring some advantages to your organization.** As a CSAB member, you will be among the first organizations to have access to the project outcomes and exploit them in the long term. You will have higher visibility at the European level and connect with relevant practitioners and other civil organizations.
- All you need to do to become a CSAB member is to **sign the attached Non-Disclosure Agreement and e-mail it back to us.**

Since we improved the CSAB recruitment process by including this FAQ list in the initial contact email, we observed a slight improvement in the positive answers' return rate, with the CSAB currently counting 46 members. We are estimating that around 450 CSAB invitations have been sent to potential candidates since the beginning of the project. Thus, this would translate into a rough 9.3% positive return rate.

8.4.3 Engaging the Two Advisory Boards

Since PROACTIVE is a Research and Innovation Action (RIA) focusing on HF and Social Science and Humanities (SSH) research methods, most of the project desk research activities consist of surveys, workshops, focus groups, and in-depth interviews, which allow the project to collect quantitative and qualitative data. The desk research phase is then followed by an experimental phase consisting of several full-scale field exercises employing real-world scenarios and actual interactions between practitioners and members of the public. The members of the two boards actively engage with the project by systematically participating in all these activities.

Regarding the Crisis Communication System development process, these series of events are the backbone of the co-creation process with practitioners and citizens. These events helped the project team members (i) collect and validate essential end user requirements toward the beginning of the project, (ii) test and evaluate intermediate versions of the system during the first half of the project, (iii) test and validate the revised version of the system in realistic conditions in the second half of the project, and (iv) facilitate the Crisis Communication System uptake by end users after the end of the project.

In the following part of this chapter, we will explain in detail the first two steps of this process, which are now completed, and also discuss steps 3 and 4, which are upcoming.

Steps 1 and 2 were carried out as a series of workshops/focus groups and the input was collected, documented, and validated using the MoSCoW (Must have, Should have, Could have, and Won't have) methodology (Clegg and Barker 1994). At each of the stages referenced in Figure 8.3, the Crisis Communication System was optimized in preparation for the next phase of feedback, adopting an iterative approach to the development in the roadmap to commercialization.

8.4.3.1 The Pre-Exercise Workshops

The project planned at least two initial workshops with the PSAB and CSAB members to identify and validate initial requirements for the PROACTIVE Crisis Communication System.

On 19 March 2020, the project held its online PSAB workshop with 40 participants from 17 different countries: Bulgaria, Canada, Czech Republic, Estonia, France, Germany, Greece, Italy, Latvia, Lithuania, Netherlands, Norway, Poland, Spain, Sweden, the United Kingdom, and Ukraine. The attendees covered all the main categories of the PROACTIVE PSAB.

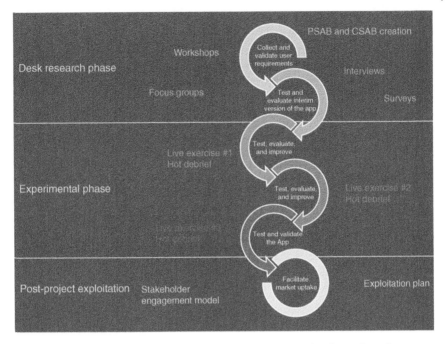

Figure 8.3 The PROACTIVE Stakeholder engagement process leading to iterative development of the Crisis Communication System.

On 1 October 2020, the project held its online CSAB workshop with about 40 participants from 14 different countries: Belgium, Bulgaria, Finland, France, Germany, Greece, Italy, Lebanon, Montenegro, Norway, Poland, Spain, Sweden, and the United Kingdom. The attendees covered the main categories of the PROACTIVE CSAB, including representatives of key vulnerable groups: deaf, blind, mental and physical disabilities, older persons, and research groups.

These two workshops allowed PROACTIVE to develop the first set of core requirements for the Crisis Communication System (Table 8.1):

These workshops also helped define the minimum limited functionality for the PROACTIVE CBRNe Crisis Communication System to be usable during the field exercises, in order to enable users to provide more in-depth feedback on usability and content, based on a realistic scenario. Table 8.2 describes the various functionalities and how the system will meet them.

8.4.3.2 Mobile App Workshops

At a later stage, during the project implementation, once the first Mobile App prototype was developed, two PROACTIVE "Mobile App" Workshops were held.

Table 8.1 Validation of initial Crisis Communication System requirements during the initial workshops according to the MoSCoW methodology.

Must have	Should have	Could have	Won't have
• A privacy policy, consent form, and disclaimer • Call 112 in case of emergency Two access levels: – Registered – Nonregistered • Downloadable data, cache data, and automatic update • FAQ page • Subscription to emails and text notifications • A secure REST API • Settings for accessibility	• Novelty • Useful advice • References to existing apps and other relevant sites (providing links where possible) • Find and contact family and friends	• A system wide avatar	• Direct integration with other apps (to prevent privacy and security issues)

Table 8.2 Functionality requirements for the field exercises.

Functionality	PROACTIVE CBRNe Crisis Communication System
Pre-incident information	PROACTIVE pre-incident materials will be available in the system for users to reference
Post-incident information	Information post-incident to be provided to stakeholders, specific to the scenario exercise as a lesson learnt
Links to available national apps	Countries where the field exercises are taking place that have existing apps for crises events will have the link signposted in the portal
Notification alerts	Live notifications to be provided by LEAs at all stages of the exercise
Existing news feeds	News feeds from the relevant countries/areas will be linked to the app, creating a central hub for information
Data analysis	LEAs will have access to data, specifically the number of users on the platform and at what stages the platform was used, etc.
Inter-agency information sharing	The ability to converse directly with relevant stakeholders to discuss operational aspects in terms of information sharing

Their goal was to provide a first evaluation of the tool by the expert groups and to collect detailed feedback following a short usability test.

The first workshop was conducted with 18 PSAB participants representing all categories of CBRNe practitioners on 25 February 2021; and the second one involved 10 CSAB members representing mainly experts or researchers on 26 February 2021.

The workshops took the form of an incident-based discussion followed by a presentation of the Mobile App and then a live questionnaire. Participants were provided with a fictitious CBRNe scenario, involving a suspected chemical attack set on a train carriage, and asked questions about their reactions to such situations. The live questionnaire asked questions specifically concerning the app's functionality, design, and accessibility.

The incident-based discussion and live questionnaire allowed for the further elaboration of the requirements. First of all, we collected detailed feedback on the usefulness of existing features. These are shown in Table 8.3.

Further, these two workshops allowed us to collect new input, including additional features that the app must, should, or could have. These are shown in Table 8.4. Lastly, during the live evaluation session of the workshops, when asked to rate the app out of five stars, the PSAB workshop participants gave it four stars while the CSAB participants gave it three. This symbolic exercise was used to give an overall impression about the app quality perception within each group of users and provide a baseline for how the rating is going to change over time.

8.4.3.3 Data Breach Workshop

The PROACTIVE Data Breach Tabletop Exercise (TTX) took place on 4 March 2021 and had 10 participants, including security experts from LEAs and ethics experts. It was a scenario-based discussion and took the form of a focus group.

Table 8.3 Feedback on the existing features collected during the first Mobile App workshops.

Must have	Should have	Could have	Won't have
• Live alerts during an incident • Pre-incident information/ communication materials • Possibility to share information, including location and images	• Contact details of LEAs and vulnerable citizen organisations	• Forum and/or direct messaging between LEAs and citizens	• Not applicable (N/A)

Table 8.4 Additional features collected during the first Mobile App workshops.

Must have	Should have	Could have	Won't have

• Better accessibility features, including:
  – Text-to-speech
  – Translation
  – Big text
  – Basic wording
  – Uncomplicated structure
  – Pictures, pictograms
  – Big buttons, icons and symbols
  – Color blind mode for images/ mapping
• Specific information on what is happening and how to act
	• Less text
	• Mental health support message
	• A symptoms checklist
	• Hospital lists
	• Links to other useful apps
		• Social media integration (post-information to a given social media account)
		• Ways to contact relatives/loved ones
		• Proof of decontamination
			• Live camera feed to app for transmission to first responders

This workshop allowed for the development of requirements related to the prevention and mitigation of data breaches (Table 8.5).

8.4.3.4 Focus Groups with the CSAB

Next, three events titled "PROACTIVE Mobile app Focus Group with CSAB" were held in May–June 2021 in the following order:

- 12 May 2021 with four participants representing the blind/visually impaired, autistic, and mobility restricted;
- 26 May 2021: with nine participants representing the blind/visually impaired, the deaf/hard of hearing, the LGBTQ community, and the mobility restricted; and
- 8 June 2021: with six CSAB members representing the homeless, pregnant women, senior citizens, visually impaired guide dog users, and immigrants.

The goal was to separate the CSAB into smaller working groups and collect their inputs separately once they had a hands-on experience with the app during an incident-led discussion. Discussions within the focus groups concentrated on the accessibility and ease of use of the app, which led to the following requirements (Table 8.6). Moreover, the focus groups gave the app a rating of 2.6 stars out of 5 on average.

Table 8.5 Requirements related to the prevention and mitigation of data breaches.

Must have	Should have	Could have	Won't have
• A means to secure the integrity and confidentiality of personal data • Anonymization, pseudonymization, and encryption • A means to provide information about the potential source of the data breach and data subjects involved • The ability to communicate the breach to the supervisory authority based on data regulations and, in some cases, also the data subjects (the citizens) • The functionality to preserve the leak's circumstances, as preservation is a key aspect of digital forensics	• Ability to switch off the false data source • Ability to detect if the data breach is human error, misuse or an intentional attack • A tool within the app to rapidly report leaks to users • The protocol to be followed in case of data leaks	• Include a system to catalogue received information according to the source in some way; • A way to register logs to the system integrated into the platform • A data breach communication protocol	• Direct integration with other apps

8.4.4 Integration of the MoSCoW Findings in the Crisis Communication System

Once gathered, the MoSCoW findings are translated to design and functional requirements, promoting the customization elements needed to address the demands for each user group. This method ensures a core set of key functionalities are developed to build the overall system architecture ensuring a modular, flexible, scalable, robust, and secure system is built. The architectural definition process focused on the following four principal objectives:

• To clearly present a description of the PROACTIVE system and how it addresses the stakeholder needs (including LEAs and vulnerable citizens);

Table 8.6 Accessibility requirements collected during the three focus groups.

Must have	Should have	Could have	Won't have
• Compliance with international standards for accessibility (e.g. WCAG 2.1) • Accessibility features, including: – Translation – Ability to zoom for the partially sighted – A high contrast option – Audio information – International Sign Language – An Easy Read mode • A less chaotic interface	• A search button • Less confusing icons (e.g. contact icon should be an envelope, not an arrow) • Less reliance on maps	• N/A	• N/A

- To provide a clear description of the critical aspects that need to be taken into consideration to ensure the system is modular, flexible, extensible, scalable, robust, and secure;
- To provide enough details to allow technical teams to build instances of the system that share a common structure and consequently are interoperable by design;
- To ensure consistency for the MoSCoW findings by using this architecture design as a baseline input.

By identifying these core requirements, it is then possible to create the Crisis Communication System. This is done by taking each requirement and applying it to the system. Take for example accessibility. As seen in the MoSCoW results, accessibility during the development stage is paramount to ensuring the Crisis Communication System can be used by multiple vulnerable groups. However, it is important to divide accessibility into two categories: accessibility through development and accessibility through content. The former accounts for the adaptations needed in HTML coding. To accommodate non-sighted users, a number of design features had to be considered during the development phase including the formatting of headings, lists, graphics and logos, sequences and hierarchies as well as color contrast ratios and self-speaking links. Once developed, the engineers were able to use a number of available tools to test the accessibility, in particular, a screen-reader and keyboard. Further, in order to allow for risk and crisis messages to use a mixture of text, pictographs, and images, the PROACTIVE Crisis Communication System supports free text for live alerts and the option to upload multiple data formats for sharing information. When it comes to content, the data, where possible, will be available as plain text built into the web page to support screen readers and as a downloadable document, for printing and dissemination. Another example can be taken from the "Must have" of "a means to secure the integrity and confidentiality of personal data," which has been implemented by making sure that to access the Crisis Communication System, no personal data is required and to make a registered account, you will only need an email address.

As previously stated, this type of implementation of the MoSCoW findings directly into the Crisis Communication System will continue in an iterative manner.

8.4.5 Three Field Exercises

The PROACTIVE project is now preparing several field exercises for 2022–2023 where the Crisis Communication System will be tested to continue its co-creation process. PROACTIVE intends to carry out three field exercises to test project outcomes in controlled settings, which simulate real-life conditions. These exercises will allow CBRNe practitioners to interact with actual members of the public, including vulnerable citizens as role play volunteers which – to the best of our knowledge – has rarely been done before. These citizens will be both members of the CSAB as well as local volunteers, of which 10–15% will be from vulnerable groups. Citizens will be active participants in each exercise as opposed to fellow first responders or actors "playing" the role of victims, as is the usual case. Furthermore, members from both the PSAB and the CSAB will be invited to attend as observers to these exercises, to provide even more inputs.

During the exercises, the practitioners involved in the actual exercise and those PSAB members who will act as observers will use the PROACTIVE Crisis Communication System during a simulated CBRNe incident. This will allow for controlled hands-on trials to test the tool in naturalistic (yet safe) settings in order to further improve it. Although this depends on the specific scenario for each exercise (which is now under development), we anticipate that practitioners will use the app to send out notifications to role-play volunteers, accept submitted reports, and test other crisis communication features.

Further, the PROACTIVE Crisis Communication System will also be used by the citizens during a simulated CBRNe incident, hence the exercises will help test and validate the system in a realistic environment, also from the citizen's point of view. Those CSAB members who are there as observers will also be able to check out the app for citizens and observe how it is used.

Each exercise will be followed by an evaluation workshop utilizing the "hot debriefing" method to get inputs from the participants immediately following the exercise, as well as those advisory board members who have acted as observers. Hot debriefing will take the form of questionnaires and focus group discussions, offering insights from both practitioners and vulnerable citizens. The accessibility of the app, the usefulness and clarity of the information available on the app, and the two-way communication capabilities (e.g. push notifications) will be key points of discussion during the focus groups. The findings will then, once again, be used to improve the design and functions of the Crisis Communication System.

In the general scheme of things, the three field exercises take place over the course of the project at optimal time intervals, with at least four months between exercises. This allows for an iterative learning process and presents the opportunity to transfer lessons learnt from one exercise to the next one. The three exercises were conceived as a process composed of three phases: (i) running the exercise and its evaluation workshop, (ii) analyzing all the results generated by the exercise and workshop and producing a dedicated deliverable, and (iii) post-processing and transfer of all relevant lessons learnt into the next exercise. These phases are sequential and are part of the iterative co-creation and development process in our Stakeholder Engagement Model.

8.5 Lessons Learnt About the Stakeholder Engagement Model

Developing a Crisis Communication System to be used by citizens and first responders during a CBRNe incident required a sustained engagement of various stakeholders through various co-creation activities and at all development stages. The PROACTIVE Stakeholder Engagement Model aimed to achieve this by creating the PSAB and the CSAB and by involving their members in surveys, workshops, interviews, focus groups, and live field exercises. Until this point in time, the stakeholders have contributed by providing functional and design specifications. They also evaluated the first version of the app and provided insightful usability feedback on how to improve it.

8.5.1 Positive Impact on the Crisis Communication System Development Process

The engagement activities completed until now revealed several points of consensus between independent groups. In some cases, the same requirements were mentioned by separate groups of experts (e.g. providing live alerts or including references or links to existing apps and other relevant sites). In essence, this is a good thing and proves the importance of that point from the end user's perspective. Other groups provided more insightful feedback in one specific area according to the group's expertise; for instance, how to improve the App's data security or how to make it more accessible to all citizens. All in all, engaging repeatedly with separate and smaller groups of stakeholders proved very useful for the app development process.

8.5.2 Challenges Identified

One of the biggest challenges that we faced and that we are still confronted with is the difficulty of recruiting CSAB members. It is much more difficult to have CSOs sign up for the CSAB than practitioners sign up for the PSAB. This is maybe because CSOs are more unaware of EU project processes compared to practitioner organizations. With the start of the H2020 work program, the involvement of practitioners in project consortia became mandatory for some topics, and over the last years, these organizations got used to being involved in research projects or cooperating with ongoing ones. We assume that CSOs are still quite unfamiliar with EU projects and their management is still reluctant with respect to the potential resources to be allocated. There is also the misconception that the project would create a mandatory amount of workload for their representatives and that there are no real gained benefits.

A second challenge we faced in the implementation of our Stakeholder Engagement Model was related to the COVID-19 pandemic. Many project events inevitably had to be postponed or conducted in a virtual format. Therefore, all our stakeholder workshops and focus groups were in a virtual format and we believe that face-to-face interaction with the consulted advisory board members would have been an advantage.

8.5.3 Recommendations

Based on the challenges faced by the PROACTIVE team, we identified several actionable recommendations that could further improve the stakeholder engagement in our project and facilitate similar processes for other projects:

1) **Do not send long invitation emails.** When inviting a stakeholder to engage with the project or one specific project activity, write a short and clear invitation email. You can provide more information as separate attachments or through embedded links.
2) **Anticipate questions from the start.** There are always some questions or concerns which are raised systematically. Anticipate and answer them with a FAQ section, which can be included on a website or in a flyer.
3) **Demystify the organization of an EU project.** Make clear what the engagement process consists of: how the project is organized and what it requires from the stakeholders as well as what the project has to offer and how the stakeholder can benefit.

4) **Run small-scale engagement activities.** This is particularly important during an online activity when participants do not have direct contact with each other. We observed that smaller focus groups lead to better engagement than large workshops. Our online activities which did not exceed 10 participants were much more dynamic compared to the ones with many participants. In a small group, every participant can talk out loud, use the chat, or be engaged by the moderator.

5) **Cooperation between heterogeneous stakeholder groups can start at the project level.** A collaborative research project can bring together experts from different domains, who do not know each other very well. Each engagement activity can be composed of a heterogeneous and ideally representative panel of participants representing different areas of knowledge and practice (e.g. different categories of first responders or citizens representing different disabilities). The next step for PROACTIVE is to create interaction between the two macro groups: practitioners and members of the public.

6) **Engagement should be a continuous process.** Stakeholder engagement is a process which starts when the project proposal is being drafted and continues until the end of the project implementation and even beyond it. This is particularly important when new solutions or technologies are being developed with the help of stakeholders. Therefore, engagement should not only be initiated but also maintained.

7) **Be aware of new emerging technological solutions.** New technologies are emerging all the time. Therefore, it is important to keep the pace with the newest research in the field, the updated state of the art, the rapidly developing technologies, and possibly evolving expectations of end users.

8.6 Going Forward: Ensuring the Crisis Communication System's Market Uptake

Project PROACTIVE aims that the tools that compose the Crisis Communication System become long-term key exploitable results beyond the life of the project. Therefore, the PROACTIVE Stakeholder Engagement Model also takes into account the exploitation of the PROACTIVE Crisis Communication System (as shown in Figure 8.3). The exploitation process actually starts with the co-development of the system in an iterative manner as this ensures that the developed product will match and exceed end users' expectations, leading to market uptake. To further the co-creation process beyond what is elaborated in this chapter, it is currently under discussion to integrate with sister projects and even directly with an existing LEA system during a future tabletop exercise. As stated previously, the best way to ensure app sustainability is to include users in the development process.

Beyond the co-creation process and having a tailor-made product, there are several other barriers to market uptake that the Stakeholder Engagement Model will help overcome. These are cost (buying a new system), time (to implement and train), and reluctance to change. Both the PSAB and the CSAB will provide inputs and feedback on what they perceive to be an acceptable cost, how much time they would be willing to put into using the system and also ways that would enable their organization to accept change. This will ensure that these barriers are perceived as insignificant when the final product is put on the market.

A report describing the exploitation strategy will also be developed by the project and reviewed by PSAB and CSAB members, ensuring that their viewpoints are taken into account. It is also envisioned to get official support for the PROACTIVE Crisis Communication System from the organizations, who are members of the advisory boards to lend legitimacy to the product.

Since all technology evolves and changes rapidly, there is a risk that a given tool (in this case, the Crisis Communication System) loses user interest or becomes replaceable by the next innovative tool. Our Stakeholder Engagement Model allows ongoing input from a plethora of stakeholders possibly also in the long run to ensure the system can be updated even beyond the life of the project. This may involve interaction with other technologies to expand the functionality at minimal cost or integration with existing systems to ensure the technology is embedded. Most importantly, practitioners may require continuous support for existing or new operational processes to be carried out more efficiently and effectively.

Finally, recent events such as the COVID-19 pandemic or as well more isolated national incidents, attacks, or plots involving hazardous materials led to a more general awareness of CBRNe incidents amongst the public. How to use such incidents to encourage uptake of the Crisis Communication System will also be part of the wider exploitation strategy.

Acknowledgments

Project PROACTIVE has received funding from the European Union's Horizon 2020 research and innovation programme under grant agreement no. 832981.

References

Bachmann, D.J., Jamison, N.K., Martin, A. et al. (2015). Emergency preparedness and disaster response: there's an app for that. *Prehospital and Disaster Medicine 30* (5): 486–490. https://doi.org/10.1017/S1049023X15005099.

Carbon, D., Arnold, A., Siemens, M., and Görgen, T. (2021). Common approaches between the vulnerable members of the civil society. Deliverable D3.4 of the PROACTIVE project.

Carter, H. and Amlôt, R. (2016). Mass casualty decontamination guidance and psychosocial aspects of CBRN incident management: a review and synthesis. *PLOS Currents Disasters 27* (1): https://doi.org/10.1371/currents.dis.c2d3d652d9d0 7a2a620ed5429e017ef5.

Carter, H., Drury, J., Rubin, G.J. et al. (2014). Effective responder communication improves efficiency and psychological outcomes in a mass decontamination field experiment: implications for public behaviour in the event of a chemical incident. *PLoS ONE 9* (3): e89846.

Clegg, D. and Barker, R. (1994). *Case Method Fast-Track: A RAD Approach*. Addison-Wesley. ISBN: 978-0-201-62432-8.

Davidson, L., Weston, D., Dennis, A. et al. (2019). Findings from systematic review of current policy for mitigation and management of CBRNe terrorism. Deliverable D1.2 of the PROACTIVE project.

DHS (2014). *Patient Decontamination in a Mass Chemical Exposure Incident: National Planning and Guidance for Communities*. US Department of Homeland Security.

Eid, A., Di Giovanni, D., Galatas, I. et al. (2019). Mass decontamination of vulnerable groups following an urban CBRN (chemical, biological, radiological, nuclear) incident. *Biomedicine & Prevention 1* (207): https://doi.org/10.19252/0000000CF.

European Commission (2017). Action plan to enhance preparedness against chemical, biological, radiological and nuclear security risks, Brussels, COM (2017) 610 final.

EUROPOL (2019). European Union Terrorism Situation and Trend Report (TE-SAT). https://www.europol.europa.eu/activities-services/main-reports/terrorism-situation-and-trend-report-2019-te-sat (accessed May 2021).

Hall, C., Williams, N., Gauntlett, L., et al. (2019). Findings from systematic review of public perceptions and responses. Deliverable D1.1 of the PROACTIVE project.

Hall, C., Weston, D., Long, F. et al. (2020). Guidelines and recommendations for mitigation and management of CBRNe terrorism. Deliverable D1.3 of the PROACTIVE project.

Havârneanu, G.M., Petersen, L., Arnold, A. et al. (2022). Preparing railway stakeholders against CBRNe threats through better cooperation with security practitioners. *Applied Ergonomics 102*: https://doi.org/10.1016/j.apergo.2022.103752.

Hughes, A.L. and Chauhan, A. (2015). Online media as a means to affect public trust in emergency responders. *Proceedings of the 2015 Information Systems for Crisis Response and Management Conference (ISCRAM 2015)*, 171–181. https://idl.iscram.org/files/onlinemediaasameanstoaffectpublictrustinemergencyresponders/2015/1226_OnlineMediaasaMeanstoAffectPublicTrustinEmergencyRespond ers2015.pdf

Kaufhold, M.-A., Haunschild, J., and Reuter, C. (2020). Warning the public: a survey on attitudes, expectations and use of mobile crisis apps in Germany. *Proceedings of the 28th European Conference on Information Systems (ECIS), An Online AIS Conference* (15–17 June 2020). https://aisel.aisnet.org/ecis2020_rp/84 (accessed May 2021).

Kouadio, S.J.A. (2016). *Les Technologies Smartphone Comme Outils d'Aide à L'alerte Face aux Crues Rapides en France: Expérimentations Dans Le Vaucluse Et Le Var*. Français: Géographie, Université d'Avignon France. tel.archives-ouvertes.fr/tel-01513549/document.

NATO (2008). The international CBRN training curriculum. https://www.nato.int/docu/cep/cep-cbrn-training-e.pdf (accessed May 2021).

Nilsson, E.G. and Stølen, K (2011). Generic functionality in user interfaces for emergency response. *OzCHI '11: Proceedings of the 23rd Australian Computer-Human Interaction Conference*, 233–242 (November 2011). https://doi.org/10.1145/2071536.2071574

Pylvas, K., Kankaanranta, T., Sofuoglu, Z., et al. (2018). NEXES user requirements, needs and gaps. EU H2020 project NEXES deliverable D2.3.

Slovic, P. (2002). Terrorism as hazard: a new species of trouble. *Risk Analysis 22* (3): 425–426.

Slovic, P., Finucane, M.L., Peters, E., and MacGregor, D.G. (2004). Risk as analysis and risk as feelings: some thoughts about affect, reason, risk, and rationality. *Risk Analysis 24* (2): 311–322.

Steelman, T.A., McCaffrey, S.M., Velez, A.L.K., and Briefel, J.A. (2015). What information do people use, trust, and find useful during a disaster? Evidence from five large wildfires. *Natural Hazards 76* (1): 615–634. https://doi.org/10.1007/s11069-014-1512-x.

Swain, S. and Kelly, D. (2019). Formation of the Practitioner Stakeholder Advisory Board. Deliverable D2.1 of the PROACTIVE project.

Tan, M.L., Raj, P., Hudson-Doyle, E. et al. (2017). Mobile applications in crisis informatics literature: a systematic review. *International Journal of Disaster Risk Reduction 24*: 297–311. https://doi.org/10.1016/j.ijdrr.2017.06.009.

Tan, M.L., Prasanna, R., Stock, K. et al. (2020). Modified usability framework for disaster apps: a qualitative thematic analysis of user reviews. *International Journal of Disaster Risk Science 11*: 615–629. https://doi.org/10.1007/s13753-020-00282-x.

Upland (2021a). 21% of Users abandon an app after one use. https://uplandsoftware.com/localytics/resources/blog/21-percent-of-users-abandon-apps-after-one-use/ (accessed May 2021).

Upland (2021b). Mobile app retention rate: what's a good retention rate? https://uplandsoftware.com/localytics/resources/blog/mobile-apps-whats-a-good-retention-rate/ (accessed May 2021).

9

Crime Mapping in Crime Analysis

The Developments in the Past Two Decades

Gorazd Meško, Katja Eman and Rok Hacin

Faculty of Criminal Justice and Security, University of Maribor, Maribor, Slovenia

9.1 Introduction

Criminological and criminal investigative research are an integral part of criminal justice studies. Crime and criminal behavior analyses (e.g. data collection, links between different behaviors and crime, sample analyses, etc.) have been a subject of interest throughout history. However, the first scientific attempts to determine links between crime, criminal behavior, and space go back to the nineteenth century (Weisburd and McEven 1997). In 1844, a department was established within the London Metropolitan Police, with the task to identify patterns of crime. Investigators therefore collected, compared, and analyzed police information, which also led to the collection and management of crime statistics. Crime analysis has been evolving ever since and takes several different forms, which can be classified into one of the three types of analytical techniques (Hart and Zandbergen 2012): (i) administrative crime analysis,[1] (ii) tactical crime analysis,[2] and (iii) strategic crime analysis.[3]

---

1 Administrative crime analysis covers long-term projects and aims to provide economic, geographic, and crime data to the police, city councils, neighborhoods, concerned citizens, and/ or the media (Hart and Zandbergen 2012).

2 Tactical crime analysis emphasizes data collection, pattern identification, and the development of possible clues, which contribute to the solving of crimes. It usually involves analyzing individual data on specific events (e.g. robberies, burglaries, etc.) (Hart and Zandbergen 2012).

3 Strategic crime analysis focuses on operational strategies to develop solutions to problematic recurring crime. Analysis of geographical units, such as areas of jurisdiction and patrol districts, is usually included in such analysis (Hart and Zandbergen 2012).

Security Technologies and Social Implications, First Edition. Edited by Garik Markarian, Ruža Karlović, Holger Nitsch, and Krishna Chandramouli.
© 2023 The Institute of Electrical and Electronics Engineers, Inc.
Published 2023 by John Wiley & Sons, Inc.

Crime analysis, as a part of a broader research area of different forms of crime, crime trends, and criminal behavior, comprises detailed data on the development of crime. Having once relied on human observation and memory of crime incidents, contemporary crime analysis uses complex computer systems that perform various analytical techniques. These range from simple sample analysis to complex statistical data analysis and crime mapping to identify crime hotspots or areas (Eman et al. 2013, p. 288).

Chainey (2014) described crime mapping as the direct application of data based on two particular characteristics of crime: (i) it has an inherent geographical quality, and (ii) it does not happen randomly. Crime mapping can be defined as an integral tool of various law enforcement agencies, enabling them to present crime on a map or regional network visually. Criminological exploration of geographical characteristics of crime requires the use of a Geographic Information System (hereinafter GIS), a computer tool that identifies the characteristics of crime, based on which various criminological theories can be verified, and police activities can be planned[4] within the model of problem-oriented policing[5] (Cordner and Perkins Biebel 2005). With such an organization of criminal offences, misdemeanours, and other security phenomena (e.g. traffic accidents), law enforcement authorities can identify patterns, problem areas, and additional relevant information on crimes or other events that enable them to perform more effectively. Klinkon and Meško (2005) argued that crime mapping is an integral part of crime analysis. Six types of crime analysis are known: (i) tactical, (ii) operational, (iii) strategic, (iv) analytical, (v) intelligence, and (vi) investigative, and each of them has a specific purpose and method of analysis (Ahmadi 2003, pp. 6–7).

The advantages of crime mapping can be seen in support of policing, visual presentation and communication, overcoming inaccurate perceptions of problem areas, developing an integrated approach to crime analysis, easier identification

---

4 Crime mapping is a support activity that facilitates the implementation of the following police activities: (i) responding to calls, (ii) collecting crime location data, (iii) using patrols and targeted responsiveness, (iv) analyzing and obtaining police intelligence, (v) exchanging information with partner agencies, and (vi) reassurance of the public (Home Office 2005).

5 Tilley (2003) argued that the priority of modern police and policing is to reduce crime and disorder, based on problem-oriented policing where the police move away from reactive work (i.e. response to events) to proactive work, which includes event analysis and response planning, as crime prevention methods.

of links and other factors,[6] and knowledge-based preventive responses to crime (Home Office 2005; Klinkon and Meško 2005). However, a particular weakness of crime mapping can be observed in the form of: (i) generalization errors, (ii) irregularities in the creation of maps to conceal specific data, (iii) manipulation of statistical data, (iv) irregularities in the creation of maps, due to the poor quality of data, and (v) the GIGO effect (i.e. Garbage In, Garbage Out) (Ostrožnik 2012, pp. 31–34).

Boba Santos (2013, p. 37) provided a more detailed and narrowly focused definition of crime mapping. It is seen as the process of using GIS to perform spatial analyses, crime analyses, and other problem-orientated analyses related to policing. Burrough and McDonnell (1998) defined GIS as a set of tools that enable the collection, storage, searching, transformation, and display of spatial data. GIS enables the identification of: (i) the perpetrators' places of residence, (ii) the location of the most vulnerable communities, (iii) determining the methods of movement/transportation of perpetrators to their destinations, (iv) identification of causes of repeated crime in certain areas, and (v) identification of problematic areas with a higher crime rate (i.e. hotspots[7]) (; Reddy 2018). Crime data are presented with thematic maps,[8] which can be divided into quantitative (displaying numerical information of study areas) and qualitative ones (displaying the qualitative characteristics of an individual area). Thematic maps can also be classified as (Klinkon and Meško 2005):

- statistical (displaying raw data of individual units);
- point (using points to display individual crimes or grouping of crimes that occur more often);

---

6 Studying crime and its distribution requires the consideration of the influence of demographic and other factors, such as population density, the specifics of certain forms of crime (e.g. drug-related crime, ecological crime, etc.), lifestyle in research areas (i.e. urban vs rural areas), lack of informal social control, daily migration of people, occurrence and migration of tourists, organization of police and policing and other security organizations (e.g. municipal wardens, private security, etc.), and police techniques of detection, investigation and sanctioning of crime (Meško et al. 2010).

7 Clarke and Eck (2008) distinguish between acute and chronic criminal hotspots. Ratcliffe (2004a, b) defined the three basic forms of chronic hotspots as (i) hot dots (locations with a high crime rate, where dots indicate places, such as individual building, parking lots, etc., with a higher concentration of crime), (ii) hot lines (streets where crime is concentrated), and (iii) hot areas (neighborhoods or areas [usually] outside the cities where crime is concentrated).

8 Thematic maps are not only used to display spatial patterns of one or several variables and geographic attributes, as they also helpful for comparing patterns between the samples (Slocum et al. 2005).

- choropleth (displaying separate distributions into individual administrative areas);
- isopleth (connecting areas of equal values with lines); and
- linear (displaying linear symbols illustrated by the difference in line thickness).

The primary goal of crime mapping using GIS is to synthesize and display the research findings on clear and transparent maps (Kraak and Ormeling 2003). Klinkon and Meško (2005, p. 136) argued that such maps and mapping began to be used as tools to merge cartography with GIS. The latter is a particular asset of the police, as it enables the display of data on maps and makes it easier to understand where, when, and who committed a crime. The data are most commonly shown on maps in the form of dots, as they allow for very accurate location display and effective planning of police operational activities (Harries 1999). GIS, in a broader sense, has replaced the traditional tagging of locations with a high crime rate (i.e. hotspots) on maps using pins or magnets to make it easier for police to analyze crime. Filbert (2004) listed three goals of using GIS in policing: (i) analysis and understanding of crime and with related social problems in a particular community, (ii) efficient planning of police work and allocation of resources on the basis of crime analyses, and (iii) informing the community on crime hotspots, crime trends, crime statistics, and so on.

Crime mapping began to develop intensively in Slovenia in the 1990s, and in the last two decades, GIS has become the primary tool to achieve this in both the Slovenian police and academic research, enabling the creation of transparent maps with advanced functions and a detailed analysis of crime (with geographical maps representing an integral part of the crime analysis). However, the development and use of GIS as a tool and method of crime analysis had already begun in the 1960s (Verbovšek 2012), and the use of GIS in crime analysis and mapping has played a significant role in related education in Slovenia since 2012 when Meško et al. (2012) included crime analysis and crime mapping in the Faculty of Criminal Justice and Security curriculum at the University of Maribor. Students have thus been trained in the use of GIS to solve specific tasks in the context of crime analysis, such as: (i) modeling and display of the distribution of security phenomena and processes (e.g. mapping crime, display of spatial data, 3D display, and temporal analysis of data), (ii) identifying correlations between parameters (e.g. frequency and time course of studied phenomena in individual areas), and (iii) in-depth analysis of individual security phenomena in selected areas (e.g. criminal hotspots, potential targets, etc.) and the planning of solutions (i.e. situational prevention methods).

The aim of this chapter is to present the development of crime mapping in Slovenia. The first part will include the application of the GIS in the Slovenian police and a review of past studies focusing on or including crime mapping. In the second part of the chapter, the development of crime mapping within academia will be highlighted, which eventually led to the establishment of the GIS Lab at the Faculty of Criminal Justice and Security, University of Maribor. Moreover, a presentation on cooperation between the Faculty of Criminal Justice and national (i.e. police) and international organizations and scholars will be provided. In the discussion part, the authors will tackle the present issues of crime mapping in the Slovenian police related to addressing antisocial behaviors and planning police preventive activities.

9.2 Introducing Crime Mapping to the Slovenian Police

The human need to display geographic data is essential and enduring, and thus we have seen maps for thousands of years. The beginnings of crime mapping saw pins stuck in large maps as early as the mid-1800s, showing the locations of recorded crimes. Still, they had several limitations, most notably the loss of previous data that came with updating the maps, archiving problems, static maps, difficulties in monitoring a series of events through longer periods of time, and difficulties with understanding the events, due to the simplistic presentation of different crimes with pins of different colors. Virtual crime maps have more or less tackled these limitations, as pins were replaced by specific points or symbols (Harries 1999), and today, crime mapping has become an integral part of any modern police force and system of knowledge-based policing.

GIS was introduced to the police in the late 1980s and early 1990s when computers and software became more affordable, accessible, and user-friendly. Analysts were the first users of the mapping of crime, while police officers were rarely involved in the process (Harries 1999). Today, in addition to analysts, police officers, commanders, and criminal investigators are engaged in crime mapping procedures, using mapping programs on a daily basis to facilitate the visualization of crime, identify trends and patterns of crime, predict possible crime locations, plan prevention operations, and so on (Environmental System Research Institute [ESRI] 2020).

The Slovenian police began introducing GIS in 1992 to provide the quality of information necessary for the efficient and rational implementation of police operational tasks. In 1992, the decision of the Ministry of the Interior introduced the GIS produced by the Slovenian provider Mikrodata. Specifically, a Spatial Data Management System or Spatial Information System (hereinafter SDMS program) was introduced to the police, and this is software that enables the management of computerized information systems by entering, storing, searching, analyzing, displaying, plotting, and distributing spatial data. The essence of the operation is in the interaction between various descriptive and numerical data, equipped with arbitrary and/or standard graphic attributes, which are systematized in a layer at particular geographical coordinates or spatial locations (Drevenšek 2005).

The police introduced GIS as one of the information subsystems that allow the integration of pre-existing alphanumeric databases with the spatial maps of Slovenia (Urh 2007, p. 55). In 1993, the second set of applications was developed, which enabled the spatial processing of data on traffic accidents. A transition to the software produced by the US company ESRI took place. The decision to switch to this software package was made because 90% of all spatial data in Slovenia had been created with ESRI software (Drevenšek 2005). From 1994 onward, the use of GIS has enabled various spatial analyses of criminal events in the territory of the Republic of Slovenia.

The development of crime mapping as an essential part of crime analysis in Slovenia can be divided into three periods. In the beginning, GIS was used in the Operational Communication Centre (hereinafter OCC) of the police to support decision-making in deploying officers to the crime or other incident scenes, and as a software tool used in spatial analysis and the processing of statistical geographic data. In this period, the purpose of crime mapping was to provide all police units with an analysis of crime in their area in order to improve the decision-making process and measures taken at the level of individual police stations. GIS was found to be extremely useful in making decisions based on spatially located information, as the time of response is crucial when the OCC receives emergency calls. In such situations, GIS provides adequate support, as it can shorten the time required to make appropriate decisions and improve the quality of guidance to the scene. Experts at the General Police Directorate are responsible for upgrading GIS and updating data (Drevenšek 2005).

Spatial-statistical analysis of geo-located data on crime and other security events has been recognized as one of the most valuable tools that police have at their disposal. Urh (2007, p. 56) argued that spatial statistical analysis could be used in the analysis of traffic accidents, violations of the peace and public order, various types of crime (e.g. theft, robbery, burglary, drug trafficking, etc.), and elsewhere where security problems occur, and the spatial dimension combined with the use of multilayered analysis of data allows us a better overview and understanding of such phenomena. LeBeau (2001) also pointed out that connecting events and intervention calls into a meaningful whole makes it easier to understand phenomena than if they are merely presented in the form of points at a specific location.

The second period of GIS use in the Slovenian police includes developing an application for strategic analysis based on such systems. The use of GIS at the OCC proved to be very useful in this regard, and consequently the Directorate for Informatics and Telecommunications decided to develop their own analytics program, while police forces elsewhere in Europe and beyond took similar steps. Part of the reason for creating their own application for geospatial data (which is then integrated into crime analysis) and not using existing applications, such as Google

Maps or similar applications with geospatial information, lies in the issue of data protection and the possibility of system intrusions. The primary purpose of making the application was to offer it to all police officers to help them solve crimes.

The third period of GIS use in the Slovenian police covers the last ten years, during which it has become an integral part of crime analysis. The intensive development of operational analytics also characterizes this period. The Slovenian police use a combination of applications and methods, combining their own databases with open-source data. In this context, GeoTime (2021) has become an essential analytical tool to analyze geographical data for operational purposes. The program's uniqueness is reflected in its combination of time and geographical space and 3D data display, as well as extremely useful sociograms and extrapolation systems. It should be emphasized that the proper interpretation of the obtained analyses and schemes is very important. However, it is notable that it is possible to use other data in the analysis and combine several applications, especially data such as that from GPS devices and smartphones, in finding connections between different suspects.

The brief review presented above clearly demonstrates the usefulness of GIS for police officers by enabling them to conduct an efficient and user-friendly analysis of crime and other security phenomena in a selected area. Geospatial analyses as a part of crime analysis can help them in the decision-making process at all levels, from tactical (e.g. organizing patrols) to strategic (e.g. adopting crime prevention measures on a large scale). The following section focuses on crime mapping and the use of GIS in the police to carry out crime mapping studies.

9.3 Crime Mapping Studies

Crime mapping has a long history dating back to the first half of the nineteenth century. Since then, hundreds of studies on crime and delinquency, including those using spatial data, have been carried out by sociologists and criminologists (Philips 1972). The first computerized mapping of crime using crime analysis was done in the mid-1960s when the first crime maps were made using the SYMAP program developed at Harvard University. Early efforts were limited mainly by lack of memory and speed, and the poor resolution of older computers (Harries 1999).

In different forms and using various tools, crime mapping in Slovenia has a long tradition, dating back to 1951, when the first study of the spatial distribution of crime was conducted (Bajt 1951). In the following sections, a review of crime mapping studies in Slovenia is provided. The studies are divided into two distinct time periods: (i) crime mapping studies before 2000, and (ii) crime mapping studies after 2000 (when GIS was used to analyze crime and spatial data).

9.3.1 Crime Mapping in Slovenia Before 2000

In the last 70 years, numerous studies have been carried out in Slovenia, which included analyzing crime and other security phenomena, mapping and/or using GIS. This mapping of crime began with Bajt (1951), who conducted a geographical presentation of the distribution of crime in the Socialist Republic of Slovenia in the period 1948–1950 and explained the reasons for its emergence (Figure 9.1). The first analyses and maps were very basic and had many limitations, primarily due to the lack of precise geolocations of recorded criminal offences. Nevertheless, this first attempt at crime mapping revealed the difference in crime rates between different regions in Slovenia.

More than 20 years after the first crime mapping study, Pečar (1975) conducted a study on the concentration of crime in the city of Ljubljana to identify specific causes of crime and other security phenomena in particular areas. Cartograms were used for testing the correlations among security phenomena on the one hand, and physical and demographic factors on the other. The findings showed that: (i) alcoholics, housed in old buildings in the city center presented a significant security problem, (ii) highly urbanized suburbs were faced with a higher concentration of crime and deviant behavior, and (iii) the number of young offenders and delinquents (usually committing offences concerning violations of public order) had increased, especially in residential areas and remote areas on the outskirts of the city. Pečar (1975) highlighted the uneven distribution of

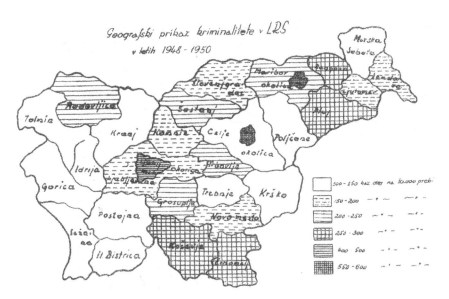

Figure 9.1 Crime in Slovenia in the period 1948–1950. *Source:* Bajt (1951, p. 292).

crime and offenders in the area of Ljubljana. Almost all forms of crime, except for sexual offences and suicides, were concentrated in the city center. Consequently, the study concluded that formal social control should be increased in this area, positively as this could reduce the extent and nature of registered crimes.

The final study of this first period was conducted at the end of the 1970s when Zemljič et al. (1979) conducted a study to determine black spots on the leading road network. They identified four main factors influencing the general problem of road safety in Slovenia: (i) people, (ii) vehicles, (iii) roads, and (iv) environment. They identified dangerous sections of major roads using the critical accident rate method and calculated the number of traffic accidents at a given location using Poisson distributions. The same methods were previously used in similar studies in the United States and Sweden. The researchers identified 323 dangerous road sections in the then Socialist Republic of Slovenia, as shown in Figure 9.2.

In the first period extending over five decades, only three published crime mapping studies were conducted in Slovenia. Some of the reasons for the lack of crime mapping studies before 2000 can be found in: (i) the lack of adequate computer

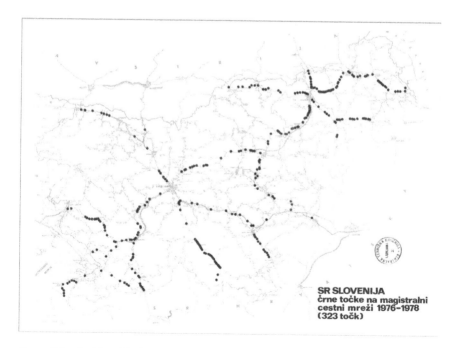

SR SLOVENIJA
črne točke na magistralni
cestni mreži 1976–1978
(323 točk)

Figure 9.2 Accident black spots on the main road network in Slovenia in the period 1976–1978. *Source:* Zemljič et al. (1979)/FAGG, Prometnotehniški inštitut.

equipment; (ii) the lack of sophisticated computer software such as GIS; (iii) the lack of knowledge, as practitioners – namely police and criminologists – conducted studies without advanced knowledge of crime mapping (besides computer knowledge, such mapping demands knowledge of statistics, geography, mathematics, etc.); (iv) no need for sophisticated analysis of crime, as crime levels were relatively low; and (v) the different nature of police work and policing (especially in the years of the socialist militia).

9.3.2 Crime Mapping in Slovenia After 2000

While GIS was introduced to the Slovenian police in the 1990s, criminologists did not begin to use crime mapping techniques until almost a decade later. Meško et al. (2003) analyzed the geographical distribution of deviant behavior in Ljubljana and used GIS for the first time to create crime maps. The findings highlighted three problematic areas in Ljubljana, for which several crime hotspots were characteristic. These locations were predominately in the city center and the areas of shopping centers. Crime hotspots in the city center were predominately identified at the locations of restaurants, discotheques, and nightclubs.

A year later, Klinkon et al. (2004) studied the influence of sociodemographic factors on the development of crime in Ljubljana. Using GIS, the spatial distribution of crime in the city was mapped, based on which the correlations between sociodemographic factors and crime rates were studied. A comparison between the study results and perceptions of crime by individuals living in Ljubljana was made to identify whether local people also perceived the hot spots identified by the police geostatistical data as areas with a higher fear of crime. The overall findings showed that sociodemographic factors influence crime rates and different forms of crime, and crime rates differ in different parts of Ljubljana (Figure 9.3).

Meško et al. (2010) used crime mapping methods (i.e. GIS) and analyzed thefts, burglaries, and robberies in Ljubljana in 2003 and 2004. The core evaluation method (i.e. Kernel Density Interpolation) showed the concentration of the focal crimes in the city center of Ljubljana (especially in areas with large movements of people, such as at the main train and bus stations), spreading along the main roads toward the city's outskirts. Clusters of such crimes were also detected in shopping and entertainment areas with large parking lots, Tivoli Park (a recreational area), and in the Tabor neighborhood, which is located close to a methadone center, and an area well-known for attracting groups of young people due to the nearby Metelkova "autonomous zone."

Eman et al. (2012) conducted the first crime mapping study focusing on environmental crime in the area under the jurisdiction of the Murska Sobota Police

Figure 9.3 Crime mapping in Ljubljana using the Isopleth technique. *Source:* Klinkon and Meško (2005).

Directorate (in the eastern part of Slovenia, with predominately rural areas). The authors analyzed statistical data on environmental crime in the period 2008–2010, and created crime maps to identify the concentration of environmental crime in the area. The findings showed that polluting and destroying the environment are the prevailing forms of environmental crime and that these are concentrated in remote locations near the state border, along the Mura River Basin, and in the area of small settlements along the main road.

Eman et al. (2013) presented the use of GIS in two studies: (i) an analysis of property crime hotspots in Ljubljana and Maribor in 2010, and (ii) project Krimistat.si. The results of the first study showed the concentration of property crimes in the city centers and their spread in the direction of the main roads toward their outskirts. At the same time, they detected a higher number of property crimes in shopping malls and entertainment areas. The Krimistat.si project is a web application that combines police statistics with Google Maps application. The purpose of the project was to create an application that would be accessible to all and user-friendly, but there was an obstacle in the form of personal data protection that prevents its use.

Hacin and Eman (2014) tested the correlations between crime levels and fear of crime in the small town of Trbovlje. Using GIS, they identified local communities with higher crime rates and compared them with the perception of fear of crime by residents of the same local communities. The findings on the comparison of the distribution of fear of crime in local communities and of crime density showed that the level of fear among the population of individual local communities was proportionate to the distribution of crime. Moreover, the findings revealed that gender does not significantly affect the perceptions of fear of crime. The highest levels of fear were observed in middle-aged individuals, followed by the oldest members of the population.

Eman and Hacin (2015) conducted the first crime mapping study in a rural area of Slovenia, analyzing the distribution of crime in the Rural Municipality of Puconci. They found that crime is concentrated in the most populated areas, and that similar to in urban areas, property crime was the prevailing kind of offence.

Hacin and Eman (2015) conducted a study on the distribution of crime in Ljubljana. Crime maps revealed property offences as a predominant form of crime in the city, with the highest concentration detected in the center, spreading along the main roads to the outskirts. Moreover, several high concentrations of property crime were detected in the commercial areas where the largest shopping centers are located. Restaurants, elementary schools, and kindergartens were also identified as areas where many cases of property damage were detected. The concentration of economic crime in the form of using counterfeit money was located in the city center, where banks, savings banks, and restaurants are located, along the main communication routes leading to the city's outskirts, where several gas stations are located, and in shopping malls. The comparison of crime rates revealed that besides the city center, residential areas also recorded relatively high crime rates.

Meglič and Eman (2015) studied the issue of thefts of various motor vehicles in the area of Ljubljana, using crime mapping in combination with an in-depth analysis of police statistics. They found that thefts of vehicles occur mainly in areas that are slightly distant from the city center but still within the proximity of the main ring road. They identified unsecured parking lots near residential buildings as the main areas where such thefts occur and proposed the following measures: (i) electronic or physical surveillance of parking lots, and (ii) increased lighting in parking lots to provide a deterrent, as most of the thefts occurred at night.

In 2016, Hacin and Eman (2016a) combined crime mapping and situational crime prevention techniques. The authors analyzed data on property crime in Ljubljana and identified two hotspots and two high-concentration areas (shopping centers and the city center). The theft was identified as a predominant form of crime in each area. In the second phase of the study, an observation of protective measures and the behavior of people in identified hotspots was conducted, and specific situational crime prevention measures were proposed for each area, including enhanced video surveillance, promoting self-protective behavior, and introducing physical security (i.e. security guards).

In the same year, Hacin and Eman (2016b) elaborated their study on combining crime mapping and crime prevention techniques, comparing areas in Slovenia's

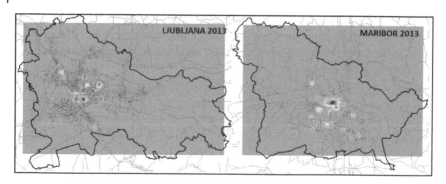

Figure 9.4 Crime distribution and hotspots in Ljubljana and Maribor. *Source:* Hacin and Eman (2016b).

two largest cities, Ljubljana and Maribor, where high property crime rates were recorded. Using GIS, they located crime hotspots in both cities, namely shopping centers and the city centers (Figure 9.4). Based on the characteristics of the hotspots, they proposed several measures that would increase safety and security by applying Clark's situational crime prevention techniques.

Due to the increased number of migrants that have crossed the Slovenian border since 2015, Eman et al. (2020) conducted a crime mapping study of the eastern part of Slovenia focusing on illegal border crossings. The study aimed to identify the characteristics of hotspots (i.e. areas where police have recorded a high number of illegal border crossings). The resulting crime maps showed that remote areas with relatively easy access, such as forests, bridges across rivers, roads, etc., experienced a high concentration of illegal border crossings. The authors proposed specific measures to tackle this situation, especially providing police officers with adequate equipment that would enable them to detect migrants at night.

The second period, extending over two decades, experienced a higher number of studies compared to the previous one. The introduction of GIS not only in the police but also at the Faculty of Criminal Justice and Security, University of Maribor, enabled criminologists to conduct crime mapping studies and to combine crime mapping with other areas of research (e.g. fear of crime, crime prevention, sociodemographic factors, etc.). This period was characterized by intensive collaboration between the police and researchers, as crime mapping was moved from the area of practice alone, in terms of the tactical and operational levels of policing, to a more complex study of crime. In the following section, the establishment and development of the GIS Lab at the Faculty of Criminal Justice and Security, University of Maribor, is presented.

9.4 Geographic Information Systems Laboratory – "GIS Lab" – at the Faculty of Criminal Justice and Security, University of Maribor and Cooperation with the Slovenian Police

Since 2011 at the Faculty of Criminal Justice and Security, University of Maribor, a particular emphasis has been given to analyzing and presenting data on crime and public disorder by using GIS for crime mapping as a component of crime analysis. Within the framework of the basic research project, "Environmental crime – criminological, victimological, crime-prevention, psychological, and legal aspects" (Meško et al. 2012), the Geographic Information Systems Laboratory (hereinafter GIS Lab) was established, in which an existing computer laboratory with more than 20 computers was equipped with the ArcGIS software, enabling students to conduct tutorials and case studies using crime mapping. Crime analysis has since become an integral part of undergraduate and postgraduate study programs. For criminal justice students, the mapping of crime and public disorder presents a new method of crime analysis and prevention. What is even more important, students obtain the basic knowledge of crime mapping, which they can then use in practice or in their future careers (assuming that they will work in the police or security sector). Students use a manual with tutorials adjusted for undergraduate and postgraduate programs and a textbook (currently in print), which indicates that the course on crime mapping has matured. In addition, several bachelor's and master's theses were written on crime mapping and crime analysis, in which the analyses were predominately conducted using GIS.

The establishment of the GIS Lab would not be possible without the well-established cooperation with the police. The Director-General of the Slovenian police and the dean of the Faculty of Criminal Justice and Security, University of Maribor, facilitated collaboration between the police and researchers. One form of assistance from the police in establishing the GIS Lab was the provision of help and partial training of researchers with the GIS software. In 2014, the cooperation was formalized by signing a bilateral cooperation agreement (Ministrstvo za notranje zadeve, Policija 2014).

In 2011, in cooperation with the Slovenian police, access was granted to geospatial data on crime that led to the implementation of crime mapping studies, as described in the previous section.[9] This granting of access to police data represented the foundation for developing and teaching the use of GIS in criminal

---

9 We have to express our gratitude to the Geodetic Administration of the Republic of Slovenia that provided the geographical data for the territory of Slovenia, without which further crime mapping analysis would not be possible.

justice studies focusing on crime, particularly methods of crime mapping and analysis. Since 2013, the Slovenian police have been unable to provide geospatial data on crime due to the new laws on personal data protection. Nevertheless, intensive cooperation with the police continued, and several researchers from the Faculty of Criminal Justice and Security, University of Maribor have since conducted studies in collaboration with the police. In these, the police analysts carried out the crime mapping and produced crime maps, while the researchers conducted in-depth crime analyses.

Researchers at the Faculty of Criminal Justice and Security, University of Maribor (GIS Lab) who were trained in the use of crime mapping have also put their knowledge into practice, as all studies after 2000 were conducted using the GIS system (e.g. Eman et al. 2013; Hacin and Eman 2015; Meško et al. 2010). Researchers also started to combine crime mapping with crime prevention techniques (e.g. Hacin and Eman 2016a, b), problems of illegal migration (Eman et al. 2020), fear of crime (Hacin and Eman 2014), environmental crime (Eman et al. 2012), and other criminological and preventative topics and methods. Moreover, the researchers slowly transcended national borders and began collaborating with foreign experts in crime mapping and analysis.

Although restrictions regarding the use of geospatial data on crime presented a key limitation to further research, the development of the GIS Lab and crime mapping in Slovenia continued. In a way, being denied access to the police data provided an opportunity for intense collaboration with the police, which has proved to be very fruitful. Several publications and debates on the use of the GIS were joint activities of police crime analysts, former police chiefs, and researchers at the Faculty of Criminal Justice and Security, University of Maribor, such as studies on crime hot spots and criminal investigation (Eman et al. 2012; Meško and Dvoršek 2003; Meško et al. 2003).

The application Krimistat.si is considered one of the best outcomes of the collaboration between the Slovenian police, the Faculty of Electrical Engineering and Computer Science, University of Maribor, and Faculty of Criminal Justice and Security, University of Maribor (predominately involving researchers working at the GIS Lab), which has never been made available to a wider population due to legal reasons. The aim of the Krimistat.si project was to combine police statistics databases and Google Maps to prepare an online application that would be user-friendly and accessible to everyone who uses the Internet. This would enable the public to be informed about the distribution of reported crimes. It was planned that the application would serve as a public information service and as a tool for the police (the internal aspect of data reuse). Krimistat.si offered a straightforward and relatively attractive application of visualizing geo-located data of crime recorded by the police in a specific time period (Figure 9.5). However, there was a legal obstacle related to protecting personal data that prevented the public use of the Krimistat.si as a free online application (Eman et al. 2013), although the Slovenian police used it for

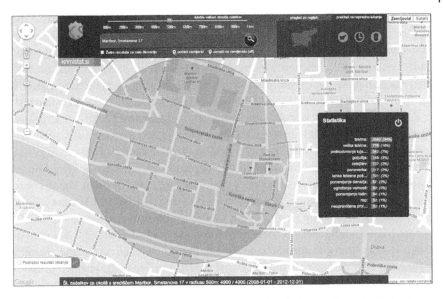

Figure 9.5 Krimistat.si. *Source:* Eman et al. (2013, p. 304)/Safety and security in local communities (2015–2018).

internal purposes for a while. Nevertheless, the online application presented progress in crime mapping, as it followed the contemporary police trends in the analysis of crime.

Despite several challenges and obstacles related to crime mapping and analysis, researchers at the Faculty of Criminal Justice and Security, University of Maribor, have succeeded in establishing GIS Lab, and transferring their knowledge of crime mapping into the faculty's curricula and practice, as seen in numerous crime mapping studies. Crime mapping in Slovenia may not yet be in its mature phase when compared to the best laboratories elsewhere in the West. However, it represents an important addition to our knowledge and understanding of crime and crime patterns in Slovenia, which is beneficial for both researchers and practitioners.

9.5 First Steps and Inclusion of Crime Analysis to Research and Teaching at the Faculty of Criminal Justice and Security, University of Maribor

The use of GIS in crime analysis by the Slovenian police was already in place in the 1990s, before researchers from the Faculty of Criminal Justice and Security, University of Maribor, in cooperation with the Police Department of Ljubljana, first carried out a research project using crime mapping techniques. The main goal of the project, financed by the Municipality of Ljubljana, was to provide the police and municipality with high-quality and up-to-date information about crime hot spots, and so increase police efficiency in the capital (Meško et al. 2003). This was the first joint research project of researchers and police analysts using computerized GIS, and the findings were presented at several meetings both nationally and internationally.

The beginnings of research using crime mapping at the Faculty of Criminal Justice and Security, University of Maribor, were related to study visits and environmental criminology meetings attended by the first author of this chapter. He attended several Environmental Criminology and Crime Analysis Symposiums (hereinafter ECCA) conferences about 20 years ago, and learned about crime analysis using GIS in the subsequent two decades. The extensive work of the ECCA was presented by Brantingham (2008) in his Introduction to the ECCA papers. Visits to Rutgers University in Newark and the University of Cincinnati in Ohio, United States, contributed to broadening knowledge and using modern technology in planning policing and crime prevention. The visits resulted in cooperation with Ronald V. Clark and John E. Eck from the Center for Problem-Oriented Policing and the translation of their manual *Crime Analysis for Problem Solvers in 60 Small Steps* into Slovenian (ASU Center for Problem-Oriented Policing 2021; Clarke and Eck 2008). The translated manual is now a helpful tool for Slovene police analytics, students, and researchers. The printed version of the manual was distributed to all police stations, regional directorates, and other departments at the Directorate General of the Slovenian Police by the Faculty of Criminal Justice and Security, University of Maribor, for free. The manual is also available on the problem-oriented policing (POP) webpage.

The Faculty of Criminal Justice and Security, University of Maribor was a consortium member of the EU–Australia project on "Governance and Security: Challenges for Policing in the 21st century/2006–2009" headed by Susanne Karstedt. In addition to many other topics, the use of GIS in policing and crime prevention was discussed as part of this with students from Australia, France, England, and Slovenia. The 2008 summer school in Piran, Slovenia, was strongly supported by the Slovenian police. During this event, the internationally renowned police scholars Andrew Goldsmith, Philip Stenning, Richard Wortley, and others shared their knowledge to facilitate police and policing research in Slovenia (Meško 2021).

In addition, the primary influence on the development of the use of GIS technology at the Faculty of Criminal Justice and Security, University of Maribor were visits to the Simon Fraser University, Vancouver, Canada, and the Jill Dando Institute of Security and Crime Science, University College of London, United Kingdom, during the last two decades. Cooperation with the latter also continued in the field of student exchanges within the Erasmus+ program. Learning about the development of crime science and analysis influenced the final decision to invest more resources in developing geographic crime analysis equipment at the Faculty of Criminal Justice and Security, University of Maribor, and training young scholars in the field of crime analysis (Meško 2021). The continuation of international cooperation resulted in further development of crime analysis in Slovenia, especially in crime mapping using GIS. Collaboration with the John Moores University in Liverpool, United Kingdom, and its School of Justice Studies contributed to the exchange of teaching staff and learning about crime analysis and other uses of the GIS technology, predominantly through our communication with Adegbola Ojo (see also Ojo and Ojewale 2019).

Since 2012, the GIS Lab has been one of the leading activities of the Chair of Criminology at the Faculty of Criminal Justice and Security, University of Maribor, in the field of teaching at all levels of studies and research, especially on local safety and security in Slovenia (Eman et al. 2020; Hacin and Eman 2015, 2016a, b). The intensive activity in research in this area can be attested by several new publications (such as Eman and Hacin 2021). Moreover, several student research projects have been dedicated to topics related to GIS, policing, and crime prevention, especially on the analysis of crime in urban areas (Česenj 2016), regional crime analysis (Felkar 2018), the perception of crime and fear of crime (Hacin 2014), car thefts in urban settings (Meglič 2014), and making GIS crime analysis more user-friendly (Lukman 2013). The inclusion of talented and highly skilled students in crime analyses research is well developed at the Faculty of Criminal Justice and Security, and this provides an additional learning experience and opportunity to collaborate with top domestic and foreign researchers and experts and contribute to the training of future practitioners and crime analysts, as well as the development of environmental criminology in general.

9.6 Discussion and Conclusion

Crime mapping as a part of crime analysis represents one of many various tools for the evidence-based responses and crime control of today's police forces. As a method of crime analysis, crime mapping has two goals: (i) responding to crime and deviant behaviors, and (ii) knowledge-based preventative responses to any issues that are detected. Crime analysis should be valid and reliable, including statistical analyses of crime and the visualization of the geographic distribution of crime and other security phenomena, as this is of great importance for policymakers and practitioners in policing and security. The use of crime mapping in crime analysis contributes to solving and preventing crimes, as it results in identifying the precise locations of hot spots or areas. For police, this means that they can develop more efficient plans and better perform their operational activities.

In the last 30 years, the Slovenian police have made remarkable progress in using GIS as an integral part of crime analysis, and it is now an essential part of their operational analytics. The use of the GeoTime presents a step forward, as the police use a combination of different applications and methods. It is worth mentioning that all police officers in Slovenia have access to the application and the information that it provides, which gives them an advantage in solving crimes, as they can obtain information on the time and location of the crime, and the movements of possible suspects. Police analysts are extremely useful in solving crimes and are constantly upgrading their knowledge. However, if a problem arises, the police can turn to an external forensic expert, especially in strategic crime analysis. It is important to note, however, that proper interpretation and reinterpretation of the results of any analysis is very important.

We support the need for constant further research and training in how to use GIS to obtain better crime analysis and crime prevention methods, based on the resulting crime maps and analysis. The most significant advantage of GIS is seeing and recognizing a new relationship between the crime and other data via the created map. Moreover, GIS enables the analysis and understanding of the occurrence of crime and related social problems, such as the distribution of poverty, drug abuse, and public disorder. It also provides information about crime statistics and trends. Evidence-based policing is, in the authors' opinion, the most appropriate and helpful way for decision making regarding crime and related issues. Its value is seen in systematic feedback to the police and continual improvement of their operating methods.

Despite several obstacles and issues regarding crime mapping, progress in his area is also evident at the Faculty of Criminal Justice and Security, University of Maribor, especially in joint projects with police departments (as seen, for example, in joint publications). Due to the complexity of the field, despite some 20 years of crime mapping, we are still at a relatively immature stage of development. While crime mapping is well-known at the Faculty of Criminal Justice and Security, University of Maribor, the path of further development is still undecided. The question thus remains: should we focus on specific crime mapping tools, or should we stay in the field of general crime analysis and the use of a combination of methods? We can conclude, however, that the use of GIS technology is promising in terms of scientific research in Slovenia.

Looking to the future reveals many opportunities and also challenges. In December 2021, Eman and Hacin (2021) published the first GIS crime analysis textbook in Slovenia, titled *Introduction to Crime Mapping*. This textbook, with tutorials on mapping, is the result of some 20 years of research at the Faculty of Criminal Justice, University of Maribor. It comprises 17 chapters, which can be divided into two parts. In the first (theoretical) part, which consists of five chapters, students are introduced to GIS, the history of mapping, and the development of crime mapping. The second part of the textbook comprises 12 tutorials, through which students will learn how to use the tools offered by the ArcGIS program in practice. These tutorials follow a natural progression in difficulty, from the first basic steps to independent work. The textbook itself is primarily intended for students at the Faculty of Criminal Justice and Security, University of Maribor, who want to get acquainted with analytics and mapping, and also for practitioners in the institutions of criminal justice, especially those interested in police crime analysis. As in many other nations worldwide, Slovenia is also developing the use of GIS and crime analytics in the direction of the use of artificial intelligence. This was also a priority of the Republic of Slovenia during its Presidency of the Council of the European Union (July–December 2021), as was especially emphasized within the European Union Agency for Law Enforcement Training (CEPOL) events and activities (Meško and Urbas 2021). Moreover, the fact that crime will never wholly disappear opens up unlimited possibilities and opportunities for GIS crime analytics.

References

Ahmadi, M. (2003). Crime mapping and spatial analysis. Master thesis. International Institute for Geo-Information Science and Earth Observation.

ASU Center for Problem-Oriented Policing (2021). About us. https://popcenter.asu.edu/content/about-us (accessed 9 June 2021).

Bajt, F. (1951). Geografski prikaz kriminalitete v Sloveniji [Geographical presentation of crime in Slovenia]. *Kriminalistična služba* 11 (1): 8–9.

Boba Santos, R. (2013). *Crime Analysis with Crime Mapping*. Los Angeles, CA: Sage.

Brantingham, P. (2008). Introduction to the ECCA papers. *Security Journal* 21: 1–3. https://doi.org/10.1057/palgrave.sj.8350065.

Burrough, P.A. and McDonnell, R.A. (1998). *Principles of Geographical Information Systems*. Oxford: Oxford University Press.

CEPOL (2021). *CEPOL Research & Science Conference 2021 MRU*, Vilnius. https://conference-digital.cepol.europa.eu/cepol-research-science-conference-2021-mru-vilnius/featured (accessed 4 February 2022).

Česenj, A. (2016). Analiza kaznivih dejanj na Policijski postaji Ljubljana Šiška med letom 2008 in 2013 [Analysis of criminal offences – police station Ljubljana Šiška between 2008 and 2013]. Bachelor thesis. Univerza v Mariboru.

Chainey, S.P. (2001). Combating crime through partnership; examples of crime and disorder mapping solutions in London, UK. In: *Mapping and Analysing Crime Data – Lessons from Research and Practice* (ed. A. Hirschfield and K. Bowers), 95–119. London: Taylor & Francis.

Chainey, S. (2014). Crime mapping. In: *Encyclopedia of Criminology and Criminal Justice*, Springer (ed. G. Bruinsma and D. Weisburd). New York: Springer https://doi.org/10.1007/978-1-4614-5690-2_317 (accessed 8 June 2021).

Clarke, R.V. and Eck, J.E. (2008). *Priročnik za policijske (kriminalistične) analitike – v 60 korakih do rešitve problema [Crime Analysis For Problem Solvers – In 60 Small Steps]* (trans. G. Meško and K. Eman). Ljubljana: Fakulteta za varnostne vede.

Cordner, G. and Perkins Biebel, E. (2005). Problem-oriented policing in practice. *Criminology & Public Policy* 4 (2): 155–180. https://doi.org/10.1111/j.1745-9133.2005.00013.x.

Drevenšek, I. (2005). Obdelava interventnih dogodkov s pomočjo programskih paketov dnevnik dogodkov OKC in geografskega informacijskega sistema [Processing of intervention events with the help of software packages event log OKC and geographic information system]. Bachelor thesis. Univerza v Mariboru.

Eman, K. and Hacin, R. (2015). Analiza kriminalitete na območju Občine Puconci z uporabo metode kartiranja kriminalitete [Analysis of crime in the area of the Municipality of Puconci using the method of crime mapping]. *Anali PAZU HD* 1 (1): 27–44.

Eman, K. and Hacin, R. (2021). *Uvod v kartiranje kriminalitete [Introduction to Crime Mapping]*. Maribor: Univerza v Mariboru, Univerzitetna založba.

Eman, K., Meško, G., and Ivančič, D. (2012). Ekološka kriminaliteta v Pomurju [Environmental crime in Pomurje]. *Varstvoslovje* 14 (1): 113–131.

Eman, K., Györkös, J., Lukman, K. et al. (2013). Crime mapping for the purpose of policing in Slovenia – recent developments. *Revija za kriminalistiko in kriminologijo* 64 (1): 287–308.

Eman, K., Ivančić, D., and Bagari, D. (2020). Nezakoniti prehodi državne meje na območju Policijske uprave Murska Sobota [Illegal crossings of the state border in the area of the Police Directorate Murska Sobota]. In: *6. Nacionalna konferenca o varnosti v lokalnih skupnostih: varnost v ruralnih in urbanih okoljih: konferenčni zbornik [6th National Conference on Safety and Security in Local Communities: Safety and Security in Rural and Urban Environments]* (ed. G. Meško, R. Hacin and K. Eman), 23–35. Maribor: Univerzitetna zalozba Univerze.

Environmental System Research Institute (ESRI) (2020). About ESRI. https://www.esri.com/about-esri (accessed 5 June 2021).

Felkar, D. (2018). Analiza izbranih oblik kriminalitete na območju PU Murska Sobota med leti 2008 in 2015 z uporabo metode kartiranja kriminalitete [An analysis of selected forms of crime in the area of police directorate Murska Sobota between 2008 and 2015 using the method of crime mapping]. Master thesis. Univerza v Mariboru.

Filbert, K.M. (2004). What is geographic information system: basic concepts and applications of GIS of criminal justice and policing. *Presentation Presented at the 7th Annual International Crime Mapping Research Conference*, USA (31 March 2004).

GeoTime (2021). Products. https://geotime.com/products/geotime (accessed 21 June 2021).

Hacin, R. (2014). Kartiranje varnostnih pojavov in proučevanje strahu pred kriminaliteto v Občini Trbovlje [Crime mapping and the study of fear of crime in the municipality Trbovlje]. Master thesis. Univerza v Mariboru.

Hacin, R. and Eman, K. (2014). Study of the fear of crime in the municipality of Trbovlje using crime mapping tools. *Revija za kriminalistiko in kriminologijo* 65 (4): 299–315.

Hacin, R. and Eman, K. (2015). Analiza porazdelitve kriminalitete na območju Ljubljane v letu 2014 [Analysis of the distribution of crime in the area of Ljubljana in 2014]. In: *Varnost v lokalnih skupnostih: Zbornik prispevkov Prve nacionalne konference o varnosti v lokalnih skupnostih [Safety and Security in Local Communities: Conference Proceedings of the First National Conference on Safety and Security in Local Environments]* (ed. G. Meško), 92–99. Ljubljana: Fakulteta za varnostne vede.

Hacin, R. and Eman, K. (2016a). Combination of property crime hot spot analysis and situational crime prevention methods – a case study of Ljubljana. In: *Criminal Justice and Security in Central and Eastern Europe: Safety, Security, and Social Control in Local Communities* (ed. G. Meško and B. Lobnikar), 148–159. Ljubljana: University of Maribor, Faculty of Criminal Justice and Security.

Hacin, R. and Eman, K. (2016b). Uporaba metod policijske analitike pri preprečevanju premoženjske kriminalitete v slovenskih urbanih okoljih [Use of methods of police analysis in the prevention of property crime in Slovenian urban environments]. In: *2. Nacionalna konferenca o varnosti v lokalnih skupnostih: Varnost v lokalnih skupnostih (29. november 2016, Murska Sobota, Slovenija) (konferenčni zbornik) [2nd National Conference on Safety and Security in Local Communities: Safety and Security in Local Communities (29 November 2016, Murska Sobota, Slovenia) (Conference Proceedings)]* (ed. G. Meško, K. Eman and U. Pirnat), 109–118. Maribor: Univerzitetna založba Univerze v Mariboru. http:// press.um.si/index.php/ump/catalog/view/144/124/201-1 (accessed 8 June 2021).

Harries, K. (1999). *Mapping Crime: Principle and Practice*. Washington: U.S. Department of Justice.

Hart, T.C. and Zandbergen, P.A. (2012). *Effects of Data Quality on Predictive Hotspot Mapping*. Washington: U.S. Department of Justice.

Home Office (2005). *Crime Mapping: Improving Performance*. London: Home Office Police Standards Unit. http://www.ucl.ac.uk/scs/people/academic-research-staff/ spencer-chainey/Slides/Home_Office_CrimeMapping (accessed 4 June 2021).

Klinkon, I. and Meško, G. (2005). Uporaba geografskih informacijskih sistemov pri analizi kriminalitete [Use of geographic information systems in crime analysis]. *Varstvoslovje* 7 (2): 133–149.

Klinkon, I., Meško, G., and Rebernik, D. (2004). Vpliv socialnodemografskih dejavnikov na razvoj kriminalitete v Ljubljani: Rezultati preliminarnega raziskovanja [The influence of socio-demographic factors on the development of crime in Ljubljana: results of preliminary research]. In: *5. slovenski dnevi Varstvoslovja [5th Slovenian days of Criminal Justice and Security]* (ed. B. Lobnikar), 836–847. Ljubljana: Fakulteta za varnostne vede.

Kraak, M.-J. and Ormeling, F. (2003). *Cartography: Visualisation of Geospatial Data.* Harlow: Prentice Hall.

LeBeau, J.L. (2001). Mapping out hazardous space for police work. In: *Mapping and Analysing Crime Data – Lessons from Research and Practice* (ed. K. Bowers and A. Hirschfield), 139–152. London: Taylor & Francis.

Lukman, K. (2013). Interaktivna predstavitev informacij javnega značaja o kaznivih dejanjih v Republiki Sloveniji [Interactive exhibition of public sector information criminal acts in the Republic of Slovenia]. Master thesis. Univerza v Mariboru.

Meglič, E. (2014). Uporaba ArcGIS programa pri analizi kaznivih dejanj tatvin motornih vozil v obdobju 2008–2012 v Ljubljani [Kartiranje varnostnih pojavov in proučevanje strahu pred kriminaliteto v Občini Trbovlje]. Master thesis. Univerza v Mariboru.

Meglič, E. and Eman, K. (2015). Uporaba programa ArcGIS pri analizi kaznivih dejanj tatvin motornih vozil v obdobju 2008–2012 v Ljubljani [Using ArcGIS program in analysing criminal offences of motor vehicle thefts in Ljubljana between 2008–2012]. *Varstvoslovje* 17 (3): 338–356.

Meško, G. (2021). Inštitut za Varstvoslovje: prvih 15 let. [Institute of Criminal Justice and Security: first 15 years] 15 let Inštituta za Varstvoslovje [15 years of the Institute of Criminal Justice and Security], Ljubljana. https://www.fvv.um.si/wp-content/uploads/2021/02/IV-15-let-Mes%CC%8Cko-28.1.2020.pdf (accessed 9 June 2021).

Meško, G. and Dvoršek, A. (2003). Kriminalna žarišča in policijska dejavnost [Criminal hotspots and policing]. In: *Dnevi Varstvoslovja [Days of Criminal Justice and Security]* (ed. M. Pagon), 106. Ljubljana: Visoka policijsko-varnostna šola.

Meško, G. and Urbas, V. (2021). Delo policije na področju preiskovanja kriminalitete v Sloveniji v času covida-19 s poudarkom na prvem valu epidemije covida-19 spomladi 2020 [Police work in the field of crime investigation during COVID-19 in Slovenia with emphasis on the first wave of the epidemic in spring 2020]. *Revija za kriminalistiko in kriminologijo* 72 (1): 21–35.

Meško, G., Dobovšek, B., and Bohinc, U. (2003). Izhodišča za preučevanje prostorskih dejavnikov kriminalitete [Foundations for studying the spatial factors of crime]. In: *Analiza porazdelitve nekaterih odklonskih pojavov v Ljubljani [Analysis of the Distribution of Some Deviation Phenomena in Ljubljana]* (ed. G. Meško), 12–63. Ljubljana: Fakulteta za policijsko–varnostne vede.

Meško, G., Dvoršek, A., Dobovšek, B. et al. (2003). *Analiza porazdelitve nekaterih odklonskih pojavov v Ljubljani [Analysis of the Distribution of Some Deviation Phenomena in Ljubljana]*. Ljubljana: Fakulteta za policijsko-varnostne vede.

Meško, G., Maver, D., and Klinkon, I. (2010). Urban crime and criminal investigation in Slovenia. In: *Urbanisation, Policing, and Security: Global Perspectives* (ed. G.W. Cordner, A.M. Corder and D.K. Das), 301–322. Boca Raton, London: CRC Press.

Meško, G., Sotlar, A., and Eman, K. (ed.) (2012). *Ekološka kriminaliteta in varovanje okolja – multidisciplinarne perspektive [Environmental Crime and Protection of the Environment – Multidisciplinary Perspectives]*. Ljubljana: Fakulteta za varnostne vede.

Ministrstvo za notranje zadeve, Policija (2014). Med Policijo in Fakulteto za varnostne vede je podpisan dogovor o sodelovanju [An agreement on cooperation was signed between the Police and the Faculty of Criminal Justice and Security]. https://www.policija.si/medijsko-sredisce/sporocila-za-javnost/sporocila-za-javnost-gpue/73169-med-policijo-in-fvv-je-podpisan-dogovor-o-sodelovanju-2014 (accessed 9 June 2021).

Ojo, A. and Ojewale, O. (2019). *Urbanisation and Crime in Nigeria*. Cham: Palgrave Macmillan.

Ostrožnik, N. (2012). Vloga geografskih informacijskih sistemov v podjetjih [The role of geographic information systems in enterprises]. Bachelor thesis. Univerza v Ljubljani.

Pečar, J. (1975). *Gostitve nekaterih deviantnih pojavov v Ljubljani [Concentrations of Certain Deviant Phenomena in Ljubljana]*. Ljubljana: Inštitut za kriminologijo pri Pravni fakulteti.

Philips, P.D. (1972). A prologue to the geography of crime. *Proceedings of the Association of American Geographers* 4: 86–91.

Ratcliffe, J.H. (2004a). Geocoding crime and a first estimate of a minimum acceptable hit rate. *International Journal of Geographical Information Science* 18 (1): 61–72. https://doi.org/10.1080/13658810310001596076.

Ratcliffe, J.H. (2004b). The hotspot matrix: a framework for the spatio-temporal targeting of crime reduction. *Police Practice and Research* 5 (1): 5–23. https://doi.org/10.1080/1561426042000191305.

Reddy, G.P.O. (2018). Geographic information system: principles and applications. In: *Geospatial Technologies in Land Resources Mapping, Monitoring and Management. Geotechnologies and the Environment* (ed. G. Reddy and S. Singh), 45–62. Cham: Springer.

Slocum, T.A., McMaster, R.B., Kessler, F.C. et al. (2005). *Thematic Cartography and Geographic Visualization*. Hoboken, NJ: Prentice Hall.

Tilley, N. (2003). *Problem-Oriented Policing, Intelligence-Led Policing and the National Intelligence Model*. London: Jill Dando Institute of Crime Science.

Urh, M. (2007). Model proaktivnega policijskega patruljiranja [The model of proactive police control]. Doctoral thesis. Univerza v Mariboru.

Verbovšek, T. (2012). *GIS v geologiji: študijsko gradivo [GIS in Geology: Study Material]*. Ljubljana: Naravoslovnotehniška fakulteta.

Weisburd, D. and McEven, T. (1997). Crime mapping and crime prevention. In: *Crime Mapping and Crime Prevention* (ed. D. Weisburd and T. McEven), 1–26. Cambridge: Cambridge University Press.

Zemljič, V., Kastelic, T., Šibenik, T. et al. (1979). *Ugotavljanje črnih točk na magistralnih cestah SR Slovenije [Identifying Black Spots on the Main Roads of the SR Slovenia]*. Ljubljana: FAGG, Prometnotehniški inštitut.

10

The Threat of Behavioral Radicalization Online

Conceptual Challenges and Technical Solutions Provided by the
PROPHETS (Preventing Radicalization Online through the
Proliferation of Harmonized ToolkitS) Project

*Ruža Karlović[1], Holger Nitsch[2], Sven-Eric Fikenscher[2], Damir
Osterman[3], Sotirios Menexis[4], Theodora Tsikrika[4], Stefanos
Vrochidis[4], Ioannis Kompatsiaris[4], and Arif Sahar[5]*

[1] Police Academy, Police University College, Zagreb, Croatia
[2] Department of Policing (CEPOLIS), University of Applied Sciences for Public Service in Bavaria, Fürstenfeldbruck, Germany
[3] Ministry of Interior, Research and Innovation, Zagreb, Croatia
[4] Information Technologies Institute, Centre for Research and Technology Hellas, Thessaloniki, Greece
[5] CENTRIC, Sheffield Hallam University, Sheffield, UK

10.1 The Growing Threat of Online Radicalization

There is no doubt that radicalization increasingly takes place in the online realm. A lot of contemporary right-wing extremist propaganda is spread that way, particularly on social media platforms such as Telegram, where much of the communication between agitators and their followers takes place (Lee 2020; Feldstein and Gordon 2021). This trend was on full display on 6 January 2021 when an ad-hoc alliance of white supremacists, nationalists and right-wing conspiracy theorists – encouraged, among other things, by the tweeting of a demagoguery President who was fanning the flames of political tensions – largely used the earlier mentioned communication tools to coordinate their march on the US Capitol, which eventually turned into a violent insurrection (Criezis and Galloway 2021). Quite tellingly, securely encrypted apps such as Telegram were downloaded way more often than usual that week. In the case of Telegram, the increase was 146% (Daly and Fischer 2021). Throughout January 2021, no less than 90 million new accounts were created (Feldstein and Gordon 2021).

Security Technologies and Social Implications, First Edition. Edited by Garik Markarian, Ruža Karlović, Holger Nitsch, and Krishna Chandramouli.
© 2023 The Institute of Electrical and Electronics Engineers, Inc.
Published 2023 by John Wiley & Sons, Inc.

Besides this singular incident, it speaks for itself that numerous high-profile right-wing terrorist attacks were carried out by individuals whose worldview was influenced by online propaganda and who even tried to further the spread of such material by posting manifestos justifying their actions. Such a pattern was particularly obvious in 2019 when the perpetrators of the infamous Christchurch shooting as well as those that were behind the attacks taking place in Poway, California, El Paso, Texas, and Bærum (Norway) all posted such manifestos (European Union, Europol 2020, p. 74).

Moreover, Islamic terrorist organizations such as the Islamic State and Al-Qaeda have increasingly tried to recruit followers and sympathizers and incite violence online. In 2016, a major study on the root causes of radicalization in the German intelligence and law-enforcement community observed that about half of those individuals that travelled to Syria and Iraq to join Islamic extremists were significantly influenced by online proceedings (Bundeskriminalamt, Bundesamt für Verfassungsschutz and Hessisches Informations- und Kompetenzzentrum gegen Extremismus 2016, p. 20).

Unfortunately, no subsequent analysis with a similarly broad focus has been conducted by German agencies (at least to the best of our knowledge). However, there are clear indications that since then, the impact of the online realm has increased even further (Vergani and Bliuc 2018). For example, a study by the domestic intelligence agency of the state of Baden-Württemberg (Landesamt für Verfassungsschutz) noted in 2019 that in most cases, the decisive proceedings in the radicalization process of women and girls that attempted to join Islamic extremists in Syria and Iraq were at least partly determined by online contacts (Ziolkowski and Kunze 2019, p. 4).

A recent analysis that casts light on why Saudi nationals engaged in the same behavior that also came out in 2019 (although the travel activities that are examined took place prior to that) even concluded that "the role of the Internet, in particular social media, in making foreign opportunities for jihad more strongly vivid to young people cannot be overstated" (Bin Khaled Al-Saud 2019, p. 35).

Interestingly, the Islamic State – after having suffered a string of defeats on the battlefield – has embarked on a new strategy to spread its ideology and cause harm to its foes. Instead of further recruiting frontline soldiers, the Islamic State has explicitly discouraged its followers from traveling to Syria and Iraq and instead shared numerous online messages that called on its supporters to carry out attacks in their countries of residence (Bundeskriminalamt, Bundesamt für Verfassungsschutz and Hessisches Informations- und Kompetenzzentrum gegen Extremismus 2016, p. 5).

This shift from aspiring to establish a Caliphate in the Middle East to inciting violence online is well underscored by a video statement that was shared by the

Islamic State's then-chief propagandist Muhammad al-Adnani, who stipulated that even "[t]he smallest bit of work that you can carry out in their countries is far better and beloved to us than any major [operations] here. [These operations] would be of much success and more harmful to them." (Counter Extremism Project 2021: Abu Muhammad al-Adnani 2021).

10.2 The Implications of Online Radicalization

The growing threat of online radicalization raises the question as to which criminal activities require special attention. The summary here alluded to recruitment as well as incitement and propaganda as focal points of online radicalization, which is fully supported by in-depth studies of inter-governmental organizations. A major report of the Financial Action Task Force (2018, p. 7) notes that "the Internet and social networks have, in the past five years, become the most commonly used tools to recruit members and supporters for terrorist organizations and disseminate their ideology." This observation is further supported by the European Union whose Directorate-General for Migration and Home Affairs (2021) draws a similar conclusion by stating, albeit in admittedly rather general terms that "Internet platforms, including social media, can be abused by violent extremists, terrorist groups and their sympathizers by providing new opportunities for mobilization, recruitment, and communication." The United Nations Office on Drugs and Crime (2012, p. 1) agrees with these overall findings. Its major report on "The Use of the Internet for Terrorist Purposes" even presents a slightly more comprehensive list of activities resulting from "the increasing use of the Internet by terrorist organizations and their supporters [. . .] including recruitment, financing, propaganda, training, incitement to commit acts of terrorism."

Admittedly, there are many different areas of terrorist Internet use, but the latter activities have turned out to be of particular relevance. Quite tellingly, all of them except for propaganda feature very prominently in the Directive (EU 2017) 2017/541 of the European Parliament and of the Council on combating terrorism. Recruitment, financing, training, and incitement are all listed in Title III of the Directive as particularly important "Offences Related to Terrorist Activities" that require special attention.

The Financial Action Task Force's (2018, p. 7) report provides some background on this in the sense of clarifying that recruitment often translates into training measures, which may involve different proceedings such as the use of video game technology. Moreover, "recruiters and individuals spreading terrorist ideology very often use the same resources not only for recruitment but also for collecting donations [. . .] [based on the] exchange [of] sensitive information such as bank accounts or the true purpose of purportedly charitable donations."

This leaves us with the propaganda notion, which still requires further clarification. Fortunately, a closer look at United Nations Office on Drugs and Crime's (2012, p. 6) report casts light on this issue. The report argues that "[i]t is important to emphasize the distinction between mere propaganda and material intended to incite acts of terrorism." More specifically, "propaganda per se is not generally prohibited, [whereas] the use of propaganda by terrorists to incite acts of terrorism is considered unlawful by many Member States. The Internet provides an abundance of material and opportunities to download, edit, and distribute content that may be considered unlawful glorification of, or provocation to, acts of terrorism." As indicated earlier, the crime of incitement – unlike the overall propaganda notion – is also covered by the aforementioned EU (2017) Directive on combating terrorism, albeit the relevant provision is officially called "Public provocation to commit a terrorist offence."

The EU has found another subcategory of terrorist and radical propaganda to be particularly worrisome, although it is not embedded into the EU (2017) Directive on combatting terrorism either, namely hate speech. In its "Counter-Terrorism Agenda for the EU: Anticipate, Prevent, Protect, Respond," the EU (2020, p. 7) committed itself "[t]o respond[ing] to the proliferation of racist and xenophobic hate speech on the Internet." In accordance with this commitment, the "Commission encouraged the signing of the EU Code of Conduct on countering illegal hate speech online in 2016 [and] will present an initiative in 2021 to extend the list of EU-level crimes under Article 83(1) of the Treaty on the Functioning of the EU to hate crime and hate speech, whether based on race, ethnicity, religion, gender, or sexuality."

The further discussion includes the conception and delineation of terrorist recruitment and training, terrorist financing, terrorist incitement as well as hate speech and elaborations on the conditions that increase the likelihood that such measures are embarked on. Factors that encourage radicalization may include a strong sense of alienation on the personal or cultural level, feelings of injustice or humiliation intensified by social marginalization, xenophobia and discrimination, limited educational and employment opportunities, crime, political factors, ideological and religious aspects, weak family ties, trauma, and other psychological problems (Silke 2008; Khosrokhaver 2014; Pauwels et al. 2015; Jacobsen 2017). Social media allows people who share extremist ideas to take advantage of such vulnerabilities.

In order for LEAs to better monitor online activities related to radicalization, modern tools and knowledge are needed. On this basis, three technical tools are presented that aim at the detection, investigation, and study of the four earlier mentioned radicalization-related online activities as well as their underlying causes. The different steps are described as follows:

10.3 Delineating Essential Radicalization-Related Online Activities

As indicated earlier, the aforementioned radicalization-related online activities can be clearly delineated in view of EU law and norms. The conception of online terrorist recruitment and training, online terrorist financing, and online terrorist incitement resembles the definitions of the European Union's (2017) Directive on combating terrorism. Accordingly, the three radicalization-related online activities are specified as follows:

Online terrorist recruitment and training: Online terrorist recruitment is understood as soliciting another person online to commit or contribute to the commission of terrorist offences,[1] whereas online terrorist training is defined as providing or receiving online instruction on the making or use of explosives, firearms, or other weapons or noxious or hazardous substances, or on other specific methods or techniques, for the purpose of committing, or contributing to the commission of terrorist offences knowing that the skills provided are intended to be used for this purpose.

Online terrorist financing: Online terrorist financing is defined as collecting funds online with the intention that they be used, or in the knowledge that they are to be used, in full or in part, to commit, or to contribute to the commission of terrorist offences.

Online terrorist incitement: Online terrorist incitement is defined as making available an online message to the public, with the intent to incite the commission

---

1 Terrorist offences are defined in accordance with the European Union's (2017) Directive on combating terrorism, which clarifies that all forms of terrorism are aimed at one or more of the following three goals: "seriously intimidating a population"; "unduly compelling a government or an international organisation to perform or abstain from performing any act" and "seriously destabilising or destroying the fundamental political, constitutional, economic or social structures of a country or an international organisation." Moreover, terrorist actors attempt to pursue at least one of the following crimes: "(i) attacks upon a person's life which may cause death; (ii) attacks upon the physical integrity of a person; (iii) kidnapping or hostage-taking; (iv) causing extensive destruction to a government or public facility, a transport system, an infrastructure facility, including an information system, a fixed platform located on the continental shelf, a public place or private property likely to endanger human life or result in major economic loss; (v) seizure of aircraft, ships or other means of public or goods transport; (vi) manufacture, possession, acquisition, transport, supply or use of explosives or weapons, including chemical, biological, radiological or nuclear weapons, as well as research into, and development of, chemical, biological, radiological or nuclear weapons; (vii) release of dangerous substances, or causing fires, floods or explosions, the effect of which is to endanger human life; (viii) interfering with or disrupting the supply of water, power or any other fundamental natural resource, the effect of which is to endanger human life; (ix) illegal system interference and illegal data interference."

of terrorist offences where such conduct, directly or indirectly, such as by the glorification of terrorist acts, advocates the commission of terrorist offences, thereby causing a danger that one or more such offences may be committed.

As further explained earlier, hate speech is not addressed in the European Union's (2017) Directive on combating terrorism. However, it is delineated by a Council of Europe's Committee of Ministers' (1997) declaration on the subject matter.

Online hate speech: Online hate speech is understood as all forms of online expression, which disseminate, promote, or justify racism, xenophobia, anti-Semitism, or other forms of intolerance based on hate, including intolerance, which is expressed in the form of aggressive nationalism and ethnocentricity, discrimination, and hostility to minorities, migrants, and people with a migrant background.

10.4 The Root Causes of Behavioral Radicalization Online: Identifying the Proper Vulnerability Indicators

As far as the underlying reasons for radicalization-related online activities are concerned, it should be clarified that radical ideology does not always have to result in criminal behavior (Khosrokhaver 2014), even though it is often associated with it. Even in case it does, radicalization as such is not a crime according to the laws of the European Union and EU member states. Having said that, the process of radicalization – as complex and multifaceted as it is and as many different risk factors as it involves (Innes and Levi 2017) – requires further study so one can detect threats of behavioral radicalization (online) quickly enough.

In this respect, the Internet comes into play again since it does not only shape the way in which online radicalization is expressed but also the trajectories of radicalization (Bayerl et al. 2020) as it provides an effective breeding ground for radicalization processes and enables terrorist networks or individuals to exploit these conditions to galvanize and carry out their objectives.

However, numerous sociologists and criminologists point out that radicalization cannot be reduced exclusively to a technological approach, but it is necessary to analyze the motivation of extremist actors (e.g. Khosrokhaver 2014). The importance of the online dimension of radicalization notwithstanding, such offline proceedings should not be dismissed too easily. A RAND study (von Behr et al. 2013, p. 24) summarized the state-of-the-art quite well by observing that "most cases involve offline activity that could have played a role in the individual's radicalization." Even in the event that almost the entire radicalization process takes place online, it rarely resembles what has been called "online self-radicalization." Instead, such incidents usually "involve virtual communication and interaction with others."

In other words, human interactions matter and so do personal encounters, experiences, perceptions, and needs. Against this backdrop, it is necessary to cast light on the rather complex process of *behavioral* radicalization online by identifying the root causes of vulnerability to engaging in radicalization-related online activities. Such vulnerability indicators are derived from the research literature.

More specifically, vulnerabilities may be related to the personal characteristics of individuals such as personal beliefs and attitudes, but also to the environment in which individuals grow up and reside, and, of course, the political and cultural characteristics of a society. Accordingly, there are three levels of analysis: micro (personal beliefs and attitudes), meso (immediate social surrounding of family, friends, and peers), and macro (system-level political, economic, and cultural factors). For obvious reasons, the specific radicalization process depends on each individual's socio-psychological traits and the context thereof.

One can further distinguish between push and pull factors. Push factors are personal or environmental conditions that make people abandon mainstream society in favor of extremist groups. Pull factors, on the other hand, increase the acceptance of extremist thoughts (Jacobsen 2017). The following list of push and pull factors has been assigned to the corresponding three levels of analysis:

1) Individual, micro-level risk factors concern personal issues such as feelings, beliefs, and needs. On the micro-level youth, mental illness, personal uncertainty, and perceived injustice/perceived grievances are the key push factors. Concerning youth (Venhaus 2010; Campelo et al. 2018), it speaks for itself that more than half of those German residents that attempted to join Islamic extremists in Syria and Iraq were not older than 25 (Bundeskriminalamt, Bundesamt für Verfassungsschutz, and Hessisches Informations- und Kompetenzzentrum gegen Extremismus 2016, p. 12). Mental illness may possibly increase susceptibility to radicalization in the sense that someone who is suffering from mental illness is likely to look for hope and eager to boost his/her self-confidence (Harpviken 2019). Personal uncertainty can easily lead to the same desires (Venhaus 2010), which radical ideologies and groups may meet by giving their followers a purpose in life. Research into the social factors of radicalization highlights that social deprivation and grievances can have a profound impact on individuals. In other words, social discrimination resulting from (perceived and/or real) injustices and a sense of alienation perpetrated by local or external actors plays a critical role in driving individuals into radical milieus (Silke 2008).

2) Moreover, a lack of self-control or inclination to risky behavior, a need for belonging, and harboring radical beliefs constitute micro-level pull factors. The impact of a lack of self-control (Borum 2014) as well as risky behavior (Cole et al. 2010), including the involvement in crime, is illustrated by the fact

that two-thirds of those whose radicalization process was examined by the German intelligence and law-enforcement community had been involved in criminal activities before (Bundeskriminalamt, Bundesamt für Verfassungsschutz and Hessisches Informations- und Kompetenzzentrum gegen Extremismus 2016, p. 18). Obviously, a need for belonging is likely to increase someone's susceptibility to joining groups with a strong, possibly even a radical ideology (Van Brunt et al. 2017), whereas radical beliefs can be expected to make someone lean toward associating him-/herself with fellow radicals (Pauwels et al. 2015).

3) Environmental, meso-level factors relate to a person's immediate social surroundings such as traumatic experiences and family dysfunction (socialization) problems that are considered push factors while radical peers are believed to be a crucial pull factor. Traumatic encounters with violence, bullying, neglect, etc., may lead to a feeling of helplessness, which might be reduced by the embrace of extremist views (Harpviken 2019), whereas family dysfunction implies the lack of a reliable social environment making someone easier to be influenced and to get recruited by extremist players (Harpviken 2019). Radical peers may exercise peer pressure or otherwise convince non-radical individuals to adopt their views (Cole et al. 2010; Scrivens et al. 2020).

4) Societal, macro-level aspects include risk factors related to society as a whole including factors such as politics, economy, and culture. Specific vulnerability indicators include social disengagement (in the sense of being detached from societal trends and values (Jacobsen 2017)), societal changes (that undermine the social bond of common values (Campelo et al. 2018, p. 11)), and social polarization (in the sense of social tensions (Campelo et al. 2018, p. 10)). The first two factors constitute push factors, whereas the latter is a pull factor.[2]

10.5 PROPHETS Tools: Preventing, Detecting, Investigating, and Studying Behavioral Radicalization Online

Accordingly, the earlier mentioned PROPHETS project has conceptualized three different tools to take on these challenges. The tools include

- the Monitoring and Situational Awareness Toolkit,
- the Policymaking Toolkit, and
- the Expert Notifications Portal.

---

2 For further details, see the summary of PROPHETS' insights into behavioral radicalisation online at https://www.prophets-h2020.eu/insights-1/training-package/concept/.

10.6   Monitoring and Situational Awareness Toolkit

The monitoring and situational awareness toolkit (MST) collects and analyzes online content. It can detect radicalization-related online activities, which is essential for criminal investigations that depend on gathering evidence. However, the MST also bridges the gap between investigative, preventive, and analytical work. Thanks to the clear conception and operationalization of the vulnerability indicators the MST can search content for proxies that imply an individual's growing inclination to go down the road of behavioral radicalization online (Theodosiadou et al. 2021).

More specifically, the platform offers three types of monitoring: social media, web crawling, and search engine monitoring tasks. The first relies on the collection of online material posted on social media platforms. The second uses an URL as a starting point in order to harvest the material contained in the respective websites. Finally, the last one exploits the power of search engines. The collected material can be categorized into different radicalization-related online activities by applying a set of appropriately trained classifiers. In addition, the material may be subjected to different types of advanced analysis proceedings, including measures that evaluate the sentiment and emotional content within the collected material (using properly trained classifiers, in a temporal and aggregated fashion) and identify the most prominent topics and their associated keywords (exploiting both clustering and hashtag extraction modules).[3]

The output of each analysis module can be used in isolation, to provide insights into certain aspects of the undergoing radicalization process, as well as in combination. The latter is related to the computational estimation of vulnerability indicators (to the extent they are measurable). These indicators constitute the ground for the identification of threats and trends in the collected online material and the provision of early warnings when an escalation is observed.

Besides the possibility to use this capability as an early warning system, detecting extraordinarily huge vulnerabilities to behavioral radicalization online can also greatly advance the systematic analysis of the overall process of behavioral radicalization online. For example, the review of online material generated by individuals who committed terrorist offences and is therefore preserved as court-relevant evidence may reveal how vulnerability-related emotions played into such violations of the law. The resultant insights might then be used to enhance preventive efforts in the form of anti-radicalization and de-radicalization programs.

---

3 For more details, see the drescription on the PROPHETS website at https://www. prophets-h2020.eu/insights-1/training-package/monitoring-and-situational-awareness-tool/.

Further efforts to advance the study – and possibly also the investigation – of behavioral radicalization online are made by facilitating the analysis of the legal and political framework and the exchange between radicalization experts.

10.7 Policymaking Toolkit

An in-depth analysis of the legal and political framework can be carried out with the support of the policymaking toolkit (PMT). The PMT has been developed to provide policymakers and LEAs with a platform to learn from one another, integrating legislation and policies from across the EU Member States. The PMT aims to recommend policy approaches to the existing and emerging threats posed by behavioral radicalization online. This enables end users to "borrow" policy best practices from the other Member States where a specific policy has proven successful.

The PMT allows for the comparison, annotation, and summary of legislation and policies in order to translate technically complex areas of interest into transparent, user-friendly data that can be used to inform relevant policies. The PMT is made up of six core pages that fulfil end user requirements and meet technical needs.[4]

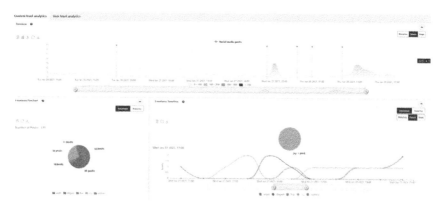

Figure 10.1 Screenshot of the MST's content level analytics visualizations. Upper panel: temporal evolution of the number of collected items. The vertical dashed lines indicate the time points where there is a possibility of radicalization-related activity. Lower panel: emotions and sentiment analysis visualization in aggregated (left) and temporal (right) forms.

---

4 For more details, see the dgrescription on the PROPHETS website at https://www.prophets-h2020.eu/insights-1/training-package/policy-making-toolkit/.

10.8 Expert Notification Portal

Besides the MST and PMT, PROPHETS has also conceptualized an ENP, which is a community-driven space designed to foster communication between law-enforcement professionals and other experts by providing real-time feedback and communication. It goes without saying that such communication can take place in the context of an ongoing investigation of one or more of the four earlier mentioned radicalization-related online activities or amidst a broader interest in understanding trends and developments that concern behavioral radicalization online.

The aim of the ENP is to improve the resilience, capacity, and agency skillset of LEAs beyond traditional boundaries. The portal has been designed from two fronts: a browser-based dashboard accessible on most modern devices and browsers, and a mobile application available on modern android and iOS devices. The rationale for this is to meet the needs of investigators both "out in the field" and within the agency. Although both versions of the portal have a different look and feel, they are functionally the same and users can log into either version interchangeably.[5]

Figure 10.2 PMT Comparator Page: Choose to view paragraphs side-by-side from documents between two countries, e.g. choose to compare sections tagged for terrorist-generated content in documents from Austria and the United Kingdom.

---

5 For more details, see the drescription on the PROPHETS website at https://www.prophets-h2020.eu/insights-1/training-package/expert-notification-portal/.

Figure 10.3 Users can post questions to the ENP. Setting the visibility of the question to specific organizations or types of organizations limits who can view the question.

10.9 Conclusion: Combining Social Science and Technological Insights

Understanding and preventing behavioral radicalization online through multidisciplinary research belongs to the priority area of the Security Union Strategy (EC 2020). The EC, through Secure societies[6] as a priority in the structure of the H2020 program, finances projects, which are supposed to ensure the security and safety of all EU citizens and protect common social values from criminal activities. Working together on consortium projects in general, including PROPHETS, is an example of knowledge transfer from different fields of science to prevent online cybercrime according to the multidisciplined approach of Community Policing (Bayerl et al. 2017).

Although the analysis of online data to detect behavioral radicalization online can be a controversial issue, the growing importance of the online dimension for radicalization and terrorist activities is clear and obvious. This applies to foreign fighters as well as to domestic terrorists that can all be indoctrinated through the Internet and social media. The mere fact that terrorist organizations invest so much time and money in complex online propaganda implies that the online realm appears to have great strategic value in the sense of advancing their goals (Schlegel 2018). The earlier mentioned assessments of the law enforcement and intelligence community on the role of the Internet in the recruitment of terrorists clearly corroborate this assumption. So do current incitement efforts.

---

6 The European Parliament and the Council reached a joint agreement on Horizon Europe as the successor to the H2020 program. More on structure and implementation is available at ec. europa.eu/info/horizon-europe_en.

Against this backdrop, the PROPHETS project was conceived. As the overview of the vulnerability indicators (informed by the project) here has indicated, the project has conducted a multidisciplinary study of behavioral radicalization online, which bridges the gap between the behavioral offline roots of radicalization and the online ramifications thereof. Moreover, a variety of tools have been conceptualized that enable LEAs to better counter behavioral radicalization online, mainly through detecting signs of such radicalization processes (vulnerability indicators) and radicalization-related online activities. The study and investigation of such incidents can then benefit from further platform tools that give end users the opportunity to study the policy environment and engage in expert conversations.

Thanks to this harmonization of different toolkits based on intense social science research PROPHETS provides a new perspective on and new options to advance the fight against behavioral radicalization online (while being mindful of privacy concerns as well as the ethical and legal standards of the European Union).

References

Bayerl, P.S., Karlović, R., Akhgar, B. et al. (2017). *Community Policing – A European Perspectives*. Cham: Springer.

Bayerl, P.S., Staniforth, A., Akhgar, B. et al. (2020). The Radicalisation-Factor Model (RFM): proposing a framework for the systematic investigation and modelling of online radicalisation. In: *Investigating Radicalization Trends* (ed. B. Akhgar, D. Wells and J.M. Blanco), 29–41. Cham: Springer.

Bin Khaled Al-Saud, A. (2019). *Saudi Foreign Fighters: Analysis of Leaked Islamic State Entry Documents*. London: International Centre for the Study of Radicalisation, King's College London.

Borum, R. (2014). Psychological vulnerabilities and propensities for involvement in violent extremism. *Behavioral Sciences and the Law* 32: 286–305.

Bundeskriminalamt, Bundesamt für Verfassungsschutz and Hessisches Informations- und Kompetenzzentrum gegen Extremismus (2016). *Analyse der Radikalisierungshintergründe und -verläufe der Personen, die aus islamistischer Motivation aus Deutschland in Richtung Syrien oder Irak ausgereist sind, Fortschreibung 2016*. Bundeskriminalamt, Bundesamt für Verfassungsschutz and Hessisches Informations- und Kompetenzzentrum gegen Extremismus.

Campelo, N., Oppetit, A., Neau, F. et al. (2018). Who are the European youths willing to engage in radicalization? A multidisciplinary review of their psychological and social profiles. *European Psychiatry* 52: 1–14.

Cole, J., Alison, E., Cole, B. et al. (2010). *Guidance for Identifying People Vulnerable to Recruitment into Violent Extremism*. Liverpool: University of Liverpool, School of Psychology.

Council of Europe's Committee of Ministers (1997). Recommendation No. R (97) 20 of the Committee of Ministers to member states on 'hate speech'. hrm.coe. int/1680505d5b (accessed 07 May 2021).

Counter Extremism Project (2021). Abu Muhammad al-Adnani. www. counterextremism.com/extremists/abu-muhammad-al-adnani (accessed 07 May 2021).

Criezis, M. and Galloway, B. (2021). From MAGA to the fringe: what was happening online before the January 06 insurrection and what can we do now? *Insights: Global Network on Extremism & Technology.* gnet-research.org/2021/01/27/ from-maga-to-the-fringe-what-was-happening-online-before-the-6-january-insurrection-and-what-can-we-do-now/ (accessed 14 May 2021).

Daly, K. and Fischer, S. (2021). The online far right is moving underground. *Axios.* http://www.axios.com/the-online-far-right-is-moving-underground-e429d45d-1b3 0-46e0-82a3-6e240bf44fef.html?utm_campaign=organic&utm_ medium=socialshare&utm_source=twitter (accessed May 14 2021).

European Commission (2020). Communication from the Commission to the European Parliament, the European Council, the Council, the European Economic and Social Committee and the Committee of the Regions on the EU Security Union Strategy. https://eur-lex.europa.eu/legal-content/EN/TXT/PDF/?uri=CELE X:52020DC0605&from=EN (acessed September 17 2021).

European Union (2017). Directive (EU) 2017/541 of the European Parliament and of the Council of March 15 2017 on combating terrorism and replacing Council Framework Decision 2002/475/JHA and amending Council Decision 2005/671/ JHA. eur-lex.europa.eu/legal-content/EN/TXT/PDF/?uri=CELEX:32017L0541&fr om=EN (accessed 07 May 2021).

European Union (2020). Counter-Terrorism Agenda for the EU: Anticipate, Prevent, Protect, Respond. https://ec.europa.eu/home-affairs/sites/default/files/ pdf/09122020_communication_commission_european_parliament_the_council_ eu_agenda_counter_terrorism_po-2020-9031_com-2020_795_en.pdf (accessed September 06 2021).

European Union, Europol (2020). *Terrorism Situation and Trend Report.* The Hague: Europol.

Feldstein, S. and Gordon, S. (2021). Are telegram and signal havens for right-wing extremists? *Foreign Policy.* foreignpolicy.com/2021/03/13/telegram-signal-apps-right-wing-extremism-islamic-state-terrorism-violence-europol-encrypted/ (accessed 07 May 2021).

Financial Action Task Force (2018). *Financing of Recruitment for Terrorist Purposes.* Paris: Financial Action Task Force.

Harpviken, A.N. (2019). Psychological vulnerabilities and extremism among wyestern youth: a literature review. *Adolescent Research Review* https://doi. org/10.1007/s40894-019-00108-y.

Innes, M. and Levi, M. (2017). Making and managing terrorism and counter-terrorism: the view from criminology. In: *The Oxford Handbook of Criminology*. https://doi.org/10.1093/he/9780198719441.003.0021.

Jacobsen, A. (2017). Pushes and pulls of radicalization into violent islamist extremism and prevention measures targeting these: Comparing men and women. Master's thesis. Malmö University.

Khosrokhaver, F. (2014). *Radicalization*. Paris: MSH PARIS.

Lee, B. (2020). Blind networks in the extreme right. *VOXPol*. https://www.voxpol.eu/blind-networks-in-the-extreme-right/ (accessed 14 May 2021).

Pauwels, L., Brion, F., Schils, N. et al. (2015). *Explaining and Understanding the Role of Exposure to New Social Media on Violent Extremism: An Integrative Quantitative and Qualitative Approach*. Cambridge, MA: Academia Press.

Schlegel, L. (2018). Online-radicalisation: Myth or reality? http://www.kas.de/c/document_library/get_file?uuid=baca4877-ac6c-4df4-ae77-28b4ba2aafac&groupId=252038 (accessed 17 September 2021).

Scrivens, R., Gill, P., and Conway, M. (2020). The Role of the Internet in Facilitating Violent Extremism and Terrorism: Suggestions for Progressing Research. In: *The Palgrave Handbook of International Cybercrime and Cyberdeviance* (ed. T. Holt and A. Bossler). Basingstoke: Palgrave Macmillan.

Silke, A. (2008). Holy warriors: exploring the psychological processes of jihadi radicalization. *European Journal of Criminology* 5 (1): 99–123.

Theodosiadou, O., Pantelidou, K., Bastas, N. et al. (2021). Change point detection in terrorism-related online content. *Information* https://doi.org/10.3390/info12070274.

United Nations Office on Drugs and Crime (2012). *The Use of the Internet for Terrorist Purposes*. New York, NY: United Nations.

Van Brunt, B., Murphy, A., and Zedginidze, A. (2017). An exploration of the risk, protective, and mobilization factors related to violent extremism in college populations. *Violence and Gender* https://doi.org/10.1089/vio.2017.0039.

Venhaus, J.M. (2010). *Looking for a Fight: Why Youth Join Al-Qaeda and How to Prevent It*. Carlisle Barracks, PA: United States Army War College.

Vergani, M. and Bliuc, A.M. (2018). The language of new terrorism: differences in psychological dimensions of communication in Dabiq and Inspire. *Journal of Language and Social Psychology* 37 (5): 523–540.

Von Behr, I., Reding, A., Edwards, C. et al. (2013). *Radicalization in the Digital Era: The Use of the Internet in 15 Cases of Terrorism and Extremism*. Brussels: RAND Europe.

Ziolkowski, B. and Kunze, A. (2019). *Deutsche muhajirat: Radikalisierungshintergründe und –verläufe von Mädchen und Frauen aus Baden-Württemberg*. Stuttgart: Landesamt für Verfassungsschutz Baden-Württemberg.

11

Blockchain Technologies for Chain of Custody Authentication

Krishna Chandramouli[1,5], Roxana Horincar[2], Charlotte Jacobe de Naurois[2], Dirk Pallmer[3], David Faure[2], Wilmuth Müller[3], and Konstantinos Demestichas[4]

[1] *Venaka Media Limited, London, UK*
[2] *Thales, Courbevoie, France*
[3] *Fraunhofer IOSB, Karlsruhe, Germany*
[4] *Institute of Communication and Computer Systems, National Technical University of Athens , Athens, Greece*
[5] *Multimedia and Vision Research Group, School of Electronic Engineering and Computer Science, Queen Mary University of London, London, UK*

11.1 Introduction

Following the developments of the past decade, the scientific and technological advancements in the field of computing have facilitated the successful handling of big-data resources, that range in the volume of a few Petabytes. In this era (Han et al. 2018), the increasing data volume places a critical constraint on the requirement of swift data processing (data velocity) leading to the extraction of timely intelligence from processing a wide variety of data types, structures, and sources. Such a computational need leads to various new challenges at which traditional data management systems have been found to be inadequate. Such limitations have been well documented in the literature (Baru et al. 2013). The need for efficient data storage and processing is at the heart of new system development leading to the development and fast emergence of various new big data systems, namely (i) Hadoop and its related systems (which includes Hadoop ecosystems including high-level languages on Hadoop and Structured Query Language [SQL] on Hadoop) have become the de facto solution for a majority of big data applications; (ii) database management systems (DBMSs) and NoSQL data stores are widely used in online transactional and analytical applications; (iii) the specific processing requirements of connected graphs, continuous streams, and complex scientific data create a need for yet another specialized systems in the big data domain. These advances in the field of computing are critical for the development of investigative platforms assisting LEAs in conducting large-scale investigations. The increasing amount of digital evidence being collected, processed, and correlated with each other requires a systematic methodology for automation. In complementary to the amount of evidence, the processing of information should comply with the legal and ethical regulations of the national and European legislation.

Addressing these requirements the overall research objective of the MAGNETO platform is to equip law enforcement agencies (LEAs) with cutting edge-scientific tools and complex algorithms that enable the efficient and effective collection, aggregation, and processing of forensic evidence for the crimes under investigation. When a crime is committed, police officers carry out investigative activities to collect information and (physical or digital) items that would eventually become the evidence supporting a conviction in court. Part of the evidence that police officers may need to rely on may consist of information generated, distributed, or stored on electronic devices. Under the European legal framework, certain rules and procedures must be followed during the criminal investigation such that the probative value of the evidence collected is not affected. In this respect, evidence collected or processed through electronic means needs to offer robust traceability.

The chapter aims to summarize the best practices for evidence lifecycle management by addressing three main organizational policies often encountered by LEAs, namely (i) organizational processes and procedures; (ii) evidence collection process and procedures; and (iii) an AI toolkit for evidence processing. The interaction between the stakeholders is presented in Figure 11.1. As the MAGNETO project brings together several LEAs from European member states, with each organization responsible to follow the national guidelines, it is important to acknowledge the different processes and procedures followed by different LEAs in the project. The compliance with national and European regulations also plays a crucial role in generating the digitalized version of evidence collected from both the crime scene and information requested and processed from external national registry of databases (such as residency status, vehicle registration, etc.). These legal frameworks and the way they relate to the MAGNETO platform are therefore described in more detail. After the digitalization process, the MAGNETO platform offers the LEAs several tools (Pérez et al. 2021). It is important to note that the MAGNETO platform generates new information from the processing of digital evidence.

The two forms of data sources namely (i) the original source collected from the crime scene and information requested from the national registry; and (ii) the new forms of digital evidence generated through the analysis of information processed within the MAGNETO platform are being indexed and stored within

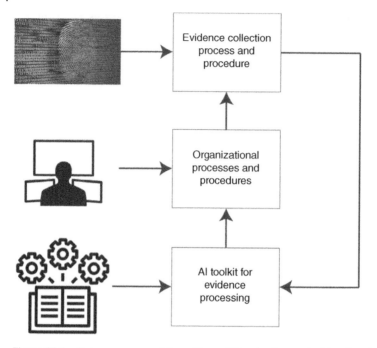

Figure 11.1 Data management for evidence lifecycle. *Source:* Andrius Gruzdaitis/ Adobe Stock.

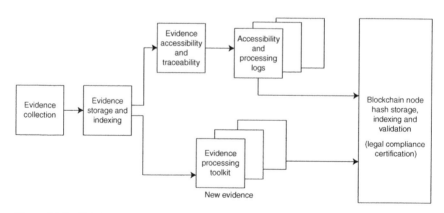

Figure 11.2 Evidence data flow management.

an immutable file repository system. The hash value generated from such an immutable data store is further stored within the Blockchain module to enable audit logs for any digital discrepancies noted in the system. An overview of the high-level approach adopted within the project is presented in Figure 11.2.

The complexity of the MAGNETO platform has been reported in (Behmer et al. 2019; Pérez et al. 2021) with the tools and services developed for advanced semantic reasoning involve the use of heterogeneity of data sources that are processed within the platform. The algorithmic development carried out for processing the heterogeneous data sources are complemented by the high-level semantic information engine. The resulting outcome is the release of the MAGNETO Common Reference Model, which supports the formalization of different crime categories, threat actors, and the associated representation of metadata extracted from the evidence collected by MAGNETO end users. Building on the semantic representational model for modeling the crime, the research activity presented in the chapter formalizes the process of documenting the investigative procedures adopted within the MAGNETO platform. The objective of the chapter contribution is to provide a detailed outline of the scientific activities carried out in the project toward the development of tools and software components that comply with European laws and criminal procedure rules concerning the processing/handling of digital evidence generated by computational algorithms. To achieve this objective, the chapter starts with a review of the principles of chain of custody as adopted within the European legal framework. Considering the principles of admissibility, reliability, and interpretability of evidence, three technologies are considered to play a key role in the court-proofness of the MAGNETO outcomes, namely:

1) semantic framework for tracking and recording the processing of information within the MAGNETO platform, which extends the use of PRO-V (Lebo et al. 2013) ontology to distinguish physical and digital activities as carried out within the platform.

2) the use of distributed immutable storage that protects against malicious attacks. This is a crucial requirement to be addressed within the platform to ensure that the outcome generated by computational tools is not manipulated and is compliant with the European rules and regulations on evidence. The use of immutable storage is built based on the use of the interplanetary file system (IPFS) (Benet 2014) peer-to-peer hypermedia protocol, which is designed to support distributed storage of different file formats.

3) the creation and storage of digital hash automatically extracted based on the algorithmic processing of the digital evidence is stored within the blockchain to protect and enable audit of the evidence presented in court for a criminal conviction. In addition, to protect the multimedia content against the application of deep-learning-based data manipulation, the use of block-based image steganography has been integrated within the multimedia processing components.

The chapter also includes a detailed summary of evidence lifecycle management to be integrated within the MAGNETO platform that ensures transparency of the algorithmic application upon the documentary evidence processed within the platform. Finally, the chapter summarizes a series of attacks against which the proposed court-proof evidence framework is evaluated in compliance with the law.

11.2 MAGNETO Architecture

The conceptualization of multimedia analysis and correlation engine for organized crime prevention and investigation (MAGNETO) was led by the need for LEAs to undertake large-scale investigations for a multitude of crimes ranging from theft, violence against property and person, and terrorist attacks to name a few. The overall architecture of the MAGNETO platform is presented in Figure 11.3 (Han et al. 2018), which highlights the different sources of information sets available for the LEAs to consider while conducting criminal investigations. While the quality and quantity of raw data have increased significantly over the years, there still exist limitations on the human capacity to process such a large volume of content effectively and efficiently. More specifically, the correlation of evidence across different modalities which are captured in isolation presents a unique set of challenges. Addressing this critical need to assist the investigators in correlating evidence, the MAGNETO project has developed a common representation model using Web Ontology Language (OWL) and stored using the Fuseki server. The instantiation sequence process has been further elaborated in (Baru et al. 2013). A full list of features and technologies adopted in the development of the MAGNETO architecture is reported in (Demestichas et al. 2021).

11.3 Literature Review

The term processing evidence in the context of criminal proceedings refers to collecting, preserving, using, and exchanging evidence while safeguarding the chain of custody. As an increasing number of stakeholders take part in the investigation, it is vital to ensure that all the interactions between the respective stakeholders are appropriately logged within digital systems used in the processing of any evidence. Evidence collection refers to gathering items that contain potential electronic evidence that could support the facts presented in a court of law. While that process is mostly performed by LEAs alone, the evidence collection may also involve information or items initially captured by the private sector (as illustrated by the examples of such data sources within MAGNETO as mentioned earlier). Once the evidence is collected, it needs to be preserved for it to be used during the criminal trial. Preservation is the process of maintaining and safeguarding the integrity and/or original condition of the potential electronic evidence, meaning that (i) it needs to be stored in a secure way to safeguard against alterations, (ii) that the chain of custody needs to be logged, and (iii) that access to the evidence needs to be restricted to persons authorized to process the evidence.

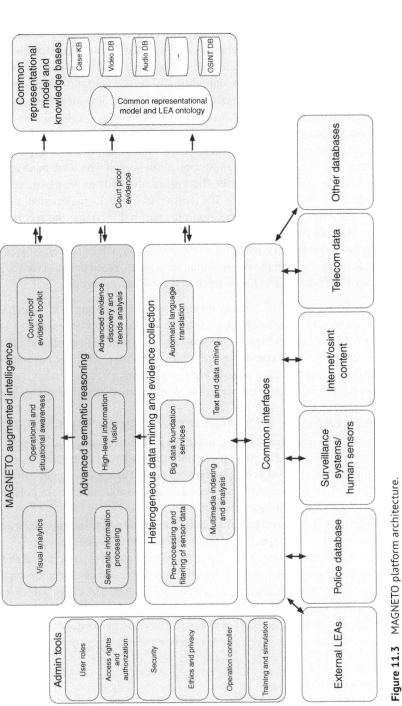

Figure 11.3 MAGNETO platform architecture.

The challenge of handling digital evidence has been addressed within the EVIDENCE project,[1] in which several stages of evidence processing have been identified (status quo assessment and analysis of primary challenges and shortcomings[2]). The first phase includes the identification, collection, and anti-contamination precautions (such as searching the crime scene, collecting the evidence, packaging, and labeling and creating documents reporting the activities performed at every step) of electronic evidence. In the second phase, the acquisition of the source of evidence takes place, determining which items are most likely to serve the purposes of the investigation, which are the most time-sensitive, and which are most at risk of being lost or corrupted. During the third phase, the findings are evaluated and interpreted, by the judicial authority. The fourth phase includes the essential step in the electronic evidence life cycle because the court will examine the report that should contain all relevant findings as well as guarantee the preservation of the evidence: every precaution must be taken when collecting evidence. The same principles must be followed for the documenting procedures. Based on the evidence life cycle, the EVIDENCE project has formalized the following concepts:

- Crime is an act, default or conduct prejudicial to the community, for which the person responsible may by law be punished by a fine or imprisonment.
- Sources of electronic evidence: comprise any physical, analogical, and digital evidence (computer or computer-like device) capable of creating information that may have a prohibitive value in legal proceedings.
- A process is a series of actions taken to achieve a particular end within the electronic evidence lifecycle.
- Electronic evidence is any information (comprising the output of analogue devices or data in digital form) of potential prohibitive value that is manipulated, generated through stored on or communicated by any electronic device.
- A requirement represents principles or rules related to legal rules and handling procedures that are necessary, indispensable, or unavoidable to make potential electronic admissible in legal proceedings.
- A stakeholder (interested party) includes people or organizations governing conduct in or playing a specific role in the electronic evidence lifecycle.
- A rule contains a set of explicit or understood regulations or principles governing conduct or procedures for the identification, collection, preservation, analysis, exchange, and presentation of electronic evidence in cross border and national dimensions.
- Digital forensics is the application of forensic science to electronic evidence in a legal matter.

---

1 http://www.evidenceproject.eu/.
2 http://s.evidenceproject.eu/p/e/v/evidence-ga-608185-d3-2-412.pdf.

These main classes of semantic hierarchy proposed in the EVIDENCE project have been further considered within the MAGNETO platform in compliance with the common representational model (CRM).

Building on the literature review and past project outcomes, the MAGNETO project has adopted a systematic approach for tracing the data processing abilities integrated within the MAGNETO platform addressing the need for handling various data modalities and information sources. This chapter will report on the scientific innovation activities carried out within the project in this connection.

11.4 Semantic Framework for Recording Evidence Transactions

Addressing the requirements of court proof evidence outlined in Section 11.1 on European regulations on the chain of custody, the MAGNETO project has developed a semantic framework leveraging the ontology concepts formalized for tracking the provenance of information. "Provenance is a record that describes the people, institutions, entities, and activities involved in producing, influencing, or delivering a piece of data or a thing. In particular, the provenance of information is crucial in deciding whether the information is to be trusted, how it should be integrated with other diverse information sources, and how to give credit to its originators when reusing it. In an open and inclusive environment such as the Web, where users find information that is often contradictory or questionable, provenance can help those users to make trust judgements" (Garrie 2014). The PROV Ontology (PROV-O) defines the OWL2 Web Ontology Language encoding of the PROV Data Model (PROV-DM). Among the many semantic representation models, this ontology specification provides the foundation necessary to implement provenance applications in different domains that can represent, exchange, and integrate provenance information generated in different systems and under different contexts, which is crucial for the evaluation of the MAGNETO platform. The ontology supports three categories of information structures, namely (i) starting point terms; (ii) expanded terms; and (iii) qualified terms.

The starting point terms are a small set of classes and properties that can be used to create simple, initial provenance descriptions. There are three classes defined in the starting point terms, which are summarized as follows:

- An prov:Entity is a physical, digital, conceptual, or another kind of thing with some fixed aspects; entities may be real or imaginary.
- An prov:Activity is something that occurs over a period of time and acts upon or with entities; it may include consuming, processing, transforming, modifying, relocating, using, or generating entities.

- An prov:Agent is something that bears some form of responsibility for an activity taking place, for the existence of an entity, or for another agent's activity.

In the context of MAGNETO, these three classes are mapped against the digital evidence represented within the platform as prov:Entity, while the operation performed upon the digital evidence is mapped with prov:Activitiy and finally the human agent enabling the activity is identified as prov:Agent. It is important to note that the responsibility of the agent stops with the creation of an activity, while the activity of information being processed is carried out by digital agents, which are considered as algorithms integrated within the platform.

In addition to these classes, there are several object-type and data-type properties associated with the classes to model the end-to-end lifecycle of digital evidence management. For instance, as mentioned earlier, prov:Activity refers to the action either carried out by a human agent from LEA or perform an operation using the AI algorithms developed in the project. Therefore, activities are referred to have a **start** and **end** timestamp associated to particular points in time (described using properties prov:startedAtTime and prov:endedAtTime, respectively) and during their lifespan can **use** and **generate** a variety of Entities (described with prov:used and prov:wasGeneratedBy, respectively, which could represent the new forms of digital evidence resulting from processing). In addition, the semantic formalization aids in sequencing multiple processing with chained representations allowed within activity using the association of prov:wasInformedBy another activity to establish interdependency of information without explicitly providing the activities' start and end times. A prov:wasInformedBy relation between Activities suggests that the informed Activity used an Entity that was generated by the informing Activity, but the Entity itself is unknown or is not of interest. So, the prov:wasInformedBy property allows the construction of provenance chains comprising only Activities.

Provenance chains comprising only Entities can be formed using the prov:wasDerivedFrom property. A derivation is a transformation of one entity into another. For example, if the Activity that created the bar chart is not known or is not of interest, then we can say that the bar chart prov:wasDerivedFrom the dataset. Arbitrary Resource Description Framework (RDF) properties can be used to describe the fixed aspects of an Entity that are interesting within a particular application (for example, the file size and format of the dataset, or the aspect ratio of the bar chart).

While the properties prov:used, prov:wasGeneratedBy, prov:wasInformedBy, and prov:wasDerivedFrom can be used to construct provenance chains among Activities and Entities, Agents may also be ascribed responsibility for any Activity or Entity within a provenance chain. An Agent's responsibility for an Activity or Entity is described using the properties prov:wasAssociatedWith and prov:wasAttributedTo, respectively. Agents can also be responsible for other Agents' actions. In this case of delegation, the influencing Agent prov:actedOnBehalfOf another Agent that also bears responsibility for the influenced Activity or Entity.

The properties rdf:type and rdfs:label are used to express prov:type and prov:label, respectively.

The use of the semantic framework developed within MAGNETO will achieve the following key objectives:

- To track the use of each module in the Magneto Platform
- For the court-proof evidence, it is important to identify the algorithm not only as a software component but also to identify the respective features and associated version to identify the features of the algorithm and tag the subsequent improvements reported in the algorithm. As a computational algorithm, the performance of the algorithm should be inspected by humans to ensure the validity of the analyzed outcome prior to integration of the same within the report preparation.
- To track the input and the output of each module
  - Two forms of indexing are developed within the MAGNETO platform that supports both entity-based retrieval and activity-based retrieval of information analysis carried out within the project.
- To link the input data and output data with the data source
  - The historic values of processing digital evidence using specific algorithms as integrated within the platform will play a crucial role in establishing the trust and transparency of the MAGNETO platform in court.

An example scenario integrated (and demonstrated) within the MAGNETO platform relates to the multimedia processing which represents the extraction of ANPR from the images captured in CCTV. The prov:Entities are instantiated as a list of each single media asset collected as evidence, while the activity to be performed relates to Automatic Number Plate Recognition (ANPR) extraction, to be triggered by the prov:Agent. The collection of information from different CCTV footage is depicted in Figure 11.4. The metadata extracted from the ANPR algorithm based on deep learning is furthermore translated into MAGNETO Common Ontology representational model for subsequent instantiation. An overview of the ontology instantiation schema is presented in Figure 11.5.

The rationale for the choice of PROV ontology relies on the availability of extended terms that extend the formalization MAGNETO semantic framework. Extending upon the starting terms, the first category of the extended terminology leads to more fine definition of prov:Agent class with prov:Person; prov:Organization, and prov:SoftwareAgent. In addition, the prov:Entity class is further refined to include three additional subclasses, namely prov:Collection, prov:Bundle, and prov:Plan. A prov:Collection is an Entity that provides a structure (e.g. set, list, etc.) to some constituents (which are themselves Entities). The prov:Collection class can be used

Figure 11.4 ANPR analysis carried out on CCTV footage collected as evidence and ingested into MAGNETO platform.

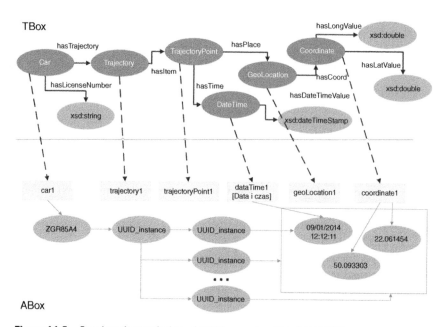

Figure 11.5 Ontology instantiation of ANPR records within MAGNETO common representation model.

to express the provenance of the collection itself, e.g. who maintained the collection, which members it contained as it evolved, and how it was assembled. The prov:hadMember property is used to assert membership in a collection. A prov:Bundle is a named set of provenance descriptions, which may itself have provenance. The named set of provenance descriptions may be expressed as PROV-O or any other form. The subclass of Bundle that names a set of PROV-O assertions is not provided by PROV-O, since it is more appropriate to do so using other recommendations, standards, or technologies. In any case, a Bundle of PROV-O assertions is an abstract set of RDF triples, and adding or removing a triple creates a new distinct Bundle of PROV-O assertions. A prov:Plan is an entity that represents a set of actions or steps intended by one or more agents to achieve some goals.

More general and more specific properties are also provided by the expanded terms. More generally, the property prov:wasInfluencedBy is a super property that relates any influenced Entity, Activity, or Agent to any other influencing Entity, Activity, or Agent that had an effect on its characteristics. Three subproperties of prov:wasDerivedFrom are also provided for certain kinds of derivation among Entities: prov:wasQuotedFrom cites a potentially larger Entity (such as a book, blog, or image) from which a new Entity was created by repeating some or all of the original, prov:wasRevisionOf indicates that the derived Entity contains substantial content from the original Entity (e.g. two results generated by an algorithm for two configuration parameters), and prov:hadPrimarySource cites a preceding Entity produced by some agent with direct experience and knowledge about the topic.

The **second** category of expanded terms relates Entities according to their levels of abstraction, where some Entities may present more specific aspects than their more general counterparts. While prov:specializationOf links a more specific Entity to a more general one (e.g. today's BBC news home page versus BBC's news home page on any day), prov:alternateOf links Entities that present aspects of the same thing, but not necessarily the same aspects or at the same time (e.g. the serialization of a document in different formats or a backup copy of a computer file).

The **third** category of expanded terms allows further description of Entities. The property prov:value provides a literal value that is a direct representation of an entity. For example, the prov:value of a quote could be a string of the sentences stated, or the prov:value of an Entity involved in a numeric calculation could be the xsd:integer four. The property prov:atLocation can be used to describe the prov:Location of any Entity, Activity, Agent, or prov:InstantaneousEvent (i.e. the starting or ending of an activity or the generation, usage, or invalidation of an entity). The properties used to describe instances of prov:Location are outside the scope of PROV-O; reuse of other existing vocabulary is encouraged.

The fourth category of expanded terms describes the lifetime of an Entity beyond being generated by an Activity and used by other Activities. Similar to how Activities have start and end times, an Entity may be bound by points in time for

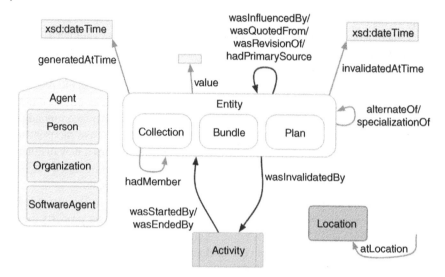

Figure 11.6 PROV-ontology expanded terms build upon the starting terms.

which it was generated or is no longer usable. The properties prov:generatedAtTime and prov:invalidatedAtTime can be used to bound the starting and ending moments of an Entity's existence. The Activities that led to the generation or invalidation of an Entity can be provided using prov:wasGeneratedBy and prov:wasInvalidatedBy, respectively. prov:generated and prov:invalidated are the inverses of prov:wasGeneratedBy and prov:wasInvalidatedBy, respectively, and are defined to facilitate Activity-as-subject as well as Entity-as-subject descriptions.

The fifth category of expanded terms describes the lifetime of an Activity beyond its start and end times and predecessor Activities. Activities may also be started or ended by Entities, which are described using the properties prov:wasStartedBy and prov:wasEndedBy, respectively. Since Entities may start or end Activities, and Agents may be Entities, then Agents may also start or end Activities.

An overview of these additional categories of concept formalization is visualized in Figure 11.6.[3]

The extended terms offer additional flexibility in performing repeated processing of digital evidence (prov:Entity) with different configurations of the algorithms integrated within the platform. The PROV ontology also supports the formalization of prov:Entity being invalidated resulting from human error or otherwise. The prov:Entity reference to prov:hadPrimarySource object property links the digital assets associated with a case as initiated by prov:Person in the system.

---

3 https://www.w3.org/TR/prov-o/diagrams/expanded.svg.

While the authentication and authorization of the human agents have been addressed with the integration of Keycloak[4] service as outlined in T9.2 and reported in D9.2, the authentication and authorization of prov:SoftwareAgent is relied upon the use of security keys that authenticate the requests generated from MAGNETO client which are subsequently processed by the components integrated within the platform.

11.5   Evidence Lifecycle Management

In the context of evidence lifecycle management, it is critical to authenticate digital evidence along with the reliability of the said evidence as processed within the MAGNETO platform. In the literature, there are two general approaches proposed to assess whether digital evidence can be relied upon in court. The first approach is to focus on whether the computer that generated the evidence was functioning normally, and the other approach is to examine the actual digital evidence against tampering and other damage.

In the past, most of the legislation across national borders adopted the first approach, instructing courts to evaluate computer-generated records based on the reliability of the system and process that generated the records. For instance, the section in the Federal Rules of Evidence 901 (b) (9) titled "Requirement of Authentication or Identification" includes "evidence describing a process or system used to produce a result and showing that the process or system produces an accurate result." Similar observations from the ECtHR have been reported in Section 11.2. In the United Kingdom, under Section 69 of the Parliamentary Assembly (PACE), there was a formal requirement for a positive assertion that the computer systems involved were working properly. The rationale for this approach is that because records of this type are not the counterpart of a statement by a human declarant, which should ideally be tested by cross-examination of that declarant, they should not be treated as hearsay, but rather their admissibility should be determined on the basis of the reliability and accuracy of the process involved.

However, the reliability of a computer system or process is difficult to assess, and, in practice, courts are not well equipped to assess the reliability of computer systems or processes. The increasing variety and complexity of computer systems make it "increasingly impractical to examine (and therefore certify) all the intricacies of computer operation" (Garrie 2014). Furthermore, requiring programmers and system designers to establish that computer systems are reliable at the lowest level (such as file system management) is untenable thus according to the authors has led to, "overburdening already crowded courts with hordes of technical witnesses." An added difficulty in certifying a computer or even a specific process is that even a process that is

---

4 https://www.keycloak.org/.

generally reliable can malfunction under certain circumstances. Computer systems can have unforeseen operating errors, occasionally resulting in data corruption or catastrophic crashes. Therefore, it is not safe to presume that mechanical instruments were in order at the material time. Furthermore, because programs can be upgraded to fix bugs and modify functionality, it is not safe to assume that a process on the current system functioned in the same way at the time of the offense. This approach also breaks down when the computer system in question is under the control of the perpetrator. It is not feasible to rigidly categorize types of evidence in general – it is not valid to claim that all NT event logs are reliable. These logs can be tampered with and there may be signs of tampering such as deleted log entries in a computer intrusion case. Even if it were possible to determine that a computer system or process is generally reliable, this does not necessarily imply that the evidence at hand has not been tampered with to conceal a crime or misdirect investigators.

To address these challenges regarding the validity of the evidence analyzed and processed within the MAGNETO platform integrating several algorithms to process the digital evidence, the project has adopted the use of immutable file systems, namely the IPFS.[5] The IPFS is released as a protocol and peer-to-peer network for storing and sharing data in a distributed file system. IPFS uses content-addressing to uniquely identify each file in a global namespace connecting all computing devices. In contrast to the traditional file system, IPFS offers immutability as an inbuilt feature. In addition, to store files of large size that are too big to fit within one block (such as video files), IPFS splits the data into multiple blocks and uses metadata to link it all together.

The ability to share the content in a distributed, decentralized manner has further enabled LEAs not only to keep a local copy of the digital evidence but also to store the information extracted from processing in a distributed decentralized repository. However, as opposed to a centrally located server, IPFS is built around a decentralized system of user-operators who hold a portion of the overall data, creating a resilient system of file storage and sharing. Any user in the network can serve a file by its content address, and other peers in the network can find and request that content from any node that has it using a distributed hash table (DHT).

11.6 IPFS Storage

Following these advantages offered by IPFS, it has been chosen as a testbed to store the relevant documents generated from the MAGNETO platform within the IPFS infrastructure. An example of the IPFS installation adopted within the project is presented in Figures 11.8–11.12.

---

5 https://docs.ipfs.io/.

In Figure 11.7, the details of the IPFS infrastructure setup have been presented with the IP address associated with the underlying service referenced. The support for IPV4 and IPV6 provides support for the global discovery of the hosted services registered across the peer network. However, for security and safety reasons, the configuration of the installation requires to be limited to local access or a preconfigured installation within an LEA organization. In Figure 11.9, an overview of the

Figure 11.7   MAGNETO IPFS immutable document store.

Figure 11.8   MAGNETO IPFS setup.

Figure 11.9 IPFS explores document repository among peers.

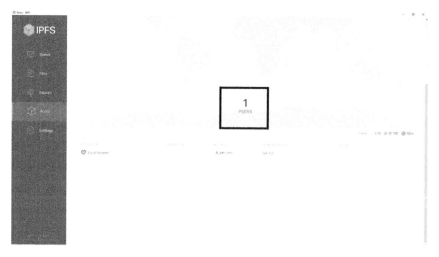

Figure 11.10 Preconfigured MAGNETO immutable document repository shared with one other peer within the local network.

files uploaded to the platform is presented. The upload process is carried out using the secure web communication authenticated by the MAGNETO Keycloak service.

In Figure 11.10 the IPFS explore document repository across registered peer network is presented followed by the global visualization of registered peers within the network in Figure 11.10, which highlights the restricted access to which the IPFS service interfaces. As mentioned earlier, the decentralized file-sharing

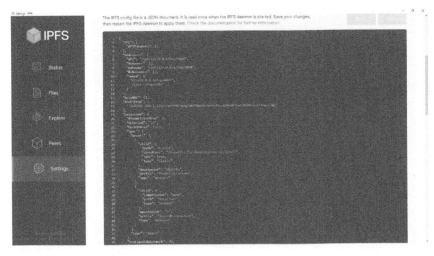

Figure 11.11 MAGNETO IPFS distributed data repository settings to secure the configuration of the network.

system could be configured for global access or to a restricted access among selected peers within the network (highlighted as one peer in Figure 11.10). As the details stored within the MAGNETO IPFS are expected to be sensitive and thus require additional security to restrict external access, the use of "bootstrap" option available within the IPFS infrastructure setting is utilized. The configuration settings for the IPFS are presented in Figure 11.11.

11.7 Accessibility and Evidence Traceability

Following the systematic development of the semantic framework and immutable IPFS file system for securing the new evidence generated within the MAGNETO platform, in this section, the accessibility and evidence traceability is formalized using the Ethereum[6] blockchain environment (described in the rest of the section), which has been configured to be operated as a private network. An overview of the network setup has been presented in Figure 11.12.

Among the several features supported by Ethereum, the use of smart contracts to be deployed that can be monitored and regulated has been identified to satisfy the MAGNETO requirement on tracking accessibility of prov:Agent against prov:Entity. For simplicity, a smart contract is considered a simple

---

6 https://ethereum.org/en/.

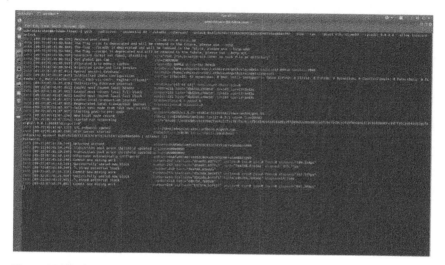

Figure 11.12   Ethereum network configuration and operation with blocks mined.

computer program that facilitates the exchange of any valuable asset between two parties. By definition, the contract consists primarily of the terms and conditions mutually agreed on between the parties (peers). In the context of MAGNETO, such an agreement is established between the users operating the platform and the platform itself. The organizational regulations limiting the authentication and authorization of different personnel in gaining access to different evidence recorded for a case within the platform are constantly monitored against any anomalies. The key feature of a smart contract is that once it is executed, it cannot be altered, and any transaction done on top of a smart contract is registered permanently – it is immutable. The verification process for the smart contracts is carried out by anonymous parties of the network without the need for a centralized authority using consensus algorithms as defined in the configuration of the environment.

The accessibility and evidence traceability smart contract as defined and deployed within MAGNETO is presented in Table 11.1. The smart contract definition has been defined using the Solidity programming language,[7] which is an object-oriented, high-level implementation. The smart contract definition as outlined here governs the behavior of the accounts within the Ethereum state.

---

7 https://solidity.readthedocs.io/en/v0.7.1/index.html.

Table 11.1 Solidity smart contract for accessibility and evidence traceability in MAGNETO platform.

```
pragma solidity ^0.4.0;
contract MagnetoEvidenceTraceability {
    mapping (bytes32 => uint256) public evidenceAccess;
    bytes32[] public entityList;
    bytes32[] public agentList;
    function MagnetoEvidenceTraceability(bytes32[] memory entityList, bytes32[]
memory agentList) public {
        entityList = entityList;
        agentList = agentList;
    }
    function traceabilityEntities(bytes32 entity) view public returns (uint256) {
        return evidenceAccess[entity];
    }
    function evidenceTrace(bytes32 entity, bytes32 agent) public {
        require(validCandidate(agent));
        evidenceAccess[entity] += agent;
    }
    function validAgent(bytes32 agent) view public returns (bool) {
        for(uint i = 0; i < agentList.length; i++) {
            if (agentList[i] == agent) {
                return true;
            }
        }
        return false;
    }
}
```

The smart contract is initialized using two main attributes a list of prov:Entities and prov:Agents as outlined in the semantic framework (Section 11.3). The list of prov:Agents includes both the registered users in the platform as authorized by Keycloak along with a list of prov:SoftwareAgents integrated within the platform (as reported in WP3 and WP4 outcomes). The list of prov:Entities are the instances reported in the semantic framework that cites each of the evidence collected and processed within the platform for criminal investigation. Both of these attributes are instantiated as an array. As the smart contract provides immutability as a feature, the smart contract should be refreshed or redeployed following the generation of new evidence from the processing outcome. The implementation of the overall traceability component offers synchronization of metadata between the semantic framework, which is instantiated within the Apache Jean Fuseki server[8] followed by the IPFS immutable file system in which the new generation of large-volume file objects are being stored. Finally, the accessibility of the evidence from the authenticated and authorized personnel from LEA is recorded within the Ethereum smart contract environment.

The compilation of the smart contract outlined in Table 11.1 results in the generation of a binary string, which is then deployed within the Ethereum network as outlined in Table 11.2. The transactions are being logged and recorded using the remix-ide[9] to interface with the blockchain to generate audit reports.

Blockchain is a broad and versatile technology that is context-dependent and not separately regulated and should therefore follow the rules applicable to every application. In this case, the data protection provisions, thoroughly discussed under D9.1 and D9.3,[10] as well as the criminal procedural requirements analyzed within this chapter, should be respected. In accordance with the description of the blockchain application detailed earlier, the logs generated by all the components reported in the chapter are evaluated to follow the European legal framework for court-proof evidence, as outlined in Section 11.2.

More specifically, by focusing on individual evidences gathered from different sources, including the different file formats collected in the process of investigation, and shielding them separately instead of focusing merely on the entire computer system, the digital form of evidence and the chain of custody is shielded in an over-arching manner. The decentralized system of storage and sharing allows for greater resilience against unauthorized access or alterations. Moreover, the use of metadata regarding files and linking the blocks, and the use of smart contracts for tracking and accessibility which cannot be altered, better safeguard the chain of custody. Audit trails and detailed reports on how the data have been collected and are being handled are in this way kept, allowing for the provenance, authentication, and originality of the data, and therefore the evidence, to be preserved and proved before the court.

11.8 MAGNETO Features Against Cognitive Biases

A formal definition of confirmation bias was provided by Wallace in (Wallace 2015) in which the author states that "confirmation bias occurs when a person believes in or searches for evidence to support his or her favoured theory while ignoring or

---

8 https://jena.apache.org/documentation/fuseki2/.

9 https://remix.ethereum.org/.

10 See MAGNETO D9.1 "Ethical and Legal Guidelines for the use of the Forensic Tools" and MAGNETO D9.3 "Interim Ethical and Legal Impact Assessment."

Table 11.2 The binary format of contract processed within Ethereum.

60806040523480156100105760008 0fd5b50604051610367380380610
367833981810160405260208110156 1003357600080fd5b8101908080
5160405193929190846401000000000 8211156100535760008 0fd5b90
830190602082018581111561006857 600080fd5b825186 60208202830
11164010000000008211171561008 557600080fd5b8252508151602091
820192820191028083836 0005b838110156100b2 57818101518382015
260200161009a565b50505050509190 910160405250508251 6100d49250
6001915 060208401906100db565b5050610143565b82805482 8255906
00052602060000209081019282156 10116579160200282015b82811156
1011657825182559160200191906 00010190610 0fb565b506101229291
5061012 6565b5090565b6101409190 5b80821115610122576000815 56
0010161012c565b90565b6102158061 01526000396000f3fe60806 040
52348015610010576000 80fd5b506004361061061 00575760003560e01c
80632f265cf714610 05c578063392e66781 461008b5780637021939f
146100bc578063b13c744b146100 d9578063cc9ab267146 100f6575b6
00080fd5b6100796004803603602081 1015610072576 00080fd5b5035
610115565b60408 0519182525190 81900360200190f35b6100a8 60048
0360360208110156100 a157600080fd5b503 561013f565b60408 051911
515825 2519081900360200190f35 b6100796004803603 602081101561
00d2576000 80fd5b5035610 18756 5b6100796004 80360360208 1101
56100ef5 76000 80fd5b5035610199565b61 011360048036 0360208110
1561010c5 76000 80fd5b50356101b7565b005b6000 6101208261 013f
565b6101 0129576 00080fd5b5060 008181526020819 05260409020545b
91905056 5b60008 05b60015 481101561017e57 82600182815481106 10
15b57fe5b906 0005260 2060002 001541415610176576 0019150506101
3a5 65b60 0101610143565b5060 00092915050565 b6000602081905290
8152604 090205481565b6001 8181548110610 1a657fe5b6000 9182526
0209091200154905 08 1565b6101 c0816 1013f5 65b6101c9576 00080fd
5b6000908 152602081 905260409 0208 054600 10190 5556fea26 5627a7
a72315820951975101 d0082d2e29441e 16281ccf 56d188a8cd 6aa59bf8
c43f559d5 17a4de64736 f6c634300050b00 32

excusing disconfirmatory evidence and is disinclined to change his or her belief once he or she arrives at a conclusion." In the context of criminal investigation, such a bias has been shown to impact the investigative procedure and processes which have been followed resulting in questionable outcomes (Meterko and Cooper 2022). The early literature on handling uncertainty and cognitive biases in knowledge engineering can be traced back to the 1993 publication by Donnell and

Lehner (1993). The authors argue that knowledge engineering is the process of eliciting knowledge from human experts and encoding that knowledge in machine-usable form. Additionally, the hypothesize argues that irrespective of the domain being modeled by the formalization of knowledge, it requires interviews and interaction with experts to encode the expert-derived procedures. Furthermore, the authors state that in any decision support system (DSS) development effort, the specification of the analytical procedures to be embedded in the DSS will inevitably be, at least in part, based on the encoding of procedures elicited from experts.

In 2017, Dror (2017) published a taxonomy citing the sources of cognitive bias being introduced into the criminal investigation. The proposed taxonomy has been subjected to further revisions (Donell and Lehner 1993) and is presented in Figure 11.13. The confirmation bias resulting from human nature is also referred to as "tunnel vision," which denotes selective seeking, recalling, weighting, and/or interpreting information in ways that support existing beliefs, expectations or hypothesis, while simultaneously avoiding or minimizing inconsistent or contradictory information.

The environment and culture influence the direction of criminal investigation, which are mitigated against using different types of training activities delivered within an organization. The modalities of these training activities aim to stimulate a constructive environment, in which different hypothesis areas are allowed to be generated and undertake several forms of actions to collect an extensive set of evidence that is relevant to the investigation at hand. Another factor that has shown to influence the outcome of an investigation refers to the individual

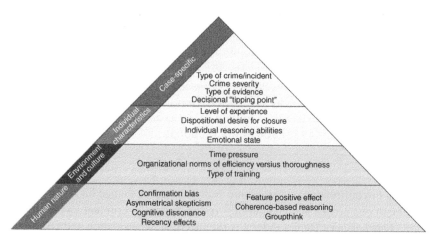

Figure 11.13 Organizational framework for case evaluation studies, adopted from Dror's (2017) taxonomy of different sources of potential bias that may cognitively contaminate forensic observations and conclusions.

characteristics, which could range from professional experience when it comes to assessments of potential criminal cases and assumptions of guilt. The final influencing factor is related to the case under investigation. Among the several factors, there is the perceived reliability of some of the evidence reviewed such as DNA vs. photo evidence vs. witness reports. When encountered with ambiguous and often contradictory information, the experience of the investigator is often required to make judgmental decisions upon which evidence to be considered and which evidence could be ignored or considered not relevant for the subsequent investigation.

In addition to the four categories which are identified as the cause of cognitive (also confirmatory) bias, the use of technology for evidence processing is also considered a source following the close integration of investigation practices with outcomes obtained from AI tools. In the MAGNETO platform, the use of advanced evidence processing components has been integrated for the analysis of textual, video and audio, CDR, financial reports, and other forms of evidence. To mitigate against the impact of cognitive bias, two methodologies have been adopted within the project as follows:

- to quantify the reliability of the algorithms integrated within the platform using accepted metrics
- to deliver a training program for the platform utilization to the end users.

As an example of the transparency in the algorithm output, the results from face recognition are presented in Figures 11.14–11.17. The appearance of the

Figure 11.14 Face recognition component with a confidence level associated with the person identity.

Figure 11.15   Person identity presented with 82.5%.

Figure 11.16   Person identity presented with 85.5%.

labels is highlighted in the red circle. As the person is seen approaching the camera, the confidence level in the person's identity is increased from 70 to 98%. Such transparent outcomes included in the visualization of the results allow for the investigator to inspect the evidence and be aware of the pitfalls of confirmatory bias.

The data and text mining tools do not use sensitive data categories such as ethnic group, religion, or sexual orientation to deliver their results. The text-mining

Figure 11.17 Confidence of the person identity presented as 98%.

component is based on publicly available corpora that have been approved not to contain any bias. The rules for semantic reasoning cannot obtain biases regarding religion, ethnicity, and sexual orientation because the design of the ontology excludes specifying these sensitive data categories.

The trajectory fusion tool does not use sensitive data categories such as ethnic group, religion, or sexual orientation to deliver their results.

11.9 Conclusions

The chapter presented in detail the research and activities carried out in the MAGNETO project for the development of robust and court-proof evidence component. The different technologies reported in the chapter are in response to the detailed analysis of the European legal framework on the court-proofness of evidence provided by legal experts within the consortium. The use of a semantic framework built on the formalization PROV concepts is extended for the operation considered within the MAGNETO platform. The semantic distinction between the physical activity carried out in the platform against the automated computing performed by the various algorithms integrated is facilitated with the use of extended classes provided by PROV ontology, namely prov:Person and prov:SoftwareAgent. The authentication and authorization of the human agents are carried out using Keycloak authentication services. The use of an immutable filesystem for the storage of new digital evidence produced by the MAGNETO platform is supported using IPFS and the traceability of evidence accessibility transaction logs are monitored using smart contracts embedded with the private network of Ethereum. Finally, the chapter also reports on the use of LSB algorithms for securing the media data generated within the MAGNETO platform against external data sources. The visual quality of the resulting prov:Entities is evaluated against the PSNR values.

References

Baru, C., Bhandarkar, M., Nambiar, R. et al. (2013). Setting the direction for Big Data Benchmark Standards. In: *Lecture Notes in Computer Science (Including Subseries Lecture Notes in Artificial Intelligence and Lecture Notes in Bioinformatics)*. Springer https://link.springer.com/chapter/10.1007/978-3-642-36727-4_14.

Behmer, EJ., Chandramouli, K., Garrido, V. et al. (2019). Ontology population framework of MAGNETO for instantiating heterogeneous forensic data modalities. In: *IFIP Advances in Information and Communication Technology*, vol. 559, 520–531. Cham: Springer 10.1007/978-3-030-19823-7_44.

Benet, J. (2014). {IPFS} – content addressed, versioned, {P2P} file system. *CoRR* abs/1407.3. http://arxiv.org/abs/1407.3561.

Demestichas, K., Remoundou, K., Loumiotis, I. et al. (2021). Evolving from data to knowledge mining to uncover hidden relationships BT. In: *Technology Development for Security Practitioners. Security Informatics and Law Enforcement* (ed. B. Akhgar, D. Kavallieros and E. Sdongos), 57–71. Cham: Springer International Publishing 10.1007/978-3-030-69460-9_4.

Donell, M.L. and Lehner, P.E. (1993). Uncertainty handling and cognitive biases in knowledge engineering. *IEEE Transactions on Systems, Man, and Cybernetics* 23 (2): 563–570.

Dror, I.E. (2017). Human expert performance in forensic decision making: seven different sources of bias. *Australian Journal of Forensic Sciences* 49 (5): 541–547. https://doi.org/10.1080/00450618.2017.1281348.

Garrie, D.B. (2014). Digital forensic evidence in the courtroom: understanding content and quality. *Northwestern Journal of Technology and Intellectual Property* 12: https://scholarlycommons.law.northwestern.edu/njtip/vol12/iss2/5/.

Han, Rui, Lizy Kurian John, and Jianfeng Zhan. 2018. "Benchmarking big data systems: a review." *IEEE Transactions on Services Computing.* vol. 11, no. 3, pp. 580–597. doi: https://doi.org/10.1109/TSC.2017.2730882.

Lebo, T., Sahoo, S., McGuinness, D. et al. (2013). PROV-O: the PROV ontology (W3C recommendation). *World Wide Web Consortium.* http://www.w3.org/TR/2013/REC-prov-o-20130430/ (accessed 27 March 2022).

Meterko, V. and Cooper, G. (2022). Cognitive biases in criminal case evaluation: a review of the research. *Journal of Police and Criminal Psychology* 37 (1): 101–122. https://doi.org/10.1007/s11896-020-09425-8.

Pérez, F. J., Garrido, V. J., García, A. et al. (2021). Multimedia analysis platform for crime prevention and investigation. *Multimedia Tools and Applications* 80 (15): 23681–23700. https://doi.org/10.1007/s11042-020-10206-y.

Wallace, W.A. (2015). The effect of confirmation bias on criminal investigative decision making. *Walden Dissertations and Doctoral Studies*. 407. https://scholarworks.waldenu.edu/dissertations/407.

12

Chances and Challenges of Predictive Policing for Law Enforcement Agencies

Sebastian Allertseder[1], Guenter Okon[2], and Thomas Schweer[2]

[1] Department Police, University of Applied Sciences for Public Services in Bavaria, Fuerstenfeldbruck, Germany
[2] Institut für musterbasierte Prognosetechnik, ImfPt., Oberhausen, Germany

Fortunately, terrorist attacks in Europe are rare events, and thus hardly predictable by statistics due to their low number. Therefore, it makes more sense to develop instruments for analyzing the risk potential of supporters of extremist groups or individual radicalization patterns, in order to be able to forecast terrorist activities and initiate suitable operational measures in a timely manner. This leads to a methodology focusing on a personalized forecasting procedure.

In addition to the undeniable advantages of such personal prognosis methods, like the increase of internal security and the prevention of politically motivated acts of violence, we have to consider data protection and ethical questions as well. The question arises – in which way false prognoses (false positive, false negative) could affect individuals and groups or internal security? To what extent may governmental intervention affect the freedom and personal rights of citizens? What effects do labeling and stigmatization processes (ethnic, racial profiling) have on vulnerable communities?

This contribution aims to provide answers to these questions. It deals not only with the opportunities but also challenges of predictive policing for the law enforcement agencies (LEAs) of the European Union. It furthermore gives an insight into the research results and technical developments from the H2020 project PREVISION.

Security Technologies and Social Implications, First Edition. Edited by Garik Markarian, Ruža Karlović, Holger Nitsch, and Krishna Chandramouli.
© 2023 The Institute of Electrical and Electronics Engineers, Inc.
Published 2023 by John Wiley & Sons, Inc.

12.1 Next Generation Policing by Prediction of Crime

Absolute security, however it might be a dream, is a target, which cannot be achieved in reality. Every society is confronted with deviant and criminal behavior. Crime unfortunately is a normal social phenomenon within human societies. Nevertheless, every country has the obligation to protect its citizens from crime and terrorist threats, as physical protection is identified as one of the main responsibilities of the state in Germany and worldwide (Fieseler and Haubner 2005, p. 13). However, this fundamental task is becoming increasingly difficult in the age of globalization and increasing technological development. Threats must be analyzed quickly and objectively by the relevant state authorities in order to be able to react promptly. In addition, the preparation for future risks and the general prevention of crime are becoming an increasing part of the risk mitigation strategies of modern police forces. Policing on the basis of forecasts is therefore one of the big trends in this field. The so-called predictive policing offers a huge opportunity of making police work more efficient. However, predictive policing, based on the analysis of huge amount of data, has to be integrated in a comprehensive manner into the workflow and the internal culture of a police authority. If this is not happening in an adequate way predictive policing is ineffective and therefore will face a lack of acceptance by the police officers and those who have to implement the measures in their daily operations.

In the context of this paper, the methodical approaches, which are relevant for predictive policing will be outlined. In a second step, psychological, sociological and criminological theories, which play a prominent role in predictive policing, will be examined in general terms. After this, the factors and indicators that can be derived from theories and further empirical research are outlined and finally it will be shown how Law-Enforcement Agencies will be able to use this in the context of radicalization and terrorism. The basis for this are the research and developments made in the context of the European Commission H2020 project PREVISION[1] (grant agreement no. 833115).

12.2 Lessons Learned from Previous Mistakes

In general, predictive policing is still a rather young but very dynamic branch of criminological research and police work. Especially in the United States, but also in European countries such as Germany and Switzerland, more and more

---

1 For further information, please visit: www.prevision-h2020.eu.

authorities are working with predictive tools such as Predpol, Hunchlab or Pre-cobs. Although, the advantages of preventing crime by fighting it before it could happen are huge, not all practical experience in past was positive.

There are a number of bad examples, which produced problematic and ethically, morally and legally questionable results. Police departments in some of the largest cities in the United States have experimented with predictive policing to predict criminal activity. Predictive policing uses computer systems to analyze large volumes of data, including historical crime data, to decide where to deploy police or to identify people who are more likely to commit or be victims of a crime. Supporters argue that predictive policing can help predict crime more accurately and effectively than traditional policing methods. Critics, however, have raised concerns about transparency and accountability. Although Big Data companies claim, their technologies can help eliminate bias in policing decisions, algorithms that rely on historical data risk reproducing that very bias again.

Predictive policing is just one of many ways police departments in the United States have incorporated big data methods into their work over the past two decades. Others include the introduction of surveillance technologies such as facial recognition and social media monitoring. These developments have not always been accompanied by adequate protective measures.

For example, the Chicago Police Department was one of the first police departments to use predictive policing software. The focus was on particularly dangerous individuals and repeat offenders. Therefore, the Strategic Subject List (SSL) was introduced in 2013. This database was designed to keep track of potential future criminals, as well as particularly dangerous citizens.

The idea behind this was: If a limited group of people are particularly likely to be involved in violent acts, it is more efficient for security authorities to focus on them. Citizens classified as a risk are visited by police and forewarned in order to prevent the prediction from occurring. Social support should also initially catch the targeted individuals. An algorithm calculates the likelihood of individuals becoming perpetrators or victims in a shooting and assigns a heat score of up to 500 points. At the top of the list are people at particularly high risk. The SSL database, which initially contained around 1000 people, has also ballooned. About 1400 people are currently recorded as high-risk and in total, more than 400 000 people have been assigned a risk score (Peteranderl 2018). Critics accused the authorities of establishing a system of mass surveillance. The 2015 version of the SSL included nearly everyone who had ever been arrested. The problem, however, is that policing and arrests are not equally distributed across the population as a whole. Even though ethnic background and gender do not play a role in risk assessment, according to the police, social inequality, and racism are reflected in the system. For example, because police focus on patrolling and raiding hot spots, more Latinos and African Americans are arrested and recorded than white citizens.

A study by the military-affiliated think tank Rand Corporation concluded that arrests, in particular, are increasing. "Individuals on the SSL are no more or less likely to be victims of a homicide or shooting than the comparison group," it said. However, targeted individuals are more likely to be arrested for a shooting, according to the Rand study (Saunders et al. 2018). Crime rates in the city, on the other hand, were not positively impacted. Meanwhile, contrary to criticisms and reservations about the effectiveness of the software being used, digital policing continues to expand in Chicago.

In 2017, the Chicago Police Department established so-called Strategic Decision Support Centers to serve as hubs for high-tech policing. In the future, their number is expected to double. In these centers, all the threads come together (Douglas 2018). By networking tools such as predictive mapping and predictive policing software, systems for real-time analysis of gunshots, surveillance cameras, and tips from citizens, police can identify high-risk areas (Douglas 2018).

Similar experiences have been shared in other cities in the United States. In April 2020, the Los Angeles Police Department (LAPD) discontinued its "PredPol" program. The PredPol software, developed by a UCLA professor in collaboration with LAPD, was intended to predict in real time where and when crimes were likely to occur in the next 12 hours. In October 2019, the police department announced changes to the program, seven months after the LAPD's inspector general said he could not determine how effective the program was in reducing crime. Officials cited funding shortfalls related to the Corona pandemic as the reason for discontinuing the program.

There are also similar findings from England regarding person-oriented predictive policing. Researchers at the Royal United Services Institute (RUSI), commissioned by the government's Centre for Data Ethics and Innovation, looked at predictive crime and individual risk assessment and found that algorithms trained on police data can replicate, and in some cases, amplify, biases present in the dataset, such as over- or under-policing of certain communities. "The effects of biased sampling could be amplified by algorithmic predictions via a feedback loop, predicting future policing, not future crime," the authors said (Babuta and Oswald 2019, p. 12).

The briefing paper cites individuals from disadvantaged socioeconomic backgrounds for whom algorithms "calculate a greater risk of criminal behavior." This bias is due to the fact that individuals from this group are more likely to come into contact with public services, generating more data than police often have access to, according to the paper. This has serious implications both for police resource allocation, which may be ineffective because it is based on incorrect calculations, and at the legal level, where "discrimination claims could be brought by individuals who have been 'negatively' assessed in comparison to others of different ages or genders," the paper continues. The briefing paper also highlights the risk of "automated bias," where police officers rely too heavily on the use of analytics tools, which undermines their discretion and causes them to disregard other relevant factors. The paper, "Data Analytics and Algorithmic Bias in Policing," by Alexander Babuta and Marion Oswald, summarizes the interim findings of an ongoing independent study of the use of data analytics for policing in England and Wales and examines different types of bias that can arise (Babuta and Oswald 2019, p.12).

In addition to the fight against ordinary crime, which was the starting point and main aim of predictive policing, it is nowadays becoming increasingly important in the field of fighting terrorism. In this field, the main target is not only the prediction of terrorist attacks but also the prediction of the course of individual radicalizations.

12.3   A Question of Methodology

In the light of these mixed results in practical use, the most important question is how can a methodology ensure a reliable assessment and a multifactor analysis. Therefore, a combination of both, different prediction/forecasting methods and criminological theories are needed to provide a solid basis for any data analysis. According to Schwind, the term "crime prognosis" means "(well-founded) probability statements about the (total) future development of crime (or about the development of individual forms of crime) in the total population (or in parts of the population)" (Schwind 2006, p. 93). This definition shows that Schwind defines the prognosis as a collective phenomenon. In contrast, individual prognosis aims to predict the future delinquency of a single person. By using crime forecasts, it will be possible to counteract the future development of crime at an early stage, as measures can be planned in good time (Schwind 2006, p. 94). Three different methodological approaches to criminal prognoses can be distinguished: the intuitive prognosis, the statistical-nomothetical prognosis and the clinical-idiographic prognosis. These three forecast methods are presented hereunder:

12.4   Intuitive Method

The intuitive method starts with an emotional assessment of an individual. Personal and professional experiences of an individual are the key elements of every assessment. Hereby the mainly subjective "feeling" about a person which can also be linked to wider "intuition," i.e. something that is difficult to grasp objectively (the so-called "good feeling") plays the most important role. The intuitive method is therefore closely linked to the knowledge of reliable experts. This very traditional approach still is commonly used, as it is still inconceivable to many people that a machine or an algorithm can deliver higher quality analyses and forecasts than experienced people who have been dealing with a phenomenon area for years. Nevertheless, numerous studies prove the supremacy of algorithms. The psychologist and Nobel Prize winner Daniel Kahneman comments as follows:

> The number of studies comparing clinical and statistical predictions has increased to about 200, but the state of competition between algorithms and humans has not changed. In about 60% of the studies, the algorithms proved to be much more accurate. The other comparisons resulted in a draw, but a draw is tantamount to a victory for the statistical rules, which are generally much less expensive than expert judgment. No exception has been credibly documented.
>
> *(Source: Kahneman 2011, p. 276).*

The reluctance to make decisions about algorithms has to do not least with the fact that we give too much weight to the statements of experts. In this context, Kahneman refers to a study by his colleague Tetlok that exposes the "competence illusion" of experts. After collecting more than 80 000 predictions from so-called experts it turn out the probability of getting true results was lower than the probability of getting the correct answer by randomly selecting among three options. Tetlok summarized this by saying that: "[. . .], people who spend their time – and make a living – thoroughly studying a particular subject make worse predictions than dart throwing monkeys who would have distributed their 'decisions' evenly across all options. Even in the field they knew best, experts were no better than nonexperts" (Kahneman 2011, p. 271). This clearly outlines the problems of a forecasting process in which experts play a major role (e.g. scenario technique. To make matters worse, "those with the most knowledge [. . .] are often less reliable." This is because someone who acquires more knowledge develops an increased illusion of his abilities and overestimates them in an unrealistic way (Kahneman 2011, p. 271).

12.5 Statistical-Nomothetical Prognosis

The statistical-nomothetical prognosis is a rule-guided procedure for the compilation of individual criminal prognoses using predefined algorithms. The basic objective of this method is the identification and systematic compilation of personal and factual characteristics that are empirically significant related to recidivism (Dahle 2010, p. 41). With the statistical-nomothetical prognosis, a deductive conclusion is drawn from empirically proven average correlations, which are determined within the framework of large-scale relapse studies, to the individual case (Bliesener 2007).

Various forecasting instruments are used, such as forecast tables, in which individual characteristics are taken into account, or structural forecast tables, which also include interrelationships between the individual characteristics. By using algorithms or the summation of risk and protection factors, the risk analysis is carried out while the adjustment to the individual case is carried out exclusively by allocation to a standardized risk group (Bergmann 2018, p. 41; Dahle 2010, p. 42)

The statistical-nomothetical prognosis includes relapse predictors whose predictive quality is empirically proven, which is why an objective assessment of the case is possible with this type of prognosis method (Bergmann 2018, p. 41). However, since they are based on group statistical average experiences, individual and case-specific peculiarities cannot be taken into account (Dahle 2008).

12.6 Clinical-Idiographic Prognosis

The clinical-idiographic prognosis strategy is linked to individual cases and assesses the personality of perpetrators by contextualization of this individual development (Dahle 2008, p. 74ff). This assessment is based on general rules and standards, although the exact procedure does not follow precisely defined rules but can always be adapted to the individual case (Bergmann 2018, p. 40). In the first step of the clinical-idiographic prognosis, the relevant factors of the delinquency of an individual as well as the personal background and framework conditions are identified. From this starting point, an individual theory of action (previous delinquency of the considered individually) can be derived (Bergmann 2018, p. 40; Dahle 2010, p. 74).

In the second step, the changes in these factors are displayed in order to identify any personality changes or therapeutic effects. This step is of particular importance if the person under consideration has spent time in prison after the last offence. Personal factors that are stable over time are particularly relevant here since they determine a person's individual risk potential (Dahle 2010, p. 75). Finally, these factors are weighted and integrated into the forecast, which is a rough estimation of the future risk potential of the individual under consideration (Bergmann 2018, p. 40).

12.7 Methodology of Criminal Forecasting

The implementation of reliable crime prognoses requires the combination of different methodologies. This could include, for example, the simple extension of time series into the future or qualified approaches that can be used to make statements on future developments of crime, taking into account demographic developments and social factors that may favor criminal development (Schwind 2016, p. 94). In addition, expert surveys and a scenario-based approach could also contribute to a higher validity of the prognoses (Schwind 2016, p. 94). A common method to integrate the experts' opinion is the so-called Delphi method, which suggests interviewing experts independently in order to give their opinions on various issues (Görgen et al. 2010, p. 42). Instead of considering expert opinions on future developments isolated and individually, the Delphi method achieves more accurate forecasts via structured group processes (Grime and Wright 2016, p. 1). Precisely, the method suggests conducting an expert survey, then aggregating and returning the survey to the respondents, giving them the opportunity to revise it based on the feedback received. This iterative process leads to a defined endpoint, in which a consensus or a confirmed dissent is reached (Grime and Wright 2016, p. 1).

The basic idea of the scenario-based approach is to develop a scenario for the future by taking into account quantitative and qualitative influencing factors. The aim is to record and illustrate all possible courses of action, alternatives, and their probable consequences (Anders et al. 2004, p. 97). Normally, three scenario types are developed – one in which current developments are realistically projected into the future and two contrasting corresponding scenarios for the best case and worst case (Anders et al. 2004, p. 98).

With the help of a time series analysis as a form of regression analysis, one of the aims is to predict the future values of a time series in order to be able to make statements about future developments based on this data. The continuation of temporally collected data series, which can relate to a wide variety of application areas, enables the making of forecasts. In the context of time series analyses, data series are used which consist of interdependent observation values, obtained in chronological order (Vogel 2015, p. 9).

Time series analysis can also be a suitable method for forecasting crime. In this case, the data basis represents the offence quantity per day, per month, per quarter, or per year over a certain period in a limited geographical area. Based on this data, it will be possible to make predictions about future crime incidence and thus future crime development for this geographical area.

At the first glance, the prediction of terrorist attacks by means of time series analyses seems problematic, in particular, due to the low data basis. In addition, the occurrence of terrorist attacks appears to follow neither trends nor seasonal fluctuations. For this reason, the quality of a time series analysis for predicting terrorism must be subjected to empirical verification.

Sociological and psychological theories investigate in different ways the causes and phenomena of crime or investigate the related fields of prevention, investigation, and fight against crime. Criminology additionally includes law, sociology, pedagogy, ethnology, anthropology, and economics to show a bigger picture of the patterns of crime. In addition, also geography plays an increasingly important role in criminology, especially in the field of predictive policing.

12.8 Rational Choice Theory

Systematically acting perpetrators act according to a cost–benefit principle. They weigh up whether they can successfully carry out an act without having to fear criminal consequences for themselves. The Rational Choice Theory is thus quite capable of explaining certain forms of crime. In principle, the approach is based on the consideration that not only standard-compliant behavior of a cost–benefit analysis but also deviant and criminal actions are determined by cost–benefit considerations (Clarke and Felson 1993).

The problem is that, for example, criminal offences committed out of effect cannot be explained using the rational choice approach. Another criticism is that hardly any individual has all the relevant information at his or her disposal to carry out an objective cost-benefit analysis. In addition, it should be noted that framing effects could significantly influence perception and decision-making processes (Kahneman 2011, p. 447ff).

The advantages and disadvantages of action do not necessarily have to be of material nature. The desire for social status within a criminal subculture, which can be achieved by committing crimes, can be a motivation for criminal behavior. This applies to mafia groups as well as rockers and violent football fans.

The social objective therefore is to increase the cost of crime and minimize its usefulness in order to prevent it from being committed. Formal and informal sanctions can help achieve this purpose, i.e. by punishing antisocial behavior and rewarding socially accepted behavior.

What is the value of Rational Choice Theory for predictive policing? The aim is to identify the benefits and costs of specific criminal activities. By identifying characteristics, which are conducive to an offence and thus recognizing exemplary behavior, it is not only possible to forecast future offensive behavior but also to prevent it by means of appropriate police measures. Even an increase in the penalty level for gang burglary can induce perpetrators to relocate their operating room.

12.9 Learning Theories

Learning theories assume that deviant and criminal actions are learned through interactions. Lamnek explains that in the context of the learning process "not only the actual behavior patterns are learned, but also the attitudes, motives, and rationalizations, which make this possible or produce it in the first place" (Lamnek 1988, p. 216).

In the sense of the learning theory approaches, every member of a society or a group has the opportunity to orientate himself toward conforming or deviating behaviors, to identify oneself with conforming or deviating peers or to experience an intensification of conforming or deviating behaviors through reactions (Lamnek 1988, p. 187). Individuals identify themselves in different ways with conform or deviant or criminal behavior patterns and learn them through interactions with other members of society or groups. Deviating and criminal behavior occurs in situations when the learned deviant behavior patterns outweigh the conformal behavior patterns and individuals identify strongly with the deviant behavior patterns within a society or a group (Lamnek 1988, p. 188).

The theory of differential association according to Sutherland represents one of the most important approaches to learning theory (Sutherland 1939). Sutherland's main point is that "a person becomes delinquent when violations of the law outweigh favorable attitudes towards attitudes that negatively evaluate violations of the law" (Lamnek 1988, p. 188). Overall, Sutherland assumes that criminal behavior is learned through interaction, especially in groups and therefore cannot be inherited. The learning of techniques for the execution of a crime takes place in the context of such a learning process in the same way as the internalization of motives and attitudes (Lamnek 1988, p. 190; Schwind 2016, p. 133). In addition to contact with criminal milieus, the opportunity to carry out deviant and criminal acts also plays an important role, in the same way as the intensity of the needs of the (potential) perpetrator and the lack of legal alternatives (Cloward and Ohlin 1960; Lamnek 1988, p. 192).

With the help of the theory of differential amplification according to Burgess and Akers (1966), statements of Sutherland were concretized. The authors argue that amplifiers influence the frequency of certain behavior. A positive influence in this context is attributed to praise or money (Lamnek 1988, p. 195). Concerning deviant or criminal behavior, an uncovered execution or prey can act as a positive booster. In the context of radicalization, biographical aspects and previous criminal convictions can be used as indicators of a problematic socialization and a further exposition of criminal behavior.

12.10 Routine Activity Approach

The Routine Activity Theory goes back to Cohen and Felson (1979). Their intention was, in particular, to explain how social change processes the opportunities for criminal action and thus causes fluctuations in the crime rate. Although the focus of this theory lies on the macro level, it is assuming that crime depends significantly on opportunities (Siegel 2000, p. 113). Within the framework of the Routine Activity

Theory, Cohen and Felson examined the spatial and temporal conditions, under which victims and perpetrators are coming into contact and a criminal act is likely to happen, specially considering the everyday routine activities. Routine activities in this context are, for example, employment and leisure activities.

According to Cohen and Felson, the following central factors must be present for a criminal act to occur:

1) A motivated perpetrator,
2) A suitable victim or object of crime or opportunity, and
3) The absence of a protector. (Cohen and Felson 1979, p. 589)

A motivated perpetrator, on the one hand, is important for the occurrence of crime as the likelihood increases if this person lacks legal alternatives to committing a criminal act; on the other hand, the attractiveness of a potential victim or object of the crime is also decisive for the occurrence of crime (Brandt 2004, p. 6). Concerning the victimization risk of objects, Felson and Clarke formulated four main risk factors (Felson and Clarke 1998, p. 5): Value, Inertia, Visibility and Access (VIVA). The value of an object determines its attractiveness for the potential perpetrator. Smaller and lighter objects (inertia) and visible objects (visibility) are more attractive. In this context, the possibility of accessing the object plays a decisive role (Brandt 2004, p. 6ff; Felson 1998, p. 59). It can be assumed that potential perpetrators are often looking for opportunities in their immediate environment (Siegel 2000, p. 113). Siegel noted, for example, that criminals usually pursue crime opportunities on their everyday journeys, for example between work and home. But the presence of a suitable protector in the form of persons or technical aids can prevent the occurrence of a criminal act.

A motivated perpetrator, a suitable victim and the absence of a protector are increasing factors for the occurrence of crime and the risk of victimization. If only one of these conditions is not met, the offence may potentially not be committed (Brandt 2004, p. 7).

The validity of this theory has already been proven by numerous studies. Cohen and Felson extended their theory to other typical routine activity risk factor. For example, they proved that women's increasing employment and the existence of single households had a effect on the rise in crime rates, because households are more often unattended for longer periods of the day (Brandt 2004, p. 8).

12.11 The Ecological Approach

The relationship between the location and delinquency has been subject of criminological research for a very long time. The descriptive approach was an outcome of the early works of the Chicago School, whose subcultural studies had a decisive influence on American and international (criminological) sociology. Researchers such as Thrasher (2000) and Whyte (1996) mainly dealt with questions of how space favors socially deviant behavior. In terms of methodology, the researchers primarily used qualitative methods, including participatory observation and open ethnographic interviews.

The zone model of Ernest W. Burgess, also a representative of the Chicago school, became very popular, as Burgess stated, that cities spread out in a circle around their center, with the social status of the citizens increasing with growing distance from the center (Burgess and Park 1921; Park et al. 1925). In this context, he named the two outer zones as community zone and residential zone. While the community zone is mainly inhabited by middle-class people, the residential zone is mainly inhabited by very well-off commuters.

Hoyt, a student of Burgess, modified the zone model and designed the so-called sector model (Hoyt 1939). Based on his studies of the rental structure in various metropole regions in the United States, he came to the conclusion that cities are developing along transport routes, with the higher-status population being the main driver of urban development. Furthermore, Hoyt explained that if areas are left by higher privileged groups, groups with the next lowest social status are taking their place.

The multicore model was developed by Harris and Ullman (1945). Unlike Burgess and Hoyt, whose models were still based on one urban center, Harris and Ullman emphasized that with the size of the cities the number of centers and cores are also increasing. Because of its decentralized structure, the multi-core model is likely to show the reality of life in modern (large) cities in the best available way. Especially in areas with different, formerly independent, municipalities, which grew together over the last centuries – e.g. the Rhein-Ruhr-Area in Germany – the multi-core model can describe and explain the geographical distribution of crime in much more realistic way than the zone and sector model. However, this does not mean that zone and sector models are obsolete per se. If cities grow organically (such as Chicago), one can very well assume that there is only one center, but this does not apply in the same way to the development of every city.

Based on the research of the Chicago School of Sociology, Shaw and McKay founded the so-called ecological approach (area approach) (Shaw and McKay 1942). In this approach, residential areas and city districts are typically characterized by different crime rates. The reasons for this can be both social and economic. For example, social disorganization due to a lack of formal control can encourage criminal behavior. Affected social spaces then threaten to develop into so-called delinquency areas. These are often residential areas characterized by an unfavorable social structure (high unemployment, lack of leisure opportunities for young people, high proportion of migrants, etc.). In criminology, such spaces are also called "breeding areas." This term refers to the fact that an above-average number of people with a criminal background living there. The concentration of "multi-problem groups" makes the social integration more difficult and favors the development of criminal subcultures (ganglands), although it is not the architecture of an area itself, but its social structure that is the determining factor for deviant behavior.

The Routine Activity Theory, which was further developed by Felson and Clarke also deals with the question of ecological and temporal characteristics and their influence of the delict-rates (Brandt 2004, p. 8; Felson and Clarke 1998, p. 6ff). Based on the central assumptions of Routine Activity Theory, the Crime Pattern Theory has identified different factors including nodes, paths and edges to describe the patterns of crime (Brandt 2004, p. 8). Nodes are places between which individuals move, for example, public transport points and the directly surrounding places. According to Felson and Clarke, an increased crime rate can be expected at these points. The link between the nodes and the daily paths of an individual provides information about the individual's risk of becoming a victim. For example, an increased risk of victimization can be assumed on everyday routes between work and home, since individuals are targets for potential perpetrators on these everyday routes. This is a close link to the assumptions of the Routine Activity Theory. The risk of victimization is particularly high on the edges between the place of residence and places of work and entertainment, as individuals are foreign in these areas and are very likely to meet strangers, and their areas of activity may therefore overlap with those of potential perpetrators (Brandt 2004, p. 8).

Therefore, in the light of Crime Pattern Theory, it can be assumed that space and time are mainly influencing the occurrence of crime and that the movement patterns of individuals are important factors in this context. The Crime Pattern Theory has not only contributed significantly to changes in urban planning but also provides a solid basis for the development of area-based predictive models.

12.12 The Technological Dimension and Data-Protection Challenges

Working with modern predictive policing software is often associated with prejudices. Every use is always accompanied by the consideration of moral and ethical aspects. By using spatial predictive policing models, the risk that people who temporarily stay in or live in a location declared as a risk area by the software have to fear being stigmatized as potential criminals is immanent. Such an approach can lead to a consolidation of prejudice and discrimination: If the police patrols more frequently in a risk area, more criminal offences are discovered and these registered offences will again be weighted in future forecasts.

In addition, police control practices are selective. It is not unusual for (individual and institutional) stereotypes to be reproduced in this way. In this context, a common criticism of predictive policing is that these stereotypes are reflected in police data and can ultimately be incorporated into the crime predicting algorithms. In the worst case, when using AI and ML, developers or analysts could reach a point, from which they can no longer understand the results of the forecasting software. In this context, critics point out that police measures in such a situation are based on a "black box." In addition, the collection of large amounts of data (keyword: BIG DATA) from different data sources increases the danger of spurious correlations, i.e. statistical correlations that are technically unfounded.

The use of personal predictive policing approaches is accompanied by the consideration of various ethical and moral aspects, whereby criticism often refers to the classification of persons as extremists or potential terrorists. According to critics, this can lead to serious invasions into the privacy of those concerned (monitoring of chat histories, observation, etc.) because the probability that all predictions are correct is almost unrealistic. Even a success rate of 95% would result in 5% of those affected being suspected wrongly. In monitoring the social media of suspects or people classified as "dangerous," also innocent people can get into the attendance of LEAs. Here the disproportionality and the threat that the security authorities falsely accuse people can be seen as the most important points. There are also concerns that collected data is not promptly or completely deleted and thus innocent persons remain permanently in the system.

In addition, critics point out that it has not been sufficiently clarified which (parliamentary) supervisory bodies will monitor the use of predictive policing software in order to keep "freedom" and "security" in a reasonable relationship with each other. After all, the benefits of predictive policing in protecting citizens from crime can also serve as a pretext for "socially disciplining" people, which can even result in social exclusion, as in China, for example.

In addition, data protection experts refer to the amount of data collected by the security authorities and the risk that criminal or unauthorized persons could misuse these data. This has already happened in the past when authorities have been victims of hacker attacks, which makes it particularly important to protect such sensitive data.

Despite the criticism mentioned earlier, the use of predictive policing also has advantages for security authorities and contributes to better protection of citizens. Predictive policing helps reduce complexity by enabling law enforcement experts to analyze large amounts of data in a timely manner and identify patterns contained within, which would be impossible without the use of such technology. In addition, AI and ML can be used to identify the patterns and relationships that would not have been discovered manually. Algorithms do not use prejudices and stereotypes; they are not racist or discriminatory. Predictive policing speeds up the investigative process and based on scientific methods, the forecast made by software solutions is more effective than human prognosis.

12.13 Predictive Policing in the Field of Radicalization and Terrorism

A common target of all radicalization theories was to develop models of the radicalization process that trace cognitive and behavioral changes as indicators of radicalized behaviors and interpret how this leads to violence and finally to the committing of terrorist acts.

In any case, the process of radicalization is not a process that happens at an instance (Christmann 2012). As Campelo et al. (2018) propose, "There is no predefined pathway leading to radicalization: radicalized individuals come from various backgrounds, have different origins, different family beliefs, social status, or gender." Moghaddam proposed a model inspired by Islamic communities in both Western and non-Western societies that describes the radicalization process as an ascending step-shaped model with six steps, including dispositional, situational, and environmental factors (Moghaddam 2005). Each individual questions the treatment received from the society and wonders if it is has deserved it. From this basic statements, some people start climbing up the stairs looking to change the unfair conditions of their lives by showing aggressive behavior. A moral disengagement from the society, a legitimate acceptance of terrorist acts and the final recruitment to commit acts of terrorism complete the pathway of a small number of individuals toward the fifth step of the process (Schmid 2013).

Based on the 2010 Report on "Guidance for Identifying People Vulnerable to Recruitment into Violent Extremism" (Cole et al. 2010), each individual mainly experiences three distinct phases until they reach the final stage of extremism and/or terrorist acts. The first is passive recruitment, where daily events build upon the willingness of each individual to participate in violent acts in order to combat their grievance feelings. The second phase is the active recruitment, occurring when an individual actively seeks out and/or is sought out by violent extremists, adopting simultaneously the belief that violence is the key answer to all their problems. The third phase is the act of terror itself "best described as instrumental behavior that is used to coerce the state or groups and individuals within it." Another volume of scientific literature, impacted by school shootings, searched the radicalization incentives among childhood experiences and personal crises, which triggered the use of violence as an answer to injustice and fame acquisition (Böckler et al. 2018; Lankford and Hakim 2011).

Von Behr et al. in 2013, in their study among 15 radicalized individuals suggested that the Internet was a key source of information, communication, and of propaganda for their extremist beliefs and provided a "greater opportunity than offline interactions to confirm existing beliefs" (von Behr et al. 2013). In addition, a study by Gill, Horgan, and Deckert in 2014 showed that 35% of 119 lone-actor terrorists interacted in a virtual way with a wider network of political activists, with 46% of them learning attack methodologies from online social networking (Gill et al. 2014). In addition to the previously mentioned function of the Internet, it also offers perpetrators an unregulated and unrestricted place where they can disseminate their propaganda, through numerous social media platforms and websites, in a low-cost, easily accessible, fast, anonymous way. According to a large meta-study (2000–2019) on the role of the Internet in (i) right-wing extremism and (ii) radical jihadism, "available studies show that extremist groups make use of the Internet to spread right wing or jihadist ideologies, connect like-minded others in echo chambers and cloaked websites, and address particularly marginalized individuals of a society, with specific strategies for recruitment. However, only a handful of studies recently published have already started to create causal designs and explain (rather than describe) online radicalization processes" (Idag et al. 2019).

12.14 Personal Risk Assessment in Context of Radicalization – Findings from the PREVISION Project

However, there is no easy offline versus online violent radicalization dichotomy to be drawn (Gill et al. 2017) as the Internet does not accelerate the process but rather seems to act as a catalyst by facilitating the process (Hassan et al. 2018). It became clear that the course of radicalization is strongly related to the individual situation of persons, in which different factors play important roles. These include personal feelings or group processes that cannot be automatically recorded, analyzed, and evaluated by algorithms. Otherwise, there would be a risk of bringing persons under general suspicion. Nevertheless, the use of modern technology and algorithm to assess the level of radicalization among suspected persons by analyzing their language and the terms used offers a huge opportunity. Because of this, a predictive tool for the assessment of personal risk in the context of radicalization was developed within the framework of the PREVISION project. The basics and the design of the tools developed within the framework of the project are therefore outlined in detail.

12.15 Personal Risk Assessment

The risk assessment tools described here focuses on the risk classification of individuals or groups who are planning to commit an act of violence. In order to be able to assess the effectiveness of the tools, a distinction is made between different generations (stages of development) of risk assessment tools. The first generation describes "unstructured, professional assessments by medical staff based on their theoretical knowledge and practical experience" (von Berg et al. 2019: 4). In contrast, the second generation of risk assessment tools is characterized by their structure. This "is based on empirical data and the relationships between historical or demographic variables and the risk examined" (von Berg et al. 2019). What is meant here are biographical data or data from the past of the person in the focus. The third generation "includes measurable psychological and behavioral variables and is characterized by an increasing specialization of the instruments in specific areas of delinquency" (von Berg et al. 2019). The fourth generation of risk assessment tools includes tools that are tailored to the risk management process, i.e. intervention approaches are selected and rehabilitation processes are pursued.

In the context of the generations of risk assessment instruments mentioned earlier, there is often a debate as to whether purely statistical tools or so-called "structured professional tools" are better suited for risk assessment. "Structured Professional Judgment Tools" (SPJ) include both statistical and dynamic factors as starting points for countermeasures (von Berg et al. 2019) And are (currently) preferably used. SPJ Tools use a mixed method approach: Defined factors are queried and supplemented by further inquiries or specifications. Each factor is rated (three categories: high – medium – low). Followed by a final assessment by the user, which is justified by observations and written documentation (von Berg et al. 2019: 5).

With regard to the topic of "extremism," research has provided specific suggestions on how risk assessment tools should be methodically designed. Accordingly, a number of quality criteria for risk assessment tools can be named. These should have a certain degree of structure and standardization as well as a link to risk management. The respective risk should be specifically defined and central concepts should be used within the risk assessment tool. In addition, there should be an awareness of the relationship between the different factors and the focus should be on risk and protective factors. Comprehensive documentation of the results is also essential (von Berg et al. 2019).

In the context of the (further) development of instruments for risk assessment and assessment, a few things should also be taken into account. In this context, a certain degree of structure and standardization is just as important as the connection to risk management. The risk and protective factors must be contextually adaptable (e.g. to changes over time, the age or gender of the individual or group perpetrators) and mental risk factors must be integrated into the analysis tool. A structuring of subscales seems to make sense even if these are only characterized as theorized connections. Language and behavior are also important indicators of radicalization. Overall, extensive practice and research fund of potential risk and protective factors that can be used to further develop the instruments already exists. However, there must be an awareness that there is no consensus on a causal interplay of these factors (von Berg et al. 2019: 8).

12.16   Text Analysis

For the text analysis (supplementary image analysis could also be carried out), various sources such as publicly available websites and data from social media (WhatsApp, Twitter, Facebook, etc.) must be included. The quality of the sources is likely to vary widely. "Problematic" texts and images will also be found on sites whose owners do not have or support any extremist motives. In this context, reference should be made to information material from security authorities, publications from research institutes or press material. In order to be able to sort out such content in advance, a list of links to such sources should be stored in the background of the software.

In addition, there are websites of groups, parties, and organizations that are already banned in the EU or have been classified as extremistic in advance. In these cases, a database enabling to identify these sites directly is necessary. The user could be advised by a "flag" that the corresponding page is already on the index. Overall the functionality of the developed software aims to identify websites and accounts with extremist content that is still unknown to the security authorities and in addition, the software uses an algorithm to classify the degree of radicalization.

Therefore the text analysis focuses primarily on the following contents:

- Violence against ethnic minorities and marginalized social groups,
- Calls for terrorist or politically motivated violence,
- Glorification of terrorist actions or politically motivated violence,
- Spread of extremist symbols,
- Calls for people to leave the country for combat zones,
- Denial of the Holocaust.

12.17   Identification of Problematic Content

Official pages are usually characterized by error-free spelling, orthography, and grammar. Accordingly, the taxonomies used should be able to identify these quite easily. It becomes more difficult when evaluating texts on social media. Therefore, scene- or youth-typical language, slang terms, or code words are often used. Spelling errors are also common. The question here is how to deal with these challenges.

One possibility would be to work with a "phonetic" or fuzzy string search. Furthermore, algorithms can be developed that take into account an error tolerance determined by the developer when searching for keywords (so-called "triggers"). Furthermore, scene-typical terms and code words can be included in the taxonomies and assigned to a score.

12.18 Methodological Design

Over the past months, a variety of extremist content (right-wing, left-wing, and Islamist spectrum) from official websites, blogs, and chats were analyzed. The extremist content was compared with "unproblematic" content. In this way, the first version of taxonomy was developed that includes relevant keywords or phrases.

Each keyword or phrase is assessed to determine whether it is a trigger or neutral feature. Triggers indicate radical content. Only trigger features are included in the scoring. Each keyword or phrase marked as a trigger feature is assigned to a scoring value that lies between 0 and 1. The higher the scoring, the higher the analyst evaluates the potential radicalness of the respective text passage.

In the next step, each trigger feature occurring in the analyzed text is multiplied by the frequency of its occurrence. The product values are added and then the sum is divided by the number of "matches." This gives the scoring value. The closer the scoring value to the value "1," the greater is the probability that the content is extremist/radical in nature.

In addition to the scoring value, a second value is calculated: the "share of extremist passages in the total text." This is the proportion of text content classified as problematic in relation to the total text.

When analyzing extremist propaganda, the chosen rhetorical (linguistic) means also play an important role. For example, if "prompting/active language" or repetitions (repetitio) and tautologies are used. Certain stylistic means can give an indication of extremist content.

Figure 12.1 illustrates the interaction of the individual components for the detection of radicalization processes in the PREVISION platform.

The tools described above offer functionality to assess both the individual risk of a person and the level of radicalization shown in a text. The advantages of such prognosis methods are obviously and their chances for modern policing have been widely discussed. The different methodological approaches used and discussed in this article have risks, but also offer a huge spectrum of opportunities. The use of these technologies offers, besides all serious concerns and partly bad previous experience, a huge potential. Although the dream of absolute security will also stay a dream for the next time these technologies can and will be able to improve

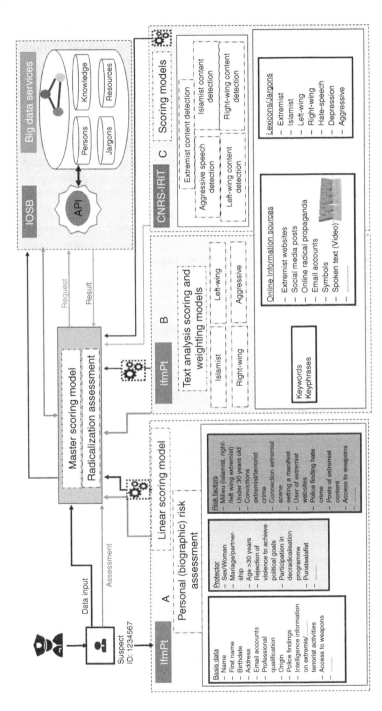

Figure 12.1 The system design of PREVISION risk assessment tools.

security in the next decades. The tool developed in the framework of the PREVISION project is an example of how modern police work can be supported by predictive policing technologies and science-driven innovation.

References

Anders, K., Prochnow, A., Schlauderer, R., and Wiegleb, G. (2004). Die Szenario-Methode als Instrument der Naturschutzplanung im Offenland. In: *Handbuch Offenlandmanagement am Beispiel ehemaliger und in Nutzung befindlicher Truppenübungsplätze* (ed. K. Anders, J. Mrzljak, D. Wallschläger, et al.), 97–104. Berlin, Heidelberg: Springer.

Babuta, A. and Oswald, M. (2019). Briefing paper data analytics and algorithmic bias in policing, https://assets.publishing.service.gov.uk/government/uploads/system/uploads/attachment_data/file/831750/RUSI_Report_-_Algorithms_and_Bias_in_Policing.pdf (accessed 9 September 2021).

von Behr, I., Reding, A., Edwards, C. et al. (2013). Radicalization in the digital era: the use of the internet in 15 cases of terrorism and extremism, www.rand.org/content/dam/rand/pubs/research_reports/RR400/RR453/RAND_RR453.pdf (accessed 9 September 2021).

von Berg, A., Korn, J., Mücke, T. and Walkenhorst, D. (2019). Einschätzungen und Bewertung von Risiken im Kontext der Extremismusprävention und Deradikalisierung. Zwischen sicherheitspolitischem "Risk Assessment" und "pädagogischem" "Resilience Assessment." https://violence-prevention-network.de/wp-content/uploads/2020/01/Violence-Prevention-Network-Schriftenreihe-Heft-2.pdf (accessed 15 June 2022).

Bergmann, B. (2018). *Expertise in der Prognose von Kriminalität. Eine Untersuchung am Beispiel der polizeilichen Einschätzung zukünftigen Verhaltens junger Straftäter.* Kiel: Christian-Albrechts-Universität.

Bliesener, T. (2007). Psychologische Instrumente für Kriminalprognose und Risikomanagement. *Praxis der Rechtspsychologie* 17 (2): 323–344.

Böckler, N., Leuschner, V., Roth, V., et al. (2018). Blurred boundaries of lone-actor targeted violence: similarities in the genesis and performance of terrorist attacks and school shootings. *Violence and Gender*, 5(2), 70–80. https://doi.org/10.1089/vio.2018.0002

Brandt, D. (2004). *Wirkungen situativer Kriminalprävention – eine Evaluationsstudie zur Videoüberwachung in der Bundesrepublik Deutschland.* Diplomarbeit Universität Bielefeld https://pub.uni-bielefeld.de/download/2306207/2306210/Brandt.pdf (accessed 9 September 2021).

Burgess, R.L. and Akers, R.L. (1966). A differential association reinforcement theory of criminal behavior. *Social Problems* 14 (2): 128–147.

Burgess, E.W. and Park, R.E. (1921). *Introduction to Science of the Sociology.* Chicago, IL: University of Chicago Press.

Campelo, N., Oppetit, A., Neau, F. et al. (2018). Who are the European youths willing to engage in radicalisation? A multidisciplinary review of their psychological and so-cial profiles. *European Psychiatry* 52: 1–14. https://doi.org/10.1016/j.eurpsy.2018.03.001.

Christmann, K. (2012). Preventing religious radicalisation and violent extremism: a systematic review of the research evidence (pdf), www.safecampuscommunities. ac.uk/uploads/files/2016/08/yjb_preventing_violent_extremism_systematic_ review_requires_uploading.pdf (accessed 9 September 2021).

Clarke, R. and Felson, M. (1993). *Routine Activity and Rational Choice.* New Brunswick and London: Transaction Publishers.

Cloward, R.A. and Ohlin, L.E. (1960). *Delinquency and Opportunity: A Theory of Delinquent Gangs.* New York: Free Press.

Cohen, L.E. and Felson, M. (1979). Social change and crime rate trends: a routine activity approach. *American Sociological Review* 44 (4): 588–608.

Cole, J., Alison, E., Cole, B., and Alison, L. (2010). *Guidance for Identifying People Vulnerable to Re-cruitment into Violent Extremism* (ed. S. o. Psychology). University of Liverpool.

Dahle, K.-P. (2008). Kriminal(rückfall)prognose. In: *Handbuch der Rechtspyschologie* (ed. R. Volbert and M. Steller), 444–452. Göttigen: Hogrefe.

Dahle, K.-P. (2010). *Psychologische Kriminalprognose. Wege zu einer integrativen Methodik für die Beurteilung der Rückfallwahrscheinlichkeit bei Strafgefangenen.* Freiburg: Centaurus.

Douglas, T. (2018). Chicago police cut crime with major upgrades to analytics and field technology, www.govtech.com/public-safety/chicago-police-cut-crime-with-major-upgrades-to-analytics-and-field-technology.html (accessed 9 September 2021).

Felson, M. (1998). *Crime and Everyday Life.* Thousand Oaks: Pine Forge Press.

Felson, M. and Clarke, R.V. (1998). *Opportunity Makes the Thief. Practical Theory for Crime Prevention. Police Research Series Paper 98.* London: Home Office – Policing and Reducing Crime Unit https://popcenter.asu.edu/sites/default/files/ opportunity_makes_the_thief.pdf (accessed 8 May 2021).

Fieseler, J. and Haubner, O. (2005). *Staat der Zukunft. Ergebnisse einer Repräsentativbefragung.* Gütersloh: Bertelsmann Stiftung www.bertelsmann-stiftung.de/fileadmin/files/BSt/Presse/imported/downloads/xcms:bst_ dms_16375_16376_2.pdf (accessed 9 September 2021).

Gill, P., Horgan, J., and Deckert, P. (2014). Bombing alone: tracing the motivations and antecedent behaviors of lone-actor terrorists. *Journal of Forensic Sciences* 59: 425–435.

Gill, P., Corner, E., Conway, M. et al. (2017). Terrorist use of internet by the numbers. *Criminology and Public Policy* 16 (1): https://doi.org/10.1111/174 5-9133.12249.

Görgen, T., van den Brink, H., Taefi, A. et al. (2010). JuKrim2020. Mögliche Entwicklungen der Jugend(gewalt)kriminalität in Deutschland. Szenarien, Trends, Prognosen 2010–2020. In: *Abschlussbericht zur Herbstkonferenz 2010 der Ständigen Konferenz der Innenminister und – senatoren der Länder*. Münster: Deutsche Hochschule der Polizei.

Grime, M. and Wright, G. (2016). Delphi method. *Statistics Reference Online* 1–6. https://doi.org/10.1002/9781118445112.stat07879.

Harris, C.D. and Ullman, E.L. (1945). The nature of cities. *The Annals of the American Academy of Political and Social Science* 242: 7–17.

Hassan, G., Brouillette-Alarie, S., Séraphin, A. et al. (2018). Exposure to extremist online content could lead to violent radicalization: a systematic review of empirical evidence. *International Journal of Developmental Science* 12 (1–2): 71–88. https://doi.org/10.3233/DEV-170233.

Hoyt, H. (1939). *The Structure and Growth of Residential Neighborhoods in American Cities*. Washington, DC: Federal Housing Administration.

Idag, O., Leiser, A., and Boehnke, K. (2019). Reviewing the role of the internet in radicalisation pro-cesses. *Journal for Deradicalization* 21: 261–300. https://journals.sfu.ca/jd/index.php/jd/article/view/289/197 (accessed 9 September 2021).

Kahneman, D. (2011). *Schnelles Denken, langsames Denken*. München: Siedler Verlag.

Lamnek, S. (1988). *Theorien abweichenden Verhaltens*. München: Fink.

Lankford, A. and Hakim, N. (2011). From Columbine to Palestine: a comparative analysis of rampage shooters in the United States and volunteer suicide bombers in the Middle East. *Aggression and Violent Behavior* 16 (2): 98–107.

Moghaddam, F. (2005). The staircase to terrorism. A psychological exploration. *American Psychologist* 60 (2): 161–169.

Park, R.E., Burgess, E.W., and McKenzie, R.D. (1925). *The City*. University of Chicago Press.

Peteranderl, S. (2018). Predictive policing in Chicago: Die Verbrecher der Zukunft stehen heute schon fest. GQ magazine (online). www.gq-magazin.de/auto-technik/article/predictive-policing-in-chicago-die-verbrecher-der-zukunft-stehen-heute-schon-fest (accessed 9 September 2021).

Saunders, J., Hunt, P., and Hollywood, J. (2018). Predictions put into practice. *A Quasi-Experimental Evaluation of Chicago's Predictive Policing Pilot Journal of Experimental Criminology* 12 (3): 347–371. https://doi.org/10.1007/s11292-016-9272-0.

Schmid, A.P. (2013). Radicalisation, de-radicalisation, counter-radicalisation: a conceptual discussion and literature review. ICCT Research Paper March 2013, The Hague: ICCT. https://www.icct.nl/app/uploads/download/file/ICCT-Schmid-Radicalisation-De-Radicalisation-Counter-Radicalisation-March-2013.pdf (accessed 15 June 2022).

Schwind, H.-D. (2006). *Kriminologie und Kriminalpolitik. Eine praxisorientierte Einführung mit Beispielen*, vol. 23. Heidelberg: Kriminalistik (edited and extended edition).

Schwind, H.-D. (2016). *Kriminologie und Kriminalpolitik. Eine praxisorientierte Einführung mit Beispielen*, vol. 23. Heidelberg: Kriminalistik (neubearbeitete und erweiterte Auflage).

Shaw, C.R. and McKay, H.D. (1942). *Juvenile Delinquency and Urban Areas: A Study of Delinquency in Relation to Differential Characteristics of Local Communities in American Cities*. Chicago, IL: The University of Chicago Press.

Siegel, R. (2000). *Criminology*. Belmont: Wadsworth Publ. Comp.

Sutherland, E.H. (1939). *Principles of Criminology*. Chicago, Philadelphia: Lippincott.

Thrasher, F.M. (2000). *The Gang. A Study of 1.313 Gangs in Chicago*. Chicago: New Chicago School Press.

Vogel, J. (2015). *Prognose von zeitreihen. Eine Einführung für Wirtschaftswissenschaftler*. Wiesbaden: Springer Gabler.

Whyte, W.F. (1996). *Die Street Corner Society (First Edition 1943)*. Berlin, New York: de Gruyter.

Index

Note: Page numbers in *italics* denote figures and page numbers in **bold** denote tables.

Security Technologies and Social Implications, First Edition. Edited by Garik Markarian,
Ruža Karlović, Holger Nitsch, and Krishna Chandramouli.
© 2023 The Institute of Electrical and Electronics Engineers, Inc.
Published 2023 by John Wiley & Sons, Inc.

Printed and bound by CPI Group (UK) Ltd, Croydon, CR0 4YY

21/12/2022

03175670-0002